GCSE/KEY STAGE 4

TECHNOLOGY

David Rees and Peter Bull

Longman

LONGMAN REVISE GUIDES

SERIES EDITORS:
Geoff Black and Stuart Wall

TITLES AVAILABLE:
Art and Design
Biology*
Business Studies
Chemistry*
Economics
English*
English Literature*
French
Geography
German
Home Economics
Information Systems*
Mathematics*
Mathematics: Higher Level*
Music
Physics*
Religious Studies
Science*
Sociology
Spanish
Technology*
World History

* new editions for Key Stage 4

Longman Group
Longman House, Burnt Mill, Harlow,
Essex CM20 2JE, England
and Associated Companies throughout the world.

© Longman Group 1994

*All rights reserved; no part of this publication may be
reproduced, stored in a retrieval system, or transmitted in
any form or by any means, electronic, mechanical,
photocopying, recording, or otherwise without either the
prior written permission of the Publishers or a licence
permitting restricted copying in the United Kingdom
issued by the Copyright Licensing Agency Ltd,
90 Tottenham Court Road, London W1P 9HE.*

First Published 1994
Second Impression 1995

ISBN 0 582 23771 8

British Library Cataloguing-in-Publication Data

A catalogue record for this book is
available from the British Library

Produced by Longman Singapore Publishers Pte Ltd
Printed in Singapore

CONTENTS

ACKNOWLEDGEMENTS

The Examination Boards are thanked for their prompt support in supplying the new syllabuses in order that the CDT-Technology Revise Guide and the CDT-Design and Realisation Revise Guide may be brought up to date for the new Key Stage Four Technology examination.

I should also like to thank Debbie Colenso, David Saddler and Natalie Stanton for permission to use some of their Design Folio work to illustrate this book.

I am also grateful to Peter Bull for his valuable contribution by writing the sections on Electronics, Pneumatics, Word Processing, Computer Aided Design, Computer aided machines, Computer Graphics and Textiles.

One final acknowledgement and grateful thanks must go to my wife Vivien who has been extremely supportive in making this book possible.

David Rees

EDITORS' PREFACE

Longman GCSE Guides are written by experienced examiners and teachers, and aim to give you the best possible foundation for success in examinations and other modes of assessment. Examiners are well aware that the performance of many candidates falls well short of their true potential, and this series of books aims to remedy this, by encouraging thorough study and a full understanding of the concepts involved. The Revise Guides should be seen as course companions and study aids to be used throughout the year, not just for last minute revision.

Examiners are in no doubt that a structured approach in preparing for examinations and in presenting coursework can, together with hard work and diligent application, substantially improve performance.

The largely self-contained nature of each chapter gives the book a useful degree of flexibility. After starting with the opening general chapters on the background to the GCSE, and the syllabus coverage, all other chapters can be read selectively, in any order appropriate to the stage you have reached in your course.

We believe that this book, and the series as a whole, will help you establish a solid platform of basic knowledge and examination technique on which to build.

Geoff Black and Stuart Wall

HOW TO DO WELL ON THE COURSE

DESIGNING AND MAKING

RESOURCE TASKS

CAPABILITY TASKS

EXTENDED TASKS

SPELLING, GRAMMAR
AND PUNCTUATION

DESIGN FOLIO

WRITTEN EXAMINATION

PLANNING AND
ORGANISATION

GETTING STARTED

Choosing a course or syllabus may not be a problem because you will
have been following a Design and Technology course at Key Stage 3
and the way forward is quite clear for you. What you should remember
is that the first part of the Design and Technology or Technology
elements are common and it is the second part which may vary and so
give you flexibility of choice. For example you may wish to do an
Extension Study in FOOD, TEXTILES, GRAPHICS, ART, BUSINESS
STUDIES, FASHION, CATERING OR ELECTRONICS, etc. It is
important therefore for you to make your choice of an Extension Study
in the early part of the course so that you can prepare and plan how you
are going to study and acquire the skills that you need for getting a
good grade at the end of the full course.

There are some new terms which may need explaining. The term
task is widely used and appears to be replacing such words as
assignment, project or problem. But do not be too worried by the
names of the different tasks you are expected to perform. Most of them
involve designing and making and they follow on from the work you did
in years 7, 8 and 9.

How well you do will mainly be determined by your motivation and
your willingness to accept guidance from your teachers.

Please note: This book will deal with **Technology** and **Design
Technology** only. **Information Systems and Information
Technology** are dealt with in a separate book in the Longman Revise
Guides series.

Pattern of Assessment

Those familiar with Design and Technology will know that a
considerable amount of time is spent designing and making. This is
done during the course and so a major proportion of the marks are
awarded to Coursework and the rest to a written examination.

Coursework 60%	Designing	40%
	Making	60%
Written examination 40%	Core	50%
	Extension	50%

ESSENTIAL PRINCIPLES

1 ⟩ DESIGNING AND MAKING

The Designing and Making element occupies a large amount of your time and in most syllabuses has a weighting value of 60%. In order to be able to do well and to show your capability, you will need to go through a number of learning activities first. They are called **RESOURCE TASKS**. These activities concentrate on small areas of learning which, when combined in a single design activity, help you do a **CAPABILITY TASK, i.e. Design and Make a product, artefact or system.**

DESIGNING SKILLS

These depend upon your ability to do well at the following:

- identifying a need or opportunity;
- writing a design brief;
- writing a product design specification;
- doing some research;
- thinking of a broad range of ideas;
- drawing these ideas;
- modelling your ideas;
- evaluating your ideas;
- developing your ideas so that they can be made;
- making your chosen idea using constructional materials;
- evaluating your final artefact or system.

2 ⟩ RESOURCE TASKS

In order to help you develop some of these skills, specimen resource tasks have been developed by Nuffield Chelsea Curriculum Trust, and are reprinted, with permission, from the trial publications of the Nuffield Design and Technology Project. Copyright © Nuffield-Chelsea Curriculum Trust 1993. Here is an example of such a resource task.

MAKING THINGS MOVE

How do things move?

You can move things yourself by pushing, pulling or turning.

An engine can do the pushing, pulling or turning for you.

Brainstorm a list of things that you pull, push or turn in a normal day.

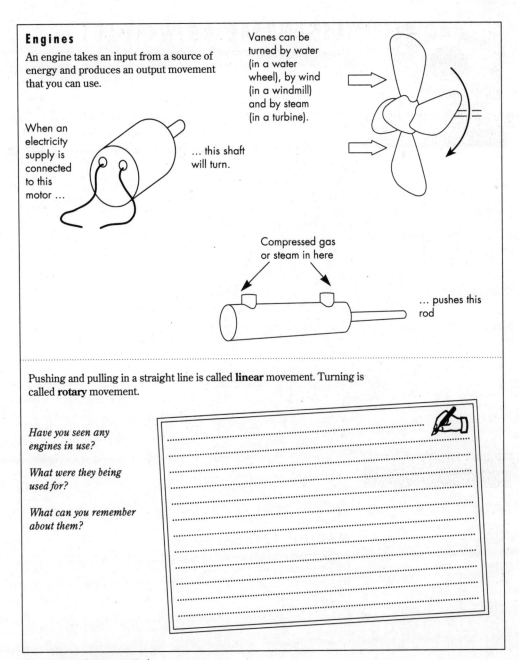

Engines

An engine takes an input from a source of energy and produces an output movement that you can use.

Vanes can be turned by water (in a water wheel), by wind (in a windmill) and by steam (in a turbine).

When an electricity supply is connected to this motor ...

... this shaft will turn.

Compressed gas or steam in here

... pushes this rod

Pushing and pulling in a straight line is called **linear** movement. Turning is called **rotary** movement.

Have you seen any engines in use?

What were they being used for?

What can you remember about them?

Fig. 1.1 Sample Resource Task
Source: Nuffield Chelsea Curriculum Trust

MECHANISMS THAT MULTIPLY DISTANCES

Test yourself on mechanisms that multiply distance. Use the Mechanisms Guide on pp 9–11.

How far does this rod move out?
With what force?

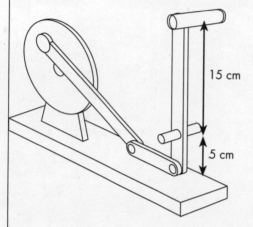

15 cm

5 cm

Each time this wheel turns, this rod moves out a distance of 10 cm with a force of 120 N.

How far does this rod move out?
With what force?

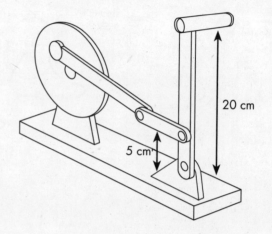

20 cm

5 cm

Each time this wheel turns, this rod moves out a distance of 5 cm with a force of 60 N.

This electric motor turns at 500 rpm (revolutions per minute) and gears can be fixed to the output shaft.
You have the following gears available:

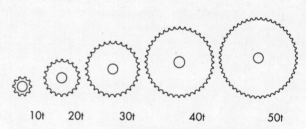

10t   20t   30t   40t   50t

Sketch the gear trains that you will need,
showing the position of the motor.

You want to use it to drive an electric fan so you want to double the speed.

You want to use it to drive a record deck that turns at $33\frac{1}{3}$ rpm.

You want to use it in a hill climbing model car so you want to increase its turning force by a factor of 100.

Fig. 1.2   Sample Resource Task
Source: Nuffield Chelsea Curriculum Trust

These activity sheets not only help to make you think, but, they also help you to focus your attention on the things you should know. In this case, 'How to make things move' (Fig 1.1) and 'Mechanisms that Multiply Distance' (Fig 1.2). Similar tasks have also been developed for 'Food' and 'Strategies'.

It is possible for you to obtain other examples from the Nuffield Design and Technology Project. When attempting these tasks you will find it necessary to have support information so that you can increase your knowledge and awareness of how things can be made to move. Here are two examples, taken from a set of ten sheets of support information on mechanisms that transfer movement.

SPECIMEN RESOURCE TASK

Guide to mechanisms

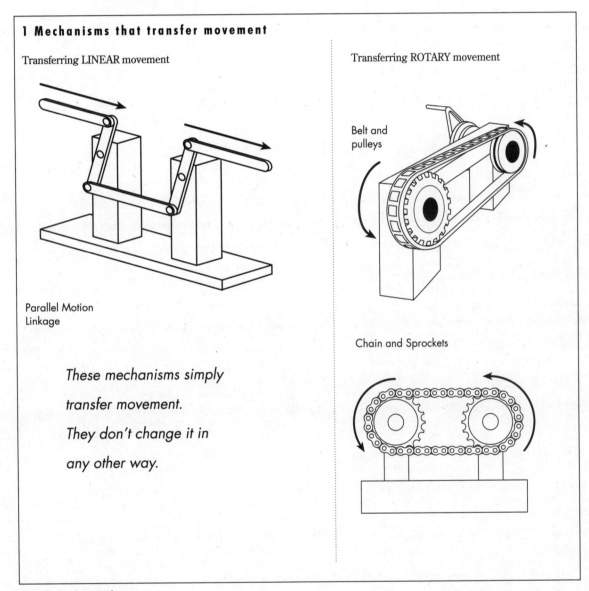

1 Mechanisms that transfer movement

Transferring LINEAR movement

Parallel Motion Linkage

These mechanisms simply transfer movement. They don't change it in any other way.

Transferring ROTARY movement

Belt and pulleys

Chain and Sprockets

Fig. 1.3   Guide to Mechanisms

2 Mechanisms that change the direction of movement

a Linear movement

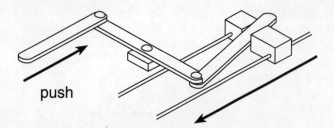

When you are pushing you need to use rigid linkages

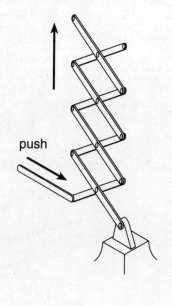

When you are pulling you can use a rope and pulley

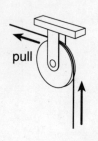
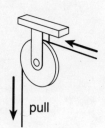
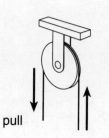

b Rotary movement

If you cross the belt in a pulleys and belt mechanism, one pulley turns clockwise and the other turns anti-clockwise.

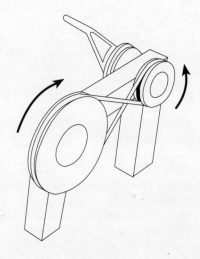

When one gear turns another they turn in opposite directions.

If you add an idler gear between the two gears, then they will both turn in the same direction.

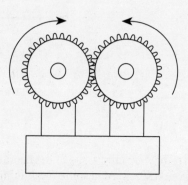
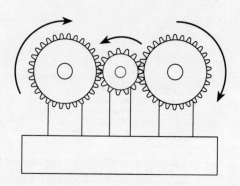

Fig. 1.3   Guide to mechanisms
continued

These three mechanisms change the direction
of rotary movement through 90°.

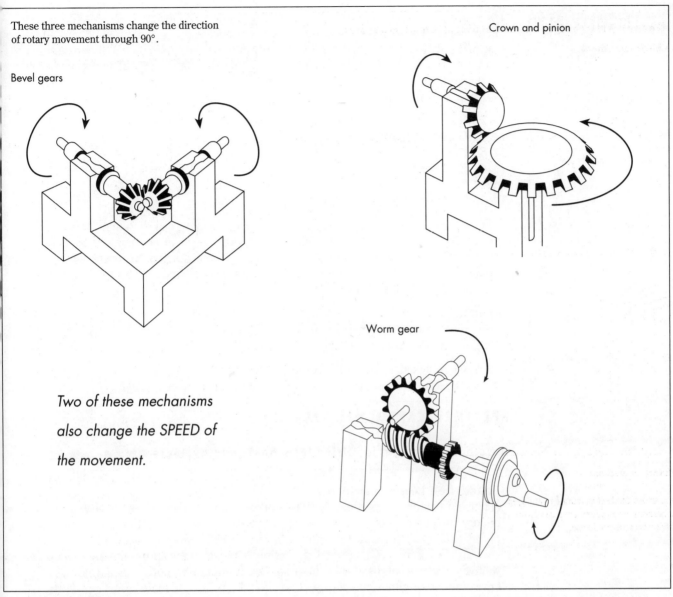

Bevel gears

Crown and pinion

Worm gear

Two of these mechanisms

also change the SPEED of

the movement.

Fig. 1.3   Guide to mechanisms
continued

You can of course turn to Chapter 12 of this book to revise your understanding of Mechanisms.

Specimen Resource Tasks are also available for other areas of the curriculum.

In using them you can work in small groups which gives you a chance to share your ideas, observations and conclusions. You will learn a lot more by *doing* these types of tasks so do try to make the most of your opportunities when working on resource tasks.

During your course you may cover a range of resource tasks, which could include any of the following topics:

- Structures
- Electronics
- Pneumatics
- Word Processing
- Computer Aided Design
- Computer Aided Machines
- Computer Graphics
- Food
- Textiles
- Graphics

All the work that you do should be kept and filed carefully for future use. It may come in use later on when you are working on a Design and Make Task. Also some Examining Boards may require you to keep such work as part of a Portfolio for assessment.

3 > CAPABILITY TASKS

These are tasks that examine your *capability* either as a Designer and Maker or as a Technologist. These tasks can be set early in the course by the examining board; in the case of the **WJEC** they are set two years in advance of the examination. Other examining boards such as **ULEAC** give you and your teacher the opportunity of setting your *own* capability tasks. However, all examining boards use the same set of criteria for assessment. These are:

Te 1. Identifying needs and opportunities;
Te 2. Generating a design proposal;
Te 3. Planning and Making;
Te 4. Evaluating;
and
Te 5. Information Technology.

The capability task must be set at such a level that you can demonstrate your best ability. You should be able to select one level from three, namely foundation, intermediate and higher. If your teacher is setting the tasks then he or she will be able to guide you as to which level they think you should choose for your capability task.

Tasks are set at three levels:

Foundation level – suitable for capability **levels 4–6**
Intermediate Level – suitable for capability **levels 5–8**
Higher level – suitable for capability **levels 7–10**

A single topic can be set at the three different levels.
The following task (set by ULEAC) shows how this may be achieved.

SPECIMEN CAPABILITY TASK

Developing museum facilities for schools and business

Foundation Level – Levels 4–6
A museum caters for parties of school children, adults and others interested in the history and contents of the museum and an allied riverside exhibition centre. As part of the development plan for the museum a series of initiatives is planned.

Using the information provided, design a picnic area and a linking riverside walkway that can be used by school parties. It should be both a pleasant and safe environment for children of all ages and should provide adequate resources for them to enjoy a meal-time, together with the opportunity to let off steam.

Your proposed outcome should be presented in both 2D and 3D forms.

Intermediate Level – Levels 5–8
A museum caters for parties of school children, adults and others interested in the history and contents of the museum and an allied riverside exhibition centre. As part of the development plan for the museum a series of initiatives is planned.

At present the Education Centre and Schools' Party Room is a bare building. Design a suitable interior structure to allow this space to be used to the maximum benefit of the visitors.

Your proposed outcome should be presented in both 2D and 3D forms.

Higher Level – Levels 7–10
A museum caters for parties of school children, adults and others interested in the history and contents of the museum and an allied riverside exhibition centre. As part of the development plan for the museum a series of initiatives is planned.

In the space available at the side of the building it is intended to build a new conference centre to be jointly used by education and business people. Design a single storey building that can be used for this purpose whose structure integrates with the existing building.

Your proposed outcome should be presented in both 2D and 3D forms.

You can see the task requires you to do quite specific things. Guidance on how to tackle this type of task is given in Chapter 3. on the topic of Product Display.

> ## CORE TASKS
> Each syllabus has a common core of knowledge that has to be learnt, understood and applied. For example, those choosing the Design and Technology route, will have to have an understanding of construction materials, construction processes and designing and making. For those choosing the Technology route, they will cover the same core content as in the Design and Technology route with the addition of computer control, robotics and related systems.

4 ▷ EXTENDED TASKS

These are tasks that *extend* into a more specialised area of the curriculum and include such courses as:-

Design and Technology and Art
Design and Technology and Graphics
Design and Technology and Textiles
Design and Technology and Food
Design and Technology and Automation
Design and Technology and Electronics
Design and Technology and Fashion
Design and Technology and Business
Design and Technology and Catering
Design and Technology and The Built Environment.

5 ▷ SPELLING, GRAMMAR & PUNCTUATION

All subjects include in their assessment criteria a percentage of marks for spelling, grammar and punctuation. This applies to coursework as well as the written examination. Your teacher will do the initial marking of your work and he or she will have to assess your ability to spell words correctly and to see how clearly you communicate your thinking through the use of the written word as well as your ability to communicate through drawing.

■ Don't hesitate to use a dictionary
With Coursework you have the opportunity of checking your work if you are uncertain of the spelling of certain words. Use a dictionary.

■ Use your 'spell check'
This book is being written with the aid of a software package called "WordPerfect" and at the end of each page or chapter the "speller" is used to check the spelling of every word. If a word is not recognised the word is highlighted and an alternative is suggested. If it is the name of a person that it does not recognise, then you have the option of accepting this word whenever it appears.

■ Let someone else read your work
You also have the opportunity of having your work checked by another person. A second pair of eyes can often pick out a simple error that you have missed. Do not feel ashamed about having your work checked. We all make mistakes and we are too often afraid to admit our weaknesses.

■ Write down words that you have difficulty in spelling
A method recommended and used for learning how to spell is known as the – **LOOK – COVER – WRITE – CHECK** method. You look at the word about which you are uncertain. Cover it with a piece of paper. Write down what you think is the correct spelling and then check it with the help of a dictionary. Copying a word from the dictionary may help you to put a mistake right but it is unlikely to help you to remember how a word is spelt. Keeping a small note book that has been divided into 26 sections, one for each letter of the alphabet, and adding words that you need to know how to spell, can be helpful in improving your spelling.

Punctuation

The rules and use of punctuation are less clear than they were in the early part of this century, mainly due to the greater use of Information Technology and the need to communicate more quickly. For example if you are hand-writing a letter to a company as part of your research, an address would have a comma after the number, a comma at the end of each line, and a full stop at the end of the address, e.g.

61, Church Road,
Yendyl,
Bristol.

However, an address need not have any punctuation if the letter is word-processed, e.g.

61 Church Road
Yendyl
Bristol
BS20 9LA

Also it might have a different position on the paper so that the address fits into the window of an envelope.

Nevertheless, certain basic rules do exist. Sentences do finish with a full stop. Short sentences may not need a comma, but long ones need to have some breathing spaces for the reader.

6 DESIGN FOLIO

To communicate clearly in a **design folio** you will use your *graphical skills* as well as your writing skills. So, there is less need to be engaged in writing lengthy prose (essay-type material). A Design Brief needs to be written using only one or two sentences. Short sentences are better than long ones and they are more easily read and understood. A *Product Design Specification* (PDS) can be a list of statements which need not be complete sentences. You can also use notes (annotation) with your sketches in the 'research and generation of ideas' sections. The only time you may need to write in prose is at the beginning when you are setting the context and at the end when you are writing your evaluation.

7 WRITTEN EXAMINATION

The **written paper** forms a very important part of the examination. It is used to test what you know and understand and your ability to communicate through good use of the English language. As with the Capability Tasks there are three Tiers (or range of levels) of written examination papers. It is important for you to know which Tier you will be taking so that you can become familiar with the layout and the type of questions you will be asked to answer. Details are given in Chapter 2.

Preparing to take a written examination

In your preparation for a written paper, no matter at what level, it is important for you to be prepared. You should, of course, have been revising your notes over the final stages of the course and not leave everything to the last moment.

You should also:

- be familiar with the layout of the paper;
- be familiar with the instructions that must be followed;
- know which questions are compulsory;
- know which questions are optional;
- know the length of time for the examination;
- know how much time to allow for each section;

Here are some more hints for you when you are actually taking the examination.

- Complete all that you have to write on the front cover, i.e. your name, centre number, your candidate number. Do not write more than you are asked.
- Read and check that you know what you are expected to do before attempting to answer any questions. **Read the instructions.**

Compulsory Section.

- Attempt the compulsory questions first. They are short answer questions and are designed to test your knowledge.
- Read the *whole* of the first section, i.e. Section A, to get a feel of the type of questions. This is a **compulsory section** and all questions have to be answered, but, you do not have to answer them in numerical order. You can answer the ones that you know best first and then tackle the remaining questions. **Attempt all questions**. You will not lose marks for wrong answers.
- If you find that you cannot complete all of the compulsory questions do not sit idly. Go to section B and only read those questions that refer to the *media you have studied,* i.e. Graphics, Food, Technology. You can always return to questions you felt you could not answer straight away.

Choice Section

- These are longer questions and they are *structured* so that you start off by answering short questions and then questions which gradually get more demanding. These questions are designed to not only test your knowledge but also to test your understanding and application of knowledge.

■ You have a choice of questions but only attempt the exact number given to you in the instructions. Attempting more will not get you extra marks.

■ Read all the questions in your section before attempting to answer them.

■ When you have chosen a question or questions in which you feel you can do well, read through the first one you are going to attempt once more from beginning to end and **underline or highlight key words and instructions.**

■ The space provided for your answers is an indication of how much writing or size of sketches you will need to provide.

■ The marks awarded for that part of the question are not only an indication of its worth but also an indication of how much time you need to spend answering it. **Spend more time answering parts of a question that have a high weighting.**

Spelling, grammar and punctuation.

■ **Use the question paper as a dictionary.** Your ability to spell is important and if you are poor at spelling this will become obvious to an examiner. You do not have the opportunity of using a dictionary to check the spelling of words in an examination. But, you do have a question paper in front of you which contains quite a number of words that are spelt correctly. Use your examination paper as a dictionary.

■ If there are specific terms used such as Anthropometric, Aesthetics, Egonomics or any other terms which you may need to check, then just glance through the paper to see if these words are present. If you have a few minutes to spare at the end of an examination use your time profitably by checking your spelling, punctuation and grammar.

Assessment of spelling, grammar and punctuation.

Each examining board is required to allocate 5% of marks to spelling, grammar and punctuation. These are the criteria that are used to assess your ability.

■ If you spell, punctuate and use the rules of grammar with reasonable accuracy; use a limited range of specialist terms appropriately, then you score **one mark.**

■ If you spell, punctuate and use the rules of grammar with considerable accuracy; use a good range of specialist terms with facility, then you can score between **two** and **three marks.**

■ If you spell, punctuate and use the rules of grammar with almost faultless accuracy, deploying a range of grammatical constructions; use a wide range of specialist terms adeptly and with precision, then you can score between **four** and **five marks.**

You may have a high level of capability in most areas of this subject, but if you are not well organised and able to plan your programme of study and realisation effectively you could get a lower grade than you expect. This would not only be a very disappointing result but one which does not reflect your true ability.

Whether it be a *core* task or an *extended* task you will be given a date by which you must complete the task. This date is most important and all your activities and how long you expect to spend on each of them will be governed by it. So work backwards and divide your designing and making activities into reasonable slots of time to enable you to complete the task on time. Remember that the completion dates for the various designing activities can be slightly flexible but the *overall* completion date is fixed and cannot be extended.

You will be assessed upon your ability to plan and organise your time, so do make sure you can show *evidence* of this in your Design Folio. In Chapter 2 we look more carefully at how you can do this.

A FINAL STATEMENT

You can only expect to do well in this demanding subject if you:

a) work consistently hard at all aspects of the course;
b) accept guidance from your teacher;
c) complete all tasks on time.

Always plan ahead so that you can make the most of your opportunities.

COURSEWORK TECHNIQUES

KEEPING A DIARY

PRODUCING A SCHEDULE CHART

PLANNING A WORK SCHEDULE

USING YOUR TIME

REVIEWING THE COURSEWORK PROGRAMME

GETTING STARTED

One of the most important parts of the course is for you to be able to demonstrate your ability in designing and making. Whether you are following the Design and Technology course or the Technology course you will be required to demonstrate your ability to design and make an artefact (object or item) that can be constructed from rigid materials such as wood, metal, plastic or clay. You will then be able to extend your designing and making skills to a task involving the use of either food, textiles or graphic media.

Do check with your teacher that what you want to do is possible and that you are able to fulfil the requirements of the course. Those following a Technology course must show evidence of having worked in construction materials and having followed a task leading to a *practical* solution that has involved the use of computer control, robotics or related systems. Again do check with your teacher so that you finish with the right kind of coursework.

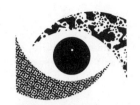

ESSENTIAL PRINCIPLES

1 ❯ KEEPING A DIARY

This is a technique used by most people who have to plan their activities well in advance. Usually the important date is the *date for completion*. If you know the date of an examination or the date by which an assignment has to be handed in for assessment, it is possible to plan each stage so that all the work is completed on time.

In the early stages of the course you will be required to complete a task. Your teacher may be the person who sets the work and will no doubt tell you the date by which it has to be finished. In the case of 'Design Task', 'Problem Solving' activities or 'Project' work, you may well expect the completion date to be ten or twelve weeks away. This may seem so far into the future that there is very little need to get started straight away. Don't fall into this trap! The first important thing to do is to write down the completion date in a diary or some other form of notebook. The second is to spend time now on sub-dividing the time you have available into the stages involved in completing your task.

❝❝ Plan your work into stages. ❞❞

In the case of a 'design task' the stages may be set out in exactly the same way as a design process, i.e.:

- identification of a need;
- design brief
- product design specification
- research/investigation;

- development of ideas;
- development of a chosen idea;
- realisation of the chosen idea;
- evaluation.

Each of the stages can then be allocated a period of time. This may seem impossible at first since you are not likely to know how long each stage will take. The important point to remember is that the dates for completion of each stage are *targets* for you to aim at. Sometimes you will find that you can meet the target very easily, and at other times you will find it extremely difficult. If you do find that you appear to be progressing well and that you are ahead of your schedule, proceed to the next stage and get started. Do *not* wait for time to pass before continuing the assignment; the next stage may take longer than you anticipated and you will need to take advantage of the extra time gained in the previous stage.

2 ❯ PRODUCING A SCHEDULE CHART

Seeing a chart on a single page helps to give you, at a glance, a picture of your programme. Turning pages in a diary or note book is more tedious and you are not able to see how you are proceeding at a glance. The presentation of the information can be done in whatever way is most helpful to you. What is important is that the information is clear and easy to follow. Though the example below is in black and white, there is no reason why you should not employ colour to give prominence to certain features, e.g. dates.

The following chart (Fig. 2.1) could be used for a ten-week assignment.

WEEK	Design stage	Activity	Completion Date
1	Identification of a need	Write a brief and analyse problem	12th Sept
2	Investigation research	Find out as much as is necessary to solve the problem	19th Sept
3 4	Development of ideas	Explore a variety of ideas before deciding which one to develop	3rd Oct
5	Detailed drawing	Draw all the detail required for the idea to be realised	10th Oct
6 7 8 9	Making or realisation	Cut and prepare material to sizes given in the detailed drawing. Construct, assemble and apply a finish	7th Nov
10	Evaluation	Test the realisation to see how well it satisfied the brief	14th Nov

Fig. 2.1 Schedule chart.

Remember that a project really starts when you *identify a need* and not what you would like to make.

You will notice from the schedule chart that the allocation of time varies from one week to four weeks. This is necessary because some aspects take longer than others. The *making* or *realisation* aspect normally takes up the most time, so a large portion of the time available is allocated to this design aspect. What is *not* shown on the chart is the time that should be devoted to the production of a 'Design Folder'. This is because the preparation of the material for the folder is *continuous* and starts on the day you receive your assignment and ends on the day given as a completion date. Ideally you should be recording information, ideas, drawings and your evaluation during weeks 1, 2, 3, 4, 5 and 10.

3 PLANNING A WORK SCHEDULE

While it is possible for you to know exactly how long you have to complete the task, you have to take into consideration the following:

- holiday breaks such as half term;
- school events such as visits, fields trips, etc.;
- illness, though this cannot be predicted, adjustments can be made so that progress is not too seriously interrupted.

The schedule must be thought of as a guide and as an aid to completing your project on time. Adjustments to accommodate visits, illness, etc., should be possible and may be done in a number of ways. The major time consumer in this subject is undoubtedly the *manufacturing process*. A careful review of the design of the product to be made and the processes chosen to enable it to be realised, may reveal that an alternative method of production may be a solution to the problem of completing a task in less time. If unexpected delays or problems are met in the method you chose, you may be able to switch to this alternative and save some time. Decisions such as these should be accepted as normal practice in any designing activity. Finding a process that can be done within a given time, and adapting to alternatives when circumstances change, is a very important aspect of the designing activity. If you have reached a stage where your recommendations *cannot* be changed, then it must be assumed that your project is very near completion.

Be flexible in your working.

4 USING YOUR TIME

Drawing up a work schedule is only the first task to enable you to ensure that you complete your work on time. Having set yourself the target dates it is now necessary to think how you are going to make the best of your opportunities.

Your time may be classified as 'contact time' and 'non-contact time'. The 'contact time' is the time you are given on your time table. It is the time when you have the opportunity to be in contact with the facilities available for DT and also the time when you will be in contact with your teacher. You should therefore plan ahead so that you know what help you need from the teacher during a lesson and to make sure that you plan the tasks that can best be done in a drawing office, workshop, studio, etc.

To be able to use the facilities 100% of the time they are available, is often the result of the preparation that you made before going into the lesson.

PREPARING TO GO INTO A WORKSHOP/PRACTICAL ROOM

It may help to make a model or mock-up of your solution in card or other suitable material.

To know what you are going to do before you go into a workshop can often prove to be most rewarding. Very few of us have ready access to lathes, drilling machines, heating facilities for softening materials so that they may be bent, twisted, etc., or to band saws. So if we know beforehand that we will need to use any of these types of equipment, we should arrive prepared, having already worked out the details of sizes, angles, or positions for holes. We can then use the equipment without too much delay. If your material has to be cut to a particular shape, say on a band saw, then you could have produced a paper 'template'. This is an outline of the shape that is required, and it can be made ready to stick onto the surface of your material as soon as you go into the workshop. You can then complete the cutting operation without delay and be ready to progress to the next stage. The 'template' could easily be made at home where the only facilities needed would be pencil, paper and scissors.

PREPARING TO GO INTO A GRAPHICS ROOM

If you do not have a drawing board and instruments, then it is wise to prepare what it is that you want to draw using instruments by first drawing in free-hand a layout of the information. You can then get down to the task of using the instruments straight away.

To *almost* finish a drawing when you had planned to complete the task before the end of a lesson can be very frustrating, particularly when a little preparation beforehand would have made certain of the drawing being completed without any bother.

PREPARING TO GO INTO A COMPUTER ROOM

If you are just wanting to use the facilities for word processing then make sure that you have some idea of what you want to produce already written down on paper. Also, if you are designing a logo or a packaging cover for a product, then do all your researching and thinking *before* sitting in front of the screen. Have a few sketches planned in rough on paper beforehand, so that as soon as you have access to a computer you can be involved with production rather than designing. In other words, know what you need to do before going into the computer room.

- If you are taking a syllabus where the Examining Group set the topics for the tasks then find out what these are as soon as you can. Ask your teacher.

GENERAL PREPARATION

Though the task of *designing* is dealt with in detail in Chapter 7, one of the most time-consuming tasks is the time taken to **decide upon a topic** for a project. If you happen to be in a school where the GCSE courses start at the end of year 9 in secondary education, then you can get off to a flying start. No doubt your teacher will be well aware of the opportunity and will use those last few weeks of the summer term to advise you on how to prepare yourself for the following autumn term. If on the other hand you are not in one of those schools, then you can still use your time wisely before the start of the autumn term by doing any of the following:

- Find out which syllabus you will be following from your teacher.
- See if you can obtain a copy of the syllabus.
- Seek advice from your teacher or teachers about tasks.
- Try to decide upon a possible topic or topics that interest you and seek the opinion of your teachers.
- If you are taking a syllabus where the Examining Group set the topics for the tasks then find out what these are as soon as you can. Ask your teacher.
- Seek advice from any one you know who may have already followed the course in the previous year or years.

By making such enquiries you may save yourself a lot of time. With the appropriate information it may now be possible for you to begin **planning** your preparation programme by doing the following:

- collecting any information that may be associated with your chosen topic;
- looking more closely at products/artefacts that appear to be related to your topic;
- making brief notes of where you saw helpful information;
- sketching products/artefacts that may be solutions to a problem *similar* to your chosen project.

The building up of a **source of information** of this kind may find its way into your Design Folio, as well as help you to develop a clearer understanding of your intended project.

WORKING DURING THE HOLIDAYS

Because *all* the GCSE courses have a percentage of marks allocated to coursework, it is essential that some holiday time be devoted to the preparation of design folios. This may seem unfair at first but in those courses where a high percentage of marks are available for coursework there will be less need for you to spend time revising for formal examinations at the end of the course.

The type of work that could be usefully carried out need not be laborious or confine you to a desk. You might visit those places that will help you discover more background information related to your project. Information may be discovered when you least expect it and may be difficult to obtain when you set out to find it, so do not be surprised or disappointed. The important point to remember is that you *live in an environment of man-made solutions,* and the very thing you are looking for may be under your nose.

SKETCHING

The ability to **sketch** quickly, accurately, and clearly is an invaluable asset. It is not only a means of recording information but it is also an extremely efficient way of developing powers of observation.

Your sketches may be on any suitable paper. It is not necessary at this stage to be worrying about where and how the sketches are going to be presented in a design folio. The most important task is to keep all your work together safely and to build up a source of information to help you solve a problem. Neatness and qualities of presentation come second in importance at this stage to the gathering, recording and storing of information.

When you return to school or college you will be better prepared for developing your ideas in solving a particular problem.

It is reasonable for you to expect over two years to complete *three* projects that have been selected by you in consultation with your teacher. A *further project* may also have to be completed in the final term of the course. The topic for this and a design brief is set by the Examining Group and forms a compulsory part of work to be assessed. For detailed requirements you are recommended to refer to the syllabus you are following.

It should be clear to you now that you will be repeating the experience of 'designing and making' at least twice. This experience and practice should prepare you for tackling a variety of situations and enable you to proceed confidently when solving problems. The time needed to solve problems should never be underestimated; it is therefore important to do a lot of the preparation work in your own time.

" Don't underestimate the time needed to solve problems. "

SCHEME OF ASSESSMENT AND PLAN OF WORK

Each of the attainment targets have different weightings and it is helpful to know what these are so that you can plan accordingly. The time you take on each attainment target should have some relationship to the marks that are awarded for each attainment target.

- Te 1   Identify needs and opportunities   (15%)
- Te 2   Generating a design   (25%)
- Te 3   Planning and Making   (40%)
- Te 4   Evaluating   (20%)

Whilst it would be unrealistic to advise you to devote exactly the same percentage of time to each attainment target as shown above, you can at least plan a sensible proportion of time on each area of designing so that you can gain the best marks possible. In practice you may identify a need very quickly and so have more time to devote to the generating of ideas. Trying to think of a good range or variety of ideas is not easy and so you may need to allow for more than a quarter of your time on attainment target 2.

Remember, although the assessment table is presented in a sequence, not all the activities have to be completed in exactly that order. For example, although Evaluation is the last attainment target, you are involved in evaluating all the way through a design task. You are making decisions about identifying a need. You have to decide whether or not the need that you have identified can realistically be met. You have to make other evaluative judgements, such as could I develop a solution in the time available, or will it be too expensive? Even when you are generating ideas you are comparing the feasibility of one idea against another and checking to see how well it suits the Design Brief and the Product Design Specification. So you are deeply involved in making decisions or evaluating right from the start. You should also make it evident to the teacher or assessor that you have gone through this process by writing this in your Design Folio.

This type of evaluation is called **formative evaluation**. In other words you are forming your opinions and ideas.

When you have completed your task you have to write an evaluation summing up how well you feel the artefact or system that you have produced fulfils the Design Brief and Product Design Specification. This is called the **summative evaluation**.

In order to get as many marks as possible you must show evidence of formative and summative evaluation.

GETTING STARTED

Throughout the course you will be required to do a number of design and make tasks. These are intended to make you more familiar with designing in a variety of situations. Sometimes you are set the specific tasks; on other occasions you have a topic set for you but *you* have to identify a need and work from there. Some of the Examining Boards set tasks in which the need has been identified for you. These are called *Core Tasks*. They are set at three different levels i.e. 'Foundation', 'Intermediate' and 'Higher.' So do check with your teacher at which core task level you have been entered. These tasks, which are common to Technology and also Design and Technology, are performed as the first of two tasks. They give you the opportunity to show your capability in designing and making, using constructional materials such as wood, metal, plastic and clay. You do not, however, have to use all four materials in a single task.

After going through the stages involved in preparing and presenting the compulsory assignment we look at an actual core task on 'product display' set at Foundation, Intermediate and Higher Levels.

CHAPTER 3

COMPULSORY ASSIGNMENTS

UNDERSTANDING THE PROBLEM

PROBLEM TO PROJECT

PRESENTATION

REALISATION OF SOLUTION

PROCEDURE

TACKLING THE PROBLEM

ANALYSIS OF THE PROBLEM

DEVELOPING IDEAS

SELECTION OF IDEA

DEVELOPMENT OF THE CHOSEN IDEA

MODELS

WORKING DRAWING

MAKING WHAT YOU HAVE DESIGNED

EVALUATION

CORE TASK: PRODUCT DISPLAY

ESSENTIAL PRINCIPLES

1 UNDERSTANDING THE PROBLEM

So that you can gain as much as possible from the assignment and not be left in too much doubt as to what to do, the Examination Groups provide more details. The **administrative** detail covers what is required; whether or not you need to present a design folio; whether or not you have to present a model or a finished product, etc. The **problem** detail provides you with more information about each individual problem. You will need to familiarise yourself with *both* aspects before attempting to tackle the assignment.

ADMINISTRATIVE DETAIL

This should tell you the following:

- the completion date;
- the format;
- the work that has to be submitted.

PROBLEM DETAIL

The type of information you will receive here could be similar to the following three examples:

EXAMPLE 1 'Learning Aids'

The theme is to be interpreted widely. Candidates should investigate a number of situations that might require the use of 'learning aids' and the associated problems before deciding on a specific problem to develop further. A range of possible solutions should be explored before developing in detail a design that will be realised. All work relating to this broad-ranging investigation must be included in the candidate's folder along with all the written and graphical work, e.g., identification, investigation and analysis of the problem, ideas and their development, working drawings, models, trial materials, etc., relating to the chosen problem.

EXAMPLE 2 'Energy Conversions'

PROBLEM: MOTOR POWERED TOY

Fig. 3.1 gives details of the basic system available to give a safe power source for a toy having moving parts. The toy is to be self-contained in that battery, switch and motor are on, or within, the toy itself. The toy can be designed for any particular age group, but **the age group must be specified in your design brief**.

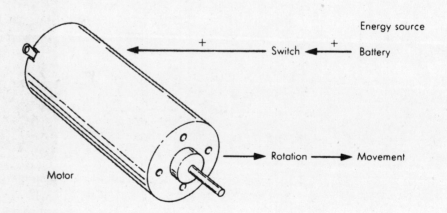

Fig. 3.1

EXAMPLE 3 'A fun money box'

Using any suitable combination of materials or processes, design and build a collecting box that could be used in your school entrance, or similar indoor site, to collect money for a charity.

The collecting box must be sturdy and secure so that it cannot be easily damaged or stolen. It must also be visually attractive and show clearly the name of the charity.

Include in your design one (or more) interesting or amusing feature(s) that operate when a person places a coin in the slot.

These novel features may be mechanical, electrical, electromechanical, or operated by **any** other method you choose. **If electrical components are used all usual requirements must be strictly adhered to**.

You may also choose the effect that is produced, for example, mechanical movements, a noise, lights or anything else you think will be interesting or amusing.

With this additional information you should be left in no doubt about the *nature* of the problem. The major concern is of course with actually *solving* the problem.

2 FROM PROBLEM TO PROJECT

Having understood the nature of the particular problem you have been *set*, or that which you have chosen, you will need to prepare, as you would in most problem solving tasks the following:

- a design brief;
- an analysis of the problem;
- an outline of all the specifications.

From now on the compulsory design and make assignment can be treated like a piece of coursework. Though it is an examination, in that the work will be assessed by an external moderator, you *can* consult with your teacher to confirm that your choice of study area and your possible solutions are appropriate and feasible to produce in the time available and with the facilities available within the school.

3 PRESENTATION OF THE COMPULSORY PROJECT

OBEY SPECIFIC INSTRUCTIONS

Read any specific instructions and work within them, e.g. The Midland Examination Group requires all design work to be presented 'in the form of an A3 or A4 design folder (not in ring-binders)', *CDT Notes for Guidance of Teachers* 1987. Though there is a choice of folder size the A3 size is by far the most suitable. The ULEAC actually supply A3 printed paper on which the candidate answers the design question. Spaces are allocated for each stage of designing, so giving a guide as to what is required and the order in which it is to be presented. There are *four sheets* in all and work can be carried out on *both sides*. One sheet has an *isometric grid* printed to assist candidates to illustrate their proposed design in three dimensions (See Fig. 3.2).

66 Make sure you know what you are expected to do. 99

In order to present the information to go on these sheets it is advisable to keep all your research work in a folder. You can also use this folder to develop your ideas, so it should be regarded as a *working folder* where you record and store information and develop your ideas. When you have developed your ideas to a level that makes you confident that you have a viable solution, you can then consider the best way to present this information on the four design sheets provided by the Examining Group.

The working folder can be presented with your coursework for assessment at the end of the course, because your research will be more evident in the folder than on the design sheets where you are only required to produce a summary.

Whichever Examination Group sets your compulsory assignment make sure that you obey any specific instructions similar to these.

PHOTOCOPY THE WORKING DRAWING

It may be that the work you have done on any of the design sheets provided by the Examination Group has to be sent away to be assessed by an external examiner. If so, it will be necessary for you to keep a copy of the details of your solution so that you can make what you have designed. This certainly applies to ULEAC candidates, but *not*, for example, to those following the MEG syllabus. For these students a copy will not be necessary, because the folder is not assessed until a month after completion of the design work, by which time you will have had the opportunity to make your solution.

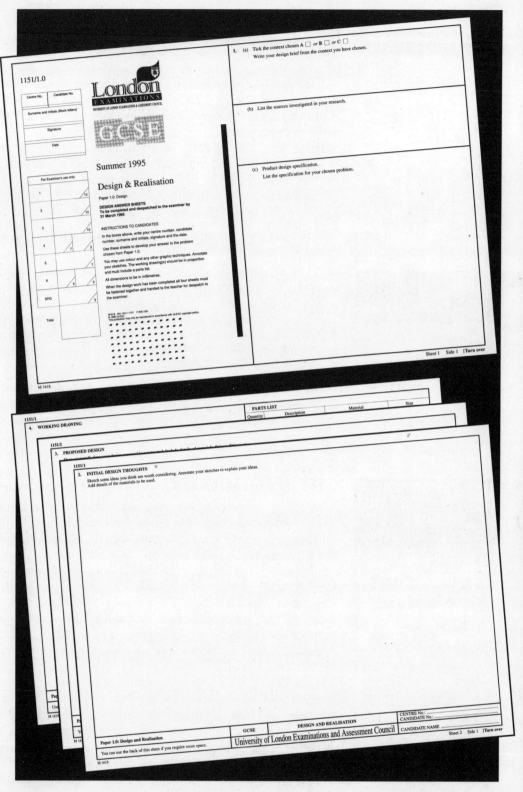

Fig. 3.2

4 ▶ REALISATION OF YOUR SOLUTION

If you have read the requirements of the examination you will soon see that little time is made available for making your solution, a maximum of 20 hours with MEG and a minimum of 5 hours with ULEAC. If you have taken these constraints into consideration at the design stage of your solution you will have chosen wisely the type of construction that will enable you to complete the work in the time available.

The wording in the instruction given by ULEAC can be interpreted to mean that you may spend as much time as you wish on the realisation, in contrast to the instructions given by MEG where you can spend more than 20 hours. It may work out that you need approximately 15 hours to make your solution, so no matter which syllabus you follow you will have a reasonable amount of time to produce your design.

PREPARATION BEFORE GOING INTO THE WORKSHOP

Good planning will save time.

As recommended earlier for the practical sessions for completion of coursework, you should be able to go into the workshop knowing what it is that you are going to do. Planning the stages of production for your compulsory project *beforehand* will save time. You could benefit considerably by doing the following:

- Make a list of the tools that you will need.
- Cut out a template in card of a shape that needs to be produced in a more resistant material.
- Produce a full-size drawing of the true shape of each component. This will provide you with a quick means of checking the sizes without needing to use a rule.
- If you made a model in the designing stage make sure that it is with you in the workshop.
- When you need to use a specialist piece of equipment such as a vacuum former or a milling machine, check with your teacher that it will be available for use when you require it.
- If you require assistance with casting in aluminium, make sure you tell the teacher in advance. He or she will need time to prepare the crucible and the furnace.
- Plan any stage that is going to take many hours to complete. For instance make sure that any gluing, painting, polishing, etc., is done so that the drying and curing time does not prevent you from continuing with another component or part of your work. These processes could be done *towards the end* of a lesson so that the drying and curing time, etc., takes place *between* lesson times.

Depending on the nature of the tasks that have to be performed in the production of your solution, you will have to decide what is the most appropriate preparation that you can make before going into the workshop. There is nothing more frustrating than to have gone into a workshop with good intentions only to find that you cannot get on with your work because a piece of equipment was not available or the teacher had not got everything ready for casting because you had not given enough notice. Any preparation is better than none, but some careful planning can be invaluable.

WORKING IN THE WORKSHOP

Knowing what you are going to do and knowing that the equipment is ready and available to use are vital first steps. However you must make sure that you plan your **sequence of operations** to fit in with other pupils in the class. The drilling machine, lathe, strip heat bender and other equipment is often in constant use. If any of these pieces of equipment are *not* available when you are ready to use them, it would be helpful if you had an alternative process to carry out until the equipment becomes available for you to use. Queueing to wait your turn is not a good use of time. Always try to ensure that your time is being used in a productive way.

A CASE STUDY

Because the conditions vary from one Examination Group to another, it is necessary to follow the procedures set out by the Examining Group to show how a problem is answered. The example chosen was set by ULEAC, but the approach is of general application.

5 PROCEDURE

The following is an extract taken from *Notes of Guidance to Teachers in Preparation for Paper 1: Design and Realisation* 1987.

The Planning Booklet must be completed by 25 March.

Each candidate will require a copy of his/her solution to be used in the Practical Realisation. The copy can be taken off the original within three days following Booklet completion date. Any suitable means of copying the working drawing which is convenient to the school/candidate may be used. Working drawing implies that information which the candidate will require for the Practical Realisation.

The Research Folio will be required for internal/external assessment and should be retained by the school until the Assessor's visit.

In the period between the Planning Booklet completion date and the Practical Realisation:

a) Modifications, if required may be made by the Teacher. Such modifications should be restricted to the availability of materials, suitability of sizes and constructional details, and will allow the candidate to complete the artefact in the time allowed. Amendments to the candidate's design in terms of functional or aesthetic improvements are not permitted.

b) Candidates should prepare all the necessary materials to size in readiness for the practical realisation.

c) Candidates who need specialised jigs, fittings, formers, moulds or castings should ensure that these are ready for the practical realisation.

d) Candidates must NOT attempt any of the practical work until the examination session(s). Where the design involves injection mouldings, vacuum forming, or GRP work, a 'trial' run can take place – but such trial material MUST be available for assessment.

In the examination session(s) on 18 May candidates should, using the materials and design they have prepared, make, clean up, and finish the practical work to their specification and fulfilling the given brief.

AN EXPLANATION OF THE PROCEDURES

As soon as you are informed of the problem questions and you have made a choice you may start gathering information. This may be recorded in a folder in the same manner as you employed for your coursework projects. The Examining Group also requires you to complete a 'Planning Booklet'. A date is given for its completion. Before it is sent away (your teacher is responsible for doing this) you must make sure that you have a photocopy of the working drawing and a cutting list of the materials required. This will be required by you when making your solution to the problem.

Should your design include a size of material that is not available in the school stock, adjustments may be made by selecting an alternative size to ensure that you are able to complete the realisation. Such modifications are acceptable and you would not be penalised because the final product did not match your drawings exactly. Making alterations to its function or appearance is not acceptable and you may be penalised for doing so.

You are responsible for preparing the material to size, so take care with the preparation to be sure that you will have no problems in the making stage. If your design includes a casting, moulding, etc., you make the pattern or mould before the period allowed to complete your solution begins.

You may also have a trial run to see if the casting will turn out as you wish, but the resultant pieces must not be used in the manufacture of your design. You must do the casting as part of the examination.

If you are still unsure of what you may or may not do, then ask your teacher.

SELECTING THE PROBLEM

You must attempt one question only from a choice of three. The questions, though based upon a theme, are presented in such a way that they give you the opportunity of choosing one that suits your interests and your ability. If you think of yourself as being on the creative side rather than the technological side, look for the question that gives you the chance of demonstrating that skill. The question that follows certainly provides the opportunity to show a creative ability.

<table><tr><td>6</td><td>**TACKLING THE PROBLEM**</td></tr></table>

PROBLEM: A KINETIC SCULPTURE

A kinetic sculpture is required for a small leisure garden to the rear of a house. The owner of the house wishes to install in the garden, an attractive centre piece that has movement as well as an aesthetic appeal.

The overall size must not exceed 450 mm x 250 mm x 250 mm. To create movement only natural sources may be used, i.e. water or gentle wind. The finished design must be free-standing and can be placed at ground level or on a pedestal if desired. The pedestal need not be made during the practical examination, but ideas for the pedestal should also be included in the design folio. The method of fixing the sculpture, whether it be on a pedestal or at ground level must be resolved.

STAGE 1: design a kinetic sculpture using the specification given above.
STAGE 2: make the kinetic sculpture and fixing that you have designed.

FIRST STEPS

Read the details given to make sure that you understand the problem. If such terms as 'kinetic' present you with a problem, then do not hesitate to check the meaning in a dictionary. Sometimes even the definition in the dictionary is confusing, so ask someone on whom you can depend to give you a good explanation. If you read into the question further you will find an explanation that will help you: 'To create movement only natural sources may be used, i.e. water or gentle wind.'

Creating movement by natural sources is not new. The energy from the movement of water and wind has provided, and still does provide us with other forms of useful energy, e.g. electricity. Examples of windmills and water wheels that are still to be found in parts of the country offer an excellent starting point for you to begin your study of movement. By drawing any examples you may be able to discover, you will be acquiring the type of information that is going to be helpful when you begin to develop your ideas.

You will find that many Garden Centres have a section on artefacts that are designed to be placed in a garden and to act as an item of attraction and interest. Some employ the use of movement to attract interest. Though the mechanical details are sometimes quite ingenious, the aesthetic qualities are often not so good. There might be examples of a woodman chopping wood, with the movement having been converted from the gentle wind via a propeller. You might believe this is an answer to the problem! It certainly is an example, but it is not your idea, and the examiner will be well aware that such things are on the market and will be able to recognise how much your solution is the result of you developing your ideas, and how much your solution is the result of direct copying. Learning from existing solutions is to be commended, provided that you are able to evaluate what you see and extract all the good features from those that need improving or even discarding.

Look around to see other examples and begin to look discerningly at artefacts. When you see something that appeals to you, try to identify those features that are appealing and state a reason. Similarly, do the same with those features that you dislike. In this way you will learn more about the qualities of the artefact and begin to express your thoughts clearly.

You may of course have to look elsewhere for your research, such as libraries, magazines, museums, catalogues, etc., in which case be prepared to make the effort to gather as much information as you can from as wide a range of sources as possible. When you have collected a wide range of material you will be able to make a selection of what you think you will need. Do not throw away any information that is not going to be used.

Keep this in a Research Folder. You will need this source material to form part of your exhibition of coursework. The Research Folder will not only provide evidence of the study that you made, for your Practical Project, it will also play an important part in your coursework assessment.

Remember that this material is not sent away to be assessed, it stays with you at your school. All you are required to do in the Design Answer Sheet 1.1 is to write a summary

This summary should be written as a list 1, 2, 3, etc.

of your investigation. Make a note of all the visits you made so that you will be able to complete this section of the Design Answer Sheet.

ANALYSIS OF THE PROBLEM

You are required to write a list of all the important points that you will consider in preparing your design. This can be done in the Research Folder first of all and copied later into the Design Answer Sheet.

The details of the analysis can be extracted from the details given in the statement of the problem on page 27. Start by writing 'The kinetic sculpture must:...' as an opening statement. Then list the analysis a), b), c), etc.

For example your analysis could read like this:
'The kinetic sculpture must:

a) have an aesthetic appeal;
b) have movement created by a natural source, i.e. water or wind;
c) be free-standing;
d) be placed either on the ground or on a pedestal;
e) have a means of fixing to either the ground or the pedestal.'

The remaining detail that has not been included in the analysis is of a specific nature and may be listed under the heading 'Specifications'. Hence a second list is to be compiled.

SPECIFICATIONS

1. The overall size of the sculpture must not exceed 450 mm x 250 mm x 250 mm.
2. The pedestal must not be made.

You may feel the need to add to the analysis and the specification list some important detail that you feel essential to this problem. By doing so you will show the examiner that you have not only been able to extract information from the given problem, but that you are also aware of other information relevant to the successful execution of this project. You may feel it important to mention the following:

a) The sculpture must be able to be made with the facilities that are available.
b) The design must be able to be made by me.
c) The design must be able to be made within the time available.
d) The design must be able to be tested so that an evaluation can be made.

This evidence of further thinking around the problem will gain credit over other candidates who considered these aspects, but failed to produce any evidence of having done so. Though these points are relevant to all projects, it is still worthwhile mentioning them for this particular project.

DEVELOPING IDEAS

You may wish to attempt the important stage of developing ideas in your Research Folder before committing your ideas to be illustrated in the Design Answer Sheet. This may help you feel more confident when the time comes for you to put down your ideas in the Design Answer Sheet.

The quality of your sketches should be just sufficient to record your thinking and for it to be understood by the reader. High quality drawings are not required at this stage. The most important aspect that should concern you is the development of your ideas. Reproduced below is an example of a copy of a sketch produced by Leonardo da Vinci of an Inclinometer. Measurements and some constructional detail had to be assumed by the craftsman who made it but none-the-less there was sufficient information contained even in a sketch of this simple outline of an idea for it to be made. You would be able to understand the annotations on the original if you were able to read Latin and read mirror writing. The point to learn from this is that the quality of sketching comes second to the quality of the idea.

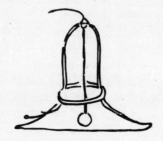

Fig. 3.3 Inclinometer

VARIETY OF IDEAS

When an assessment is being made of this section the examiner is looking mainly to see if you have examined a wide range of possibilities. You should endeavour to begin to explore at least three alternative ideas. The important word here is 'alternative'. If you have shown that you looked at three alternative ideas and not just three variations of a single idea, then you will gain credit. The important points to remember then must be:

1. Produce at least three ideas.
2. The ideas should be quite different from each other.
3. More credit is given for alternative ideas than for variations on a single theme.

ANNOTATION OF SKETCHES

The purpose of adding notes to sketches may be twofold. The first is to provide information that cannot be communicated by drawing, e.g. surface treatment, paint, polish, etc.; name of the material, plywood exterior quality, etc.; pinned and glued, brazed, silver soldered, etc. The second is to express design detail such as, 'more support required here', 'appearance could be improved if this detail could be hidden', etc. Statements such as 'good idea' or 'I do not like this', do not convey helpful and constructive information and as such gain very little credit. If the comments were qualified by saying why the idea is a good one, then this will be more informative and will gain credit. Reasons for an idea being a good one could be that:

Always try to give reasons.

- 'The construction is adequate and possible to make in the time available.'
- 'Materials are readily available and should cause no delay in manufacture.'
- 'The processes required to manufacture this component can be carried out with the facilities that are available.'
- 'This idea is the best because less material and less time is required.'

These types of comment are informative and give an indication of your design reasoning.

You should not be too concerned with presentation. Communication and speed are more important; you must obviously try to get your ideas and thoughts down on paper in a way that can be understood by the reader and in the time available. You will not be assessed on your graphical skills at this stage, therefore concentrate on the development and communication of your thinking and ideas.

SELECTION OF AN IDEA FOR DEVELOPMENT

The detail in the sketches and notes of the 'Development of Ideas' stage should be only such that the idea is recorded visually, similar to the sketch by Leonardo da Vinci shown on the previous page. But before an idea can be developed it is necessary to choose the best information that you consider worth developing. This information may be contained entirely in one of your ideas or it may be spread over several ideas. Whichever it is you will have to decide which information is to be developed.

If you look at the sample of ideas for the 'kinetic sculpture' on page 31 you will see four ideas presented in annotated sketches. They each give an outline of a possible shape, some detail of the components and an indication of how the movement is created by water or wind. It now remains for you to make a selection from just the information in front of you. To set about this task you need to know what you should look for to ensure that your selection is the right one. One way of setting about the task is to compile a list of questions:

a) Does the basic idea potentially fulfil the Design Brief?
b) Is the concept simple?
c) Is the concept one I could possibly make?
d) Could I make the solution within the time available?
e) Is the idea free from possible snags?

The answers to these questions could be YES/NO for each of the ideas. Using the four examples shown you may arrive with the results looking like this:

QUESTION	IDEA			
	A	B	C	D
a)	NO	YES	YES	YES
b)	NO	YES	YES	YES
c)	YES	YES	YES	YES
d)	NO	YES	YES	YES
e)	NO	YES	YES	NO

Only ideas B and C have a total positive response to these initial questions. It would appear from this that one of these two will be selected for further development. However before making the selection it may be helpful to see how the YES/NO answers were decided.

IDEA A

Question a) The problem set did not indicate whether an electric pump could be used. Since this may be interpreted as employing another energy source it could be argued that this idea does *not* satisfy the 'brief' in every aspect. Therefore because of this area of doubt the answer must be 'NO'.

Question b) The idea uses at least six separate components which though not difficult to make could present a problem in assembling them together. Not really a simple concept to solve the problem, especially when it is compared with idea B. The answer must therefore be 'NO'.

Question c) The basins could be made using a resin casting technique and the remaining components could be manufactured on a lathe. I have the knowledge and the experience of casting and working on a lathe. I am confident that I have the necessary skills to make this design. The answer based on this reasoning must be 'YES'.

Question d) There is quite a lot to do and considering the limited time in which it has to be completed it is very doubtful whether I could complete it in time. The answer must be 'NO' to play on the safe side. Had I been doing this as a piece of coursework I would have been more confident and said 'YES'.

Question e) The problem of not knowing whether an electric pump may be incorporated in the design does present a snag. The balancing of the basins is critical to the movement that is intended and may take a long time to achieve. The answer must be 'NO'.

IDEA B

Question a) Movement can be created by a gentle breeze and there does not have to be any other source of energy to create this movement. 'YES' this idea does comply with the details given in the problem.

Question b) There are very few components and the shapes are plain. A resounding 'YES'.

Question c) Again, the idea is so simple that it would even be possible to learn a new process and still be able to be made. Casting in concrete should not cause too many problems. A confident 'YES' must be the answer.

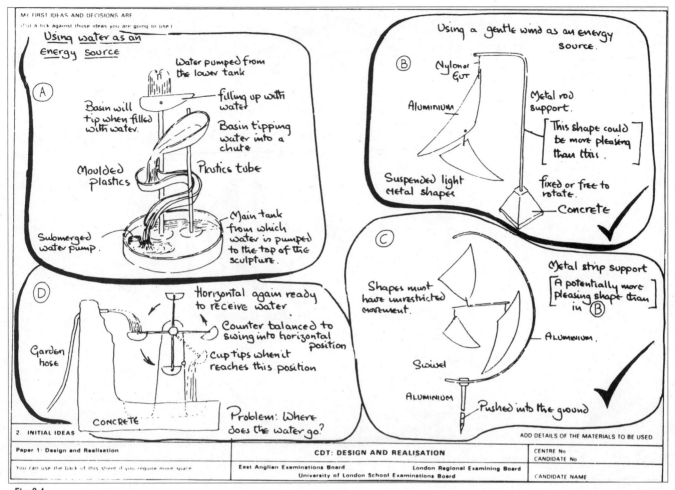

Fig. 3.4

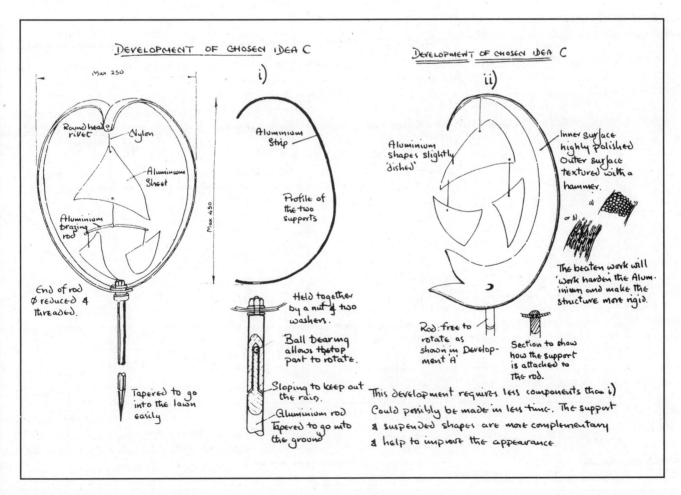

Fig. 3.5

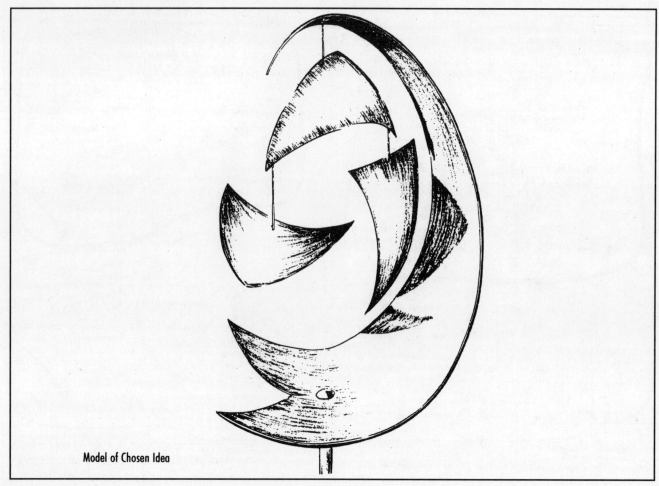

Model of Chosen Idea

Fig. 3.6

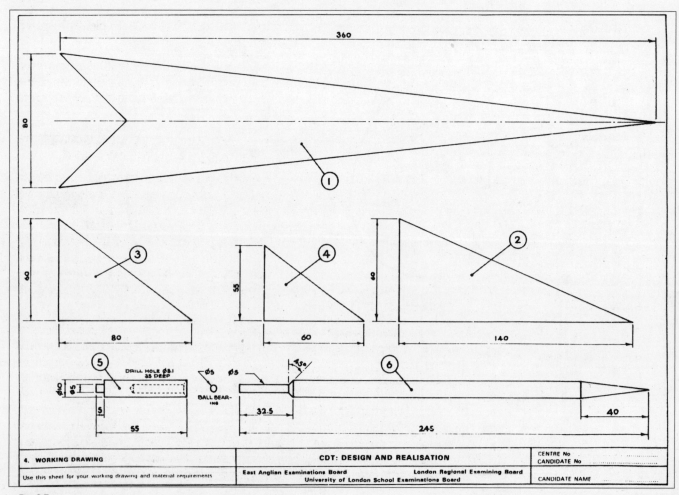

4. **WORKING DRAWING**

Use this sheet for your working drawing and material requirements

CDT: DESIGN AND REALISATION

East Anglian Examinations Board   London Regional Examining Board
University of London School Examinations Board

CENTRE No
CANDIDATE No

CANDIDATE NAME

Fig. 3.7

Question d) The method of production requires marking out, cutting out, and some right-angle bending. The method of fixing the upright to the base needs to be resolved. A 'fixed' solution is acceptable but a rotary movement could be achieved if time is available. Accepting that there are no heavy time-consuming activities this design could be made quite easily in the time available. A confident 'YES'.

Question e) There are no apparent difficulties in the execution of this idea. Therefore 'YES', the idea is free from possible snags.

IDEA C

Question a) There is a free movement for the entire sculpture. It is free standing and can be readily fixed in the ground. A resounding 'YES' is given to this aspect.

Question b) There are a few more components in this idea than in B, but nowhere near as complex as those in idea A. 'YES' this is a simple idea.

Question c) The techniques required to produce this idea are similar to those for idea B. Answer 'YES'.

Question d) Since the design is quite simple there appears to be no obvious reason why it should not be completed on time. Answer 'YES'.

Question e) Provided materials and the necessary equipment is available, the production of this idea is free from any snags. Answer 'YES'.

IDEA D

Question a) Movement is caused by water flowing from a tap and no other energy source is necessary. Given the right conditions, this idea could receive its supply of water from a stream. No matter in which situation it is to be sited it could have a base that is free standing. So far this idea fulfills the 'brief'. Answer 'YES'.

Question b) Even though aspects of being free standing have not been clearly resolved the concept is simple. Answer 'YES'.

Question c) The techniques required to produce this idea are well within the expected range in the syllabus. They include working in metal for the arms of the water wheel, thermosoftening plastics for the basins and possibly concrete for the support. Answer 'YES'.

Question d) There is not an awful lot to do and it would be reasonable to expect this idea to be completed in the time available. Answer 'YES'.

Question e) If this idea is to be placed in the garden there will be a restriction on where it can be positioned. The supply of water from a garden hose should not cause too much of a problem. Where the water goes from the sculpture is a problem. For it to disappear down a drain is both wasteful and totally unacceptable, and for it to just soak into the surrounding ground could prove to be very messy. The obvious site is in a rockery garden that has a natural stream flowing through it. But since such sites are rare this idea must be limited in its application. This restriction is a snag and the answer must be 'NO'.

The question that has been saved until last is concerned with appearance. The first set of questions could be classified as being 'objective'. In other words the answers could be achieved logically. A question about appearance cannot always be answered by logical reasoning. What appears to be attractive to one person appears ugly to another and we often have to accept that much-quoted phrase, 'beauty is in the eye of the beholder'. Even viewing the idea in terms of balance, proportion, texture, colour, etc., can cause a wide variety of opinions to be expressed. Therefore a 'subjective' reason has to be acceptable in making a judgment about appearance, which leaves you to make a decision of selecting one of the two remaining ideas. The choice could depend upon which one appeals to you most since in every other respect there is very little difference.

66 Some subjective opinion is inevitable at times. 99

From reading the annotations placed in the table it would appear that a decision has been made and idea C is the selected idea.

The reasons why 'Idea C' was chosen all depended upon aesthetic appeal. The curved support was a more sympathetic shape for the suspended components and curved lines throughout the design provided a feeling that the components belonged to each other.

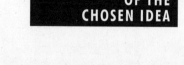

10 > DEVELOPMENT OF THE CHOSEN IDEA

This is the stage of making the idea work, i.e. putting theory into practice. The outlines on the paper have got to be translated and transformed into a three-dimensional, material form.

The development can be achieved by:

a) drawing in proportion all the detail that would enable at least a model to be made;
b) making a scale model.

The details that must be clearly communicated in the developed drawing are:

1. materials;
2. construction;
3. sizes;
4. surface treatment.

These are all the details you would expect to find in a working drawing but the difference here is that some of the details may be changed as you work through the development, while the details given in the working drawing are final. The example given on page 31 shows you the type of development that is necessary and how this information may be communicated. You will also notice that alternative methods of construction are drawn, so leaving the final selection of how the idea is to be made until all options have been considered.

The 'Development Drawing' is still a theoretical solution to the problem. The balance of the suspended shapes is important for each to hang in the required position, but so far the drawing is based upon speculation only and it is necessary to try out the 'idea' in practice.

11 > MODEL OF THE CHOSEN IDEA

A model or models can be made from any suitable material. The important factor is to be able to produce a three-dimensional version of the idea in as short a time as possible, using a relatively inexpensive material. Such materials as card, wire, clay, plastiscine, string and perhaps balsa wood could be used. Of these materials, balsa wood is the most expensive. Make use of any waste materials, such as thin sheet plastics, found in detergent bottles and much of the packaging that is used round many products.

Make the model to scale. In most situations this means that the model will be smaller than the proposed idea. Be prepared to make modifications to your developed idea. In working with a three-dimensional model it is inevitable that you will discover that some alterations will be necessary. When you have made the necessary amendments, you should record these, either on the drawing from which the model was made or on a new drawing if considerable alteration was necessary.

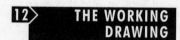

12 > THE WORKING DRAWING

The details of the solution to the 'kinetic sculpture' are not going to be easily represented in a two-dimensional drawing such as an 'Orthographic Projection'. So a more suitable method has to be chosen. You may be able to illustrate the details successfully by using a combination of methods, i.e. 'Two-Point Perspective' and 'Orthographic Projection'. The working drawing on page 32 is a combination of 'Two-Point Perspective' and 'Third-Angle Projection'. Where appropriate, British Standards recommendations have been used.

Much of the work you have so far completed in answering this 'paper' will be in your Research Folio and will need to be transferred to the Design Answer Sheets. The Examining Group does not give you this type of guidance because it is left to you to decide how you wish to prepare your work. The important point is that you are able to complete the Design Answer Sheets, showing the essential details at a level of presentation that is a true reflection of your ability. Therefore by doing it in rough in your Research Folio first, you can then concentrate on presentation in the Design Answer Sheets. Since you are being assessed upon your ability to design and to communicate your ideas graphically, the time spent in taking care with presentation will receive credit.

❝❝ It is worth taking care to present your work well. ❞❞

PRESENTATION TECHNIQUES

The medium you use for illustrations in the Design Answer Sheets is left entirely up to you. You are advised to use only those with which you are familiar and most successful. This is definitely not the time to try a medium that is new to you.

Pencil is perhaps the most useful medium and used well is quite suitable. A 2H pencil is useful for the preliminary stages of setting out the page and the outline of the ideas you wish to illustrate. A darker line may be produced by using a softer pencil such as a 2B. This will help your drawing to stand out more clearly and used well will indicate not only good drawing ability but will also begin to add quality to the presentation.

There is a very wide range of materials and equipment that may be used to illustrate your booklet and you should be encouraged to employ some of them. The list may include:

- coloured pens;
- coloured pencils;
- water colours;
- highlight pens;
- fibre tipped pens;
- coloured inks;
- dry transfer lettering;
- airbrushes.

You may be familiar with those listed and with others used during the course. You will therefore be in a position to select just what you feel is going to help present your Design Answer Sheets. Do not be tempted to overdo it by showing an example of everything. An overuse of 'highlighting' pens can soon begin to make a mess of what may have started out to be a well-presented piece of work.

MAKING A COPY OF THE WORKING DRAWING

Because you are expected to make what you have designed, and because in the case of this project the booklet has to be sent away before you make your solution, it is necessary for you to have a copy of the details of the working drawing. You need to know:

- all dimensions;
- material from which each component is made;
- constructional detail;
- assembly details;
- details of any fittings that may be necessary;
- details of any adhesives, solders, nails, screws, rivets, etc.
- details of surface treatment, paint, polish, preservative, spraying, etc.

As part of the working drawing you will have prepared a 'Cutting List', and much of the information may have been included. The example layout of the cutting list on page 101 is one that you may find helpful to follow.

There was a time when all candidates had to make an examination piece. The details were set by the Examining Board and the 'piece' had to be made under strict examination conditions in a given time. This was known as the 'Practical Examination'. Your teacher may refer to the making of what you have designed as the practical examination. The major differences with GCSE are:

a) You have set the details of what you have to make.
b) The time allowed is not just confined to 5 hours.
c) You have an opportunity to complete your design.
d) Everyone will be doing something different.
e) Such practical processes as casting, gluing and finishing are possible activities that can be performed.

You will be given an opportunity to prepare, i.e. cut to size, the material you require. You will also be given a choice of when you would like to use the period of 5 hours that the Examining Group states that you must be given. Would you want it soon after you have prepared your material? Or, would you prefer to have it nearer the end of the course?

The allocation of 5 hours by the Examination Group is intended to ensure that you have:

a) a period in the workshop free from other classes;
b) the constant supervision of a teacher;
c) a long continuous period in which lengthy processes may be completed;
d) the best possible circumstances for making what you have designed.

Because all the candidates are making different solutions to one of three problems, there will be a variation in the time required to make them. So if you estimate that your design could be made within the time of 5 hours, you may wish to do your 'practical' as soon as possible after you have prepared the material. Then any time afterwards you could see whether or not you need to do any finishing touches.

On the other hand, your design may include a lengthy process such as casting and it would be beneficial for you to get this process completed before the 5-hour period so that you could do all the machining processes in the best possible circumstances. However, the final decision will have to be made in consultation with your teacher, who will be familiar with the needs of all the candidates.

When you know the date on which the period of 5 hours falls, it is your responsibility to plan your programme. If there are processes involved such as casting, or the need to make a mould for plastics forming, or a jig for laminating, etc., then the time before the allotted 'practical' examination is the time to get these important tasks completed. You will no doubt find that your teacher has a commitment to teach other pupils in the school at the same time as you would like to get on with your work. Therefore you must expect that sometimes your plans may not be practical, and you must be prepared to do alternative work, even for another subject, in the time you had allocated! Sometimes you will be able to work at the back of a class, but again it may not always be convenient for the teacher to give you the attention that you would wish. A lesson to be learnt from this situation is to resolve the problem with a good but simple solution, one that can be made easily and is not too demanding of time.

> **Again, try to be flexible in how you work.**

14 EVALUATION

This cannot be carried out until you have made the solution and been able to give it a trial. In the case of the 'kinetic sculpture' there can be no better trial than to place it in the surroundings for which it is intended and to observe it in a gentle wind.

Your evaluation must be based on how well it fulfils the requirements you listed in the analysis. If you turn to pages 27–28 you can remind yourself of what was written in the analysis and use this as a set of criteria for making a judgement about its levels of success.

If you use the list of items a)–e) of the analysis as questions, and add the details given in the specification, also on page 28, you will have an excellent set of criteria against which you can evaluate your solution.

EVALUATION SHEET

Fig. 3.8 gives an example of how an evaluation sheet may be set out:

Each of the questions in Fig. 3.8 requires an honest answer and though it would be very easy to give a 'yes' or 'no' answer to most of these questions, a much fuller answer is required. So your response could be 'yes, but…', giving a reason as to why it fulfilled the criteria.

Possible answers to the ten questions given in the Evaluation:

1. The balance and proportion is quite pleasing. The shiny surfaces of the three suspended shapes reflect the sunlight and moving shadows are cast on the curved support and the nearby ground, providing an added interest. The curved outline of each component and the changing patterns help it to blend naturally into its surroundings.

2. A gentle wind produces a movement that allows each suspended component to move freely. A stronger wind unfortunately causes the pieces to clash and make it necessary for it to be removed until the conditions are suitable again.

3. This design is intended for a lawn and it is held in place by pushing the spiked end into the ground. It can be easily moved to any part of the lawn and it does not need any other support. Yes it is free standing.

4. Because the method of support relies on a spike it can only be placed where the ground is soft, yet firm enough to accept the spike. Unfortunately a mallet or hammer cannot be used on this design.

Topic:	KINETIC SCULPTURE	
	CRITERIA	EVALUATION
1	Is it aesthetically appealing?	
2	Is movement created by a natural source?	
3	Is it free standing?	
4	Can it be placed on the ground or on a pedestal?	
5	Is there a suitable means of fixing to the ground or pedestal?	
6	Does it fit within the overall size of 450 mm × 250 mm × 250 mm?	
7	Could the solution be made within the available facilities?	
8	Were you able to make the solution without help?	
9	Was it made in the allotted time?	
10	Are you able to make an objective evaluation?	

Fig. 3.8 An evaluation sheet.

5. The spike is not too difficult to get into a lawn and it provides an adequate support for the sculpture. It has the added feature of being able to rotate so that the sculpture gets the maximum benefit of the wind as it changes direction.

6. The overall size of the sculpture, excluding the spike, is

440 mm x 250 mm x 250 mm.

7. All the materials and equipment were readily available for the production of this design.

8. Some assistance was required to set up the lathe for centre drilling but I was able to carry out the process on my own after my teacher had checked the lathe and was quite happy to let me make the swivel. All the other components were made without any assistance.

9. Because I did not have to use any processes that took a long time to complete, I was able to finish my work well before completion date and I was able to spend more time polishing and cleaning up.

10. Because I was able to complete the work in good time, I was able to set up my sculpture in the garden and observe what happened in gentle wind and slightly stronger wind. The results were noted and I was able to make some recommendations for improvement. They were:

    a) The suspended shapes could be made from a thicker gauge aluminium sheet to give a little more weight, so that the movement of the stronger winds would not blow them into the support. They could of course be made smaller but this might change the appearance, and I do not want to do that.

    b) It would be an advantage to use a mallet to drive the spike firmly into the ground and I suggest this could be overcome by using the device shown in Fig. 3.9.

    c) I have seen the reaction of my parents and some of my friends when they first saw it in the garden. They stared at first then tried to guess what it was supposed to be. One suggestion was that it was a bird scarer. This was not too far from the truth because when the wind was strong the sound of the metal parts clashing did have the same effect as a bird scarer. There was a remark about the sunlight and how it reflected as the pieces of metal swung round. So I could say that some interest was shown but I could not be sure that the sculpture was accepted as 'an attractive centre piece'.

The Evaluation is to be placed in the back of the Research Folio before the visiting assessor is due to arrive to see the coursework, and the compulsory project.

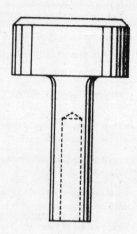

Fig. 3.9 Device used when hitting
the spike into the ground.

ANSWER PLAN

1. Make a Design Folio to keep all research material together and in which to develop your ideas.
2. Select a problem and place a copy of the question paper on the first page. A copy of all the instructions should also be conveniently enclosed in the folio.
3. Collect research material and arrange in the folio.
4. Write an analysis.
5. Develop your ideas.
6. Select an idea.
7. Develop your chosen idea.
8. Make a model of the developed idea.
9. Make a working drawing.
10. Write out a cutting list.
11. Complete the Design Answer Sheets.
12. Make a copy of 9 and 10.
13. Prepare material to the sizes given in the 'cutting list'.
14. Make your solution to the problem.
15. Evaluate your solution and enter the details in your Research Folio.

The examples of candidates' work in Chapter 21 should help you to understand more fully what is required, and at the same time show you that the 'paper' may be presented in a number of ways.

We now look at a 'Core Task' set by a major exam group and consider how you might approach it, bearing in mind the points made in this Chapter.

Here are some Core Tasks set by ULEAC at three different levels.

TASK A – PRODUCT DISPLAY

Foundation Level – Levels 4–6

Many visitors come into a shop in a tourist area to buy postcards to send to their friends..

Investigate ways of displaying postcards so that the full range is displayed. Remember that there will need to be a quantity of each card so that more than one person can select one, take it to the counter and pay for it.

The people in the shop tell you that the design should blend in with the character of the shop.

The shop manager tells you that they are going to increase the range of postcards to 24.

Each of the postcards is 200 by 120mm in size. They are 0.5mm thick.

The manager wants there to be enough space for at least 40 of each card to be in the display.

(a) Decide how your postcard display is going to fit into the shop and show its position on a sketch plan.

(b) Design the display to hold the right number of products to meet the requirements of the shop manager.

(c) Remember that people of all ages will require to use the display.

(d) Make a clear set of drawings that you can use to make your design at school. Remember to specify the materials that you are going to use so that they can be made available.

If you need any special components, such as screws etc, give full details so that you could purchase them.

Analysing the task

Read the task from beginning to end. You may have to do this several times before you feel that you have understood the problem.

The following points should become clear:

- The problem is about displaying postcards in a shop.
- There is a range of postcards, the number is not specified.
- The range is to be increased to 24 postcards.
- There are 40 cards of each kind.
- The cards are 200 x 120 x 0.5mm.
- The design should blend in with the character of the shop.

You need to make a list like this so that it is easy for you to follow and it can also form part of your Product Design Specification.

The task tells us also that:-

Many visitors who come into a tourist area buy postcards to send to their friends.

This is the context in which the problem is being set and helps you to get a feel for the problem you are going to attempt to solve. The fact that most of the people are tourists suggests that they need not all have an understanding of the English language and therefore a design which is easy to understand and use may be important.

You are also told that the design must blend in with the character of the shop. You have a choice here of:

either   a) presenting a hypothetical situation, i.e. one that you have made up,
or   b) identifying a shop that really exists in your area.

If you have a choice then it is much easier to design a display for a shop that already exists because you can:

1. do some primary (first hand) research;
2. see what the place looks like to identify its character;
3. identify a suitable position for the card display;
4. find out what you can from the shop owner or manager about the type of people who come into the shop; where the best place is for a card display and have your initial ideas evaluated by this person before developing your ideas.

Designing for a customer is how designers mostly work and presents a real situation.

Next you are being given guidance about what areas you should investigate.

Investigate ways of displaying postcards so that the full range is displayed. Remember that there will need to be a quantity of each card so that more than one person can select one, take it to the counter and pay for it.

Having done your research you can begin to be quite sure what the Design Brief should be.

DESIGN BRIEF:

Design and make a postcard display.

That is all you need to state. The Product Design Specification will state all the specific details and this will come mainly from your analysis of the problem. So now you can write these details as a:

Product design specification

The Product display must:

- display a range of 24 postcards;
- display 40 cards of each kind;

- display cards that are 200 x 120 x 0.5mm. in size;
- blend in with the character of the shop;
- be accessible to people of all ages.

You will have to work within a range of constraints and you can write a heading CONSTRAINTS and write this also in the form of a list. A list is easier to follow and also enables you to check to see if everything has been done.

Constraints

The Product Display must:-

- be able to be made in a school workshop;
- be able to be made by me in the time available;
- not cost more than £...;

There may be other constraints which relate to the availability of materials, tools and specialised equipment.

Once you have established all this information and written this up neatly in your folio you can begin to set about designing a product display unit.

Generating ideas

Whilst you have to only design a display for a single product, a postcard, you must still put down on paper a broad range of ideas. You must show the examiner that you have kept an open mind and looked at a variety of ideas. You should also annotate (write brief notes on) your drawings to show that you have referred to your Design Brief, Product Design Specification and Constraints and evaluated each idea in terms of how well it might fulfil all these requirements. There is no need to refer to all of them individually but just give a general comment to say why an idea is feasible or not feasible. These formative evaluations must be evident so that you can be credited with the marks that are available.

Development of an idea

After you have evaluated your potential solutions you will select a design proposal and make a detailed drawing to show how it might be made. Here you will have to consider the use of different materials, methods of construction, likely processes needed, etc. You may wish to make a three dimensional mock-up using off cuts of card to see if your ideas on paper really do work in practice. If you do model your idea in three dimensions do keep the model for assessment no matter how unfinished it may look to you.

Working drawing

This is the drawing which will have all the details that are necessary for it to be made. You may know how you want to make it without bothering to make a working drawing but you must do a working drawing if you wish to be given the credit. The drawing must:-

- be drawn to scale;
- show all the constructional detail;
- show all the sizes;
- have a cutting list, naming the materials and their sizes (this may also include a components list);

The type of working drawing is left for you to choose. When you are working in resistant materials like wood, metal, plastic, the most commonly used working drawing is presented in Orthographic Projection. Here you have to do your drawing according to British Standards. There are examples on pages 32 and 101. If you require specific details then you should refer to any of the following publications:

PD 730   Engineering drawing practice.
PD 1192 Construction drawing practice:
PD 7303 Electrical and electronic graphical symbols for use in schools and colleges.
PD 7307 Graphical symbols for use in schools and colleges.

The next stage is to make your solution. You will need to show evidence of planning as well as making.

Planning the making

The most important thing to know is how much time you have in which to not only complete the design in whatever materials you have chosen but also to allow yourself time for the solution to be tested and tried so that you can write a valid summative evaluation. Give yourself a target by setting a completion date.

First, write down the completion date at the bottom of a page. Then write down the starting date at the top. Now divide the space in between into the number of weeks that you have available.

After receiving the materials shown on your cutting list your activities are most likely to include:

- Checking that all the materials are cut to the correct size.
- Preparing the material for marking out.
- Marking out.
- Cutting out.
- Fitting/assembling (no permanent methods of joining used).
- Modifying any components that were found to be ill-fitting in the assembling.
- Assemble permanently.
- Clean up and apply finish if needed.

These activities will not necessarily require equal lengths of time, so take advice from your teacher.

For each activity just briefly state what has to be done.

You may wish to use a chart to show when each activity is to take place. The making time for this task is approximately 10 hours and the chart below shows how the ten hours may be divided so that each activity can be completed.

Date	Time	Design stage	Activity	Design stage
21st Jan	1hr	Check materials. Cut to size. Mark out construction	See if it is correct according to my working drawing. Begin marking out and checking details against the working drawing	Do this thoroughly to avoid making errors later
24th Jan	2hrs	Cutting out all the parts	Cut to shape ready for joining	Check thoroughly
28th Jan	2hrs	Fitting and assembling	Assemble everything together to see if it fits. Clean up and adjust if necessary	Do not join anything permanently yet
4th Feb	1hr	Final fitting	Final check before final fitting next lesson	Check that facilities are ready
7th Feb	2hrs	Final fitting	Assemble everything together permanently	
11th Feb	2hrs	Finishing off	Clean all parts and apply a finish	Leave in a safe place so that it does not get damaged

Fig. 3.10

Summative evaluation

When the product is completed you have to test it, see if it works and assess how well it satisfies the Design Brief, and Product Design Specification. Since you made a list of details in the Product Design Specification you will find it easy to make your evaluative judgements against each detail you have stated. Start by changing the specifications into questions e.g.

- **Specification**
  - display a range of 24 postcards;
  - display 40 cards of each kind;

- **Evaluation**
  Does the solution display 24 postcards?
  Does it display 40 cards of each kind?

In answering these questions it will be insufficient simply to say just 'yes' and 'no'. You will need to qualify your 'yes' or 'no' with how well it displayed the cards. In doing this you will be demonstrating to the examiner that you have been assessing the effectiveness of your solution.

■ Recommendations

In the light of your experience you will have encountered difficulties in constructing that you may not have envisaged in the early days of designing. You should therefore be in a position of saying what you would do if you had the chance of doing the task again. You may have chosen another material because it would be easier to work. Or you would have chosen a different process, one which could have been done with just as good results but more quickly.

You should give quite a lot of thought to writing an evaluation because there are 20% of the marks available.

INTERMEDIATE LEVEL and HIGHER LEVEL TASKS

The activity of designing is the same for each of the levels but the process gets more demanding. You are given more intricate tasks to perform which give you more problems to resolve. You have to think more deeply and show evidence of a higher level of innovation and imagination. In doing so you will also be expected to be able to present your work at a higher level, i.e. your graphical and presentation skills will need to be that much better than that expected from a foundation level candidate. Also your making skills will demonstrate a higher level of accuracy and finish.

TASK A – PRODUCT DISPLAY

Intermediate Level – levels 5–8

There are three different toy kits which are displayed for sale in the local toy shop.
They are:

Finger Puppets,
Cuddly Toys and
Articulated String Puppets.

The shop needs a free-standing display which will clearly display the whole range of these products.

Investigate free-standing displays that could be used in the shop.

When you return and talk to the Manager of the shop she tells you that it is very important that the image of the shop should be expressed right the way through the design.

The following important features must be met:
■ the design must be stable so that it will not tip over and cause an accident,
■ it must be easy to manufacture and be in keeping with the image of the shop.
In addition, the pack sizes are as follows:

Finger Puppets	180 x 100 x 30mm
Cuddly Toys	220 x 120 x 15mm
Articulated String Puppets	200 x 150 x 50mm

There is a slot (25 x 10mm) at the top of each package, in the centre, for fitting to the stand.

Design a display stand that will hold the maximum amount of stock in the most convenient way possible. The design should incorporate the key design features identified by the manager. You must be able to make it using the school facilities. There is a possibility that the product could be marketed to other retailers.

Analysing the task

If you have read Task A Foundation Level and this one you will soon realise that more is being asked of you to think about and to resolve. The major difference is that in this task you are asked to design a display for three different items all of different sizes compared with a single item, postcards, that were all the same size in the foundation task. The other, and quite important detail that you will need to consider is how far your design could be marketed to other retailers.

The design process, however, is just the same as that described in the analysis given for foundation level.

Now compare the Task A set for the Higher level.

TASK A – PRODUCT DISPLAY

Higher level – Levels 7–10

During the summer holidays you work in a shop as a sales assistant. Part of your job is to unpack the new deliveries and put them out for display. It is necessary to keep an accurate record of what arrives and what is sold, the rest should be in stock.

It becomes obvious that many of the compact discs that have been specially purchased for the shop, have been stolen by shoplifters. The directors of the shop instruct the manager to only put out the cases on display. The customers then ask an assistant to put the compact disc in the case when they purchase them.

Even this strategy does not seem to be working! Thieves are still stealing empty cases!

In desperation the shop manager asks you if you can investigate the problem and report back to her offering a system that could solve the theft problem.

Investigate a method of displaying compact discs that allow the customer to select the product without the cases being stolen.

After giving your presentation to the manager she decides that what the shop needs is a display that:

fits in the design of the shop;

allows customers to select their choices and come to the counter and get the assistant to give it to them;

has some sort of customer interaction, movement or remote control as examples;

fits the special boxes that the shop uses i.e. 142 x 124 x 10mm; and does not allow the boxes to be stolen.

Design a solution to the problem, together with the presentation material, so that you can get funding from the directors to produce your design. You must be able to manufacture your design using the school facilities, but you are able to buy specialist components as necessary.

Analysing the task

Here the designing activity is wide open. You really need to do some Primary Research and to consult with your client, the manager, on a regular basis. You may not only arrive at a solution with a product but also a system. The system has to include movement or remote control that is activated in some way or another. This type of open ended comment given in the requirements is something that would need clarification from the manager. However, it is always possible that the manager does not know what she really requires and may expect you to come up with a suggestion or suggestions. What is clear is that there is a problem of theft which needs to be resolved without hindering the honest customer who wants to buy a particular compact disc.

To show the assessor that you know how to analyse the problem is important and this will be shown in the wording of your **Design Brief** and a **Product Design Specification**.

The **Design Brief** could read like this:

Design and make a display that allows a customer to select a compact disc.

The **Product Design Specification** would then include the specific details that need to be fulfilled. You extract the details from the Task Sheet.

The solution must:

- fit in the design of the shop;
- prevent the theft of compact disc cases;
- prevent the theft of a compact disc;
- suitable for presentation to the directors.

Listing the details like this helps you to focus your attention upon what is really required. The details on the Task Sheet about customer interaction, movement or control has more to do with the generation of ideas and perhaps you will incorporate remote control in your possible solutions.

Constraints

There appears to be only one specific constraint and that is that the solution must:-

■ fit the special boxes that the shop uses i.e. 142 x 124 x 10mm.

Why this should be necessary is not clear and you would need to have this clarified by the manager. However, the Task is set round a hypothetical situation and you may not have worked in this type of shop. You would be able to innovate your own situation so long as it closely matches the one you have been given.

The more general constraints which are not included on the Task Sheet, but which you will have to consider, are time and cost. There must be a limit on how much you can spend and of course you have to make your solution which also includes a Design Folio by the date given by the examining board.

Once you have analysed the task and you have written the Design Brief and Product Design Specification you can continue with the other designing activities such as generating ideas, investigation, developing ideas etc.

EXAMPLES OF OTHER ASSIGNMENTS

The following assignments have been set by Examining Boards in the past and are likely to appear again in the future. They may appear worded differently but the activity you have to perform will not change very much. This subject is all about two main elements, **DESIGNING AND MAKING**.

1. Simple energy conversions:

    MOTOR POWERED TOY using a small 5-volt d.c. electric motor.
    WORKING MODEL ELECTRIC GENERATOR using a small d.c. motor as a dynamo.
    A KINETIC SCULPTURE to be located outdoors in a small leisure garden

    (ULEAC)

2. Learning aids: no specific problem was set. The candidates were free to identify a need and to write a Design Brief

    (MEG)

3. Areas of study: no general topic was set, instead candidates were able to select one area of study from four topics:

■ A table decoration
■ A fun money box
■ Designing for the needs of the disabled and the handicapped
■ Designing for the needs of younger children

    (WJEC)

THE WRITTEN EXAMINATION

MULTIPLE CHOICE QUESTIONS

SHORT ANSWER QUESTIONS

STRUCTURED QUESTIONS

REVISION

IN THE EXAM ROOM

ANSWERING THE QUESTIONS

GETTING STARTED

The written examination forms a very important part of your overall assessment. As you will have seen from the introduction and the syllabus and assessment charts, the majority of the written examinations last 2hrs. But there are variations from forty minutes to two and a half hours. You will also notice that there are three examinations for each syllabus. You only take *one* of these because each written paper is set at three different levels or *tiers*. The examining boards are inconsistent with the names they have given each tier but the terms used are given below and shown against the levels as set in the National Curriculum.

	Terms used			Levels	Grade Equivalent
Basic	Foundation	A	P	4–5–6	G-F-E-D
Standard	Intermediate	B	Q	6–7–8	B-C-D
Higher	Higher	C	R	8–9–10	B-A-A*

A* is higher than an A awarded in the pre-1994 GCSE.

The front of each written paper will give the title of the subject and the tier level for which it is set. Do check that you know which tier level you are taking *before* the examination and then, when in the examination, read the cover very carefully to see that you have got the correct paper. If you believe that you have been given the wrong paper then raise your hand for the examination invigilator to see. If you have been given the wrong paper the invigilator will change it for you.

Most examinations are in the form of a booklet and you will be required to write your answer in the spaces provided against each question. Remember, the size of the space is an indication of the length of response expected. Small space, short answer; big space, long answer.

STRUCTURE OF THE WRITTEN PAPER

The written examination paper is divided into two parts. The first part deals with the *core content* of the subject and you are required to answer *all* questions in this section. The second part deals with the *extension study* and you are only required to answer a question or questions from the extension materials you studied. The three extensions are Textiles, Food and Graphics.

ESSENTIAL PRINCIPLES

1 ▷ MULTIPLE CHOICE QUESTIONS

2 ▷ SHORT ANSWER QUESTIONS

There are a number of different *types* of written question.

At the moment these are only used by the IGCSE Examination. They are considered more fully on page 48, and examples are presented there. Since you receive no penalty for a wrong answer, you should make an attempt on each question. Even if you do not know the correct answer, you may be able to *eliminate* some of the possible answers that are incorrect.

These questions should take only a minute or two to answer and if you read the rubric (set of instructions) you will see that *all* questions in this section must be attempted.

The **short answer** type questions rely on a *brief* response, but there is a danger that the response could be *too brief* or *imprecise*. Suppose the question was:

■ From what material is a nail punch made?

The answer could quite well be 'metal'. Though this would not be wrong, a *better* answer would have been 'steel', but a still more informative answer would have been 'Carbon steel'. Each of these answers would have received some credit, but more credit would be given to the second answer than the first and still more to the third answer.

❝❝ Be as specific as you can in your answers. ❞❞

The more informative answers gain more marks so when answering questions about **materials** always be specific. Give as much identification as you possibly can. When dealing with **wood** name the *type* of wood you think is appropriate, e.g. 'African Mahogany'. Even the answer 'hardwood' is more informative than just 'wood' and so is given more credit. Similarly, when dealing with **plastics**, name the *material* as fully as you can. If the response requires a *thermosoftening* plastics material to be named then state it as 'Acrylic', 'Nylon', 'Polystyrene', etc. If, however, a *thermosetting* plastics material has to be named, then state 'Polyester Resin', 'Melamine Formaldehyde', etc. If you cannot remember the specific name, even using the terms 'thermosoftening' or 'thermosetting' will gain more credit if correctly applied than just using the term 'plastics'.

Being **specific** about **constructional detail** is also very important. Naming a *joint* as 'Mortice and Tenon' is not so specific as a 'Stepped Haunched Mortice and Tenon'. Neither is the term 'welding' as specific as the name of any of the *types of welding* that can be used.

Because the answers are short a *lot* of questions are asked in this section. This enables the examiner to set questions over a *wide range* of the syllabus. Short answer questions will mainly concentrate on *knowledge* rather than on understanding, therefore it is important that you *know* the correct technological terms and where they apply. The examiner will usually be more concerned with what you have learnt through *experience* rather than with what you have *remembered* from things you have read.

Therefore make sure that you become familiar with the *technical terminology* used in design activities; it will certainly help you to answer these short questions.

3 ▷ STRUCTURED QUESTIONS

The **structured** questions are *much longer* and form the second section of the examination paper. You are given more time to answer them and you only have to answer two questions from a choice of approximately ten questions. However, within a *single* question there are *many smaller questions* and the further you get into the question, the more detail is required in answering any part. It could be said that the first part of the question is easy, and that each successive part gets progressively more difficult, hence the name 'Structured Question'.

The early parts of a *structured* question are similar to short answer questions, in that the responses required are generally brief and are designed to test your *knowledge*. However the emphasis changes as you progress through the question from that of testing knowledge to that of testing *understanding*.

The spaces allowed for answering these questions are much larger and a single space may cover several pages. Each space should give you an idea of the length of the expected response. Because of the nature of the subject you should take every opportunity to **illustrate your answers with annotated sketches** (freehand drawings with notes). Again the space provided should indicate the size of the illustrations expected.

QUALITY OF ILLUSTRATIONS

Because you are working under the pressure of *time* in an examination you have to get down as much information as you can in the time available. This may mean that your drawings will not have the finish and quality that you would hope for. The most important function of the drawing is to *communicate clearly* to the examiner *what you know*. Shading or colouring the drawing is unlikely to be a vital element in communicating the information more clearly to the examiner! Besides which, the time spent shading and colouring might be more profitably spent in *checking* your answers to see if they could be improved.

The examiner is interested in detail. Use the *dotted line* to show hidden detail or use *section views* where appropriate.

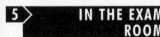

The *written* examination is just as important as the coursework and the design paper and should be prepared for in the best way that you can. Your experience in working with materials and in covering a range of processes should also be of help to you in preparing to take the written examination.

There are no hard and fast rules about revising for this written paper. The questions are mainly concerned with the **application of knowledge** rather than the regurgitation of facts. The *areas of knowledge* that should concern you are as follows:

a) **materials** – wood, metal and plastics;
b) **tools** – hand and mechanical;
c) **mechanisms** – gears, levers, etc.;
d) **energy** – electrical, electronic and mechanical;
e) **construction** – methods of joining materials;
f) **processes** – lathework, soldering, casting, finishing, etc.;
g) **ergonomics** – the influence of environment on man's behaviour;
h) **anthropometrics** – the measurement of human beings;
i) **aesthetics** – pleasing shape, form, proportion, etc.;
j) **conservation** – economic use of resources;
k) **information technology** – use of computers.

Many of these topics will be very familiar to you. You can also find information on these topics in the various chapters of this book. However, the only reliable way to assess how well you can *communicate* your knowledge is to try the following:

1 Rewrite the **headings** of the notes you compiled during the course.
2 **List** important names, functions, etc. in shortened form.
3 Use a coloured 'text-marker' to **highlight important points** in your course notes.
4 Try writing the important points **from memory**.
5 **Check** what you have written from memory against your course notes.
6 Try **answering questions**, both short and structured.
7 Practise answering questions **in a limited time** without reference to your course notes.
8 Practise answering a **complete examination paper** in the time allowed.

Though you have become familiar with the format and the requirements of the paper in your preparation you should still read all the **rubric** that is on the front page. You should note the following requirements:

■ the time allowed;
■ how many questions have to be answered;
■ which questions are compulsory and which questions have a choice;
■ the time recommended for each section (not always given);
■ the units of measurement used on illustrations (usually millimetres);
■ where you must answer the questions.

You should also fill in the details requested, such as candidate number, centre number, surname and initials. If there is an instruction to indicate the questions answered in 'boxes' provided at the front of your answer booklet, try to remember to do this towards the end of the examination. You may also see on the front page some space with a statement 'For the Examiner's use only'. Do *not* write anything in that space.

ALLOCATION OF MARKS

Each question and part of a question has a number of marks allocated to it. This information can help you to decide how much time to allow yourself on each question. But remember it can only be a *guide*. Because *structured questions* are often long and made up of several parts, marks are awarded *to each part* of the whole question. They are usually to be found in the right-hand column written in brackets, e.g. [8] or (8 marks).

While the space allocated for the answer can give you an indication of the *amount* you may need to write, the mark allocation will give you an indication of the *depth* of detail that is required. Where you have a *choice* of questions, all of them must carry the same number of total marks.

6 > **ANSWERING THE QUESTIONS**

Before attempting to answer a question, **read the question more than once** to make sure that you have fully understood what you are being asked. This applies to the multiple choice and short answer questions just as much as it does to the structured questions.

ANSWERING MULTIPLE CHOICE QUESTIONS

You are required to select the correct answer from four given answers. You indicate your choice by placing a tick against the answer. If you put a tick against an answer and you wish to change your response, make sure that you cross out the unwanted tick so the examiner is in no doubt about the answer you believe to be correct. If you leave two ticks you will get no marks at all even if one of the ticks is marked against the correct answer.

ANSWERING THE SHORT QUESTIONS

All the short questions in the compulsory section have to be answered. Though they are numbered there is no strict order in which they must be answered. Therefore if you come across a question that you are not sure about, go on to the next question. You can always come back to an unanswered question later. You should attempt all questions in the compulsory section and it is advisable that this section is completed before moving on to the next section that has a different style of question, usually structured questions that take much longer to answer.

You can have worked out how much time you have available for the whole of the compulsory, short answer, section *before* the examination. If 50 out of 150 marks are given to this section, then $1/3$ of the *total time* should be spent on it. In a 2-hour exam, you should then spend no more than 40 minutes on this section. At the end of this time move on to the *next section*, returning to finish any unanswered questions if you have any spare time at the end.

Whenever possible, attempt the question even if you are not sure whether you are correct or not. You have a better chance of gaining marks by *attempting* a question than by leaving a space! The examiner will not take marks off for a wrong answer. In fact, the examiner is looking to see where marks can be awarded. So no harm will be done if in your attempt you give a wrong answer.

ANSWERING THE STRUCTURED QUESTIONS

You may have read as many as ten questions before selecting two to answer. This is very time consuming and your examination time is passing by. Some Written papers have an **index** of the questions in section 'B' printed on the front page. This enables you to see at a glance the topics of each question and on which page the question is to be found. See the example below.

INDEX TO SECTION B QUESTIONS

Questions
B1 STRUCTURES (stool) starts on page 14.
B2 PRODUCTION EVALUATION (calculator stands) starts on page 18.
B3 PLANNING (hopper manufacture) starts on page 22.
B4 DESIGN & FABRICATION (table tennis net clamp) starts on page 26.
B5 CONTROL SYSTEMS (valves) starts on page 28.
B6 TURNING (wheels) starts on page 32.
                                                    etc.

If your Examination Group *does* provide such an index, do make use of it. This should help you decide which questions to **read** first. Before deciding which questions you **answer** do at least glance at *all* the questions to make sure that you have selected the ones you wish to attempt. Having made your decision you can answer whichever of the two questions you selected in any order. As a general rule, attempt the question you think you can answer best first, and the one you feel less confident about last. It is always encouraging to feel you have 'got marks in the bank', and the confidence this gives may help you make a better attempt at your less preferred question.

Do not attempt more questions from this section than is required. You will not gain more marks. If you do attempt more questions than required they will usually all be marked, but only the two with the highest marks will be accepted. The marks you may have obtained from the remaining questions will not be counted and you will have wasted valuable time.

MAKING A CORRECTION

To **change** an answer or to **correct** it is perfectly acceptable, but it is vitally important that you:

a) erase or cover over the part that you believe to be wrong and clearly indicate the answer you wish to be accepted;
b) do not confuse the examiner; and
c) only make a correction when you are absolutely certain that the answer you have given in the first place is wrong and the correction is correct.

What has been written in this chapter has been mainly concerned with revision and examination techniques in the final stages of the course. Though the effort you make at this point may help to improve your performance, it cannot be a substitute for a high level of commitment *throughout* the course. You are much more likely to achieve a mark consistent with the true level of your potential ability by working hard and conscientiously throughout the whole course than by relying on a heavily committed revision programme in the final stages.

CHAPTER 5

GRAPHIC MEDIA

APPROACHING
COURSEWORK

GRAPHIC TECHNIQUES

GRAPHIC MATERIALS

GRAPHIC EQUIPMENT

BASIC DRAWING
TECHNIQUES

SHADING TECHNIQUES

SHADOWS

MODELLING

GETTING STARTED

Graphic Media is one of three extensions that you can take with either Design and Technology or Technology as the core subject. The other two extensions are Textiles and Food.

The important theme in Graphic Media is still the activity of *designing and making*. You may, in some designing activities, *realise* a solution in a two dimensional form. In other design activities you may need to produce a combination of two and three dimensional solutions, such as a graphic illustration and a model, made from card, of a design of a room or a building.

The illustrations have been drawn in pen and ink to help you follow the constructional detail and to provide you with precise information that would have been blurred using other media. You should use a variety of media which may include a selection of pencils, felt pens, fibre tipped pens, crayons and technical pens etc. Even so, the basic principles of drawing will be the same as those illustrated in this chapter.

As in all syllabuses, the three tier levels of performance and assessment exists and you will be required to select (or be guided by your teacher) the tier which is appropriate for you. The three tiers are:

- Foundation.   Levels 4–5–6
- Intermediate.   Levels 5–6–7–8
- Higher.   Levels 7–8–9–10

You will be required to complete a coursework task and answer a question from the Graphic Media section of the terminal written examination paper.

ESSENTIAL PRINCIPLES

Planning your research work

A simple list of tasks to be completed by certain dates is helpful. It helps you to see what has to be done by certain dates and it also helps you to check if you are on target for completing the project on time. If you have been set a *theme*, it will have been given you quite some time before you are actually time-tabled for the project.This means that you have an opportunity to do some research and begin collecting resource material to read and look at *before* the date for beginning the task. When researching, you often get more material than you require. It may also fall into different categories, so adopt a *filing system*. Using an A4 lever arch file is very helpful for storing research information. It can be subdivided into sections and you can always add research material to these sections as and when you collect more and more information. Much of the information that you get from magazines and catalogues can be carefully selected and put into this type of file.

Types of Design Problem

The problems set are often very open ended. This means that you have the opportunity of developing your own interest within the topic. Such topics as 'Interior Design'; 'Advertising a product'; 'Advertising a special occasion' and 'Designing the documenta-tion for a company', offer you quite a wide choice of activity within one topic. The opportunities under say 'Interior Design' means that you can choose the *situation*. You may select any of the following: an office, your own study bedroom, the entrance to the school or any room of your choice. Once having chosen a specific situation you can then concentrate on the specific area of research that will help you to decide how you are going to tackle the problem.

What will you be required to do?

If the examining board has set the theme or topic, then your teacher will have received a set of *instructions*. These will tell you what you are expected to produce. Because this is a design and make task you will be expected to show evidence of designing in a folio and a product.

The folio should show all the elements of designing. A well organised folio will have the following:

1. a cover with a title, your name and the centre's name;
2. a contents page and each page numbered;
3. a context;
4. a Design Brief;
5. a Product Design Specification;
6. evidence of primary and secondary research;
7. generation of initial ideas;
8. development of a chosen idea;
9. an artistic impression of the proposed solution;
10. details from which the solution can be produced;
11. a planning schedule for the production of the solution;
12. a summative evaluation of the solution.

This should all be completed on paper of the same size, either A4 or A3, and bound down one side so that the folio can open like a book.

FOUNDATION LEVEL

You will be demonstrating your ability to draw in two and three dimension throughout your folio. You will also be demonstrating your ability to print neatly and to present information in an interesting and attractive manner.

At **foundation level** you will be required to show evidence of being able to draw lines of different thickness, and to show how light and shade can be used to give depth to

---

1 APPROACHING THE COURSEWORK TASK

❝❝ Aspects of a well organised portfolio. ❞❞

2 GRAPHIC TECHNIQUES

three dimensional artefacts. Also you will be required to use techniques to simulate texture such as rough and smooth.

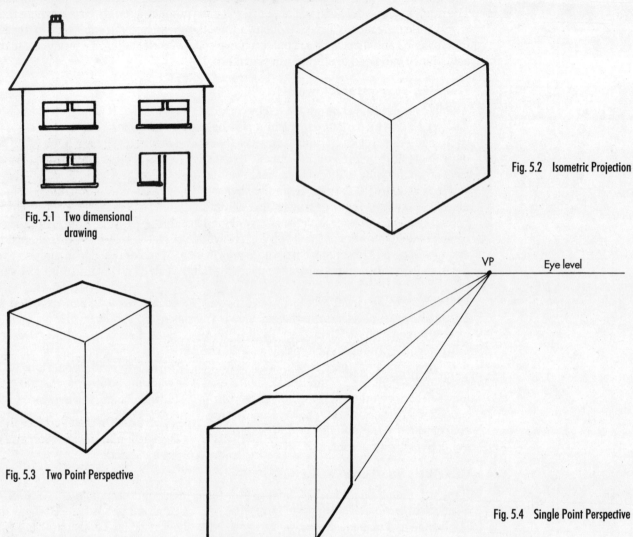

Fig. 5.1   Two dimensional drawing

Fig. 5.2   Isometric Projection

Fig. 5.3   Two Point Perspective

Fig. 5.4   Single Point Perspective

Thick and thin lines. Notice that the outline is thicker than other lines. This helps to make the drawing stand out from the paper.

Light

When light falls on a three dimensional object some areas receive more light than others so it is possible to shade those areas that receive little light to make it appear dark. Some areas receive full light and do not need shading and other areas receive half light and need to be shaded lightly.

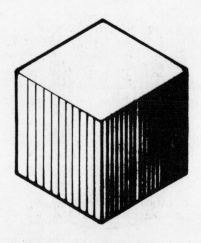

Fig. 5.5   Light falling on a cube

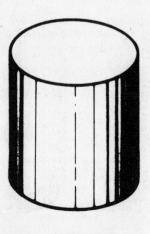

Fig. 5.6   Light falling on a cylinder

Fig. 5.7   Light falling on a cone

Texture

You will also be expected to indicate the difference between rough and smooth surfaces. The random movement of a pen or pencil will often produce a rough surface where there is very little reflection of light. To obtain a smooth appearance you can shade in the area first in pencil and then, with a rubber, remove some of the shading. To produce a textile appearance you need to show a woven pattern.

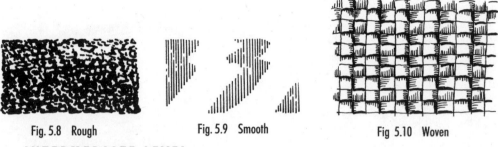

Fig. 5.8   Rough   Fig. 5.9   Smooth   Fig 5.10   Woven

INTERMEDIATE LEVEL

At **Intermediate level** you will be expected to do all those things expected for foundation level plus the following:

- use rendering to show how light reflects on surfaces;
- draw in Orthographic Projection using British Standard conventions;
- use appropriate techniques to show hidden detail.

Light

Light reflects at different levels according to the type of surface. On matt surfaces there is little to no reflection. On medium gloss surfaces there is a hint of reflection and on smooth glossy surfaces there is a strong contrast of light and dark.

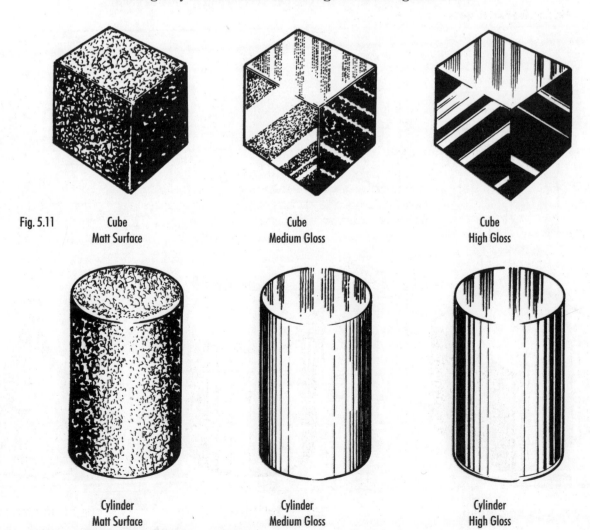

Fig. 5.11   Cube   Cube   Cube
             Matt Surface   Medium Gloss   High Gloss

             Cylinder   Cylinder   Cylinder
             Matt Surface   Medium Gloss   High Gloss

Water Tap
Example of High Gloss

Fig. 5.12

Orthographic projection

There are two types of Orthographic Projection drawings, but you only need to know one type. They are sometimes referred to as Working Drawings because they have all the details of sizes, joints, materials etc. drawn to scale. They often have four views which show a side view, two end views and a plan view. These have to be laid out in a particular way so that lines can be projected from one view to another. The difference in the arrangement of these views gives you the two types of Orthographic Projection.

First Angle Projection

The three views are laid out as shown in the figure below.

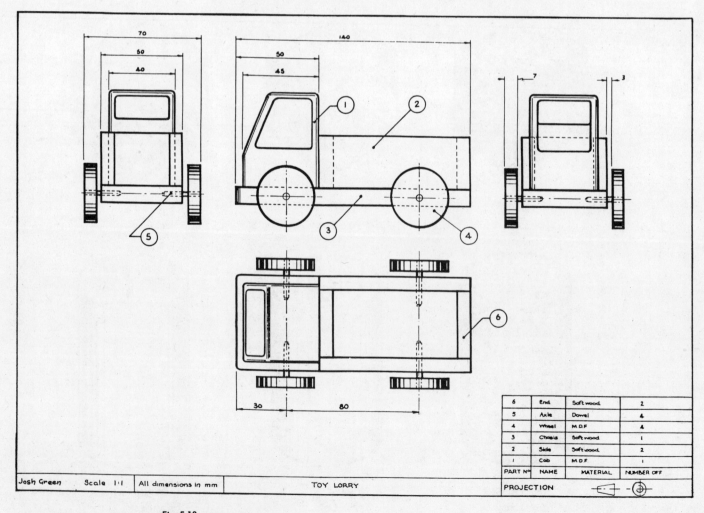

PART Nº	NAME	MATERIAL	NUMBER OFF
6	End	Softwood	2
5	Axle	Dowel	4
4	Wheel	M.D.F.	4
3	Chassis	Softwood	1
2	Side	Softwood	2
1	Cab	M.D.F.	1

Josh Green   Scale 1:1   All dimensions in mm   TOY LORRY   PROJECTION

Fig. 5.13

A simple way of remembering where the views should go is to think of the word *opposite*.

What you see from the **left** you draw on the **right**.
What you see from the **right** you draw on the **left**.
What you see from the **top** you draw on the **bottom**.

Third Angle Projection

Again four views are used and laid out as shown in the figure below.

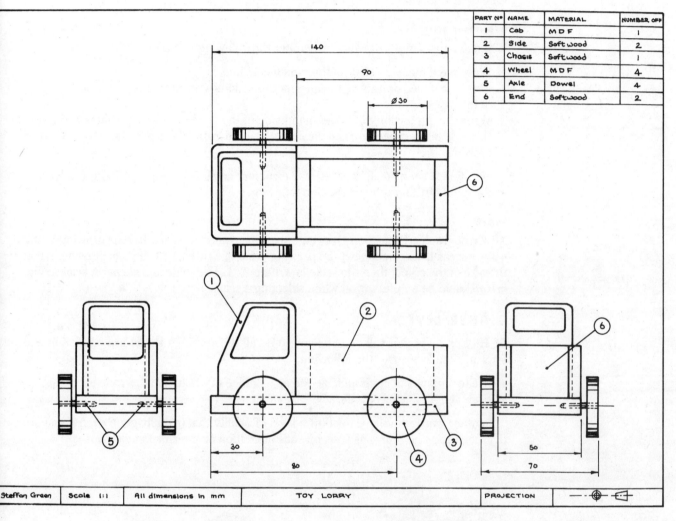

PART N°	NAME	MATERIAL	NUMBER OFF
1	Cab	MDF	1
2	Side	Softwood	2
3	Chasis	Softwood	1
4	Wheel	MDF	4
5	Axle	Dowel	4
6	End	Softwood	2

Steffon Green   Scale 1:1   All dimensions in mm   TOY LORRY   PROJECTION

Fig. 5.14

A simple way of remembering where the views should go is to think of the word *same*.

What you see from the **left** you draw on the **left**.
What you see from the **right** you drawn on the **right**.
What you see from the **top** you draw on the **top**.

Drawing Conventions

All Orthographic Projection Drawings must have a standard set of rules. These rules are standardised by the British Standards Institute, BSI. There are a number of publications which you can use such as, PP 7308 Engineering Drawing and Practice or PP 7302:1978, Compendium of British Standards for Design and Technology in Schools. There are also many books published on this specialised topic which you should read to fully acquaint yourself with graphical techniques and methods.

If you look carefully at Figs. 5.13 and 5.14 you will have examples to follow. The arrangements of the views, the use of thick and thin lines, dotted lines for hidden detail and the thin long and short chain centre lines and the dimensioning are all done according to British Standards.

Parts List

The parts list is always written such that if you had to add an item the numbers would flow in numerical order.

Cutting List

An extra column could be added to the parts list so that the size of each part could be written. Remember that the size of a piece of material is given in a certain order, i.e. Length, Width and Thickness. A useful way of remembering this is to think of **L**ondon **W**eekend **T**elevision.

Dimensioning

When dimensioning a drawing remember the following points:

1. Write the dimension clear of the dimension line.
2. Write the dimension above the line for dimensions written parallel to the bottom edge of the paper.
3. Write the dimension on the left-hand side of the vertical dimension lines and round through 90 degrees so that they can be read from the right-hand edge of your drawing.

   Attention to such detail impresses an examiner and lets him/her know how much you know about Orthographic Projection Drawing.

Scale

All Orthographic Projection Drawings must be drawn to scale. If your drawing is the same size as the actual object the drawing scale is written 1 : 1. If your drawing is half the size of the object then the scale is written 2 : 1. The following sheet on scales (Fig. 5.16) should be helpful to you when selecting a scale.

HIGHER LEVEL

At **Higher level** you will be expected to do all those things stated in Foundation and intermediate levels *plus* the following:-

■ use techniques to communicate the appearance of wood, metal, textile etc.;
■ draw at a high level of accuracy.

   In other words you have to show a level of quality that is really good even if you are drawing the same things as someone at Foundation or Intermediate level.

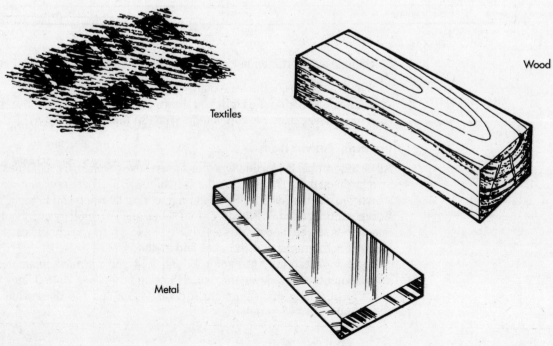

Fig. 5.15

SCALES

EVERY THING SHOULD BE DRAWN IN PROPORTION, I.E. TO A UNIFORM SCALE AND THE SCALE USED SHOULD BE STATED ON THE DRAWING AS A RATIO.

ON DRAWINGS SMALLER THAN FULL SIZE.

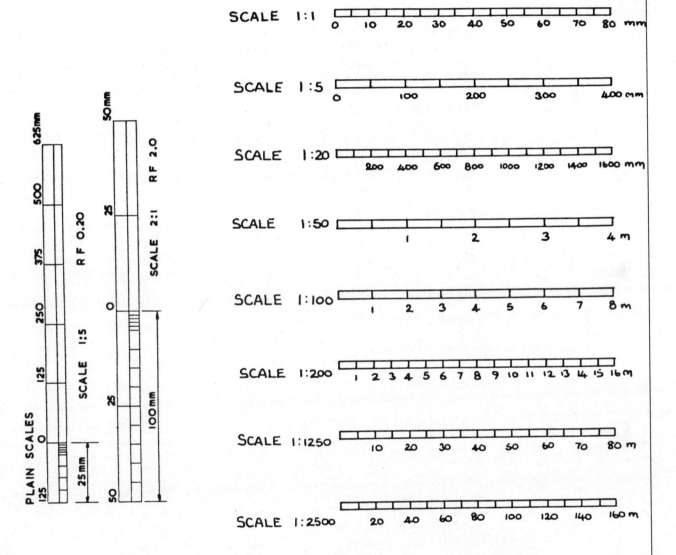

SCALE 1:1

SCALE 1:5

SCALE 1:20

SCALE 1:50

SCALE 1:100

SCALE 1:200

SCALE 1:1250

SCALE 1:2500

ON DRAWINGS LARGER THAN FULL SIZE.

SCALE 2:1   5:1   10:1   20:1   50:1   100:1 Etc

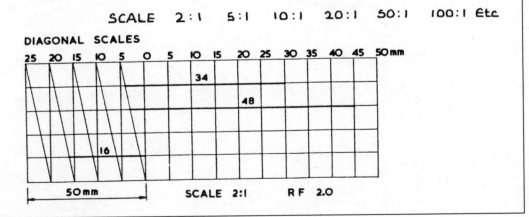

DIAGONAL SCALES

SCALE 2:1   R F 2.0

Fig. 5.16

3 > GRAPHIC MATERIALS

Everyone is expected to use a good range of graphic materials. This applies to all the tiers. You are expected to show evidence of having worked with:

- colouring pencils, felt and fibre tipped pens;
- card, foamboard, and associated modelling materials.

Your own level of competence in using these materials will be obvious in the graphics work that you produce.

4 > GRAPHIC EQUIPMENT

FOUNDATION LEVEL

At **Foundation level** you are expected to know when and how to use a drawing board, setsquare, compass, and standard templates for drawing circles and ellipses. When modelling you should know when and how to use a cutting mat, a safety straight edge and a paper-card cutting knife. You should also know the meaning of and be familiar with the terms 'one off', 'batch' and 'long production runs'.

INTERMEDIATE LEVEL

At **Intermediate level** you are expected to be able to do all those things listed for the foundation level plus being able to:

- show a capability of making models in two and three dimension;
- produce computer aided drawing.

Computer aided drawing. For more guidance read Chapters 15–17.

HIGHER LEVEL

At **Higher Level** you are expected to do all those things listed above but at a more sophisticated level.

An example is this *Two Point Perspective* drawing of an injection moulding machine.

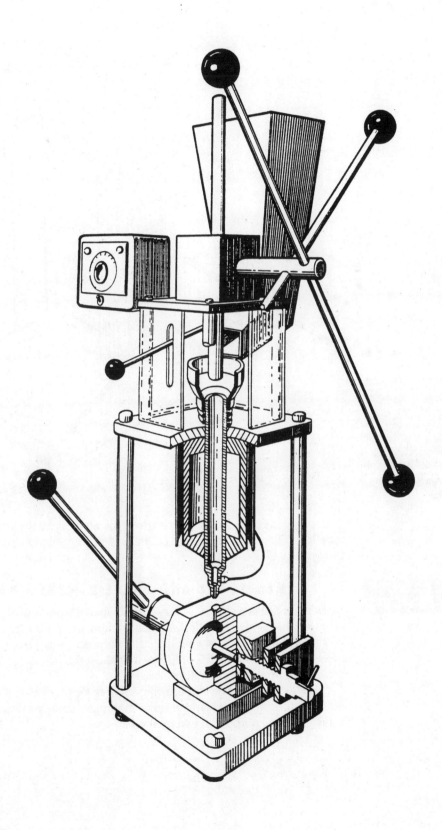

Fig. 5.17 Injection moulding machine

If you look carefully you will see that thick lines are used to emphasise the outline, and parallel lines are used to provide a dark tone to the sides that are on the opposite side to the source of light i.e. in the shade. The spherical handles are rendered to give the feeling of a smooth surface and the high light spots give the feeling of roundness. Thin broken lines on the acrylic guard are used to give the illusion of transparency. Some parts have been sectioned to show detail that would otherwise be hidden. The distance apart of lines on curved surfaces such as the end of the plunger are graduated to give the feeling of roundness.

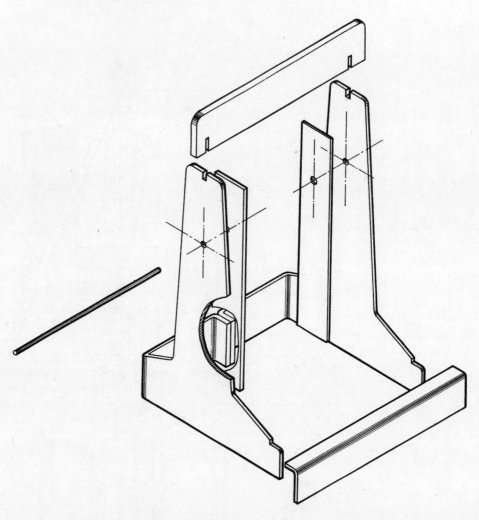

Fig. 5.18 Exploded Isometric of a
design for a two tone
chime

Drawing in Exploded Isometric gives you an opportunity to show how all the parts go together. They are kept in line so that if you were able to push them in a straight line they would all fit together.

5 **BASIC DRAWING
TECHNIQUES**

TWO DIMENSIONAL AND THREE DIMENSIONAL DRAWING

Drawing in *two dimensions* is very useful when a true view of a surface is required as in orthographic projection, designing a pattern for a garment, planning a layout for a poster, or the plan view of a building. But if the drawing is to be of an object that is already three dimensional then the only way to make a realistic graphical representation of that object is to draw in three dimensions.

There are several ways of drawing in *three dimensions* and they will be dealt with in order of difficulty. You could assume that many students doing foundation level would make good use of the first two methods.

OBLIQUE PROJECTION

Draw a square and from that square project a line, at approximately 45 degrees, from three corners. Now join these with two more lines that are parallel with two edges of the square. Do not draw the 45 degree lines too long. Draw them approximately half the length of those in the square. This will then make the drawing look more realistic. You can use the same technique for drawing a cylinder on its side. Draw a circle then project two lines at 45 degrees. Complete the drawing by drawing a semi-circle to join up the two lines.

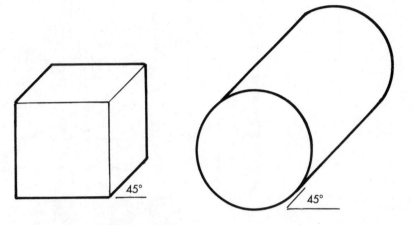

Fig. 5.19 Oblique Projection of a cube and a cylinder

PLANOMETRIC PROJECTION

Another name for this type of projection is **Axonometric Projection**.

This technique is very useful when you want to change a two dimensional plan of a room into a three dimensional image. Rotate the plan through 30 degrees or 45 degrees. (These two angles are chosen because they are the angles of the set squares used for projection drawing.) This is best done under a sheet of tracing paper so that it stays in position while you draw. Trace the plan in its new position and project lines up from the corners. This will begin to give you the three dimensional effect of the walls of the room. Furniture, and fittings can be completed to give the overall three dimensional effect.

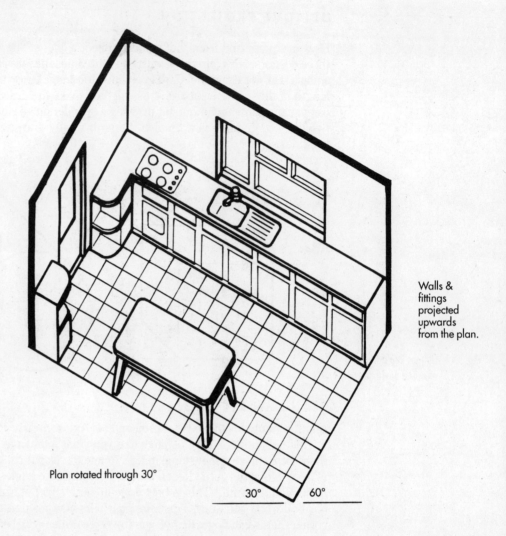

Walls &
fittings
projected
upwards
from the plan.

Plan rotated through 30°

30°   60°

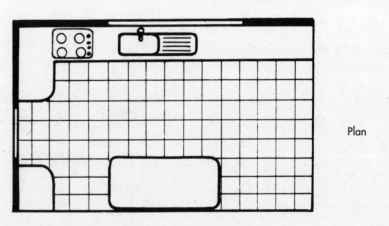

Plan

Fig. 5.20   Planometric Projection

ISOMETRIC PROJECTION

As with the other two techniques this is basically quite simple, with quite pleasing results.

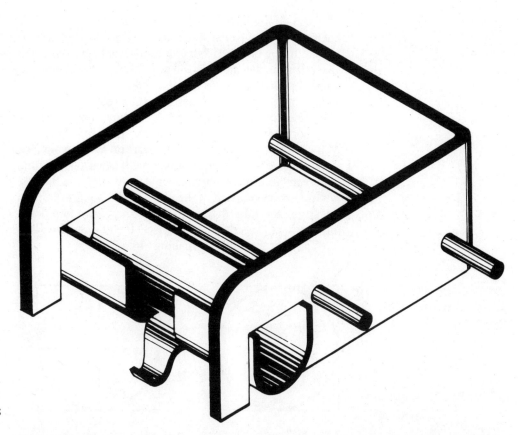

Fig. 5.21   Example: Buggy chassis

What you must remember is that lines representing vertical planes are drawn vertically and lines that are drawn to represent horizontal planes are drawn at an angle of 30 degrees.

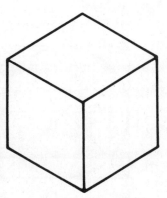

Fig. 5.22   Isometric cube

Drawing ellipses can be done using an ellipse template. But the important thing is to know the correct way round to place your template. An ellipse has a major axis and a minor axis. If you know which way round to have the major axis then the minor axis will take care of itself. The drawing below shows you the major axes drawn on the sides of the cube. If you have an ellipse template then you select the appropriate size ellipse, line up the marks on the template with one of the major axes, hold the template steady and draw the ellipse. Do the same with the other two sides so that you have an example of one ellipse drawn in a horizontal plane and two ellipses drawn in a vertical plane.

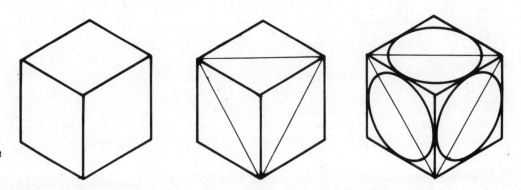

Fig. 5.23   Isometric cube
and ellipses

If you do not have an ellipse template you can still draw ellipses using the following technique. First remember that an ellipse is the view of a circle at an angle. You can check this by holding a circular dinner plate in front of you and gradually rotate it in any direction you like and you will see its shape change from a circle to an ellipse. One more thing for you to notice is that if you draw two lines, with a felt pen, that pass through the centre of the plate and cross at right angles the diameter of the circle always remains the same in one direction. This is the line that represents the major axis and the other, the shorter one, represents the minor axis. To be able to extend your knowledge so that you can draw an ellipse, you can start off by drawing a circle with a diameter of 50mm. Now enclose the circle in a square with sides also of 50mm in length. Next draw the two diameters that cross one another at right angles in the centre by measuring and marking the mid point on each of the sides of the square. Join the opposite mid points. Where these join the sides of the square you now have four points of the circle that touch at the mid point of the sides of the square. If you draw the diagonals you can get another four positions on the circle so making eight in all.

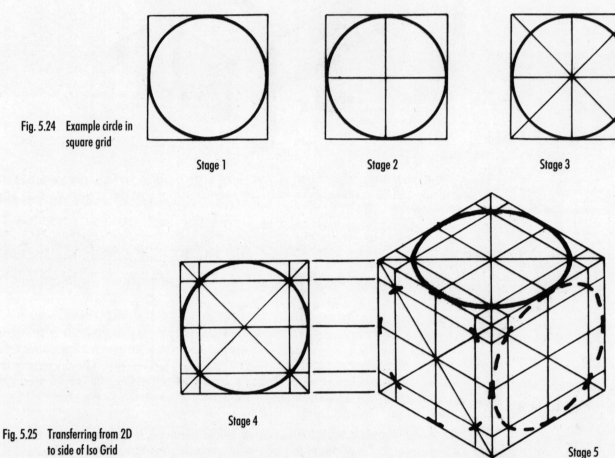

Fig. 5.24   Example circle in square grid

Stage 1   Stage 2   Stage 3

Fig. 5.25   Transferring from 2D to side of Iso Grid

Stage 4   Stage 5

If you follow the instructions you can make a two dimensional grid so that you can complete the ellipses.

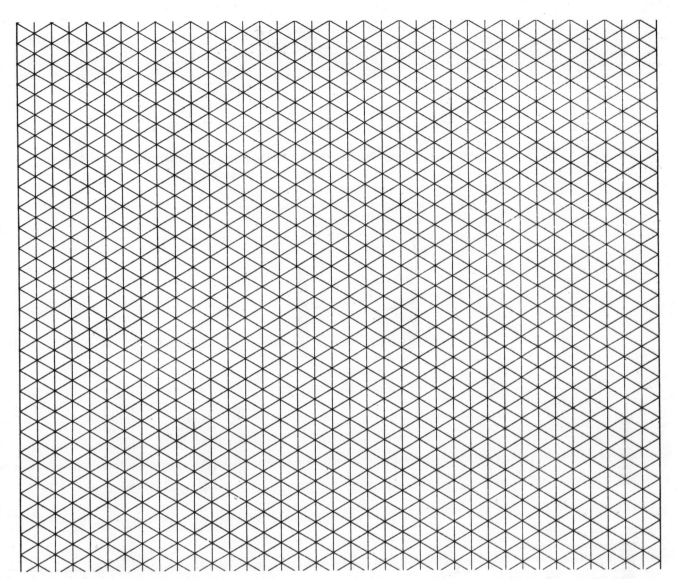

Fig. 5.26 Isometric grid

The grid contains the vertical lines for the vertical planes and the lines at 30 degrees for the horizontal planes. The grid is placed underneath a sheet of tracing paper or any other quality paper that will allow the lines of the grid to be seen. The drawing is then done on the top sheet and not on the grid. This means that the grid can be used many times for many different drawings.

Fig. 5.27 Example grid and simple drawings

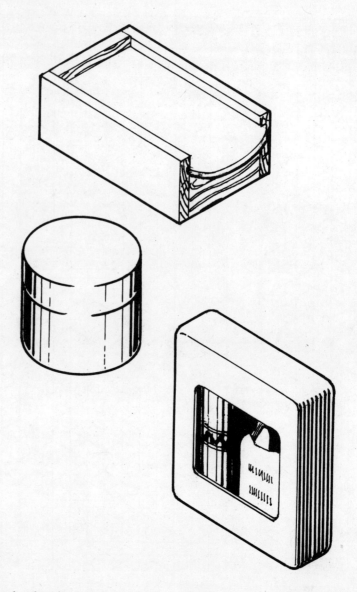

Fig. 5.28 Examples of a package drawn using an Isometric Grid

Note that the drawings may not seem perfectly correct to the eye. This is because, although you may have employed the techniques correctly these drawings do not include perspective or foreshortening of objects. The further objects are away from you the smaller they appear.

The next two methods of drawing in three dimensional do have foreshortening and enable more realistic drawings to be produced.

SINGLE POINT PERSPECTIVE

This technique is also sometimes called interior perspective because it is commonly used for drawing the inside of rooms. Here are a few examples.

Fig. 5.29 Example of single point perspective drawn with the aid of a grid

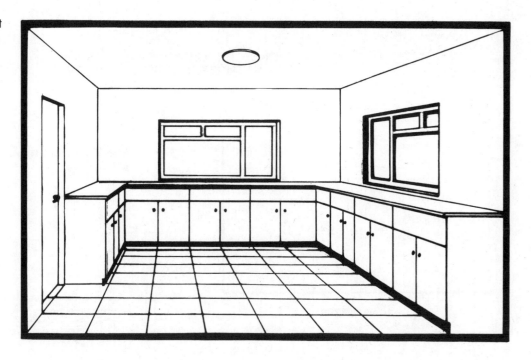

Single point perspective can of course be used for indoor and outdoor scenes.

Eye Level

Fig. 5.30 An exterior drawing

Basic Principles of perspective drawing

■ the vanishing point is always on the eye level.
■ all horizontal lines meet at a vanishing point.

How to draw in single point perspective

If you are drawing something as large as a room on an A4 size drawing paper you will need to draw to scale. A suggested scale of 1:20 will enable you to draw a grid as shown in Fig. 5.31.

ONE POINT PERSPECTIVE GRID
INTERIOR PERSPECTIVE

1. Draw room to scale

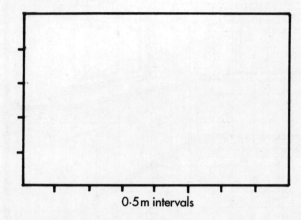

0·5 m intervals

A grid for a room 4 m × 4 m
& 2·5 m high

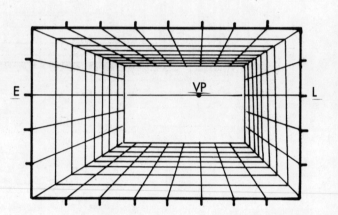

2. Draw Eye level & vanishing Point

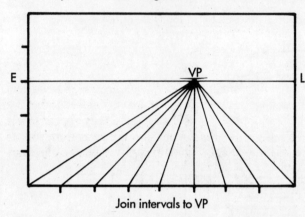

Join intervals to VP

3. Extend eye level to represent 2 m.

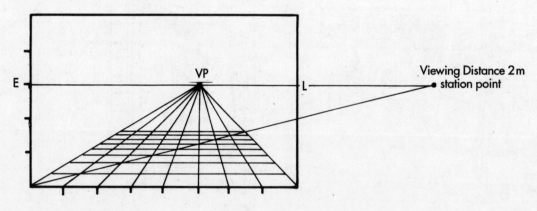

Viewing Distance 2 m
● station point

Fig. 5.31   An interior drawing

Follow the sequence given in Fig. 5.31 to obtain your single point perspective grid. When you have drawn your grid place it under a sheet of detail paper to draw an interior scene. Fig. 5.29 is an example of a fitted kitchen and a tiled floor to show clearly that it fits the grid that was used.

SINGLE POINT PERSPECTIVE (INTERIOR PERSPECTIVE)
SCALE 1:20

EYE LEVEL ABOUT 1·5m WHICH IS STANDING OF AN ADULT

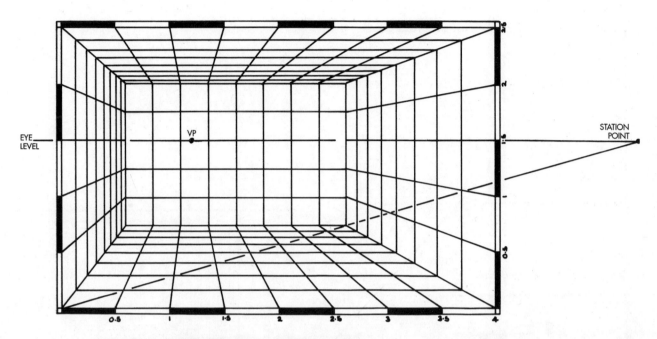

Fig. 5.32 **TWO POINT PERSPECTIVE**

Two point perspective is perhaps the most commonly used type of three dimensional drawing and it is the one method which produces images that are very close to what the object looks like in real life. As objects recede into the background they appear to get smaller. Even the sides of a cube appear smaller the further they are away from you, as can be seen in the drawings (Fig. 5.33) below. This Figure also shows you how to draw in Two Point Perspective.

How to draw in Two Point Perspective

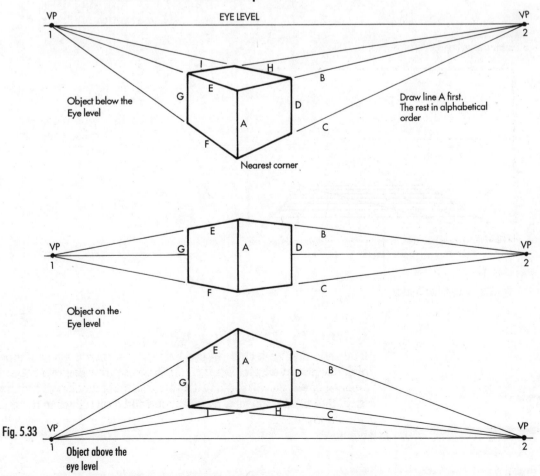

Fig. 5.33

The shapes below are drawn in two point perspective as a concept drawing of buildings. Shading has been used to emphasise the three dimensional effect.

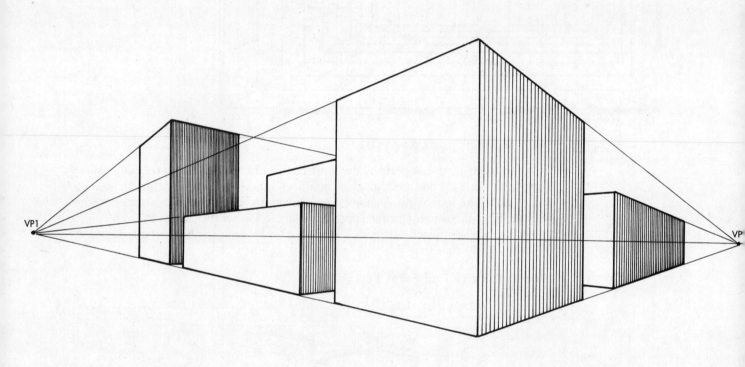

Circles in Two Point Perspective

Being able to draw a circle in two point perspective is also an important skill. You may think it is just an ellipse. But if you look at how the side of a cube changes when drawn in perspective you will see how the foreshortening effect of a circle takes place and the half of the circle furthest away from you will be smaller than the nearest half. Follow the instructions in Fig. 5.35 and you will see that the circle in perspective is not the same as an ellipse.

DRAWING A CIRCLE IN ESTIMATED PERSPECTIVE

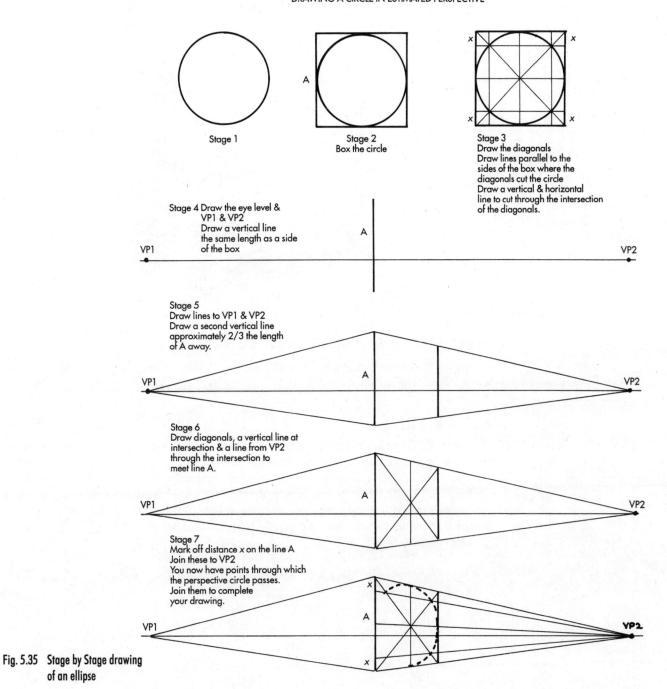

Fig. 5.35 Stage by Stage drawing
of an ellipse

This method of drawing can be used to present cylindrical shapes in a vertical or horizontal position

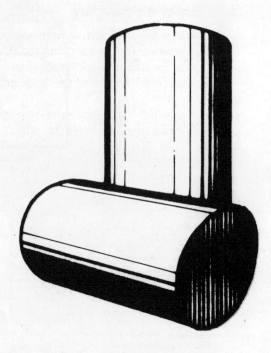

Fig. 5.36   Two cylinders

MEASURED TWO POINT PERSPECTIVE

There are two ways that you will find straight forward to follow. There are of course very complicated and advanced methods of drawing in measured two point perspective and these are used by architects and designers.

Visual Ray Method

You start this type of drawing as you would an estimated two point perspective drawing by drawing an eye level or horizon line and placing two vanishing points VP1 and VP2. Where you place them is up to you, but, you are recommended to keep them as far apart as possible. Again, where you view the object is left up to you to decide, but of course it must be between the two vanishing points and near, but not necessarily on, the centre of the horizon line. From here on you have to follow a set of instructions and they are produced in the figure below.

Step by step procedure.

1. Draw a line of sight at right angles to the Horizon Line.
2. Draw a plan view touching the Horizon Line with the near corner.
3. Fix the station point S on the line of sight when the cone of vision is 30 degrees. (You can do this by sliding the 30 degree angle of a 30–60 degree set square over the plan view.)
4. Draw the Visual Ray from the Station Point S through A and C on the plan view.
5. Draw a line from the Station Point S, parallel to AB to obtain VP1.
6. Draw a line from the Station Point S, parallel to BC to obtain VP2.
7. Draw the true height of the object on the Line of Sight i.e. where the corner of the plan view touches the Horizon Line.

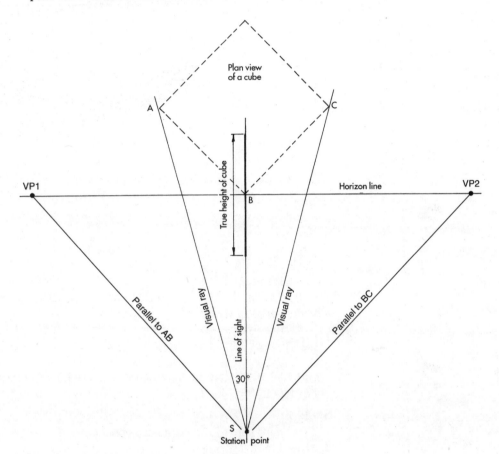

Fig. 5.37

You have now got the leading edge of the cube drawn. To complete the sides.

8. Draw lines to VP1 and VP2 from the true height line to complete the top and bottom of the cube.
9. Where line SA intersects the Horizon Line draw a vertical line to touch the lines going to VP1.
10. Where the line SC intersects the Horizon Line draw a vertical line to touch the lines going to VP2.

You have now completed a drawing of a cube in Two Point Measured Perspective.

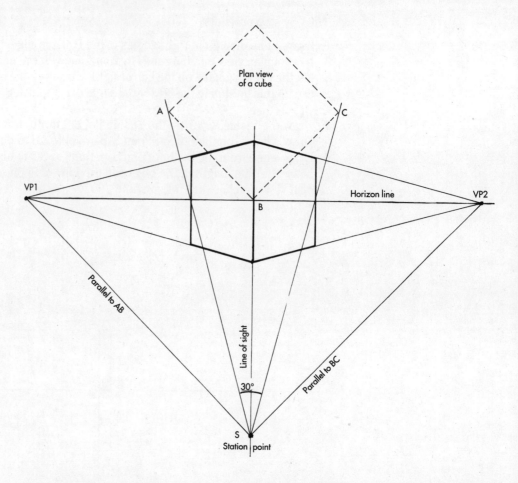

Fig. 5.38

You may use this method to draw more complex objects such as a flat roof garage shown below in Fig. 5.39.

Alternative Method

An alternative method of drawing in Measured Two Point Perspective is shown in the following figures.

Stage 1
1. Place your paper in the landscape position.
2. Draw the measuring line.
3. Draw two true views of the object touching below the measuring line and more to one side than the other. This is so that the object will look more interesting than if it was drawn in the middle. The two views must be touching as shown:

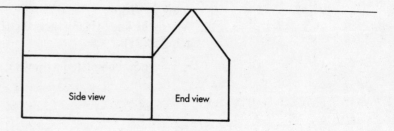

Fig. 5.40 Stage 1 drawing

Stage 2
The next task is to find the eye level, the two Vanish Points VP1 and VP2 and the two Measuring Points MP1 and MP2.

■ **Finding the eye level**
1. Draw a thin line from the Measuring Line at an angle of 30 degrees in the position shown (Fig. 5.41).
2. Draw a thin line at an angle of 45 degrees in the opposite direction.
3. Draw the eye level line to intersect the two lines you have just drawn as shown.

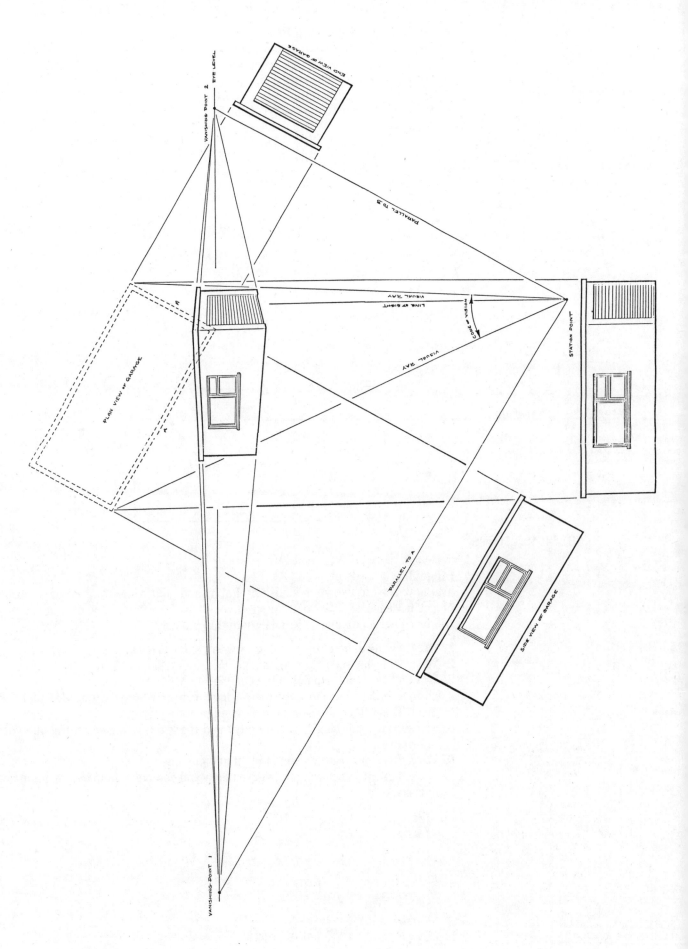

Fig. 5.39

■ Finding the Vanishing Points
1. At the points of intersects mark off vanishing point 1, VP1 and vanishing point 2, VP2.

■ Finding the Measuring Points
1. Measure the length of the 30 degree line.
2. Mark this length on the eye level from VP1.
3. Write MP2.
4. Measure the length of the 45 degree line.
5. Mark this length on the eye level line from VP2.
6. Write MP1.

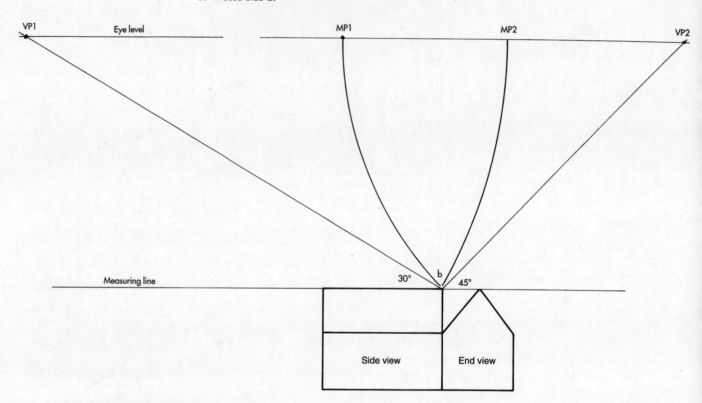

Fig. 5.41 Stage 2 Drawing

Stage 3
You now need to use your Vanishing Points and your Measuring Points to draw your object in Measured Two Point Perspective. All the lines you will be drawing in this stage will be construction lines, so make them thin but clear.

1. Draw a vertical line from the end view to the measuring line.
2. Where this line meets the measuring line draw a line to MP1.
3. Draw a line from the point of the end view to MP1.
4. Draw a vertical line above the measuring line from where the side view and end view meet. This will be the near or leading edge of the object.
5. Measure the full height of the object and mark this distance on the line you have drawn in 4.
6. From this mark draw one line to VP1 and one line to VP2.
7. Look at the lines drawn in the figure below and complete them before going onto the final stage.

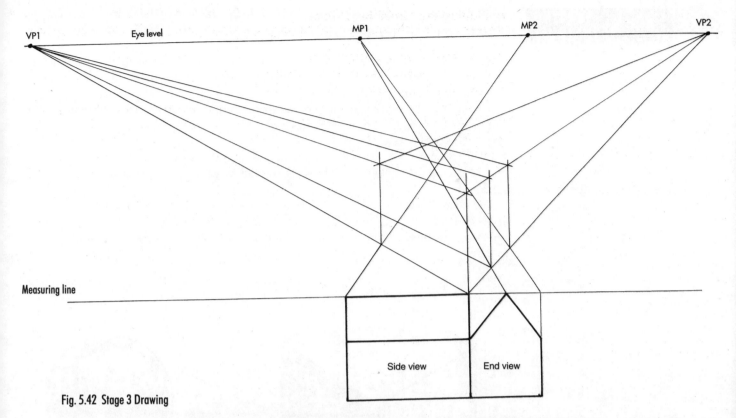

Fig. 5.42 Stage 3 Drawing

Stage 4

You can now draw in bolder lines to make the object show up from the many construction lines that you have drawn.

1. Measure the distance 'a' and mark this off on the leading edge.
2. Draw the vertical height of the object.
3. Draw the sloping height.
4. To obtain the slope on the far side first draw a construction line from the top of 'a' to VP2.
5. Draw the slope of the far side.
6. From the top of 'a' draw a construction line to VP1.
7. Draw the first part of this line bold as shown.
8. Draw the remaining sloping line.
9. Complete the drawing to produce your Measured Two Point Perspect Drawing.

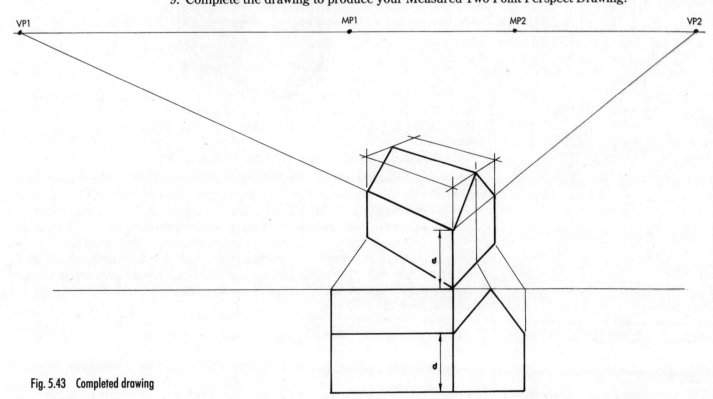

Fig. 5.43 Completed drawing

6 **SHADING TECHNIQUES**

Adding shading to a drawing helps to bring it to life. Instead of the drawing just looking like a series of lines it takes on the appearance of a more solid form. Just look at the many illustrations in this chapter.

Remember shading has nothing to do with colour. Shading is all about how light falls on to an object. So if you are drawing an object which is dark in colour this does not mean that you have to shade your drawing to try to match what you see.

In order to achieve a satisfactory result the light must come from a single source. For simplicity it is helpful to think of light coming from above, behind and to the left of the object. Look at figures 5.46 – 5.48

Light travels in a straight line and does not pass through solid opaque objects. This may be stating the obvious but it is worth reminding yourself when you are shading your work.

The areas that are in direct line with the source of light do not need shading at all. The areas that are receiving some light but not full light can be lightly shaded. The area not receiving any direct light can be shaded the darkest. The drawings below illustrate this feature.

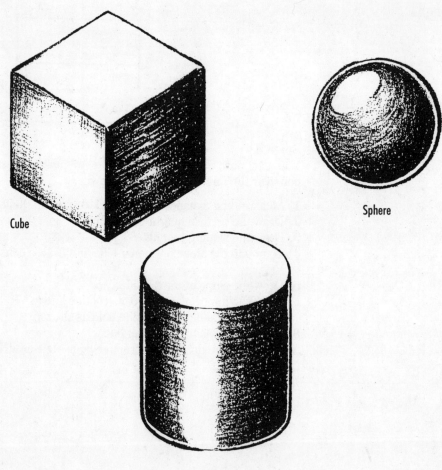

Cube

Sphere

Fig. 5.44   Cylinder

Note that the shading is not just a flat tone on the two sides. Some areas are lighter than others. The thin line of light on the outer edges of the cylinder and the sphere are areas of **reflected light**. Showing reflected light is helpful if the background is dark.

Light areas help to make greater contrast in certain positions, such as the meeting point of two planes, so that we can avoid two planes looking as though they have become merged. This sometimes happens when using colour felt pens. So highlights are added at crucial points to make the meeting points of planes much crisper and very much more obvious. Highlights are normally applied in the final stages of a coloured rendering of a drawing to give it that final touch.

Fig. 5.45   Cube   Cylinder

7 > SHADOWS

This is another technique you can use to make your graphic work look more interesting and again more realistic. When light falls on an object a shadow is cast. As for the shading, think of a single light source as coming from above behind and from the left. The shadow will then be cast on the right hand side of the object and pointing downwards and to the right.

Stage by stage construction of the shadow for Fig. 5.45

1. After you have drawn the object in Two Point Perspective select a point for the light source that is above and to the left of the object.

2. Draw a vertical line to the eye level. Where it meets the eye level is the Shadow Vanishing Point. SVP.

3. Draw construction lines from the Light Source through the corners of the top edge of the object.

4. Draw the construction lines from the SVP through the corners of the bottom edge of the object.

5. Join up where the lines intersect and you will have the outline of the shadow.

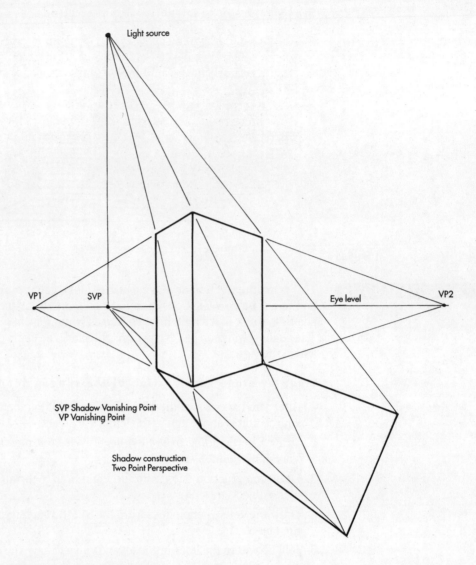

Light source

VP1   SVP   Eye level   VP2

SVP Shadow Vanishing Point
VP Vanishing Point

Shadow construction
Two Point Perspective

Fig. 5.46

6. Shade in the enclosed area.
7. Remove all construction lines.

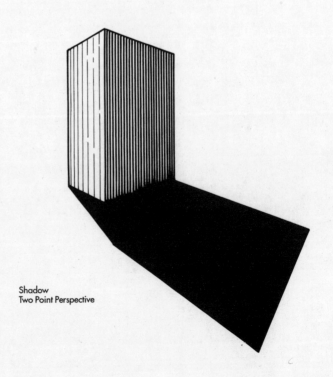

Shadow
Two Point Perspective

Fig. 5.47

Stage by stage construction for the cylinder.

1. After having drawn the cylinder in Two Point Perspective select a point for the light source which is above and to the left of the cylinder.
2. Draw a vertical line down from the light source to the eye level. This will give you the SVP.
3. Draw a series of vertical lines on the curved surface of the cylinder.
4. Draw a construction line from the light source through each of the vertical lines where they meet the top edge of the cylinder.
5. Draw a construction line from the SVP through each of the vertical lines where they meet the bottom edge of the cylinder.
6. Draw a line through the points of intersection to produce the outline of the shadow.

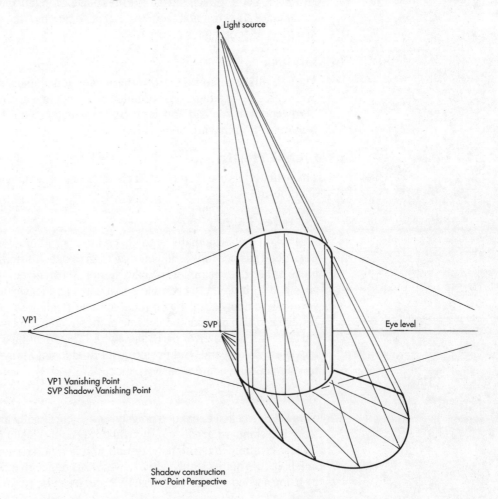

VP1 Vanishing Point
SVP Shadow Vanishing Point

Fig. 5.48

Shadow construction
Two Point Perspective

7. Shade in the enclosed area and remove all construction lines.

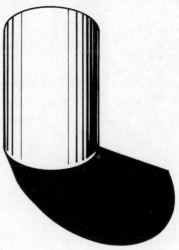

Fig. 5.49

Shadow Two Point Perspective

8 ▷ MODELLING

Making a model in an easy to work material means that you can produce a three dimensional form reasonably quickly and with care produce a quality model that looks like a finished product.

MATERIALS

Medium Density Fibre Board

This is an excellent manufactured material for modelling. It is a homogenous material (it has no grain) that can be easily shaped using most wood working tools. Its surface responds well to abrading techniques and allows a very good finish to be achieved so that, after spraying with a cellulose paint, the finished model can look like the real thing. However, some education authorities have stopped the use of MDF where there is inadequate air extraction facilities. Because much of the abrading is done on a finishing machine, a lot of dust is created.

Jelutong

Though this is a naturally grown hardwood it has many working qualities. The grain is even and allows a high quality finish to be achieved. Unfortunately, it is an expensive hardwood so if you can obtain off-cuts this may be your best way of obtaining what you require without having to pay a high price.

Foamed Plastics

These materials are readily available either as packaging or it can be purchased in large sheet form.

Expanded Polystyrene

It is a light and easy material to shape but, its rather coarse nature makes it difficult to get a good surface finish. So you may wish to use this material for developing your initial ideas rather than using for a quality model. It can be cut with a sharp craft knife or a hot wire cutter. It tends to crumble when sawn and leaves a poor quality surface finish. If you wish to apply a finish you must not use a cellulose paint. The cellulose paints have a solvent which attacks the styrene and damages the surface. You can try rubbing the surface with a plaster of paris paste to fill the small blemishes and seal it with a water based emulsion paint. But even this method is not always successful if you try rubbing the surface with a fine abrasive paper.

Styrofoam

This is a fine celled expanded polystyrene foam, usually blue or white in colour. The blue foam is a standard grade and the white is a high density foam that has a fine grain. It is far less crumbly than the polystyrene so it is much easier to get a good quality surface finish. It cuts quite cleanly when sawn or shaped with a hot wire cutter. It can be joined by using a wood adhesive such as PVA and it can be painted with a water-based emulsion paint.

WARNING. CUTTING EXPANDED POLYSTYRENE OR STYROFOAM WITH A HOT WIRE CUTTER GENERATES TOXIC STYRENE FUMES. THIS TASK SHOULD ONLY TAKE PLACE IN A WELL VENTILATED ROOM OR WHERE SUITABLE AIR EXTRACTION FACILITIES ARE AVAILABLE. YOU SHOULD NEVER USE A HOT WIRE CUTTER WITH THE WIRE RED HOT.

DESIGN BRIEF: BATTERY OPERATED WHISK

A student was given the design brief to:
Design a battery operated whisk for presentation to a potential manufacturer.

This meant that the student was required to design a whisk using drawing and modelling techniques. Since the final piece of work was a presentation model only there was no need to make it function. Should the design appeal to the potential client then the whisk would be made using mass production techniques.

First the student drew his initial ideas (Figs. 5.50 and 5.51).

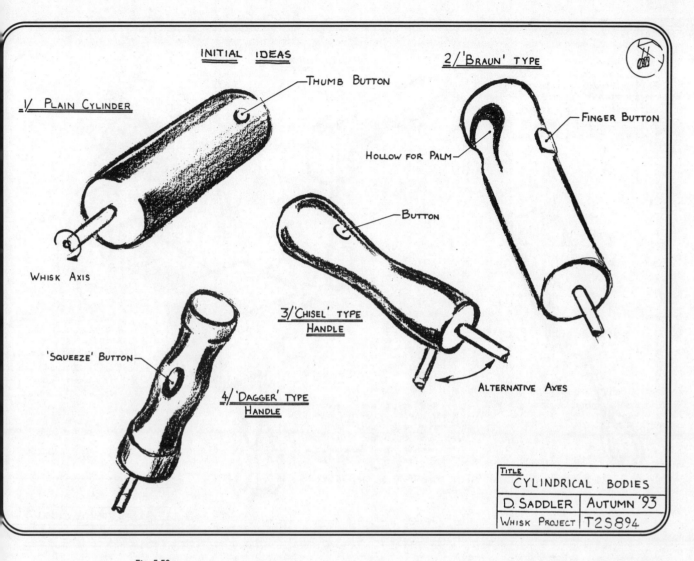

INITIAL IDEAS

2/ 'BRAUN' TYPE

1/ PLAIN CYLINDER

THUMB BUTTON

FINGER BUTTON

HOLLOW FOR PALM

WHISK AXIS

BUTTON

3/ 'CHISEL' TYPE HANDLE

'SQUEEZE' BUTTON

4/ 'DAGGER' TYPE HANDLE

ALTERNATIVE AXES

TITLE	
CYLINDRICAL BODIES	
D. SADDLER	AUTUMN '93
WHISK PROJECT	T2S894

Fig. 5.50

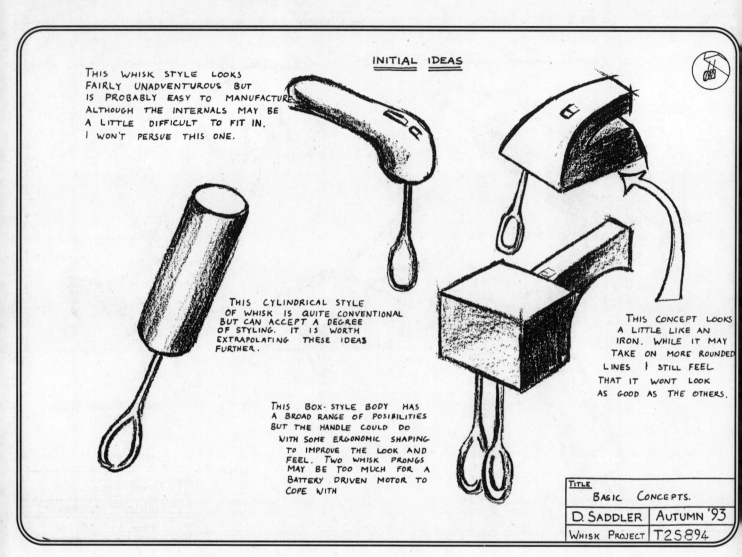

INITIAL IDEAS

THIS WHISK STYLE LOOKS FAIRLY UNADVENTUROUS BUT IS PROBABLY EASY TO MANUFACTURE ALTHOUGH THE INTERNALS MAY BE A LITTLE DIFFICULT TO FIT IN. I WON'T PERSUE THIS ONE.

THIS CYLINDRICAL STYLE OF WHISK IS QUITE CONVENTIONAL BUT CAN ACCEPT A DEGREE OF STYLING. IT IS WORTH EXTRAPOLATING THESE IDEAS FURTHER.

THIS BOX-STYLE BODY HAS A BROAD RANGE OF POSIBILITIES BUT THE HANDLE COULD DO WITH SOME ERGONOMIC SHAPING TO IMPROVE THE LOOK AND FEEL. TWO WHISK PRONGS MAY BE TOO MUCH FOR A BATTERY DRIVEN MOTOR TO COPE WITH

THIS CONCEPT LOOKS A LITTLE LIKE AN IRON. WHILE IT MAY TAKE ON MORE ROUNDED LINES I STILL FEEL THAT IT WONT LOOK AS GOOD AS THE OTHERS.

TITLE	
BASIC CONCEPTS.	
D. SADDLER	AUTUMN '93
WHISK PROJECT	T2S894

Fig. 5.51

Then the ideas were developed further by shaping and abrading Standard Polystyrene foam before the next set of drawings were produced.

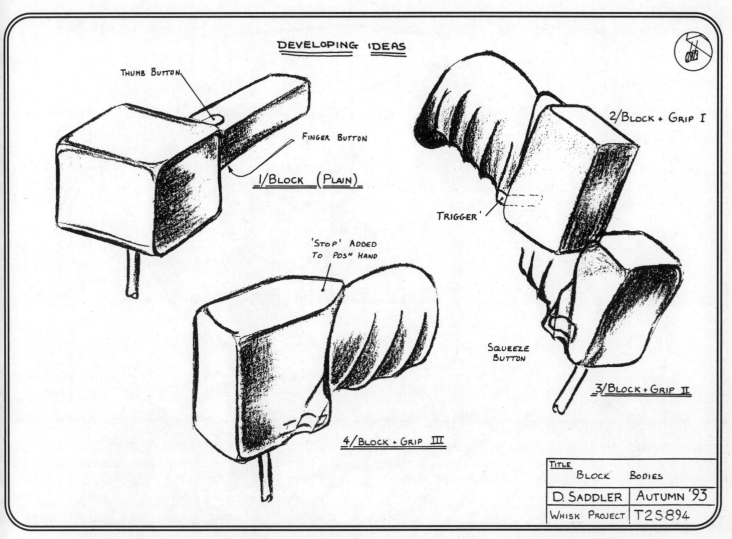

DEVELOPING IDEAS

THUMB BUTTON

FINGER BUTTON

1/BLOCK (PLAIN)

2/BLOCK + GRIP I

TRIGGER

'STOP' ADDED
TO POS^N HAND

SQUEEZE
BUTTON

3/BLOCK + GRIP II

4/BLOCK + GRIP III

TITLE	
BLOCK BODIES	
D. SADDLER	AUTUMN '93
WHISK PROJECT	T2S894

Fig. 5.52 Developed idea

Once having tried the shape in his hand to see if it was comfortable to hold and the switch was in a suitable position to operate, the final model was made in High Density Foam so that a quality model could be produced. The drawing on page 87 is his artistic impression of the final design.

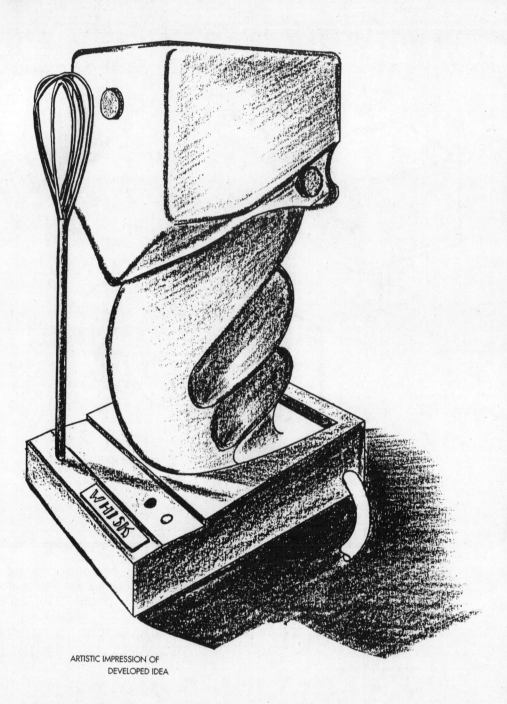

ARTISTIC IMPRESSION OF
DEVELOPED IDEA

Fig. 5.53   Artistic impression

The final model was finished with a water based paint and gave a very good impression of what a manufactured design would look and feel like.

REVIEW SHEET

To be able to draw well you will need to do a lot of practice.

- Using the cubes and cylinders shown overleaf try the following exercises.

  a) Using an HB pencil render the three cubes to emphasise their three dimensional form.
  b) Do the same for three cylinders.
  c) Using a black fibre tipped pen render the three cubes to show a) a matt finish, b) a semi-matt finish and c) a highly polished finish.
  d) Do the same for three cylinders.
  e) Using a technical pen render three cubes to simulate a) Textile, b) wood and c) metal.
  f) Do the same for three cylinders.

- Here is a Plan view of a study/bedroom which requires to be developed into a three dimensional planometric drawing. On a separate sheet of paper, draw the plan, and complete the planometric projection.

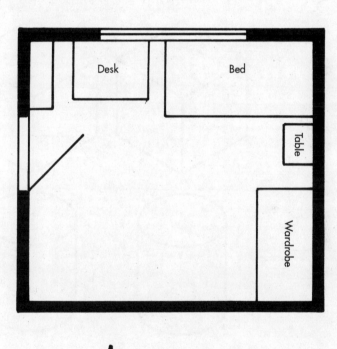

Fig. 5.54   Plan of a study Bedroom

A

From the detail you have used to do a planometric view of the study/bedroom, draw in single point perspective a view as seen from A when the wall is removed.

- For many of the following exercises you will need to draw on size A3 paper.

  a) Draw a landscape in Two Point Perspective where the buildings are below and above your eye level.
  b) Draw an artefact in measured Two Point Perspective. You can then add shading to emphasis the form of the artefact and construct the shape of the shadows when the light source is from above, behind and to the left of the artefact.

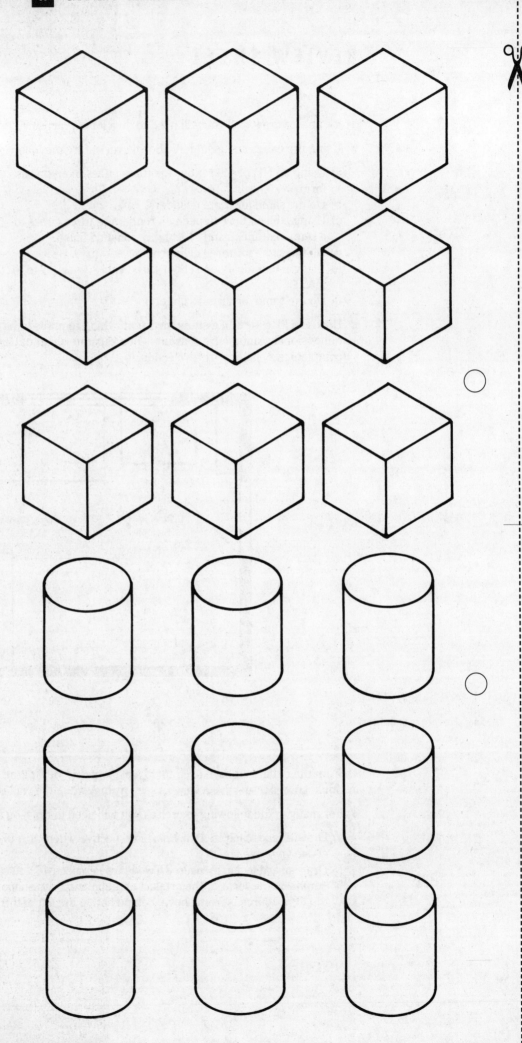

ROLE OF DESIGN AND SOLVING PROBLEMS

GETTING STARTED

Solving problems of a technological nature is what this subject is all about. The scale of the problem is immaterial. All the characteristics of solving the problem of opening a food can are the same as the problem of flying faster than sound. The only difference lies in the degree of complexity. Therefore no matter what problem faces you, in theory you will be able to arrive at a solution. It is only the complexity of the problem that will determine the suitability of the solution.

All pupils following this course will be expected **to solve several problems**. Some will form the coursework, others will be answers to problems set in an examination paper. The problem set can have as many solutions as there are attempts to solve it. Some, of course, will be better solutions than others, but none-the-less they are *all* solutions. Your main task is to become skilful in arriving at a *viable* solution to a problem.

Solving problems can be done in a number of different ways. There is a small minority of people who are highly gifted in solving problems and appear to be able to come up with a solution "off the top of their heads". You might call it inspiration. But the vast majority of people have to work extremely hard to arrive at a solution that barely meets the requirements. This can, however, become non-productive and very disheartening. If you find it to be true in your case, then there are a number of things you can try.

Solving problems without being able to discuss your thoughts with someone else is very difficult and often the results are very uninspiring. The term "more heads are better than one" is most applicable to *any* problem-solving situation. Therefore, be prepared **to work in a group** of three or four. Here are two methods you might try:

- discussing your ideas with friends;
- brainstorming.

We then move on to a more detailed discussion of design techniques and the role of design.

ESSENTIAL PRINCIPLES

SOLVING PROBLEMS BY DISCUSSION

Sharing your ideas with others and being prepared to listen to other people's suggestions often stimulates your own thinking and leads you on to new ideas. The contribution made by each person must be a serious attempt to resolve the problem. An alternative point of view does *not* mean that the first contribution was wrong. The merit of each point made can be discussed in detail until a **census of opinion** is made. The census of opinion could be that either the suggestion is worth pursuing further, or that it is not feasible and not worth pursuing further. Whatever decision is made, do not feel that it is either a "pat on the back" or that your ideas are "no good". Be prepared to accept criticism as well as praise. Keep an open mind about all suggestions, because the idea that seemed less likely to be successful may in the end prove to be a very good idea to pursue.

❝❝ Two heads are often better then one. ❞❞

The essential points to remember in using this technique are:

■ Be prepared to make a contribution.
■ Listen to other people's ideas.
■ Accept alternative points of view.
■ Keep an open mind.

Your chances of solving a problem will be much greater if you remember these points.

SOLVING PROBLEMS BY BRAINSTORMING

With this technique you need to be relaxed and feel free to say what comes into your head. Do not attempt to assess the feasibility of each response, because even the most outrageous thought may act as a stimulation for *other* possibilities. This process is best carried out with a small group of people. The members of the group do not have to be experienced in problem solving, in fact it is sometimes of value to have the group made up of people with a variety of interests and ability.

The best way to organise a "brainstorming session" is to:

■ form a small group of approximately four people;
■ state clearly the problem that is to be resolved;
■ get each member to write down as many ideas as he or shc can, or have one person writing down the suggestions while the others state the ideas that come into their heads;
■ read out the list;
■ add new ideas that come from hearing the reading of the list.

Now you will have a *list* of ideas that can be considered systematically and at a pace that gives you time to think. Give each idea careful consideration and begin to eliminate those ideas that seem unsuitable. Leave about four to six suggestions on your list and then develop each to see which is most likely to be successful. You now have the basis for starting to solve the problem.

Remember that in order for this method to be successful it is necessary for every one to feel free to make unusual suggestions. They should not be given any reason to feel awkward about any suggestion that they might offer.

EMPIRICAL RESEARCH

This sounds a rather frightening method but it is quite the reverse, and is one that is commonly used. All it means is **finding out by experience**. It is the method you would use to solve a puzzle, e.g. Rubik cube, or snake. Logical thinking is only possible after *you have made several attempts* and are then able to compare the results. At first it is a matter of *trial and error* leading to *trial and success*.

Applying this method to a real problem is quite simple. To illustrate, consider the problem of supporting a brick 50 mm above a flat horizontal surface with a single sheet of newspaper. You may start to discuss ways of tackling the problem, but you would very soon want to manipulate the paper into various shapes to see what happens. Seeing the *results* will help you to select a suitable solution.

Not all problems can be solved this way, but it sometimes helps if you handle materials and experiment a little in order to arrive at a decision.

Having come up with a number of *possible* solutions the next task is to decide *which one* to use. If you remember that the best solution is often the simplest, then you might choose the simplest possible solution first. Then try the *next* most simple if your first choice does not work.

<table>
<tr><td>3 ▷</td><td>THE BRILLIANT IDEA</td></tr>
</table>

❝❞ Brilliant ideas do happen, but they are usually the result of hard work and experience. ❝❞

Do not deceive yourself into believing that a **brilliant idea** will appear like magic. The really clever ideas come from the highly gifted and the most experienced people. The chances of you hitting upon a brilliant idea are close to nil. However, it has been known for problems to be solved by pupils, even though many attempts by highly trained people have been unsuccessful. There is the example of the lorry that became trapped under a rather low railway bridge. The top of the lorry came into contact with the underside of the bridge. The lorry could not move forward or backward without causing more damage to itself or the bridge. The problem was to get the lorry from under the bridge without causing further damage. Representatives from the railway discussed the problem with Bridge Construction Engineers, Roadworks Engineers and Transport Engineers. Each representative put forward suggestions and considerable thought was given to each proposal. A young boy standing on the roadside heard most of the discussion and became interested in the problem. "Why don't you let the tyres down", called out the boy. The experts immediately acknowledged that this *was* the solution to their problem and the lorry, with its tyres let down, moved freely from under the railway bridge.

Though the experts may have felt embarrassed that the problem was resolved by a boy who had no experience or qualifications in solving problems, it just goes to prove that "more heads are better than one" and that not everyone has to be an expert to make a valuable contribution to a problem.

The points to be learnt from this illustration are:

- Be prepared to listen to all contributions.
- Expect the unexpected to occur.
- Look at problems in a broad sense.

Only fall upon this way of viewing a problem as a *support* for a more thorough and well-tried method. It is as well to remember that you are taking a course in which you are being *assessed*, and it is necessary for you to *show evidence* of your thinking. A method *has* been devised to help you approach problem solving step-by-step and it is referred to as "A Design Process".

<table>
<tr><td>4 ▷</td><td>DESIGN PROCESS</td></tr>
</table>

When given the task to design and produce a solution you are often, in your mind, shooting ahead with possible solutions. This is perhaps the way most of us think. However, if you are designing for a client and a lot of money is going to be paid for the final product or system then it is important for everything to be right. Otherwise a lot of money is going to be lost and a lot of people may have wasted their time and energy. This particularly applies to major project such as designing space craft, aircraft, bridges, channel tunnels. But even something as small as an electric plug has to be properly designed so that it is safe and reliable to use. So it is not the size of the object or system to be designed that is important, it is how well it satisfies the need.

In order that you can demonstrate your ability to solve a problem you have to produce a Design Folio. The way in which the examining boards like you to present your **Design Folio** is quite specific and relates to the Attainment Targets given in the National Curriculum. This means that you are required to have the stages clearly identified in a prescribed order. You are advised to present your design activities in the following order:

❝❞ Stages in the design process ❝❞

- identification of a need;
- analysis of the problem;
- writing a design brief;
- writing a product design specification;
- researching the situation;
- analysing the information gathered;
- generating a range of ideas;
- evaluating your ideas against the design brief and specification;
- developing a viable solution;

- modelling and testing;
- refine the viable solution in the light of new information gathered during testing;
- produce measured and detailed drawings for production;
- plan and organise the production process;
- realise the solution;
- evaluate the solution.

Putting the *evidence* of your work in an orderly fashion helps not only the assessor to follow your work but it should also help you to know and check what has to be done. You will notice that the list has not been numbered. Because, if it were, it would suggest that everything has to be done in that order. The process of designing does not fall neatly into a logical sequence of events. When actively engaged in designing you must start at the beginning i.e. the identification of a need, but, after that you may begin thinking of a few ideas. This is fine, but you will soon find that you need to be more precise about what it is you are proposing to try and do. So you will go backwards and forwards throughout the whole process, checking your ideas against the design brief and finding out more information as and when it is required. This flexibility of moving backwards and forwards is expected. The **Design Loop** illustrated below is an attempt to graphically show this dodging about. Here again, it must be emphasised that this is not a rigid structure or pattern for designing.

> **You can vary the order of the stages**

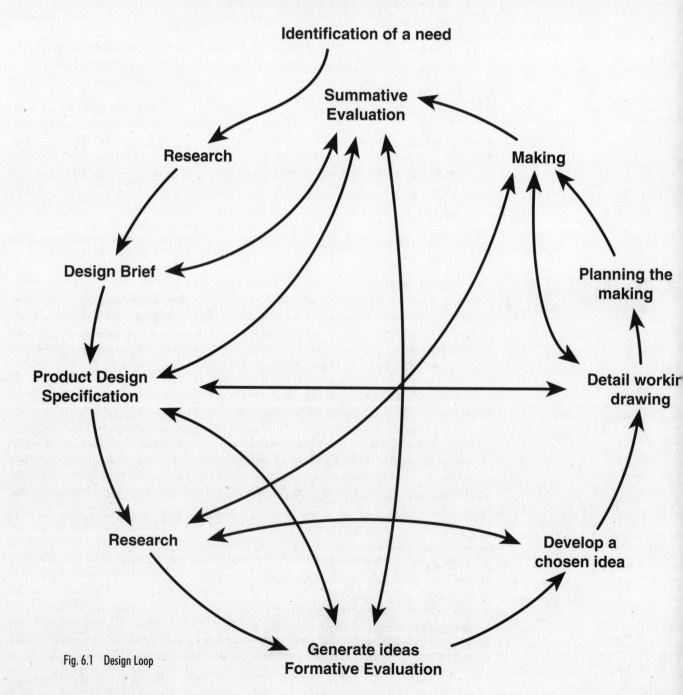

Fig. 6.1   Design Loop

5 > STAGES IN THE DESIGN PROCESS

Identification of a need

This is the starting point for all real designing processes. It is important that a true or real need is identified. Compare these two statements:

- I need a sewing box.
- I need a bicycle lock.

with

- I need a container in which to store sewing equipment and materials.
- I need a system or way of stopping my bicycle from being stolen.

I think that you will agree that the first two statements strongly suggest that you already have an answer in your mind to the need. This means that you will have a limited view of the need and may not arrive at a very good solution.

The second two statements are very much more *open ended* and will help you to keep an open mind and examine a wide range of possible solutions. Since this broadens your options you are much more likely to finish with a more rewarding solution.

Design Brief

This is a statement of intent. Again as with the identification of a need you still need to keep your options open. The design briefs for the second pair of two statements could read:

- Design and make a container in which to store sewing equipment and materials.
- Design and make a system or an artefact to prevent a bicycle from being stolen.

Product Design Specification (PDS)

The Product Design Specification (PDS) should tell you specifically what is required. The details are best written briefly, precisely, and as a list of requirements. Doing it this way helps you to check that your initial ideas are going to be satisfactory or not satisfactory. Also, when you do your final evaluation of your solution you will be able to comment on each of the specifications. For example you may have included in your list of PDS for the container;

- Must be easy to check to see if everything is in its place.

You would then be able to evaluate your proposed design to see if everything could be easily checked.

Constraints

These are restrictions that you must accept and follow. They can form part of the PDS, but it helps to keep the two apart so that they form part of a shorter list and can be more readily checked. Constraints are usually related to **time, money and availability of certain materials and equipment**. If you have been given a limited time and a limited cost for the project you must plan to work within these constraints.

Research

There are three types of research activities and you are likely to be engaged in all three in a single project. The most common of these is **Secondary Research**. This is looking at, listening to and reading information that has been produced by someone else, e.g. videos, tapes, books, magazines, etc. In other words you are researching someone else's primary research. **Primary Research** is the information that you find out for yourself. This may involve you in developing a questionnaire to obtain information that could not be found any other way. Or you may need to observe children at play to find out what really interests them, watch an elderly person trying to open a tin of food etc and recording the evidence that you have found out for yourself. You may need to have a closer look at nature to see how she has solved a problem. **Be sure that you make it clear to an assessor that what you have produced is headed Primary Research** because a lot of credit is given to this type of research. Another form of primary research is called **Empirical Research**. This is where you carry out a series of experiments or tests. You may have to make a mock up or model to see if what you have put down on paper, in the form of a drawing, really works before moving on to the realisation of the final solution. Lego kits are often used to see if an idea will work.

❝❝ Primary Research is given much credit ❞❞

Generating Ideas

It is important that the Design Brief, the PDS and the constraints are clearly defined before this activity is started. Once the objectives are quite clear then thinking can begin. This type of thinking should be broad so that a wide range of possibilities may be considered (Divergent thinking). Your ideas are best expressed on paper in the form of sketches and notes (**annotations**). Even the most outrageous idea should be given some thought. Its merits and weaknesses should be given consideration before it is accepted or rejected. Your formative evaluations should then be written near the sketch. **Evidence of formative evaluations is something that the assessor looks for in your generation of ideas.**

Development of a chosen Idea

Do check that the chosen idea fulfils all the requirements of the Design Brief, Product Design Specification, and constraints *before* embarking on thinking of ways to make your solution.

Your chosen idea now has to be translated from an idea on paper to a makeable solution. You have to think about the materials from which it could be realised; think of the type of methods of joining the materials and the processes that will need to be carried out.

Mock-up

You may have made a model or mock-up to work out a few principles at an earlier stage in the designing process. This time you will have to consolidate your ideas and it may still be necessary to make a mock-up of your idea before embarking on the final solution. A mock-up is usually made from offcut materials that are relatively soft and easy and quick to use, such as card, balsa wood, clay, fabric, etc.

Working Drawing

With all the information you have been able to find out and develop you should now be in a position to do a drawing to scale. This scale drawing will need to be very accurate so that you will be able to have all your materials cut to the correct size. The British Standards have a clear set of rules and symbols that can be used to ensure that all detail is clearly presented. For resistant materials Orthographic Projection in First or Third angle Projection is commonly used. See Chapter 5.

Realisation

This is the making stage of your solution to the problem. It may take the form of a rigid three dimensional artefact, a garment to be worn, a control system, a series of two dimensional charts and posters or a recipe that has been cooked.

Summative Evaluation

You have been making evaluative judgements all the way through the design process. You had to make decisions about your ideas, sizes, choice of materials etc. now you have to do an overall summing up about how well your solution fulfils the Design Brief, and Product Design Specification. You should also evaluate your experience in realising the solution. Where you encountered difficulties that you had not anticipated you may be in a position, through your experience, to be able to recommend alternative ways of tackling the problems. In writing this down as part of your evaluation you will be able to show how deeply you have thought about the whole project.

6 PUTTING THESE STAGES INTO PRACTICE

CHOOSING A TOPIC

You may find it difficult to **choose a topic**. If so you can ask your teacher to tell you what sort of topics had been attempted by previous candidates. Some textbooks written for GCSE Technology contain a section on Assignment Topics. These are listed to help give you a quick idea of the *sort of things* that can be done and that are suitable for this subject. Look around and you will often see *examples* of past work pinned upon the display boards and stands. Usually what you see will be the *solution* to a problem without all the work that went into it. You require to know:

■ what the need was in the first place that presented a problem to be solved;
■ how the material was researched and recorded;
■ how the ideas were developed and arrived at to achieve a viable solution.

So it is important for you to *see* projects that show the *complete package of work* if you are to gain a true insight into the demands of that particular project and to be in a position whereby *you* can make an informed judgement.

Design problems arise from a need

If you can identify a **need** you are well on the way to finding a problem to be solved. If you can find something that is needed, maybe at home, maybe by a relative or even by yourself, then this could be the *starting point* for you to discover an interesting and worthwhile assignment.

Perhaps you have some hi-fi equipment that needs to be stacked or stored, or speakers that need to be mounted on a wall, or perhaps you require a means of carrying equipment round to a friend's house. An assignment based on needs like these could prove to be demanding, interesting and profitable.

Making a *list of your interests* – whether they are sporting, reading or just going out with friends – is another way of identifying a need. Should this exercise prove to be unsuccessful in producing a topic, then start looking at the *needs of others*. Perhaps you have a younger brother or sister who would be delighted to have a toy designed and made by you. Perhaps you have an elderly relative who has difficulty in picking things up from the floor, or has difficulty in hearing the front door bell. If you designed and made something that *overcame* this kind of problem it would be rewarding for you and give pleasure to the person who was fortunate enough to receive such a useful device.

Community assignments

By now you may have chosen a suitable topic for an assignment but, if not, it is well worthwhile looking at other areas where *needs* exist. These may provide ideas for a project at a future date. The **community** depends very largely upon support from people with all kinds of skills and interests. Some of the most exciting and rewarding projects have sprung from community needs. For example, you may know of a special school in your area that is concerned with educating the severely handicapped, or a play group for the very young, or a home for the elderly.

These community activities often provide assignments in which a number of pupils will need to work in a *team*. To produce a play area for handicapped pupils or a climbing frame for very young children could be a major project; it might need three or four pupils working together to ensure that what is started can be completed. However, an assignment of this kind is more appropriate *after* you have gained experience in working through projects individually and are aware of the demands of completing a project.

Having an assignment approved

Having discovered a need and having thought of the possible demands that the project may involve you in, it is now time to **discuss your proposals with your teacher**. Your teacher will be able to advise you about the suitability of your proposal. You may have identified a very important need, but for the need to be *resolved properly* and with a reasonable degree of success there may be a number of *obstacles* to overcome, or at least consider, before you can embark on the project with certainty. For example:

- Do you have ample time to complete the project?
- Have you the necessary skills to tackle the project?
- Will you have to allow time to acquire new skills?
- Has your school the necessary resources or facilities to enable you to complete the project?

Only your *teacher* can advise you here, so it is very important that you discuss your proposals fully before going ahead. If you have any doubt about your proposals, then it is advisable for you to have a second alternative proposal ready so that time is not wasted. If a firm decision to go ahead with the project *can* be made during your discussion with your teacher, so much the better. Often there is only a set amount of time for working on a project so the sooner your proposals can be accepted, the sooner you can get down to the task of *resolving* the problem.

When *proposing* a project you must also consider the demands it will make upon *you*. A balance has to be achieved between tackling something that is over ambitious and something that is far too easy. It is important for you to be engaged in an activity that:

- makes you think;
- encourages you to examine a variety of potential solutions;
- helps you to extend your knowledge;
- provides you with the opportunity to develop your design and making skills.

All this has to be taken into account, particularly by your teacher who will be responsible for making the final decision about the suitability of the chosen project. If you still need ideas, read Chapter 5 and Chapter 21.

WRITING A DESIGN BRIEF

Once the topic for the project has been chosen it is necessary to **express clearly and briefly in writing** what is required to be resolved. Usually a single sentence is sufficient. This is then to be referred to as the "DESIGN BRIEF".

The more detailed information that follows will provide more specific information and will be referred to as the "SPECIFICATION" or "Spec" for the shortened version. Because much of this information is obtained through analysing the problem, this is sometimes referred to as the "ANALYSIS".

However, there are unfortunately a few inconsistencies in the use of these terms, depending to some extent upon the geographical area in which you live. You are therefore advised to check with your teacher which term you should use.

A Design Brief based on the topic of "Lighting" could read as follows:

> Specification and Analysis often refer to the same thing.

- A student requires some form of illumination on a desk to be able to do homework when normal daylight is inadequate.

The statement is brief and in no way suggests what the solution might be. However, the information is far from adequate to proceed with research and to think of ideas. The problem needs to be *analysed carefully* to establish *specific information* such as:

i)   What type of functions have to be performed?
ii)   Will it be free standing?
iii)   Will it be wall mounted?
iv)   Does it have to be attached to the desk or working surface?
v)   Will it be adjustable or a fixed height?

These are the type of issues that need to be resolved before going any further.

UNDERTAKING AN ANALYSIS

Assuming that you are free to decide these issues yourself it is perhaps advisable to remind yourself of the "need", in this case the need to "provide some form of illumination on a desk".

First of all it would be helpful to know something about the desk and where it is placed. If the desk is *situated in the middle of the room*, then it is more likely that the illumination will be near the desk and away from a wall, so the possibility of having a wall-mounted solution is unlikely. However, the location of the desk might suggest that some form of lighting could be suspended from the ceiling. If the *surface area of the desk top is small*, the possibility of suspending the illumination from the ceiling becomes a viable consideration and certainly not one to be discarded at this stage. The alternative of having a flex trailing along the floor is something not to be recommended for obvious reasons.

You may feel that allowing your mind to go from one consideration to another is wasting time and not making much progress, but this is what designing is all about. Perhaps you have heard the phrase "keeping an open mind". By doing this you are examining all sorts of possibilities, and when you finally make a decision it is based on sound preparation. You will find that you are then able to *support your decisions* with reasons and to state clearly *why* you selected one idea over another.

WRITING A PRODUCT DESIGN SPECIFICATION

For the purpose of illustrating how to **write** a Product Design Specification (PDS) let us suppose that a number of points have been established, in which case the PDS might be written up as follows:

a) The source of illumination is to be temporarily attached to the working surface of the desk.

b) The means of attachment must be easy to operate and must not cause any damage to the desk.

c) The electrical fittings must be standard and fulfil British Standard Safety Regulations.

d) There must be a means of adjusting the height and position, vertically and horizontally.

e) There must be a means of switching the light source on and off that is within easy reach of the person while working at the desk.

f) The final design must be able to be realised in a school workshop by a student following a Design and Technology course at GCSE Key Stage 4.

g) The total activity from identifying a need to the evaluation of a finished product must be completed in the time allowed.

Further details may be added to this list, but it is hoped that by now you are able to recognise the **type of information** that needs to be decided *before* going on to the next stage of research and investigation.

RESEARCH AND INVESTIGATION

All this really means is the **gathering and putting into some sort of order** the information that is essential and helpful to solving the problem.

Much of the information needed to solve the lighting problem is concerned with the *electrical fittings*. These are available in a variety of designs, colours, shapes and sizes. This means that at some stage a decision will have to be made about *which* fittings are going to be used.

> **If you can't get the real thing, look for an illustration.**

The best way of acquiring the information initially is through looking at catalogues. A set of *illustrations* of different types of switches, bulb holders, bulbs, tubes, flexes and plugs, etc., arranged under suitable headings for easy reference, might be collected and placed in your folder. Ideally it would be better to have a collection of the actual fittings, but this would be an unreasonable expenditure for you to bear, since you are concerned only with the design and production of a single solution to the problem. However, many of the electrical fittings you will need to examine form part of common household articles. Hence you have a readily available source of information that need not cost you anything.

RECORDING INFORMATION

Using **sketches, with notes added to give you as much information as possible**, is an excellent method of recording information. It is also an excellent method of improving your powers of observation. The sketches can be drawn quickly. Provided the details drawn are clear and sufficient to fulfil what is required of them, there should be no need to use drawing instruments of any kind. Drawing with instruments only slows down the process of recording information. A small sketch pad approximately A5 size is quite adequate for the task of recording and building up a store of information.

When you *have* collected sufficient information to put in your Design Folder you only need to cut out the drawings and paste them neatly on the much larger size paper of the folio. This also gives you a chance to *arrange* the drawings so that you have all the information you require on, say, *switches*, together on one page and all the detail you require on *light bulbs* on another, etc.

Remember that the important feature of this part of your Design Folio is to **provide relevant information in an orderly and clear manner** to assist you with the task of developing your ideas. In Fig. 6.2 you can see an example of some annotated sketches of some electrical fittings. These fittings were found around the home and details were recorded in a sketch pad. No attempt at this stage was made to put the items in any order or grouping. This will come later when the drawings are put into the Design Folio. These drawings were sketched in using an HB pencil, and then some of the outline was drawn over again with a softer but sharp pencil, a 3B. Though no further detail was added, using

❝ A drawing is usually better then a illustration taken from a catalogue. ❞

the softer pencil helped to make the drawings stand out a little more clearly. The notes and sizes were added to provide more information.

The advantage of *drawing* the actual items, as compared with *collecting* information from a catalogue, is that you are able to pick up the item and examine it closely as a three-dimensional *object*. A picture from a catalogue can only provide you with a three-dimensional *image* that is not necessarily the same size as the actual object. Therefore, it is not possible to take any measurements that will be helpful when it is necessary to make specific decisions about *proportion* and *construction*.

Taking *photographs* of relevant material is another way of recording information. This can prove to be expensive and has the same sort of limitations as the illustrations taken from a catalogue. However, that is not to say that in some projects photographic evidence of some research and investigation will not be of value. But do not take photographs simply because you think it will look better in your Design Folio!

DEVELOPING IDEAS

During the time you have been gathering information you will have begun to understand a little more about ways in which the problem may be *resolved*. In fact you may have begun to formulate ideas in your mind. This is the time to put pencil to paper and start *expressing* these ideas in two- or three-dimensional drawings. Do not worry too much about detail, or even about possible solutions with a particular material in mind. Just think in terms of *shapes* or *forms*.

Having made a number of sketches of a *variety* of possible solutions, it is important that you do not discard those ideas that you think are unsuitable. Keep *all* your work. Having unsuitable ideas in your Design Folio will *not* mean that you will lose credit in the assessment. Rather, you will gain credit for having shown that you have considered a *number* of possible solutions. Keeping an "open mind" is most important at this stage. This is how the more successful solutions are derived. It is rare for ideas to be formulated in one go.

RESOLVING PROBLEMS

Some problems can be very complex and you may find the task of resolving them daunting and find it very difficult to know where to start. It might help if you try to *break down* the *major* problem into a number of *smaller* problems contained within it. Take the task of resolving the problem of *illuminating a desk surface*; here there are a number of small problems *within* the major problem that need to be resolved. There is a need to consider the following:

a) the method of attaching the lighting unit to the desk;
b) the method of putting the light on or off;
c) the method of adjusting the position of the light vertically or horizontally;
d) the type of shade that will direct the light over the surface of the desk;
e) how the standard electrical fittings may be incorporated in your design;
f) the overall appearance of the design.

The fact that materials have *not* been mentioned at this stage is important. If you begin thinking about *materials*, the shape and form of your ideas will be strongly influenced and the results will be limited by your knowledge and understanding of the material you choose. It is far less inhibiting to think of *shape or form first*, and *then* to investigate the best way to achieve your ideas.

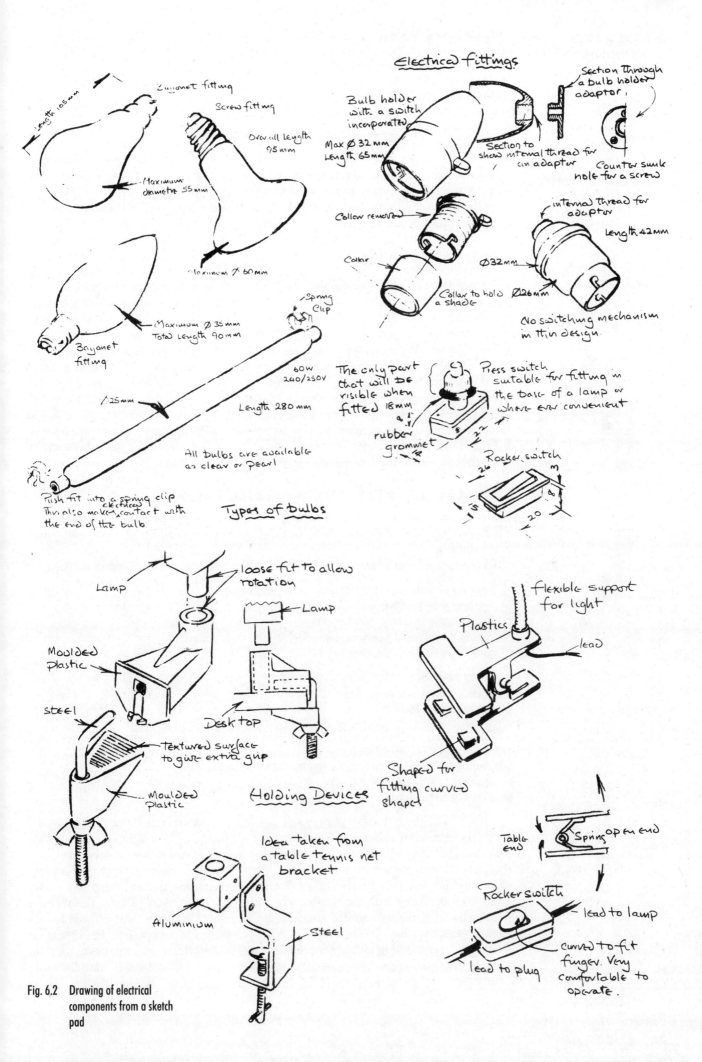

Fig. 6.2 Drawing of electrical components from a sketch pad

SHAPE AND FORM

The possible **shapes** and **forms** that may be used are endless. A look at the solutions that exist in homes, offices, shops, etc., will be sufficient to highlight this point.

There are **two basic groups** into which shapes and forms may be classified: these are **geometric** and **natural**. If you need to know more about shape and form read Chapter 20.

In your sketch pad begin to draw the shapes and forms that appeal to you most. Do not worry about neatness at this stage. The most important task is to draw *what you have in your mind*. You could say that you are "thinking aloud", only your thoughts are expressed on paper. Some people like to doodle and hope that something will emerge from the shape and form of the doodle, but this has little chance of being productive if a conscious effort is not being made to resolve the problem. Ideas do *not* come easily, so be prepared to spend quite some time drawing. When you *have* drawn a variety of shapes and forms, begin to be *selective* and elect to develop the drawing that you have chosen.

Keep in mind the shape and form of the *electrical fittings* that you wish to incorporate into a possible solution. Remember that the final design must fulfil a *function*; it must have balance; it must have the facility to be adjustable; it must be able to be attached to a desk, etc.

You may now begin to see the possibility of your solution being resolved in a *particular material or combination of materials*. Now begin to *translate* the shape and form into suitable materials. **Slender** forms may best be translated into a material that has the *strength* to carry the weight of components *without being bulky*. Most *metals* and some *plastics* would fit into this category. **Bulky** forms tend to suggest *wood*. However, some *manufactured timber* or *laminated forms* can improve the strength of the material and permit much more slender forms to be achieved *without being too weak* to carry the weight of other components. An **understanding of the structure and strength of materials is essential** if a wise choice of material is to be made.

TRANSLATING IDEAS INTO MATERIAL FORM

When interpreting an idea that so far only exists as a line drawing on paper, not only is a knowledge of materials important, but also **an understanding of processes and construction**.

To produce a **form** in a material may be achieved by one of the following methods:

a) removal of unwanted material by a cutting action;
b) reforming by melting and casting;
c) reforming by heating and bending;
d) joining component parts together;
e) applying a force to bend or twist.

You may have heard the term "deformation". This also means *re-shaping material* and is an alternative way of saying that the material shape or form is going to be changed from its original state.

Materials may be **joined together** by the following methods:

a) bonding with an adhesive;
b) holding by nails, screws, pins, rivets, nuts and bolts, etc.;
c) soldering, welding;
d) constructional joints.

When you begin to think of **processes** that will be required to change the shape of a material to agree with your idea, you may discover that your idea is unrealistic and that some modifications will be necessary. Provided the modification is relatively small, you should continue to persevere with your idea. However, if you cannot find an obvious and viable modification, then you are advised to look at alternative materials and processes. Annotate your sketch with the *reasons* why you found it necessary to make the change, so that should you meet a similar situation in this project, or in another, you will have a *reminder* that may help you to avoid following the same fruitless path again. Changing ideas as you go along is perfectly acceptable and is considered to be perfectly normal when involved in the process of designing.

> This is where your knowledge and understanding of materials and processes is going to be helpful.

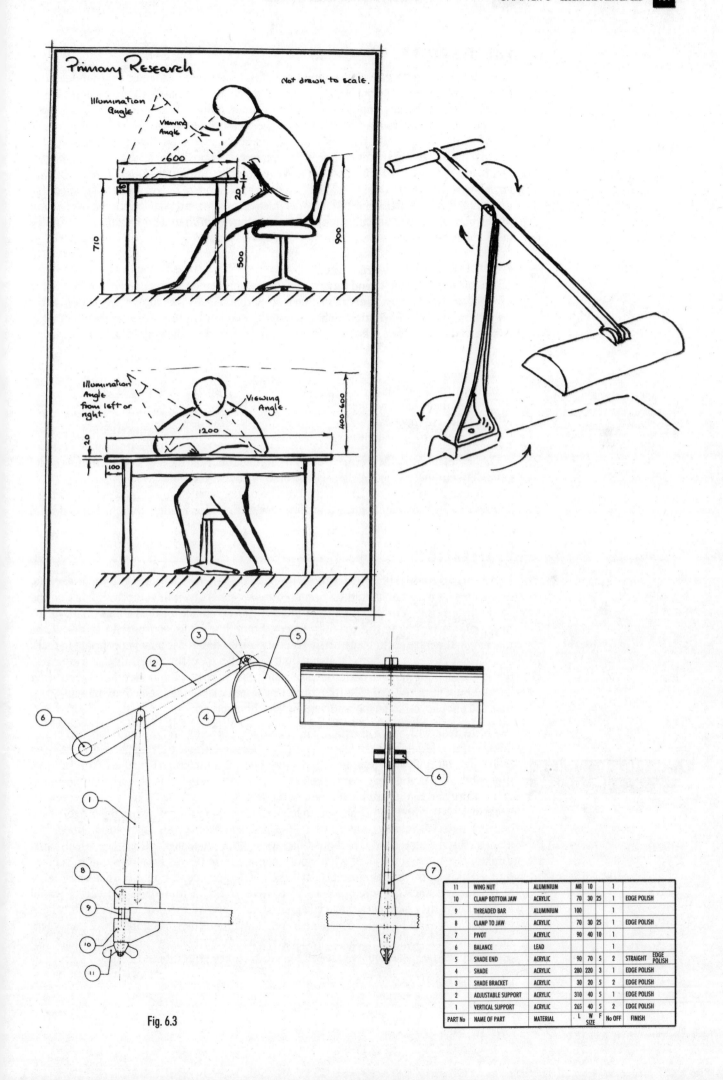

Fig. 6.3

PART No	NAME OF PART	MATERIAL	L	W	F	No OFF	FINISH
			\multicolumn{3}{c}{SIZE}		
11	WING NUT	ALUMINIUM	M8	10		1	
10	CLAMP BOTTOM JAW	ACRYLIC	70	30	25	1	EDGE POLISH
9	THREADED BAR	ALUMINIUM	100			1	
8	CLAMP TO JAW	ACRYLIC	70	30	25	1	EDGE POLISH
7	PIVOT	ACRYLIC	90	40	10	1	
6	BALANCE	LEAD				1	
5	SHADE END	ACRYLIC	90	70	5	2	STRAIGHT EDGE POLISH
4	SHADE	ACRYLIC	280	220	3	1	EDGE POLISH
3	SHADE BRACKET	ACRYLIC	30	20	5	2	EDGE POLISH
2	ADJUSTABLE SUPPORT	ACRYLIC	310	40	5	1	EDGE POLISH
1	VERTICAL SUPPORT	ACRYLIC	265	40	5	2	EDGE POLISH

THE DEVELOPED IDEA

Your detailed drawing should contain sufficient information for either a model to be produced or a working drawing to be drawn. If you feel that some of the design aspects have not been fully developed, a three-dimensional model made from card, balsa wood or a constructional kit may be the next stage to consider. A model will enable you to check all the functional aspects of your design and give you an opportunity to see what it looks like. Viewing the design from as many varied positions as you like will enable you to judge the success or failure of its visual quality. Should you feel dissatisfied with any aspect, now is the time to make the necessary changes. When you are satisfied that the "final idea" is worth realising, a "working drawing" should be completed. Keep your model if at all possible, or take a number of photographs so that you have a record to go in your Design Folder.

A working drawing

As the name suggests, this is a drawing from which you or someone else could work to produce the solution. These drawings should normally be drawn in orthographic projection, first or third angle. They should also conform to the recommendations of British Standards. A working drawing should contain the following information:

a) scale;
b) dimensions;
c) all constructional detail;
d) name of materials involved;
e) cutting list of materials;
f) list of any fixtures and fittings;
g) surface treatment;
h) title;
i) type of projection;
j) date;
k) drawn by . . .

Other details may be requested by Examination Boards, i.e. centre number and candidate number. Your teacher will be able to advise you.

Sculptured forms do not lend themselves to orthographic projection type of drawings. Therefore it is reasonable for artistic impressions and/or models to be produced from which a final product could be made.

REALISATION

Beginning to **make** the artefact that you have designed is perhaps the most exciting moment. The material should be prepared to the sizes given in your cutting list on the working drawing. The next stage is to plan the sequence of operations that will be necessary to complete the making aspect. Sometimes it is appropriate to do all the marking out before cutting any of the pieces; at other times it is only appropriate to mark out certain pieces, cut them to shape, and from these do the remaining marking out. Some component parts need to be assembled and may be joined together *before* other parts. You will have to decide this for yourself and make a list of activities in an order that will enable you to successfully complete the making.

We have dealt with ways in which you can solve problems and evaluate the success or failure of a solution to a problem. You have been looking at products that have been made by you and also products that have been manufactured in their hundreds of thousands. What you have not looked at is the effect that all this productivity has upon your future and the future for the rest of the world.

To make a product it is important to have an understanding of materials, processes to convert materials into a product and the designing skills to produce a solution that fulfils a need. But we also have a responsibility to use the materials and energy wisely. Just think of the consequences of what would happen if there was no more food to replace that existing in the shops. Just think of the consequences of no more materials being available to re-stock the school stores. The effect would be immediate and a crisis would arise. The world's supply of materials is limited. When all the coal, oil, and natural gas has gone there will be none to replace it. When all the timber has gone it will take years for it to be replaced. The effect of overusing such materials may not be immediate, but the effect will be disastrous and it will be felt by future generations.

Our responsibility as members of this generation must be:

1. to use materials wisely;
2. to make as much use as possible of those forms of energy that are not limited, i.e. solar, wind, tidal, water and geothermal;
3. to think more carefully about the needs of the future when resolving today's problems;
4. to consider very carefully when identifying a need if a need really exists. Sometimes products are designed to satisfy greed and not a need.

You will not be expected to read about this type of information in textbooks in order to help you do well in an examination. You are much more likely to read it in newspapers and hear and see it on the television. The important thing is that you are aware of the dangers as well as the advantages of using the world's resources. Being aware and acting upon those aspects that are close to you are important. So treat this section not as a means of helping you learn about the "Role of Design in Society" but, rather, to improve your awareness of the social context in which the designer works.

CONSERVATION

We live in a world that may be divided into two main categories:

1. the *natural world* of plants, insects, fish, birds, animals, etc;
2. the *man-made world* of buildings, transport, products.

The major problem is finding a way in which the two worlds can exist side by side without one adversely affecting the other. Man is much more dependent upon the natural world than the natural world is dependent upon the man-made world. Animals and plants existed long before man appeared and it is only since man arrived that animals and plants have become seriously endangered. One species of animal has always been the prey of another species, but the balance of nature has been such that the large majority of species have managed to survive. Now many species have become extinct:

1. Man's extensive use of timber has resulted in destroying the natural habitat of wild animals and wild plants.
2. Man's extensive use of insecticides, although improving the food crop, has adversely affected the insect, bird and small-animal population.
3. Man's increased provision of building land has resulted in a change of environment that is unsuitable for many species of plants and animals.
4. The industrial methods used to provide man with the products that are needed often pollute the air, land and sea at the expense of the lives of animals, birds and fish.
5. Man's need to travel has resulted in considerable pollution of the air, land and sea. It has also meant that considerable amounts of land have been used to provide roads, railways and runways.

As a result of an increasing public awareness of environmental issues, governments of many countries have been forced to pass laws to prevent the unnecessary destruction of the natural world. Very strict laws now make it illegal for waste chemicals to be deposited in rivers and seas. Waste gases also have to go through a cleaning process before being released into the air. Oil tankers are not allowed to dump unwanted oil in the sea. Other laws have also been passed to protect the natural world but unfortunately having laws is not always enough to bring about the desired results.

CONSERVATION ORGANISATIONS

Organisations have been set up by people who are very anxious that many of our endangered species may soon be extinct unless more drastic action is taken. You may have heard of some of the following:

1. Greenpeace;
2. Friends of the Earth;
3. The Wild Fowl Trust;
4. The Royal Society for the Protection of Birds;
5. The Society for the Protection of Wild Plants and Animals.

These are only a few of the organisations that have emerged in recent years. New ones are being formed all the time with the purpose of:

a) establishing ways of stopping those actions which bring about destruction;

b) educating man to live in harmony with the natural world.

c) restoring the damage that has been done, by breeding rare and endangered species of wild birds and animals in captivity so that they may be returned to the wild.

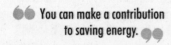 **Conservation is part of your syllabus** The very fact that the Government, through its Department for Education, has included among the eight aims of the DT course one which states:

To encourage technological awareness, foster attitudes of cooperation and social responsibility, and develop abilities to enhance the quality of the environment.

is an indication of the serious nature of the problem. You are also expected to be able to:

describe the interrelationship between design/technology and the needs of society (e. g. economic, cultural, social, ecological, industrial).

CONSERVATION OF ENERGY

The main reason for conserving energy is to ensure that future generations may have a share of the world's natural resources, such as coal, gas, oil, etc. At the moment we do not use these resources economically and efficiently. Many of our industries depend heavily upon the use of energy that either comes from the direct use of raw materials, or indirectly as in the case of electricity. Nuclear energy was hoped at one time to replace the need for coal, but the major disasters in Russia and America have brought home to many that there might be an unacceptable cost to society from increased dependence on this energy source. Other sources of energy are being developed, such as:

1. solar;
2. wind;
3. tidal;
4. geothermal;

but they are insufficiently developed to cope with present day demands. There are two main areas that need to be examined to resolve the problem:

- finding a way of using less energy;
- finding a way of increasing the output of energy from solar, wind, tidal and geothermal sources.

Much *less* energy would be needed if we could increase the scale of the following:

1. Effective insulation of buildings.
2. Greater use of waste products as a fuel.
3. Less use of "throw-away products".
4. Improvement of public transport so that there is less need for private transport.
5. Use of low wattage lighting systems.

You can make a contribution to saving energy. These are just some of the ways in which a more *economic* use of energy could be made on a national scale. Now think of ways in which you, as an individual, could cut down on the excessive use of energy. Your list might include such things as:

a) switching off a light when it is not needed;

b) closing a door after leaving or entering a room;

c) having a shower instead of a bath;

d) never using an electric toothbrush;

e) remembering to switch off the television when it is no longer required;

f) using a towel to dry your hair instead of a hair drier.

Although you could add to this list it should be clear by now that energy is wasted in the form of light and heat, and the amount wasted could be reduced if every individual made the necessary effort.

CONSERVATION OF MATERIALS

The need to make the most of our material resources has never been greater. The sources of our raw materials such as oil, coal, ores, and timber, are getting smaller by the day. There will come a time when the supply of some of these will be totally exhausted. That could happen some time in the next century. Though technology is advancing day by day, the rate of advancement is insufficient to cope with the growth in demand for energy, so that finding new ways of conserving materials is still a major concern.

Many of the large towns and cities have begun to investigate ways of using "waste materials". The methods employed vary according to the nature and character of the town. Domestic waste disposal schemes are in evidence in many towns. The most common method is the use of a refuse collection lorry that visits houses once a week to empty the rubbish bins and take all the rubbish to a large tip. When the tip can no longer accept more rubbish, earth is bulldozed over the top to restore the environment to a more acceptable condition. Trees and shrubs are also planted to improve the quality of life in that area for both humans and animals. So "waste materials" have in this way helped to fill in holes in the landscape which are then turned into acceptable sites.

The more recent schemes for waste disposal demand more effort from the individual, in that the waste materials are not collected. Instead it is the responsibility of the individual to take selected rubbish to a collection centre, and then the local authority is responsible for transporting the rubbish to a central recycling plant.

Some waste materials include glass, paper, ferrous metal and non-ferrous metal. These materials are more readily made re-usable than other materials such as plastics. It helps if the materials are separated. The task of initial separation is often the responsibility of the individual. You may have seen, and even used, the "Bottle Banks" that are sometimes sited in large car parks. Here the individual can place bottles in a large container. The containers also take the separation process one stage further by asking you to put *clear* glass bottles in one container, *green* glass bottles in another, and *brown* glass bottles in yet another container.

A similar method is used for the disposal of *drink cans*. Here again you are asked to put *ferrous* metal cans in one container and *non-ferrous* cans in another. To help you identify the metals, a magnet is fixed to the side of the container. If the can is magnetically attracted, then the can goes into the ferrous container; if it is not attracted, then it goes into the non-ferrous container.

The method of collecting *paper* is carried out in one of two ways:

1. You take it to a collection centre where it is packed and made into bundles.
2. It is collected from your house by a paper collection lorry once a month.

Both methods require the individual to sort the paper from card, so that at least two grades of paper can be produced from the recycling process. A major portion of the paper used for newspapers is recycled paper, and the stiff card used for packaging in the packaging industry is increasingly being made from recycled paper or card. It is possible now for materials to be recycled many times. In the case of paper, this lessens the need for felling so many trees.

This greater *use* of a raw material does help to lessen the demands upon the world's resources. However, we need to go much further in developing new methods of recycling and in educating individuals to be more responsible.

INDUSTRY AND CONSERVATION

The manufacturers of the products we buy are the greatest users of raw materials. They not only require a raw material to make a product, they also, in the large majority of cases, require a second raw material to provide the *energy* to process that product. In many cases that second raw material is oil or coal. The industries that are less demanding on raw materials are those that are able to use hydroelectricity.

Types of industry

■ Wood

Many of the industries that use *wood* as a raw material produce a high proportion of material that they cannot use in the product they manufacture. This material used to take the form of sawdust, shavings or chippings and was regarded as unusable. Today we have many manufactured boards that have been formed from these so-called waste materials. Chipboard is an excellent example of a manufactured board that evolved from a need to conserve wood. There were also economic reasons behind its development, but the important thing from a conservational point of view was in satisfying a demand without having to use more raw materials. Other manufactured boards also make use of this material that was once regarded as unusable. Manufactured boards are commonplace in furniture. Every household must have some piece of furniture that is made from a manufactured board. The exterior may be laminated with a veneer or covered with a plastic surface, but the hidden portion is made from a bonding agent and wood dust or chips. Technology has advanced sufficiently for these products to be of a high quality and to be so attractive that they are now used in preference to solid wood. From a product that was regarded as unusable has grown a major industry, the "Flat Pack" furniture industry. Furniture is sold in a pack ready for the DIY person to assemble at home.

The manufacturers of various *drinks* such as Coca Cola, fizzy fruit drinks, wines, spirits and beers, etc., perhaps do not do enough to encourage the return of the bottle. Some *do* provide incentives by refunding a deposit, but too many are clearly designated "nonreturnable".

■ **Car industry**

The *car industry* must be one of the heaviest consumers of raw materials. The automation processes make it possible for cars to be produced at such a high rate that we think of changing a car every year or two, knowing that there are plenty available. Many families have two or three cars and see this as normal today, while only some thirty or so years ago a single car was thought of as a luxury and it would be expected to last many years before being handed down to members of the family in just the same way as a house would be. If anything, the car industry has done most to persuade us that we need a car so that more cars can be sold. Very little has been done to design cars to last so that we need to buy fewer cars in a lifetime, and so make less demand on raw materials.

■ **Packaging industry**

The *packaging industry* is a growing industry and a heavy consumer of raw materials. Card and plastics are the two main materials if you discount glass and tin sheet. The packaging industry was at one time mainly concerned with providing a protection for the product. Now the package has to be attractive and a selling point.

Many goods are now sold as a package. This means that if you want to buy a pair of hinges you will not only receive the two hinges but also a packet. Should it be that you want to buy *three* hinges, you may find that you will have to buy two packets of two. You are then left with two packets to throw away and a hinge that you do not need! You have already paid more for the hinges because the cost of packing had to be included in the purchase price, and you have paid for a hinge that you are not going to use.

Just examine the goods bought in the weekly shop before they are unwrapped. Then see what has to be thrown away after the goods have been stored. The major content of a household rubbish bin is packages. Beyond the need to protect the goods, is there a justification for raw materials to be used so extensively in the production of packets or packages?

ROLE OF DESIGN

Design can mean different things to different people. There have been many attempts to define the meaning of design. All of them in some way are correct, but there seems to be no *single* definition that is really acceptable for all situations. Design to you may mean "solving a problem", or "providing a solution to a problem". It could, if you are more imaginatively inclined, mean something "creative". Many very distinguished people who have devoted their lives to the study of design have attempted to provide definitions:

❝❝ Some useful definitions of design. ❞❞

■ "A goal-directed problem-solving activity."

(B. Archer 1965)

■ "A creative activity – it involves bringing into being something new and useful that has not existed previously."

(Reswick 1965)

■ "To initiate change in man-made products"

(Jones 1970)

These are only a few of many definitions and it is clear that even among this small number, the definitions are different. Yet they are all acceptable as descriptions that relate to design or the act of designing.

What the definitions have *omitted* is the area of *human responsibility* that must play an important role in any act of designing and making. When you last completed a design project did you think of the *consequences* of your design? Not all consequences are predictable, though you probably did give some thought to safety. For example, when designing a child's toy you might have included in your considerations:

1. rounding all corners and edges to avoid the child cutting him or herself;
2. using a non-toxic paint because the toy is likely to be put in the mouth;
3. ensuring that moving parts are not a trap for little fingers, etc.

The less predictable consequences are the way in which the toy may be *used*. It could be an object to be thrown. The possibilities are endless. The consequences could be good as well as bad.

When designers decide on a solution they may find it impossible to anticipate *all* the consequences of their decisions. In designing a car, did Henry Ford anticipate the traffic congestion that it has caused in many of our streets and cities? Did he consider the demands it would make on our world resources (e.g. oil)? Did he consider the problems of pollution? On the credit side, however, he did provide the world with a car that could be bought by the less well-off, and so created a product that could serve the masses as well as the wealthy.

Architects are also designers, and they are responsible for the designs of the buildings in which we live, play and work. Many of the homes that have been designed by architects who are *aware* of family needs, have proved very successful. However many of the buildings designed for the community, such as high rise flats, have taken too little account of patterns of human behaviour. Many of the problems of vandalism have developed through a breakdown of community spirit. In these cases the environment has not provided for healthy relationships. It has been difficult for young children to play together and for adults to meet friends.

Today, when architects are involved on major developments they consult experts on human behaviour to try to avoid similar situations occurring again. Such consultations are an example of "designing" in a responsible way.

Design is all about introducing change that will improve the quality of life. Life here includes all forms of life, plant and animal as well as human, and the future as well as the present life.

PRACTICAL IMPLICATIONS

How, then, can you take conservation into account on your course? You can start by:

1. Looking closely at the wisdom of your **choice of material** in terms of *conservation*, as well as economic, ecological and social effects.
2. Making a list of the *processes* used and see how much energy was used, e.g. 10 minutes of electrical power on the drilling machine, and 20 minutes on the power sander, 3 minutes on the strip heater, 5 minutes on the brazing hearth, etc.
3. Making a note of the **amount of material** you started with and seeing just how much was *wasted*. Include in your list of materials such items as glue, nails, solder, glass paper, varnish, paint, etc.
4. Working out approximately **how many hours** were spent on the project and how much of this time required the use of *heating and lighting*.

Having completed this exercise you may have a better idea of what your project *really* cost. Knowing that a lot of energy and material will be used on just one project may cause you to look more closely for ways of cutting down this cost.

There are a number of ways you might use to reduce the "hidden" costs of a project:

❝❝ Ways in which you can reduce the "hidden" costs of a project. ❞❞

a) Only take *sufficient* material to complete the project.
b) When *marking out*, look for the most *economical way*, gaining the maximum use; e.g. when marking out on sheet material, always mark *as near to the edge* of the sheet as possible.
c) If a process can be carried out equally well by hand as by using a power tool, then use the *hand process* in preference; e.g. to remove waste wood, use a hand saw instead of a sanding disc.
d) Use glass paper only in the *final* stage of preparing the surface of a piece of wood, and not as an alternative way of removing unwanted material. Use the correct tool for the job.

e) Unwanted material, wood, metal, plastics, etc., should *not* be thrown away. It should be either returned to the store room, or placed in the "off-cut" box. These small pieces may still be useful for another project or for making a "model" in the designing stage.

f) Clean the surfaces of steel thoroughly *before* attempting to braze, so that you are successful *first time*. Repeating the process means not only a waste of your time but also of energy and resources.

g) Always treat paper with great respect. The more you use, the more trees need to be felled!

These are just a few suggestions for you to consider and to get you thinking. No doubt you will be able to think of other ways of reducing an unnecessary waste of resources.

Over a period of time you should acquire *attitudes* that will make it second nature for you to use your resources wisely, and to be annoyed when you see someone else being unnecessarily wasteful.

Pay careful attention to the design features of the product *you* design, to see if you can minimise its impact on resources. For example, you may have made a battery-powered toy that demands so much energy to make it "go" that the batteries have to be constantly renewed after only a short period of use.

THE EXAMINATION

You can expect a question or part of a question to relate to conservation in the written examination. It may not come under such a precise heading as conservation. For example, the following headings have been used:

- "Technological Awareness". (WJEC)
- "Design in Society". (MEG)

Sometimes there are *no* headings and you would have to rely upon your understanding of the question or part question as given below;

- "Give four examples of how the activities of designers influence our lives." (NEAB)

All the sub-parts of this question related to aspects of design. This was the *final* part; out of 20 marks it had a weighting of 4 marks.

Though the type of questions vary, and the topics change each year, you *can* expect several questions to be set on this aspect of the course. The one thing they have in common is that they test your *awareness* rather than your detailed knowledge of technical processes.

TECHNOLOGICAL AWARENESS
Q1
Children's Play Areas

Play areas in parks can be dangerous places.

a) Suggest **one** way in which slides could be made safer for children to use. (2)

b) Suggest **one** way in which swings could be made safer for children to use. (2)

c) A group of people your age are designing an adventure playground for a local primary school. They have been given
   i) 50 tractor and lorry tyres,
   ii) 100 railway sleepers.
   They are not sure whether to use these items.
   List **two** advantages and **two** disadvantages of using the tyres and sleepers. (8)

d) The group also have £500 to spend.
   List **four** factors that they should consider before spending the money. (8)

Q2
Design for the Disabled

Think of a **commercially produced** aid that you have recently seen being used by a disabled or handicapped person.

a) Using diagrams and notes describe this piece of equipment. Include in your answer reference to
   i)   how the aid helps the disabled person,   (4)
   ii) what materials it is made from,   (3)
   iii) how it is constructed.   (3)

b) You have designed and made an aid for a disabled person. It has now been in use for a month. You must now meet the disabled person to evaluate the design. List the **five** most important questions you will ask the disabled person. Give **one** reason for **each** question.   (10)

Q3
Design Analysis

The subject of Design and Technology in schools has changed a lot recently.

a) Using the experience you have gained over the last two years, think what you consider to be the **ideal** DT Department.
   List the **five** most important features. Give **one** reason for **each** choice.   (10)

b) There are many reasons why "the ideal" is not possible, but small, inexpensive improvements can often be made.
   Consider the DT Department in your own school and suggest **four** inexpensive changes that could be made to improve the facilities. Give **one** reason for **each** suggestion.   (8)

c) Outline ways in which the money could be raised to fund your ideas.   (2)

(WJEC)

DESIGN IN SOCIETY

The questions are based on the theme "Conservation of Raw Materials".

*Read the following statement carefully and then answer **either** Question 4 **or** Question 5. Wherever possible refer to the statement given below in support of your answer.*

> ■ **People are becoming more aware of the need to consider the conservation of resources especially in connection with activities that consume raw materials. This is particularly important when thinking of future generations.**

Either

Q4

a) Using examples, describe measures taken to help conserve raw materials.   (6)
b) Explain what is meant by "conservation of materials".   (4)
c) Give **two** examples of products and explain how conservation of raw materials appears to have been ignored in their design.   (6)
d) Why is it important that, when we design something, we should be concerned with conserving materials?   (4)

Or

Q5

a) From the list of materials given, name those which are raw materials and those which are non-raw materials.

   oak   polythene   gold   coal   plywood   iron ore   (3)

b) Disposable products can be wasteful. Some examples are shown in Fig. 6.4 below.
   i) Identify the raw material from which each of the above examples is made.   (2)
   ii) Name **two** other disposable products and the raw materials from which they are made.   (2)

c) Some products can be recycled. Explain, using examples, the benefits of recycling.

(6)

d) How do hardboard and chipboard contribute to the conservation of raw materials, and how do these materials influence product design?

(7)

(MEG)

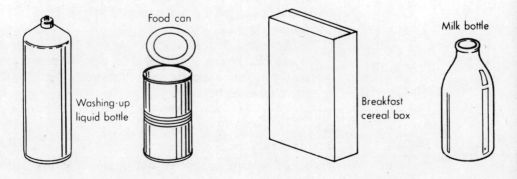

Fig. 6.4

STUDENT'S ANSWER – EXAMINER'S COMMENTS

STUDENT'S ANSWER TO QUESTION 1

Children's Play Areas

66 Good beginning with a reason given. 99

66 Valid. 99

66 A little thin on content, should say why, e.g. rubber is water resistant. 99

66 Correct but it would have been better not to repeat an answer. 99

a) By having grass around under the slide so that if a child falls it might not get hurt.

b) By making the seat of a softer material than wood.

c)   USING TYRES

Advantage	Disadvantage
1. Using a waste product.	1. Heavy
2. Withstand the weather	2. Dirty

66 BThe material should be named e.g Polypropylene. 99

66 Give a situation when this could be a disadvantage - e.g. Tyres free to roll. 99

Using railway sleepers

1. Using a waste product.	1. May have splinters.
2. Withstand the weather.	2. Could be dirty.

d) 1. What is needed, e.g. fixing material such as concrete, rope, stakes, etc.

2. Does anything have to be done to the tyres and sleepers to make them safe.

3. Give any tools required?

4. What maintenance is required, if any.

66 Here you need to name tools e.g. spade, hammer etc. 99

Fig. 6.5

REVIEW SHEET

■ Write a list of the type of details that you would expect to see in a Product Design Specification.

_____

_____

_____

_____

_____

■ Write a list of details that you would expect to find under the heading of Constraints.

_____

_____

_____

_____

_____

_____

■ Describe how making a mock up can assist you with developing a solution to a problem.

_____

_____

_____

_____

_____

_____

■ List the important features of a working drawing and state why they are important.

_____

_____

_____

_____

_____

_____

_____

■ Starting from the identification of a need, write a linear sequence of designing activities that will take you through each stage to the summative evaluation of a realised solution.

1. _____

2. _____

3. _____

4. _____

5. _____

6. _____

7. _____

8. _____

9. _____

10. _____

■ Describe, after having identified a need, how you proceed to the stage of writing a Design Brief.

_____

_____

_____

_____

■ Define the term "Design brief" and state what are the important features of a good design brief.

_____

_____

_____

_____

■ It is stated that we live in a materialistic society i.e. we love to possess manufactured products. Select a manufactured product that you possess, then a) see how far back you can go to trace the origin of the material resource that was used to make it, and b) the origin of the energy resource that was necessary for its manufacture.

Material resource. _____

_____

_____

_____

_____

Energy resource. _____

_____

_____

_____

_____

_____

■ Whilst industry is a heavy user of materials and energy it is for our material benefit and physical comfort. State two ways in which we, the public consumer, could reduce our demands upon industry so that material and energy resources could be more widely used.

1. _____

_____

_____

_____

2. _____

_____

_____

_____

■ Look round your home or school and make a list of those aspects where you believe material and energy is used wisely.

1. _____

2. _____

3. _____

4. _____

Now make a list of those aspects where you believe that materials and energy are not used wisely.

1. _____

2. _____

3. _____

4. _____

PRODUCT EVALUATION

EVALUATION OF A "ONE-OFF" PRODUCT

EVALUATION OF SEVERAL SIMILAR "ONE-OFF" PRODUCTS

EVALUATION OF A COMMERCIAL PRODUCT

EVALUATING A PRODUCT AT HOME

GETTING STARTED

There are two main classes of products:

1. the product made by an individual such as yourself;
2. the product that is manufactured by a company and is sold in the shop, store, etc.

You have already been concerned with evaluation when you were asked to make judgements about the products you made as part of the coursework.

To distinguish between the product you make and the product made by a company it is simple enough to think of the product that you or your class friends made as a "one-off" product, and those made by a company as a "commercial" product.

ESSENTIAL PRINCIPLES

**EVALUATION
OF A
"ONE-OFF
PRODUCT"**

The two main areas that require evaluating are:

1. How well does the product fulfil the Design Brief?
2. How easy or difficult was the product to make?

Fig. 3.8 on page 37 is an example of a way of setting out an evaluation sheet. However, the layout is only suitable for dealing with how well the product satisfied the Design Brief. Therefore it will be necessary to produce a different evaluation sheet, which this time will be suitable for dealing with how easy or difficult the product was to make. It should have a space for recommending where improvements could be made. See the example in Table 7.1 given below.

EVALUATION SHEET

TITLE

DESIGN BRIEF

AREAS OF DIFFICULTY   *RECOMMENDATIONS FOR
                                          IMPROVEMENT*

Construction

Were the techniques you selected easy to
perform?

Could you achieve equally good results using an
alternative technique that was easier to perform?

Was your choice of material or materials a good
one considering the available facilities and your
ability to use them?

Were you able to perform the chosen technique
without having to rush?

By using alternative techniques and materials
would your design be improved?

Table 7.1

There are many *different* ways of presenting this type of information. The tabular form (Table 7.1) helps to direct your thoughts to those areas that need commenting upon and to present them in an easy to follow manner. The example shown in Fig. 7.1 is an evaluation produced by a *student*. Many of the points listed above are included in this evaluation. In many ways this student has produced a very good evaluation with recommendations for improvement, but had it been set out using a "table", the specific detail would be easier to find.

ASSESSMENT OF THE STUDENT'S "EVALUATION"

Before assessing the content it is clear to see that:

a) the handwriting is easy to read;
b) the comments are brief;
c) care has been taken with the presentation.

PROJECT TITLE Motor driven toy

SUMMARY OF DESIGN BRIEF Age of user to be decided. Toy should be safe to use and appealing to play with. All electrical parts to be contained within toy – access should be included so as to change battery. No major restrictions on materials or size.

EVALUATION

66 Design fault identified. 99

When the toy was finished I found that the motor wasn't powerful enough to push it along. When pushed along, the movements of the toy worked, but not as well as they could.

66 Construction problem identified. 99

66 Solution. 99

The first problem that I had while constructing the toy was the head. At first the cam wouldn't push the head as it kept getting stuck so I applied plenty of wax which helped.

66 Problem identified. 99

When the head was coming out, the elastic band wouldn't pull it back again.

66 Solution. 99

So I tried attaching the elastic band to different places while I found the best one. It worked here, but it could have been better if the elastic band was stronger.

66 Design Problem. 99

The second problem was with the legs. They wouldn't sit on the cams properly. So I had to keep on adjusting the position which they were stuck. The appertures in the top shell also had to be cut wider and higher as the legs were not clearing the shell. The same had to be done with the bottom appertures as the cams were hitting the shell.

66 Solution. 99

66 Repeat of first statement. 99

If the motor was powerful enough to push to toy then it could be operated by a young child but I don't think its that suitable as its not strong enough.

66 Recommendations. 99

If designing it again I would use stronger plastics, especially for the head which is polystyrene. Also the way in which the head and legs work would have to be thought about more.

Fig. 7.1 A Student's Evaluation

Though these qualities are not directly assessed when reading an evaluation, they help considerably with the communication between you and the assessor. Read Chapter 21 for further details of the assessment of this student's evaluation, when it will be seen together with the rest of the project.

If you read the evaluation carefully you will see that:

1. Design faults have been identified.
   (Motor not powerful enough and the movements of the toy were not entirely satisfactory)
2. Construction faults have been identified.
   (The head and the cam kept getting stuck)
3. Choice of material criticised.
   (A stronger plastic for the head was required)
4. Modifications made and recommended.
   (The apertures in the top shell had to be cut wider)
5. Aspects that still need more thought.
   (The way in which the head and legs worked)

As an evaluation it could have been seen that this student had been quite critical about the end-product. Not all comments need to refer to weaknesses of design or constructional detail. It is just as important to refer to the good qualities of the product. This may seem boastful about a product that you have designed and made, so view the product as one that could have been made by another pupil and one that you did not know. In this way you can highlight the good and the poor qualities of the product.

The evaluation above could have been improved by including comments about the following details:

a) reference to the Design Brief;
b) the appearance;
c) the appeal that the toy had for the child;
d) good qualities;
e) ease or difficulty of making;
f) more precise details about modifications and recommendations that should be considered if this project were to be done again.

During the designing and making, you are learning an awful lot about the problems encountered in such an exercise. The assessor and your teacher would like to know *what* you have learnt through this experience. Therefore, think about those times that you found difficult or easy, and when you had to use a *different* material or process than that given in the working drawing. As we have seen, making changes as you progress with a project is quite normal and to be expected. You will gain more credit by acknowledging that it was necessary to make alterations than by omitting to say anything.

Check through your own evaluations of products that you have designed and made and see if you are presenting:

a) a clear and precise comment about the product;
b) an acknowledgement of all the changes that were necessary during manufacture;
c) precise recommendations for future consideration, especially if the product were to be made again;
d) a fair and sincere comment on all aspects.

Assignment

Produce an evaluation sheet that would be helpful to you when you have to "evaluate" a project.

2 ▷ EVALUATION OF SEVERAL SIMILAR "ONE-OFF" PRODUCTS

Sometimes examination questions are set which involve the evaluation of products that have been designed and made by students following a Technology course. Unfortunately you are unable to have the actual products and you have to get all your information from a drawing. The task is done under strict examination conditions; therefore it has to be done in a limited time and without consultation with anyone. This question usually forms part of the second section in which there is a choice and a time limit of approximately 25 minutes to answer.

QUESTION

Four designs for a stand to hold a pocket calculator are shown.

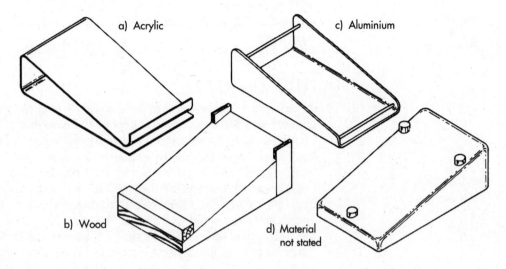

a) Acrylic

c) Aluminium

b) Wood

d) Material
not stated

Fig. 7.2

(I)   List the four main design factors common to all the stands shown.
1.
2.
3.
4.

(II) The material for design d) is not given. Specify a suitable material without repeating those given.
MATERIAL SPECIFICATION
REASON FOR SELECTION

(III) Which stand do you consider the most expensive in terms of time and energy? Show why.
STAND
Because: (6 lines available)
Under what conditions would it be worthwhile using the stand you have selected? (6 lines available)

(IV) The design chosen for manufacture will depend upon the number needed and the production facilities available.
Select the stand you consider most appropriate for each of the following:
(i) MAKING ONLY ONE STAND
(ii) MAKING TEN STANDS

Complete the table below.

	STAND CHOSEN	METHOD	REASON
Making one only			
Making ten			

(V)   You are in charge of a Group Project at your school. You have four unskilled pupils in your group, and the School CDT facilities are available to make 75 stands.
i)   Decide which stand your group will make, and give reasons for your choice.
(6 lines available)
ii) Outline your production organisation for using four unskilled workers effectively.
(8 lines available)

OUTLINE ANSWER

(I)   In answering this first part of the question you need to look at the illustration and identify **similarities**. The first observation you may make is that they all have a *sloping* surface. Therefore just write "sloping surface". The second observation you may make is that they all have a *stop* at the bottom of the slope. They all have a *flat base*. Finally, the fourth similarity may not be quite so obvious. Some of the differences are obvious but the question does *not* require you to give these so you must look more deeply. Do you think that *you* could make all of them? If so, the fourth similarity could well be that "They could all be made in a school workshop" or "They could all be made by students following a Technology course."

(II)   In order to be able to name a material you need to know the type of processes that produce a form with rounded edges and corners. Most moulding and casting techniques produce this type of finish, therefore all you have to do is to name a material that may be cast or moulded and check that it is different from the materials named in the other three examples. The most likely casting material must be "aluminium alloy" or a "polyester resin". There are other materials that could be used but the one you chose should be one that you have used while in the workshop, or one that you have seen being used in the workshop. If you have experience with vacuum forming techniques you will know that a thermoplastics material could also be made to produce the form illustrated in d) and you could give as your answer: sheet nylon, polyethylene, or PVC.
Having made your *choice* you must give your *reason* for selection. The **reason** for choosing any material must be:

a)   that it will readily take up a form that has rounded edges and corners;
b)   that it is commonly used in a workshop;
c)   the equipment required to produce this type of form is readily available.

Remember, the examiner is unlikely to ask a question that includes a material and process with which you are unfamiliar. So just try to recall some of your experience in the workshop.

(III) To answer this part of the question you need to look at each design in turn and think which process is most likely used in its production.

■ a), being made from acrylic, is likely to be cut out of a sheet, the edges filed, scraped, polished and then heat bent three times to arrive at the form illustrated.

■ b) is made from four pieces of wood. Each has to be cut to size. Two pieces have to be shaped with one surface sloping. Producing a sloping surface is never easy. The parts have to be fitted and assembled. Surfaces have to be smooth and ready to receive a coat of polish.

So far the list of functions is much longer than that given to produce a) and if you have worked in these two materials you will know that the processes outlined in b) take much longer than those outlined in a).

■ The stand in c) is also made from a number of components. Therefore besides the cutting, shaping, drilling, and bending, the parts will have to be fitted and assembled. For the parts to be assembled properly, considerable accuracy will be required. This design is obviously going to take time and energy to produce and will most certainly take longer than a) to make. But it is doubtful whether or not it will take more time and energy than design b) to make.

■ When you consider the last design d), you have to compare the answer given in part (II) of the question with the designs where the material was already named. If you choose a casting technique in aluminium alloy then you have to take into consideration the time and energy to make a pattern, to set up a flask and to prepare a furnace and crucible for making the aluminium ready for casting. If you choose a moulding technique, then again you will need to make a pattern but the process of making a moulding should be much quicker and not so expensive on energy as casting in metal.

The problem of producing the three vertical cylindrical lugs on the sloping surface has also to be considered. You have the choice of either including the lugs on the pattern or fitting the lugs as a separate operation. Either way, more time and energy is going to be taken. From the clean edge lines on the lugs it would appear that they were made individually and fitted by drilling the "body" of the stand and fitting the lugs with a tight fit. The drilling of the holes on a sloping surface also presents a problem. Mounting the "body" on the table of the drilling machine to ensure that all the holes are vertical to the horizontal demands accurate alignment and time to do the job properly. The design of stand that is going to be most expensive in terms of time and energy must be d) because of the problems already outlined. The answer could be presented as follows:

Stand d)

Because: the stand has to be made first in wood as a pattern and then cast in metal. Preparation of the furnace, crucible, and flask all takes time. The pouring process needs a teacher to participate and time is needed for cooling down. The casting has to be trimmed ready for setting up on the drilling machine. The lugs will be produced on the lathe and then fitted.

The **conditions** under which it would be worthwhile using this design of stand are:

1. where it has to withstand a lot of rough use;
2. where many stands are required;
3. where weight is an advantage;
4. where there is an ample supply of aluminium.

(IV)	STAND CHOSEN		METHOD	REASONS
Making one only	b)		1. Marking out 2. Sawing to size 3. Shaping wedge shape by sawing and planing. 4. Remove waste for uprights supports by sawing and chiselling. 5. Glue and clamp. 6. Clean up. 7. Apply a coat of polish	Beyond making templates very little could be done to assist in the manufacture of this design. In a workshop containing wood working hand tools – saws, chisels, planes, etc., this design could be easily made as a 'one-off'.
Making ten	a)		1. Marking out position of bends from a template. 2. Strip heat and bend round a wedge-shaped former made from wood. 3. Polish edges (This could be done before bending). 4. Check angles against a template.	1. The workshop has a strip heater & a supply of 3 mm thick sheet acrylic. 2. The manufacturing process can be easily adapted to using 'jigs' and 'formers'. 3. Manufacturing time is shorter than that needed to produce the other designs.

In this part of the question your understanding of the processes required to produce a single product and the processes to produce a number of products is being tested. For a small number such as ten, the term "batch production" is sometimes used. To produce a "batch" often means that a "jig" or "pattern" is needed to improve accuracy and to reduce the time needed for manufacture. For example, if a jig could be designed to ensure that the position and angle of the bends in design a) could be achieved without the need for marking out on the acrylic and using a protractor, a time-consuming process will have been eliminated. Therefore you need to look for a design of a stand that can be easily made with the aid of a "jig" etc. Design a) is suitable for manufacture with the aid of a "jig" ("former") because:

1. The number of operations are fewer than the other designs. (This was established in answering part (III).)
2. Marking out the position of the bends can be done by placing the acrylic on a piece of card that has the positions already marked on it and transferring them with a felt pen.
3. The angles can be achieved by bending the heated acrylic against a piece of wood already shaped (a former) to the appropriate angles. They can also be checked against a full size side view drawing on a piece of plywood (a template). These are good reasons why design a) is suitable for "Making Ten".

When making one only you need to look for a design that would not benefit from being produced by "jigs" etc. or any other repetitive method that is required to produce a number of identical shapes. We have already chosen a) as being suitable for jig production, so that design must not be considered again. Earlier it was stated that stand d) could be produced by a casting process, so this eliminates design d). The choice then remains between b) and c). A case could be made for choosing either of these stands when only one is required. Stand b) is made of wood and lends itself to making each part separately and assembling with an adhesive. Stand c) is made from aluminium sheet and rod and lends itself to marking out, cutting to shape, drilling two holes to locate the rods and assembling.

(V) The last part of the question is again concerned with the production of a quantity of stands but this time not only is the quantity much larger, the number of manufacturers has increased to four. Note that the four manufacturers are described as "unskilled".

i) *I have chosen design (d) made from a thermoplastics sheet e.g. P.V.C. Because 1. Provided a mould is available the operation of a vacuum forming machine is not complicated and difficult to use. 2. There are very few different operations. 3. The moulding can be produced in a short space of time. 4. All stands produced by this method will be identical in shape size and quality.*

ii) *First worker: Feeds the machine with the plastics sheet and switches the machine on.*

Second worker: Removes the formed sheet and takes it to the trimming bench.

Third worker: Trims the waste material from the moulding.

Fourth worker: Cleans and polishes the trimmed edges.

Fig. 7.3

i) When selecting a suitable design for the four unskilled workers to produce 75 stands, you should look for the following points:

1. A simple design that requires as few as possible different operations in its production.
2. The operations must be easy for the four unskilled workers to understand and acquire the necessary manufacturing skill.
3. The design must be suitable for employing the use of such processes and

techniques as casting or moulding, etc., because all the stands must be made the same shape and size.

4. The production time must not be too long. Otherwise the unskilled workers may lose concentration and enthusiasm to complete the task of producing 75 stands.

At this stage of answering the question you will be very familiar with the design details and the manufacturing processes required to produce each stand. Therefore you may have decided which stand you will make as a Group Project. It is worthwhile to just check each design against the four points listed above before making a final decision:

- Design a) has already been chosen as a stand that can be made in a small quantity. It therefore may be worthwhile considering later.
- Design b) was selected as being suitable for a "one-off" production and is therefore unlikely to be considered suitable for a quantity production. No more thought need be given to this design.
- Design c) was considered to demand a similar breakdown of operations as design b). It also required some quite difficult production skills and is therefore another design that needs no further consideration.
- Design d) could be produced using a casting or moulding process that would ensure that all stands were the same size and shape, etc. This must mean that it is worth considering.

This now means that the final decision must be made between design *a)*, made from acrylic, and design *d)* made from a material that has not been stated. If design *d)* could be produced in a single operation, i.e. the lugs and body made from a single piece of material and produced using a moulding technique, then this design must take preference over design *a)*. The major task is to produce the mould. Once this is made the act of operating a moulding machine is relatively straightforward and should not be difficult to learn and acquire the necessary skills. An ideal material would be a thermoplastics sheet, e.g. polyethylene, polystyrene, polyvinyl chloride PVC, etc., from which the design could be manufactured, and in which case a vacuum forming process could be employed. Once the mould has been made by a skilled person the remaining operations require very little skill. The operations are:

a) placing the mould in the vacuum forming machine;
b) placing a sheet of thermoplastics in the machine;
c) switching on the machine;
d) removing the vacuum formed sheet;
e) trimming the stand.

(ii) After the first production of a formed sheet the mould can remain in the vacuum forming machine until all the 75 stands have been produced. Therefore the tasks for the four unskilled workers could be divided as follows:

- **First worker:**   Place the sheet of thermoplastics in the vacuum forming machine ready for forming and switch on.
- **Second worker:**   Remove the formed sheet and take it to the bench where the mouldings will be trimmed.
- **Third worker:**   Trim the waste material from the moulding.
- **Fourth worker:**   Clean and polish the trimmed edges.

This now completes the sample answer. Though this may be an answer that would satisfy an Examiner, it must not be considered as the only possible answer. There is no such thing as a single correct answer to this type of question. There are many answers and they should be seen as answers of varying quality from very weak to excellent. Remember you are being examined to find out what you know and understand and the understanding part of this question forms a major part.

3 **EVALUATION OF A COMMERCIAL PRODUCT**

When faced with the decision of buying a product, whether it is a "tin opener" or a "car", the process of assessing the product's qualities are the same. A tin opener must be reliable and efficient at opening tins in the same way that a car must be reliable and efficient at being driven. All commercial products can be evaluated. While you would not be expected to make evaluative *judgements* about a product like a car in an examination,

> Remember function, appearance, reliability and cost, when evaluating a product.

it is possible to expect you to establish a set of *criteria* that will help to evaluate a product like a car.

Most commercial products can be evaluated under such broad headings as: Function; Appearance; Reliability; Cost; etc. All that is needed is for the appropriate questions to be asked for each aspect.

EVALUATING A TIN OPENER

The best way of course is to try it on a number of tins and to test its efficiency. But what would you be looking for if you were having to make a choice of one tin opener from a range of many such products? Under the headings listed below it is possible to draw up a number of questions which, if answered, would provide the type of answers that would tell us something about the qualities of the product.

Function

- How easy is the tin opener to use? Very easy. Quite easy. Not easy.
- Does the tin opener leave a clean edge to the tin so that there are no rough edges? Yes. No.
- Does the tin opener remove the cut portion? Yes. No.
- Will the tin opener open tins that are not cylindrical? Yes. No.

With a tick through the appropriate answer you would soon be able to see which tin opener got the most "yes's", was easy to use and produced a clean edge to the tin.

Other factors have to be considered before a purchase would be made. They include: appearance, reliability, maintenance, how long it would be expected to have an efficient life and cost.

Appearance

Appearance plays a very important part in our lives. The shape, colour, and texture may be combined to produce a product that is not only efficient but is also pleasant to look at. An attractive product is much more satisfying to have than an unpleasant one. Many products are chosen because of their colour alone. This is why identical products are presented in a range of colours so that at least one colour may appeal to your taste.

Reliability and maintenance

The life expectancy of a tin opener should be many years. It should be sufficiently well designed and made to withstand the rigours of opening many thousands of tins before needing to be replaced. It should be able to withstand coming into contact with all sorts of moist foods and not cause any contamination to the food by staining or rusting. A very cheap product may begin to rust because the steel from which it was made was either not the correct alloy or the surface treatment was inferior. Hence it is reasonable to expect a cheaper product not to last as long as a more expensive one.

Maintenance, though not a major aspect to be concerned with in a tin opener, can be a source of annoyance if it is difficult to clean.

Cost

Cost is important. As with purchasing any product you want to have value for your money. If two tin openers perform equally efficiently and look equally attractive but one costs less than the other, it is not difficult to predict which one will be sold first.

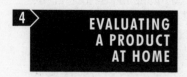

4 > EVALUATING A PRODUCT AT HOME

First draw up a set of criteria that will help you to assess a product. Use the broad headings of; function, appearance and reliability under which to list the appropriate questions. You may use Table 7.2 for assistance.

The choice of products to evaluate at home is almost endless. Here are just a few recommendations: chair, table, television set, radio, kettle, toaster, table lamp, cupboard, wardrobe, shoe polish container, toothpaste dispenser, battery torch, cutlery, garden spade, wheel barrow, garden furniture, hair dryer, electric plug, telephone, etc. With a product that you are able to examine carefully and able to make observations about how well it performs its function, what it looks like etc., you are able to make critical judgements.

EVALUATING A CHAIR

Function

Select a **chair** that you wish to evaluate. Under a heading "Function", list what you think the chair must be able to do. Your list could include the following points.

HEADING	CRITERIA (expressed as questions)	ANSWER
Function		
Appearance		
Reliability		

Table 7.2

The chair I have chosen must:

a) be comfortable to sit in;
b) match the other furniture in the room;
c) be easy to move when necessary;
d) be the correct height when watching television;
e) not easily tip over and be able to withstand my weight;
f) be made of a material that is easy to keep clean;
g) be made from a material or materials that are not highly combustible.

> 66 Try to turn these points into questions. 99

These points could now be expressed as questions and the answers given in levels of performance: Excellent, Satisfactory, Poor, as shown in Table 7.3. When answering g) look to see if there is a safety guarantee label, or design award label. Do not be tempted to carry out any testing.

Appearance

A chair could satisfy all the above requirements but it may not *look* attractive. Therefore you will need to list the criteria that it must satisfy if its appearance is going to be acceptable. One criteria listed under the heading of "Function" could equally be included under the heading of "Appearance". Criteria b) is concerned with how it looks when compared with the rest of the furniture, but an answer that may rate the chair as being an excellent match may not necessarily mean that it is a very attractive piece of furniture. Under "Appearance" you should assess the aesthetic qualities and its suitability for the environment in which it is situated.

The construction and design of the chair must:

a) be pleasing to look at;
b) be inviting to sit in;
c) be well proportioned;
d) be inviting to touch.

To turn this set of criteria into questions is easy, but to answer them can be quite difficult. Unlike answering the questions under the heading of function where you could sit in the chair and see if it was comfortable to sit in, here you have to just look at the chair and form an overall impression. Look at the detail and it may come clearer to you *why* that impression was formed. The colour of the fabric may have caught your eye. The texture of the materials from which the chair was made might have invited you to run your hand over the surfaces. The pleasing proportions may invite you to sit in the chair. These invitations can work in the opposite direction. You may not feel invited to sit in the chair. You may not feel sufficiently attracted to want to touch the surfaces of the materials from which the chair is made. You do not have to be knowledgeable about *proportion* in order to assess whether the design of the chair you are evaluating is well proportioned or not. Just remember the characteristics that you know about materials. For example, wood is acknowledged as being less strong than metal. Therefore the thickness and width of the legs of a chair made from wood can be expected to be larger than that made from a piece of steel. If the proportions are such that it is not possible to lift the chair, then the proportions may be excessive and the chair would have a heavy look about it.

Proportion is also concerned with balance. If a chair looks top heavy it may give you the feeling that it will fall over easily. The space between the legs at the point where they contact the ground may be too small, in which case the chair will topple over and prove that your feeling was justified. The space between the lower part of the legs may be excessive, in which case its stability will be excellent but the chair will require a lot of floor space. The two aspects to look for in proportion are:

1. the thickness and width of material used;
2. the space between each structure.

Reliability

Reliability is not something you often associate with a chair, but it is important that it does not start falling apart. A soundly designed and well-made chair should survive quite a bit of misuse as well as sensible general use. If the joints are appropriate for the material and are well made, there should be no problem. If the fabric is correctly applied and is of such a quality that it will not tear easily, then it can be relied upon to last a long time.

EVALUATION SHEET   CHAIR

HEADING	*CRITERIA*	*RESPONSE*		
		EXCELLENT	SATISFACTORY	POOR
	a) Is it comfortable to sit in?		✓	
	b) Does it match other furniture?	✓		
	c) Can it be easily moved?	✓		
FUNCTION	d) Is it suitable for watching TV?		✓	
	e) Is it stable and able to withstand my weight?	✓		
	f) Is it easy to clean?			✓
	g) Is it made from low combustible materials? Is it safe?		✓ ✓	
	a) Is it pleasing to look at?	Yes. The colours are bright and cheerful.		
	b) Is it inviting to sit in?	Yes. There is plenty of room and the soft furnishing makes me want to sit in it.		
APPEARANCE	c) It it well proportioned?	Yes, but it is perhaps a little heavy looking. The structure could be reduced slightly in thickness to give a lighter appearance.		
	d) Is it inviting to touch?	The cold metal parts no, but the soft fabric is very pleasant.		
	a) Is the structure sound?	It withstands my weight comfortably.		
	b) Are any joints loose?	Just one at the back is getting slightly loose.		
RELIABILITY	c) Is the fabric firmly attached?	Yes.		
	d) Are there any tears in the fabric?	No.		

Table 7.3

Evaluate a product of your own choice. Use the format given in Table 7.3 above drawn on a sheet of A4 paper, i.e. the same size as this page. Then set out the appropriate questions for the product you are evaluating in the column headed "Criteria". Once you have completed this you can then examine the product and begin to enter your findings in the column headed "Response".

QUESTIONS AND ANSWERS

You may be expected to evaluate a product from either a photograph or an annotated drawing. This may seem an unsatisfactory way of evaluating a product, but then, this is the only way an examiner can assess your understanding of "Product Evaluation".

The Figure below shows a folding picnic chair.

To what extent has the designer tried to incorporate the following five features in the chair?

The Picnic Chair must:

i)   be stored and carried easily;   (3)   iv) have an attractive appearance;   (3)
ii) withstand outdoor use;   (3)   v)   be safe to use.   (3)
iii) withstand the weight of an adult;   (3)   (Use sketches where appropriate.)

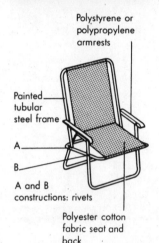

Fig. 7.4

1 **QUESTION: DESIGN EVALUATION**

Polystyrene or polypropylene armrests

Painted tubular steel frame

A

B

A and B constructions: rivets

Polyester cotton fabric seat and back

ANSWER

This question has to be answered on the lined paper that has been provided: The main task of evaluating a "folding picnic chair" is broken up into answering short answer questions related to design features. You must be sure that you identify the answers in the same manner as they are set out on the examination paper i), ii), iii), etc:

i)   The picnic chair is designed to fold flat so making it easier to carry and to take up a limited space for storage.

ii) The polyester cotton fabric used for the seat and back is not affected by rain and quickly dries if it does get wet. The armrests are also made from a water resistant material, either polystyrene or polypropylene and the tubular steel is painted.

iii) The materials used in this design are noted for their strength. The polyester cotton fabric has a strong tensile strength. Polypropylene is tough and not brittle and finally tubular steel can withstand considerable resistance to bending. However, where the holes are drilled for the rivets A and B this might cause a weakness.

iv) The outline of the chair is clean and the fabric could be brightly coloured and attractive. The armrests are generally white and the paint used on the frame could be chosen to match the colours in the fabric.

v)   A spring is used to relieve some of the tension in the fabric which occurs when someone is sitting in the chair. The frame appears to be suitable for the weight of an average person. The danger in getting the fingers caught exists with most folding chairs but with the use of a tubular frame no serious harm should be caused. The splay of the leg part of the frame should provide adequate stability.

The style and manner in which product evaluation occurs varies. It may form the *total theme* of a question like the one just answered or it may form *part* of a question like the one below.

2 **QUESTION: DESIGN FOR THE DISABLED**

Think of a commercially produced aid that you have recently seen being used by a disabled or handicapped person.

a) Using diagrams and notes describe this piece of equipment. Include in your answer reference to:
   i) how the aid helps the disabled person   (4)
   ii) what material it is made from   (3)
   iii)how it is constructed.   (3)

b) You have designed and made an aid for a disabled person. It has now been in use for a month. You must now meet the disabled person to evaluate the design.

(WJEC)

ANSWER PLAN TO PART b

1. List the criteria that a product has to fulfil.
2. Write the criteria in the form of a question.
3. Select a suitable way of presenting the five most important questions and the reasons.
4. Divide the criteria into main areas i.e. Function, Appearance, Reliability, etc.

REVIEW SHEET

■ Almost every product that you see and use has been designed. There are often a variety of solutions to a single problem. For example you require a mobile source of light to find an object in the dark and the solution is a battery operated torch. How many different designs of torch have you seen or used? Select three products that are fulfilling a similar need. Analyse each of the products and evaluate them for there intended need.

Product number one. _____

_____

_____

_____

_____

Product number two. _____

_____

_____

_____

Product number three. _____

_____

_____

_____

_____

■ Now for each of the three products write what you think may have been the Design Brief and Product Design Specification.

Product number one.

Design Brief. _____

Product Design Specification.

a) _____

b) _____

c) _____

d) _____

Product number two.

Design Brief. _____

Product Design Specification.

a) _____

b) _____

c) _____

d) _____

Product number three.

Design Brief. _____

Product Design Specification.

a) _____

b) _____

c) _____

d) _____

■ You should see that the products have similar but not identical Design briefs and Product Design Specifications.

Write a set of **general criteria** that could be used to evaluate any product.

1. _____

2. _____

3. _____

4. _____

■ Write a set of **specific criteria** that could be used to evaluate any product.

1. _____

2. _____

3. _____

4. _____

■ Write in a few sentences what you believe is "good design". In doing this state what factors influence design and illustrate your answer by referring to a chosen product.

_____

_____

_____

_____

_____

_____

_____

_____

_____

_____

_____

_____

_____

_____

_____

_____

_____

_____

■ State what part fashion plays in the design of products. Illustrate your answer by referring to specific products.

_____

_____

_____

_____

_____

_____

_____

_____

_____

_____

MATERIALS

TIMBER CLASSIFICATION

MANUFACTURED BOARDS

METAL CLASSIFICATION

PLASTICS CLASSIFICATION

SELECTION OF MATERIAL

SUMMARY

GETTING STARTED

The three main materials to be used in the realisation of a design solution in this subject will be wood, metal and plastics. Other materials such as fabric, clay, glass, etc., must not be discounted. The rather wide range of materials that could be used may be daunting but you are only expected to be familiar with the three main materials.

You will probably *not* receive formal lessons devoted to the identification of timbers, metals and plastics. So when you are working with a material make a few notes that will be helpful to you as you go through the course. If you are working in **wood** it would be helpful to know the following:

1. The full *name* of the timber, e.g. Parana Pine, Brazilian Mahogany, Scandinavian Beech, etc.
2. A brief description of *what it looks like*, e.g. colour, any distinctive markings, dark lines, wavy lines, etc.
3. Its *working properties*. Can you cut it easily, or does it split easily, is it difficult to saw, etc.
4. *Use*. Some woods are more suited for one function than another. Some are very resistant to outdoor weather conditions, e.g. Western Red Cedar, others are not so resistant and can only be used indoors, e.g. Jelutong is ideal for making toys and models where appearance does not matter.

Just a few brief notes under the headings, **Name, Appearance, Working Properties** and **Use** of three softwoods and three hardwoods should be most helpful.

You can use a similar approach when you are working in metal or **plastic**.

ESSENTIAL PRINCIPLES

Wood is classified into two groups. *Softwoods* and *Hardwoods*. The classification is determined by the *type of tree* from which the timber has derived. Trees are either *coniferous* (bears cones and has needle-shaped leaves that stay green all the year round), or *deciduous* (has flat leaves that fall in the autumn). The timber that comes from the coniferous tree is known as a "softwood" and the timber that comes from a deciduous tree is known as a 'hardwood'. Though the terms "hardwood" and "softwood" imply that woods in each group are either hard or soft there are examples where this is not true. *Balsa wood*, noted for its lightness and softness, is by classification a "hardwood", while *Pitch Pine*, noted for its weightiness and hardness, is by classification a "softwood".

	NAME	APPEARANCE	WORKING PROPERTY	USE
HARDWOODS	English Beech	Pale-brown to white, even texture grain	Turns well on the lathe Can be steam bent	Furniture School desks
	Ramin	Almost white, fine grain markings	Easy to work Only suitable for indoors	Furniture Dowelling
	Teak	Golden brown with dark markings	Hard to work by hand Machines well	Outdoor furniture
	Obeche	Pale-straw yellow Silky sheen Interlocking grain Reddish-brown heart	Easy to work Very light to handle	Most indoor work General use Furniture
SOFTWOODS	European Redwood	Pale yellow	Quality varies Can be worked well with hand tools	Paper Outdoor work when treated with preservative
	Western Red Cedar	Pale pinkish brown, distinctive grown rings	Easy to work with sharp tools Finishes well	Garden furniture Greenhouses

Table 8.1

Table 8.1 lists six timbers you should know.

Note there are woods that are suitable for indoor work and outdoor work. This is because some are very durable and can withstand the outdoor conditions, e.g. Teak, while others need treating with a preservative, i.e. a substance that soaks into the wood to make it withstand outdoor conditions. The small range of woods given in the table should enable you to answer most questions in an examination. But you are advised to find out the names, appearance and uses of woods that you have in school, and to add these to the list above.

Timber is available in a variety of shapes, sizes and finishes. The terms used to group different *sizes* of timber, starting from the largest forms are:

- plank — usually 40 mm thick and more;
- board — less than 40 mm thick, but more than 75 mm wide;
- strip — narrower than 75 mm wide;

- square   various sizes;
- dowel   round 0.25 mm and below;
- mouldings   various shapes and sizes;
- veneers   thin sheets of wood less than 0.5 mm thick.

Finish refers to the process by which the timber was prepared to size. *Sawn* timber has a *rough* finish. *Planed* timber has a *smooth* finish. The size given for any piece of timber is the size it was *when sawn*. Though the planing operation removes shavings of timber from all the surfaces, it will still be referred to as the original size it was when sawn. If you wish to have a piece of wood with a smooth surface you must state the size it is to be after planing. For example, if you want a piece of timber to be 47 mm by 22 mm it will be planed from a piece 50 mm by 25 mm and it will be referred to commercially as a piece of 50 mm by 25 mm.

2 > MANUFACTURED BOARDS

These are available in large sheets and are made up of timber arranged in different ways. The most commonly used **manufactured boards** are:

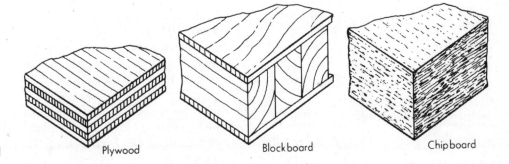

Fig. 8.1   Plywood   Blockboard   Chipboard

1. PLYWOOD

This is made from veneers (plies) of timber with the grain of each layer being at right-angles to each other and bonded together by a resin and pressure. There are always an odd number of layers so that the grain of the two outside layers is in the same direction. There are a number of grades that are designed to suit different situations. The grades are determined by the type of adhesive used to bond the plies:

a) marine plywood that is moisture resistant;   c) boil resistant plywood;
b) weather and boil proof plywood;   d) interior plywood.

The sheets are available in standard sizes 2440 mm by 1220 mm and range from 1.5 mm to 25 mm thick.

2. BLOCKBOARD

This is built up with a core of softwood strips bonded together with an adhesive and covered with a sheet of plywood on each side. There is a similar manufactured board that has narrower strips of softwood and is called laminboard. The boards are available in standard sheets 2440 mm by 1220 mm and the most common thickness is 18 mm.

3. CHIPBOARD

This is made from small "chips" of wood bonded together with resin and formed into sheets by compression. It is not as strong as plywood and blockboard but is also not as expensive. Chipboard is best used in dry conditions. Many chipboards are covered with a veneer of an attractively grained hardwood to improve its appearance and is then used to make furniture. Chipboard can also be covered with a plastic laminate and is again much used in the making of furniture, especially kitchen cupboards and working surfaces. The uncovered form is commonly called chipboard and is available in standard sheet size 2440 mm by 1220 mm. The covered forms are available in a wide range of sizes and a wide range of finishes. Common thickness is 18 mm and it is available in lengths of up to 3 metres.

4. HARDBOARD

Hardboard is made from wood fibres that have been pulped, processed and refined. The pulp is put under high pressure and temperature until the fibres bond to produce a tough board that is smooth on one side and rough on the other. The sheets are available in a standard size 2440 mm by 1220 mm and a thickness of 3 mm–5 mm.

There are two main categories of metal:

1. **ferrous:** those which contain iron;
2. **non-ferrous:** those which do not contain iron.

FERROUS METALS

Table 8.2 overleaf lists five **ferrous** materials that you should know.

NON-FERROUS METALS

Table 8.3 overleaf lists five **non-ferrous** materials that you should know.

Metals are available in sheet form or in lengths of a number of different cross-sectional shapes.

COMMON STOCK SHAPES

1. rounds	5 mm–150 mm diameter;
2. squares	5 mm–100 mm square;
3. flats	thickness: 3 mm, 5 mm, 6 mm, 8 mm, 10 mm, 12 mm, 16 mm, 20 mm, 25 mm, 30 mm, 40 mm, and 50 mm;
	widths: 12 mm, 20 mm, 25 mm, 32 mm, 40 mm, 50 mm, 60 mm, 65 mm, 70 mm, 80 mm, 100 mm, 125 mm, 160 mm;
4. hexagonal	distance across the flats: 6 mm, 8 mm, 10 mm, 12 mm, 16 mm, 18 mm, 20 mm, 22 mm, 25 mm, 28 mm, 30 mm;
5. round tube	outside diameter: from 5 mm to 40 mm;
6. square tube	outside measurement: from 12 mm to 25 mm;
7. rectangular tube	various available but not in common use in the school workshop;
8. angle	the measurements are taken on the outside: 12 mm to 25 mm in common use.

There are two main groups:

1. **Thermosetting plastics.** Once set these plastics cannot be heated to soften or remould.
2. **Thermoplastics.** This family of plastics can be heated to soften and for the shape to be bent or moulded.

THERMOSETTING PLASTICS

Many of our adhesives belong to this family. The most well known being "Araldite", which is an epoxy resin that hardens when a second chemical is added. The action takes several minutes to activate so that there is time for it to be applied and the parts assembled before it really hardens. They bond most materials which means that it is possible to bond unlike materials, e. g. wood and metal or metal and some plastics.

Polyurethane

This forms the basis of many paints and varnishes because of its tough and water resistant qualities.

Melamine formaldehyde

This is used in the production of plastics laminates because of its smooth surface and hygienic qualities. It is also used in electrical plugs, sockets, etc., because of its ease of casting and its property of being an excellent insulator.

Polyester resins

They go very hard and brittle on their own but if they are combined with another material such as fibre glass the result is the production of a very tough material. It will resist impact and this strong material, known as glass reinforced plastics (GRP) is used in the repair of car bodies, sailing boats, corrugated sheet, sculpture and furniture because of its lightness, toughness and resistance to water.

NAME	ALLOY OF;	PROPERTIES	USES
Mild steel	Carbon 0.1–0.3% Iron 99.9–99.7%	Tough. High tensile strength. Can be case hardened. Rusts very easily.	Most common metal used in school workshops.
Carbon steel	Carbon 0.6–1.4% Iron 99.4–98.6%	Tough. Can be hardened and tempered.	Cutting tools and patches.
Stainless steel	Iron, nickel and chromium	Tough, resistant to rust and stains.	Cutlery, medical instruments.
Cast iron	Carbon 2–6% Iron 98–94%	Strong but brittle. Compressive strength very high. Has a natural lubricant.	Castings, manhole covers, engines.
Wrought iron	Almost 100% iron	Fibrous, tough, ductile, resistant to rusting.	Ornamental gates and railings. Not in much use today.

Table 8.2

NAME	COLOUR	ALLOY OF;	PROPERTIES	USES
Aluminium	Light grey	Aluminium 95% Copper 4% Manganese 1%	Ductile, soft, malleable, machines well. Very light.	Window frames, aircraft, kitchen ware.
Copper	Reddish brown	Not an alloy	Ductile, can be beaten into shape, Conducts electricity and heat.	Electrical wiring tubing, pains, kettles, bowls.
Brass	Yellow	Mixture of copper and zinc 65%–35% most common ratio	Hard. Casts and machines well. Surface tarnishes. Conducts electricity.	Parts for electrical fittings, ornaments.
Silver	Whitish grey	Mainly silver but alloyed with copper to give sterling silver	Ductile, malleable, solders, resists corrosion.	Jewellery, solder, ornaments.
Lead	Bluish grey	Not an alloy	Soft, heavy, ductile, loses its shape under pressure.	Solders, pipes, batteries, roofing.

Table 8.3

THERMOPLASTICS

These all have one thing in common. They will soften when heated.

Acrylic

This is most commonly available for use in the workshops in sheet. It can be worked with most tools that are designed to cut metal. Acrylic can be obtained in a wide range of colours that are either opaque, translucent or transparent. The transparency of acrylic is better than glass. It is resistant to most acids and weather conditions.

Expanded Polystyrene

An efficient insulator used in cavity walls and as decorative tiles and coving on ceilings.

Nylon

Whilst commonly used in clothing it is also used in engineering to make gears and bearings. Its "oily" nature means that it has a natural lubricant and reduces friction between moving parts.

Polythene

Because of its excellent moulding qualities it can be moulded into almost any form. It is commonly used in the production of bottles, bowls, crates, buckets, toys, and tube. It is also available in large sheets and bags of all sizes. There are two grades: *high-density*, which is hard and rigid; and *low-density*, which is tough and flexible. Machine parts are made from the high-density polythene and detergent bottles are made from the low-density polythene.

Polyvinyl chloride

This plastic is better known as PVC. It is a tough material which is available as a hard and rigid material or as a flexible material. It can be welded or bonded with an adhesive. It is used outdoors as guttering and pipes and indoors for plumbing cold water systems. Because of its excellent resistance to electricity and its toughness it is used as a coating on electric wires and cable. PVC raincoats and long-playing records are just two more examples to show the wide usage this plastic has.

PLASTICS IN THE WORKSHOP

The most commonly used **thermoplastics** are *acrylic sheet*, used in making colourful jewellery and as a general material in the production of artefacts, and *nylon* or *polythene pellets* for injection moulding. Thin sheets of PVC and high-density polythene are used in vacuum forming.

The most commonly used **thermosetting plastic** is *polyester resin* used in glass reinforced plastics work such as boat hulls, trays, etc. The clearer and more expensive resin is used in the encapsulation of electronic components and biological specimens.

Making the decision as to *which material* to use in the realisation of a design can be a daunting task. However, if you refer back to the design brief and the analysis, you should receive some help. List the functions that are going to be affected by the choice of material. For example, will the artefact:

a) be used indoors;
b) be used outdoors;
c) need to be aesthetically pleasing;
d) be made from a hard wearing material;
e) be made from a colourful material;
f) be made from a light weight material;
g) be made from a stable material, (one that is not affected by climatical change);
h) have to have good electrical insulating properties;
i) have to be non-inflammable?

Some of the answers to such questions will come readily and will begin to eliminate many materials from the range that is available. The *design* should dictate the material, but you are always advised, particularly in the case of an examination, to work in a material or materials with which you are familiar. So, if you have to choose between two materials, then always go for the one *you* feel most confident to use.

Figs. 8.2 and 8.3 should be of some assistance in helping you to arrive at a quick decision.

THERMO PLASTICS						THERMOSET. PLASTICS				NON-FERROUS METAL					FERROUS METALS				MANUFACT. BOARD				SOLID WOOD						PROPERTY
Polyvinyl chloride PVC	Polythene	Expanded polystyrene	Polystyrene	Nylon	Acrylic	Polyurethane	Epoxy resin	Polyester resin	Melamine formaldehyde	Lead	Silver	Brass	Copper	Aluminium	Wrought iron	Cast iron	Carbon steel	Mild steel	Hardboard	Chipboard	Blockboard	Plywood	Western Red Cedar	Red wood	Obeche	Teak	Ramin	Beech	MATERIAL → PROPERTY
										✓	✓	✓	✓		✓	✓	✓	✓											Heavy weight
✓	✓		✓	✓	✓	✓	✓	✓	✓										✓	✓	✓	✓	✓	✓	✓	✓	✓	✓	Medium weight
		✓												✓															Very light weight
						✓	✓	✓				✓			✓	✓	✓	✓	✓	✓						✓			Hard
✓	✓					✓					✓									✓	✓	✓			✓		✓	✓	Medium
✓	✓	✓	✓	✓	✓					✓			✓	✓									✓	✓					Soft
✓	✓		✓	✓	✓	✓	✓	✓	✓	✓	✓	✓	✓	✓	✓	✓	✓	✓				✓				✓			Moisture resistant
																							✓	✓		✓	✓		Attractive natural finish
					✓	✓																							Colourful
✓	✓		✓						✓							✓										✓		✓	Hard wearing
✓	✓	✓	✓	✓	✓	✓	✓	✓	✓			✓	✓	✓	✓	✓	✓	✓	✓	✓	✓	✓							Stable
✓				✓	✓																								Insulate electricity
		✓																											Insulate temperature
	✓	✓																	✓	✓	✓	✓	✓	✓	✓	✓	✓	✓	Inflammable
✓							✓	✓	✓	✓	✓	✓	✓	✓	✓	✓	✓	✓											Non-inflammable
										✓	✓	✓	✓	✓	✓	✓	✓	✓	✓										Conduct electricity
											✓		✓	✓															Excellent for conducting electricity
✓	✓		✓	✓	✓																								Easily bend if heated
										✓	✓		✓	✓				✓											Easily bend cold
																						✓						✓	Will bend with treatment
✓	✓					✓	✓	✓	✓			✓				✓				✓	✓			✓	✓	✓	✓		Rigid
✓	✓				✓					✓	✓		✓		✓		✓	✓	✓			✓	✓					✓	Flexible

Fig. 8.2

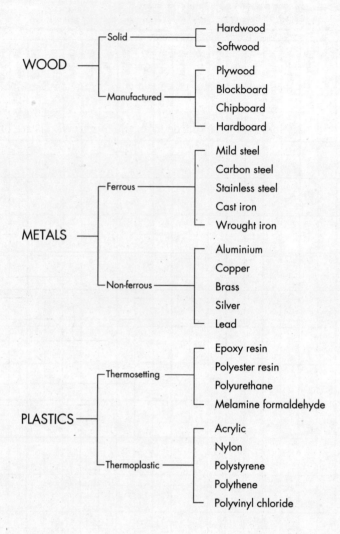

Fig. 8.3

REVIEW SHEET

- Name the type of tree from which softwoods are obtained.

  _____

- Name the type of tree from which hardwoods are obtained.

  _____

- Name two softwoods. Give a brief description of each, state a use for each and state why they are particularly suited for the purpose you have given.

  _____

  _____

  _____

  _____

  _____

  _____

  _____

  _____

  _____

- Name two hardwoods. Give a brief description of each, state a use for each and state why they are particularly suited for the purpose you have given.

  _____

  _____

  _____

  _____

  _____

  _____

  _____

  _____

  _____

- Name three manufactured boards.
  1. _____
  2. _____
  3. _____

- State three advantages of using a manufactured board over timber.
  1. _____

  2. _____

  3. _____

- State three disadvantages of using a manufactured board.
  1. _____

  2. _____

3. _____
_____

■ Metals are classified into two groups. Name the two groups.

1. _____

2. _____

■ State the main feature that distinguishes one group from the other.

_____

_____

Under the headings of the two groups of metal, list four metals or metal alloys.

Group 1   Group 2
   a)   a)
   b)   b)
   c)   c)
   d)   d)

■ Select two metals or metal alloys that you have named in group 1 and state their properties and uses.

_____

_____

_____

■ Select two metals or metal alloys that you have named in group 2 and state their properties and uses

_____

_____

_____

■ Plastics are classified into two groups, Thermosetting and Thermoplastic. Briefly describe the difference between the plastics that fall into these two broad classifications.

Thermosetting Plastics _____

_____

_____

Thermoplastics _____

_____

_____

■ Name two Thermosetting plastics, state their use and briefly describe their properties.

_____

_____

_____

_____

_____

CHAPTER 9

EQUIPMENT AND TOOLS

HAND TOOLS

POWER TOOLS

MACHINES

SAFETY EQUIPMENT

GETTING STARTED

Equipment and tools extend Man's ability to manipulate *materials*. You need to extend your ability to manipulate tools so that you can not only make what you design but also make it well.

The more familiar you become with the tools that are available, the more chance you will have of selecting the right tool for the job. Tools are solutions to a problem. A major problem in the making of many things is the removal of unwanted material. The solution to this can be a saw, file, chisel, plane, etc. But the *selection* of the right tool will depend on your knowledge and understanding of tools and materials. A tool designed to remove unwanted material from *wood* will not be the same design as one required for removing unwanted material from *metal*. As you will no doubt know from this obvious example, a tenon saw is designed to cut wood, and a hacksaw is designed to cut metal. Sawing a piece of wood with a hacksaw will not only take a long time, it may result in the blade getting clogged with sawdust and the cut (or kerf) will not be very accurate. Sawing a piece of metal with a tenon saw will result in ruining the teeth of the saw and a failure to remove the unwanted metal. So make sure that you *know* which is the correct tool for the job by reading this chapter very carefully.

Knowing the name of the tool and what it looks like is an asset. To help you, a selection of tools has been illustrated. You are given the *name*, what it is *used for*, and on *which material* it may be used. Many of them will be familiar to you, which will be a good start. Now see if any of the tools on the following pages are unfamiliar to you; this will give you the chance to extend your knowledge.

ESSENTIAL PRINCIPLES

1 > HAND TOOLS

These are tools that are held by hand when they are being used. They fall into one of five groups:

1. marking out;   4. cutting;
2. measuring;   5. miscellaneous.
3. holding;

MARKING OUT TOOLS

Not all the tools in this group are actually used to mark material. Many are used to *assist* in the *process* of marking out, e.g. a trysquare does not mark the wood, it only guides the pencil or marking knife to make the line that is required.

Fig. 9.1 provides information on the name, appearance and use of the most important **marking out** tools.

MEASURING TOOLS

These are essential for ensuring that the marking out is in the correct place. Some are used for checking that the material has been reduced to the correct size, e.g. outside callipers used to check that a bar of round metal or plastics has been turned to the correct diameter. A trysquare can also be used for checking the accuracy of an angle and could belong to this group.

Fig. 9.2 provides information on the name, appearance and use of the most important **measuring** tools.

HOLDING TOOLS

It is important for the material to be securely held when it is being worked. Using the wrong holding device can mean ruining the work or having a nasty accident.

Fig. 9.3 provides information on the name, appearance and use of the most important **holding** tools.

CUTTING TOOLS

This is by far the largest group. The variety of different cutting operations and the variety of characteristics of materials makes it essential that the tool is perfectly designed to meet the needs. Tools designed to cut along the grain of a piece of wood are different from tools designed to cut end grain, e.g. the angle of the blade in a jack plane is steeper than the blade in the block plane. Just looking at the various shapes and sizes of planes alone will give an indication of the variety of tasks that are to be performed. The designs of most of the cutting tools have been evolved over the centuries. They have been designed primarily to cut wood or metal. More recently, plastic has become a common material available for use in making artefacts and many of the tools designed to cut metal will also cut plastics. Many of the woodworking cutting tools lose their sharpness when used on plastics and should not be used on anything else but wood. The high-speed steels from which cutting tools are made to cut mild steel, have to be much harder and tougher than the mild steel and hence they are not as likely to lose their cutting edge as the carbon steels used to cut wood. Tools that have replacement blades are often suitable for cutting plastics.

Fig. 9.4 provides information on the name, appearance and use of the most important **cutting** tools. Some of the tools assist in *holding* the item to be cut.

MISCELLANEOUS

This is a group of tools that do not fit into the first four groups, and do not appear to have anything in common with each other. None-the-less they exist and they are important. The group is made up of such tools as spanners, screwdrivers, wrenches, socket keys and a variety of *striking* tools such as hammers, mallets, etc.

Fig. 9.5 provides information on the name, appearance and use of a range of **miscellaneous** tools.

NAME / WHAT IT LOOKS LIKE	USED FOR	USED ON			NAME / WHAT IT LOOKS LIKE	USED FOR	USED ON		
		W	M	P			W	M	P
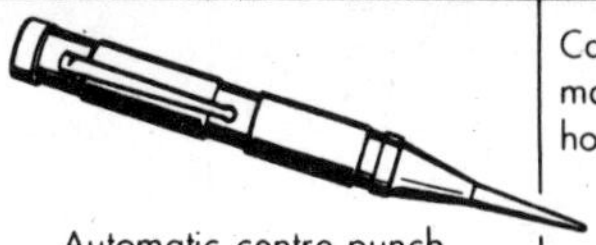 Automatic centre punch	Can be used on metal for marking the position for a hole to be drilled		✓		Round headed centre punch	Marking the centre position where a hole is to be drilled, or dot punching to show outline of metal to be removed		✓	
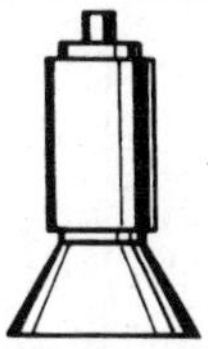 Bell punch	Marking the central position of the end of a piece of round bar. This is done when preparing a piece of metal for turning between centres on the lathe		✓		Square headed centre punch	Marking the centre position where a hole is to be drilled		✓	
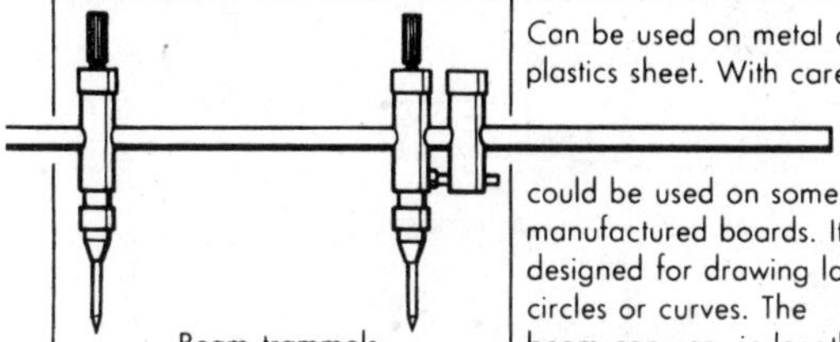 Beam trammels	Can be used on metal and plastics sheet. With care it could be used on some manufactured boards. It is designed for drawing large circles or curves. The beam can vary in length		✓	✓	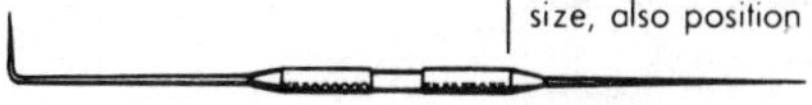 Scriber	Scribing a line on the surface to show shape and size, also position of holes. Used with an Engineers square		✓	
Centre squares	Can be used on wood, metal or plastics to find the centre on round bar	✓	✓	✓	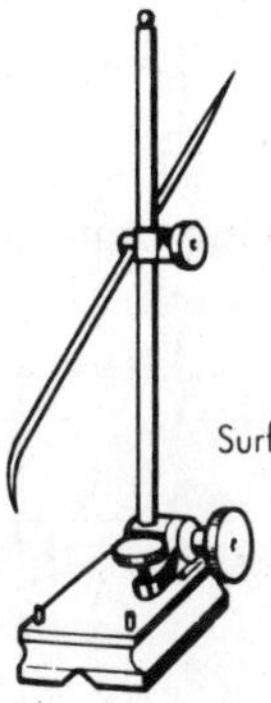 Surface gauges	Can be used on metal and plastics for marking parallel lines. It has to be used on a surface plate (not drawn) and the work held on an angle plate or in a vee block and clamp (see drawing on pg 89)	✓		✓
Dividers	Can be used on metal or plastics for transferring measurements	✓	✓	✓	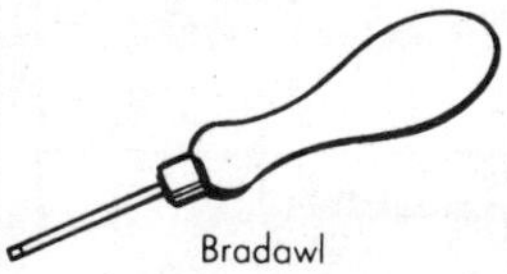 Bradawl	Marking a position for a hole. To make a small hole for a small screw or cup hook	✓		
Engineers' squares	Can be used on metal or plastics when marking a line at right angles to an edge. Can also be used to check an angle of 90°		✓	✓	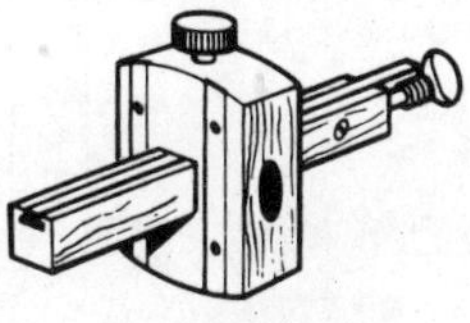 Mortice gauges	Marking two parallel lines to a face edge. Specially designed for mark out a mortice tenon joint	✓		
Jenny calipers	Can be used on metal & plastics for scribing a parallel line to an edge		✓	✓	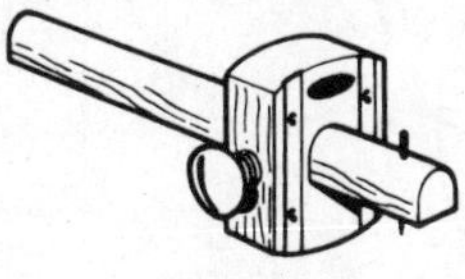 Marking gauge	Marking a single line parallel to a face edge	✓		
Chalk	Marking out on metal that is to be heated red hot		✓		 Sliding bevel	Marking lines with pencil or knife at any angle to a given edge	✓		✓
Felt pen	Marking out on acrylic. The mark can be removed so that the surface is not damaged			✓	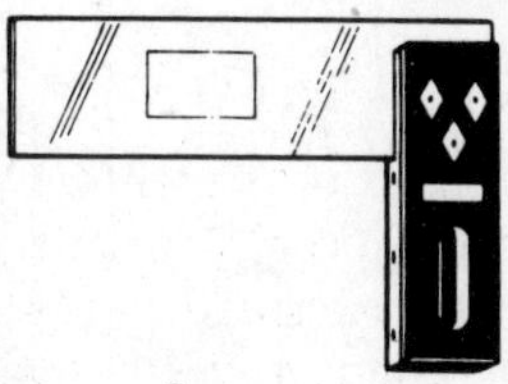 Try squares	Marking lines, pencil or knife, at right angles to an edge. Also used to check right angles for accuracy	✓		✓
Pencil	Marking face side and face edge and indicating material to be removed	✓							

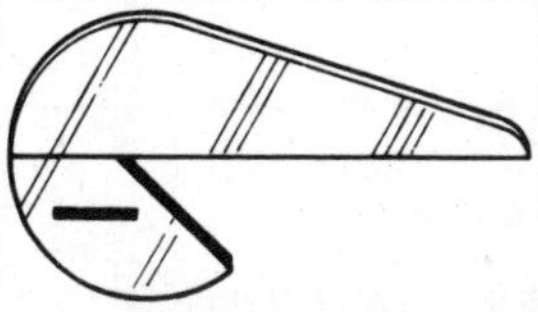

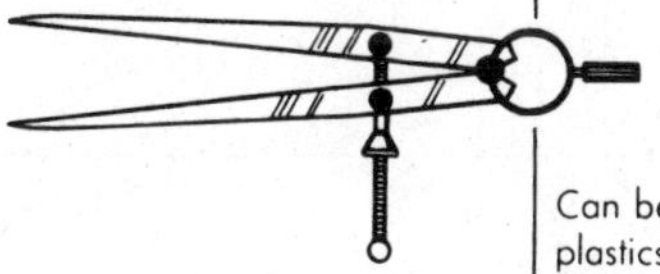

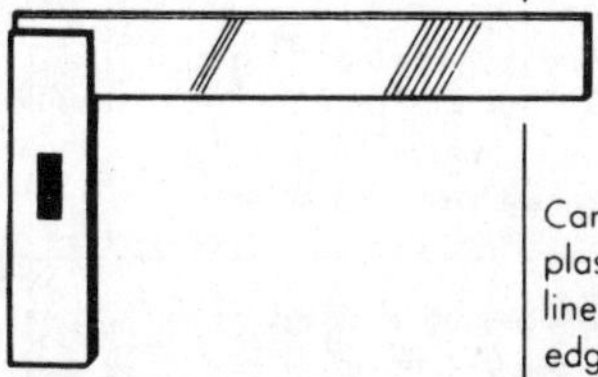

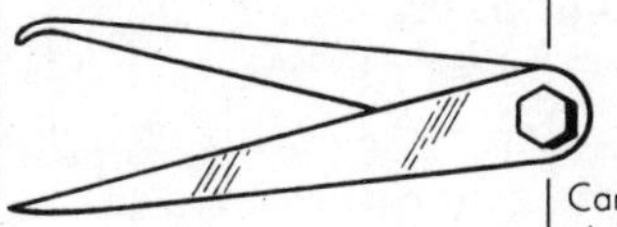

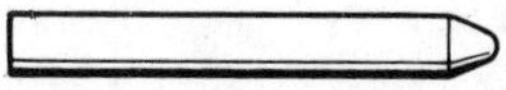

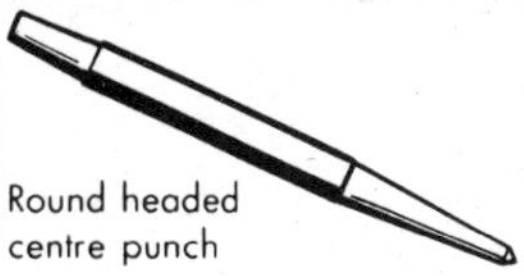

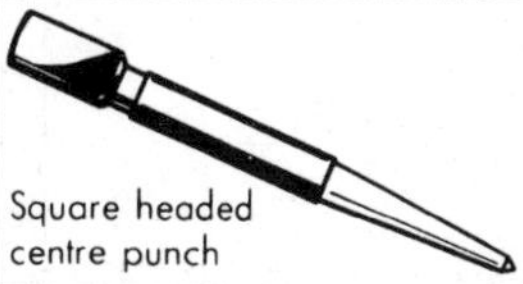

Fig. 9.1 Marking Tools

(W = wood; M = metal; P = plastic)

NAME / WHAT IT LOOKS LIKE	USED FOR	USED ON			NAME / WHAT IT LOOKS LIKE	USED FOR	USED ON		
		W	M	P			W	M	P
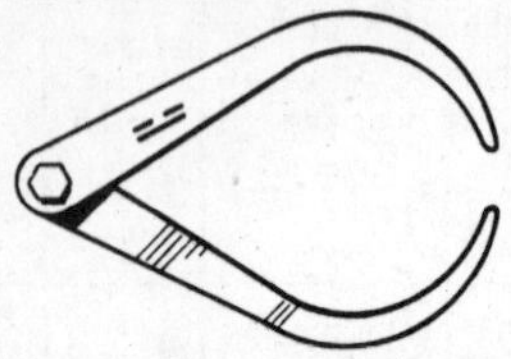 Callipers (external)	For measuring the outside diameter of round section bar	✓	✓	✓	Micrometer	For measuring the precise size of a piece of material round or flat		✓	
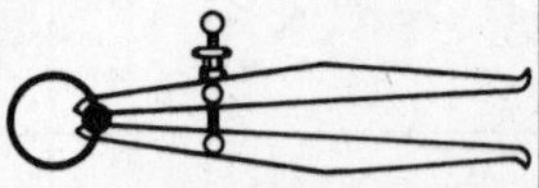 Callipers (internal)	For measuring the inside diameter of a hole or tube	✓	✓	✓	Screw cutting gauge	Checking the angle of thread cutting lathe tools. When threads are cut using a lathe the tool must cut the same profile as the desired thread		✓	
Combination set 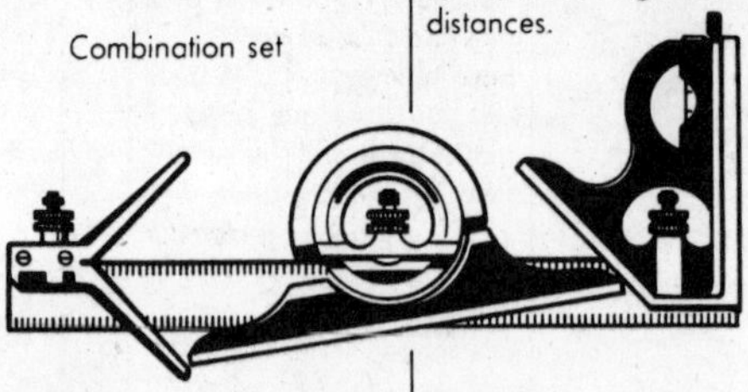	Measuring and marking out right angles 45° angles and any angle 0-90°, centre of round bar, vertical and horizontal levels, measuring linear distances.		✓		Steel rule	For measuring distances between 0·150mm or 0·300mm. Measurements start from the squared end so that accurate measurements may be taken	✓	✓	✓
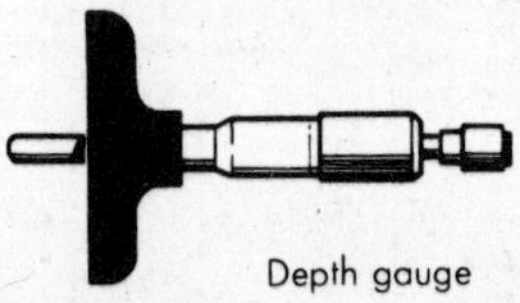 Depth gauge	For measuring the precise depth of a groove or shoulder		✓		Steel straight edge	Checking the flatness of a surface and for marking accurate straight lines. Length between 0·1 metre	✓	✓	✓
 Dial gauge	For quick checking of flatness of a surface or eccentricity of a round bar in a lathe		✓	✓	Tape measure	For measuring off lengths between 0·2 metres. Especially use for measuring on sheet material. The little right angled lip grips the edge of the sheet	✓	✓	✓
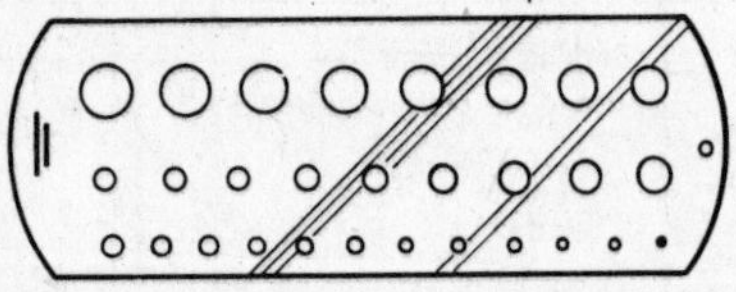 Drill gauge	Checking the size of a drill. Sometimes the size on the shank gets worn and the size rubbed away and this gauge is particularly useful for checking and identifying the size of a drill		✓		Vernier caliper	Reading and checking precise measurements of flat round or surfaces and internal diameters		✓	✓
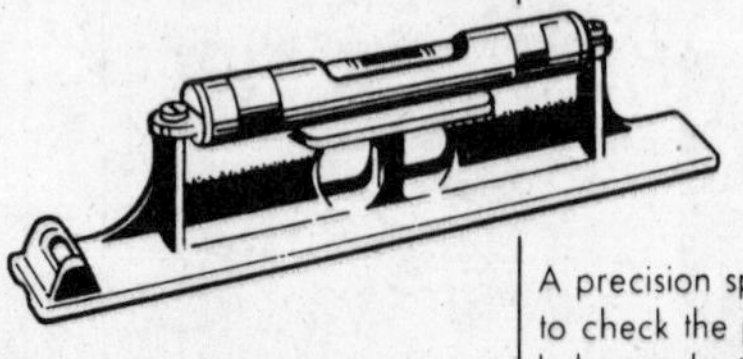 Engineers level	A precision spirit level used to check the position of lathes and milling machines etc.		✓		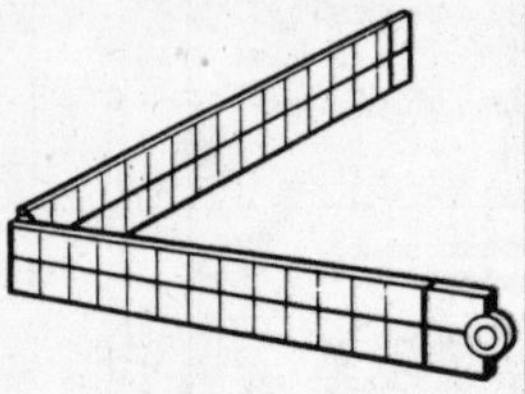 Wooden folding ruler	For measuring where precision accuracy is not required	✓		

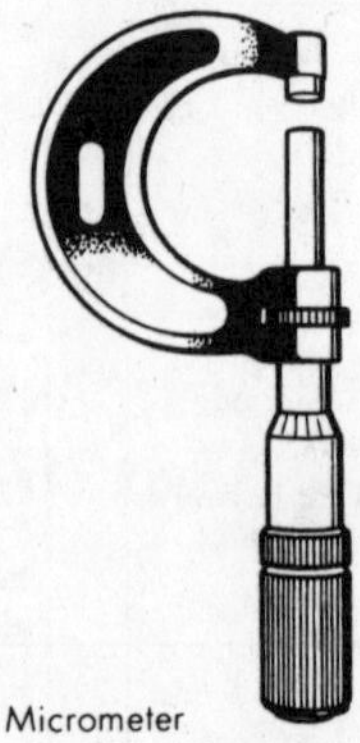

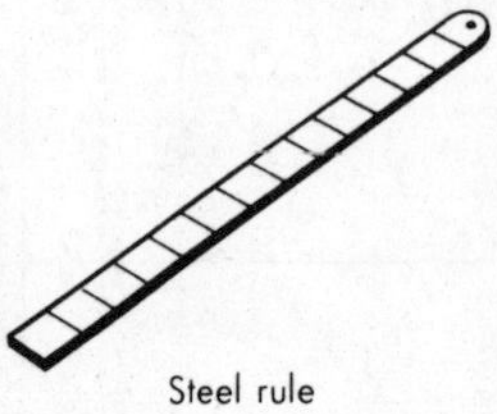

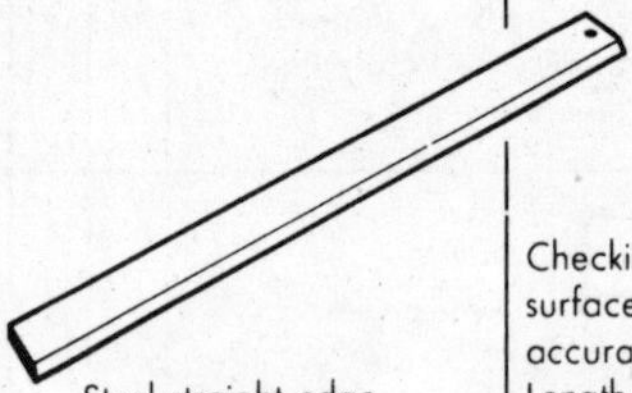

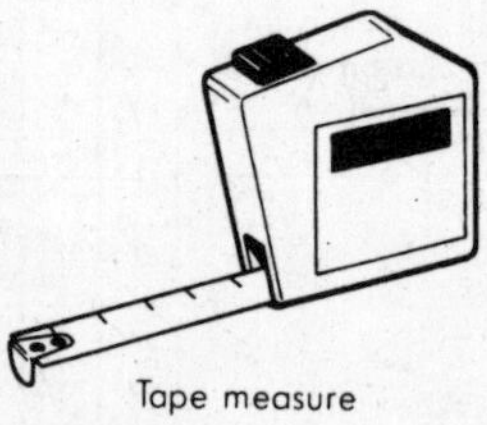

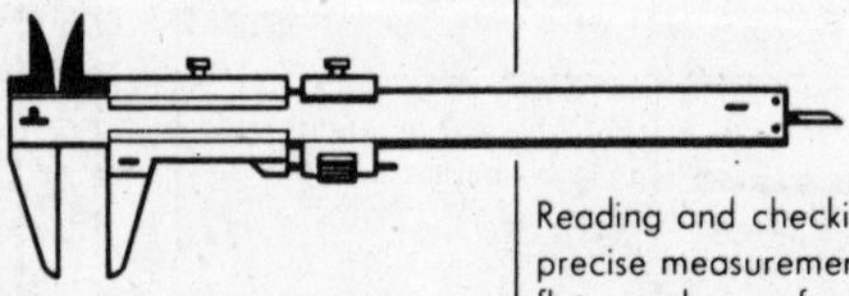

Fig. 9.2 Measuring Tools

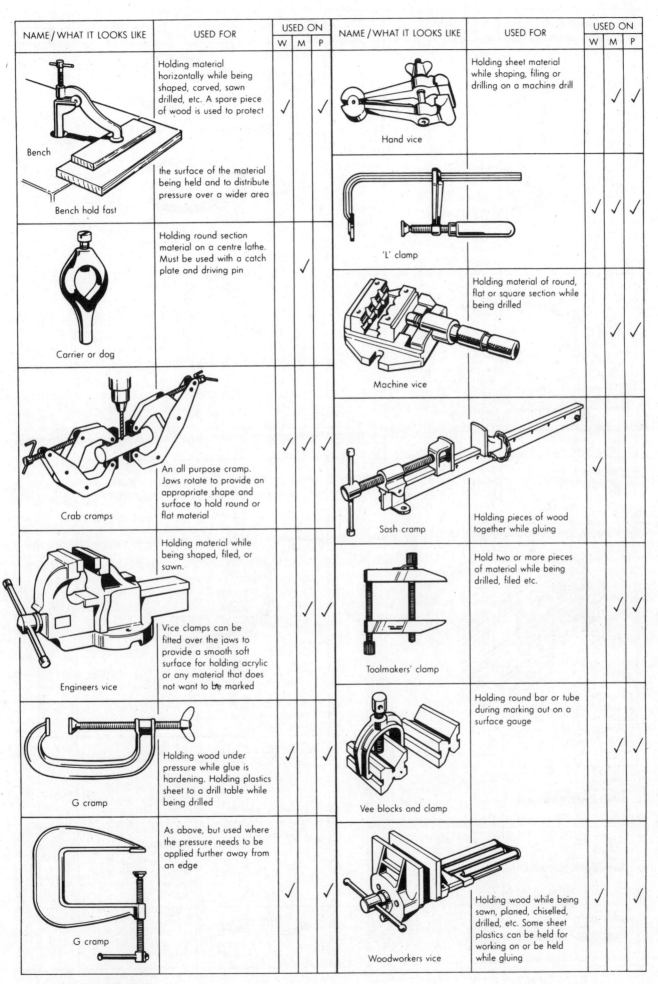

NAME / WHAT IT LOOKS LIKE	USED FOR	USED ON W	M	P	NAME / WHAT IT LOOKS LIKE	USED FOR	USED ON W	M	P
Bench / Bench hold fast	Holding material horizontally while being shaped, carved, sawn drilled, etc. A spare piece of wood is used to protect the surface of the material being held and to distribute pressure over a wider area	✓		✓	Hand vice	Holding sheet material while shaping, filing or drilling on a machine drill		✓	✓
Carrier or dog	Holding round section material on a centre lathe. Must be used with a catch plate and driving pin		✓		'L' clamp		✓	✓	✓
Crab cramps	An all purpose cramp. Jaws rotate to provide an appropriate shape and surface to hold round or flat material	✓	✓	✓	Machine vice	Holding material of round, flat or square section while being drilled		✓	✓
Engineers vice	Holding material while being shaped, filed, or sawn. Vice clamps can be fitted over the jaws to provide a smooth soft surface for holding acrylic or any material that does not want to be marked		✓	✓	Sash cramp	Holding pieces of wood together while gluing	✓		
G cramp	Holding wood under pressure while glue is hardening. Holding plastics sheet to a drill table while being drilled	✓		✓	Toolmakers' clamp	Hold two or more pieces of material while being drilled, filed etc.		✓	✓
G cramp	As above, but used where the pressure needs to be applied further away from an edge	✓		✓	Vee blocks and clamp	Holding round bar or tube during marking out on a surface gauge		✓	✓
					Woodworkers vice	Holding wood while being sawn, planed, chiselled, drilled, etc. Some sheet plastics can be held for working on or be held while gluing	✓		✓

Fig. 9.3 Holding Tools

NAME / WHAT IT LOOKS LIKE	USED FOR	USED ON			NAME / WHAT IT LOOKS LIKE	USED FOR	USED ON		
		W	M	P			W	M	P
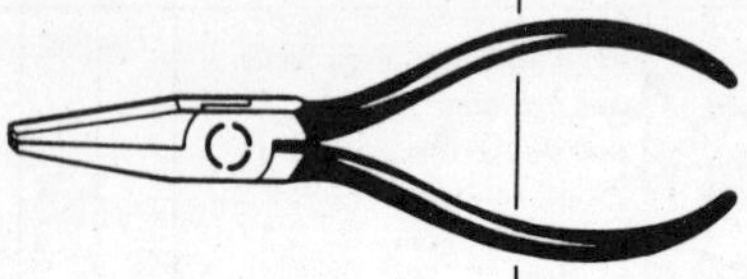 Flat nose pliers	Bending, holding and twisting wire		✓		Round nose pliers	Bending wire in loops		✓	
 Pliers	Temporary holding of sheet metal, cutting wire and small strips of metal		✓		Snipe nose pliers	Gripping, holding and bending wire		✓	
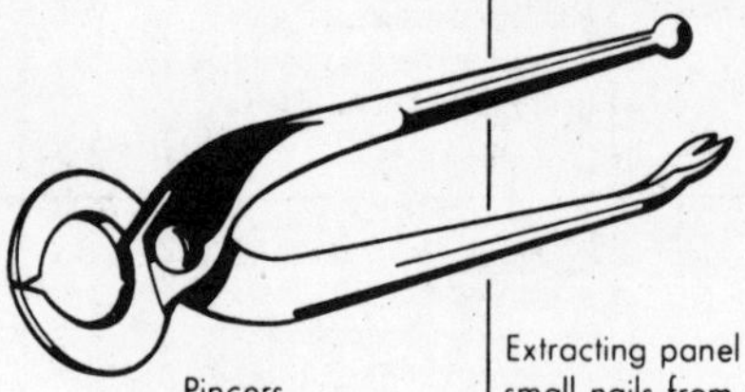 Pincers	Extracting panel pins and small nails from wood		✓		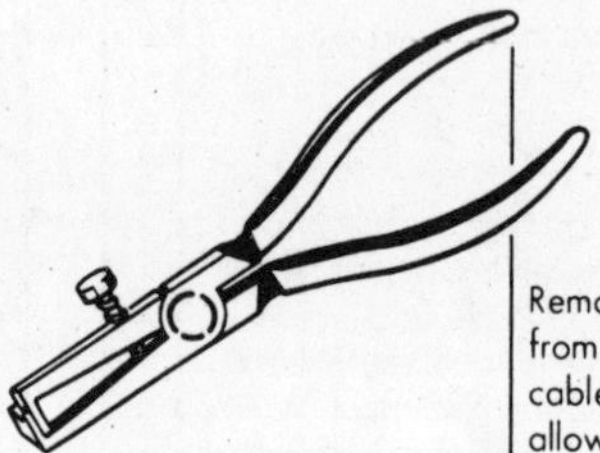 Wire stripper	Removing the insulation from electrical wire and cable. The adjusting screw allows for different size of wires to be stripped		✓	✓

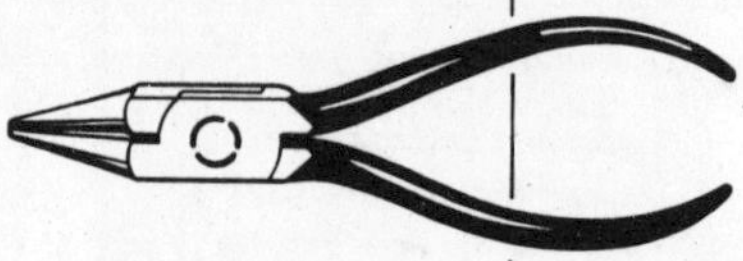

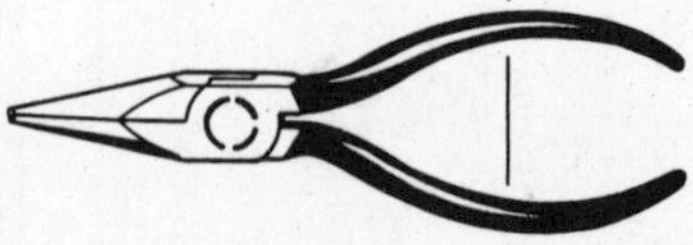

Fig. 9.3 Holding Tools (continued)

NAME / WHAT IT LOOKS LIKE	USED FOR	USED ON			NAME / WHAT IT LOOKS LIKE	USED FOR	USED ON		
		W	M	P			W	M	P
Set of taps and dies with wrench and holders. 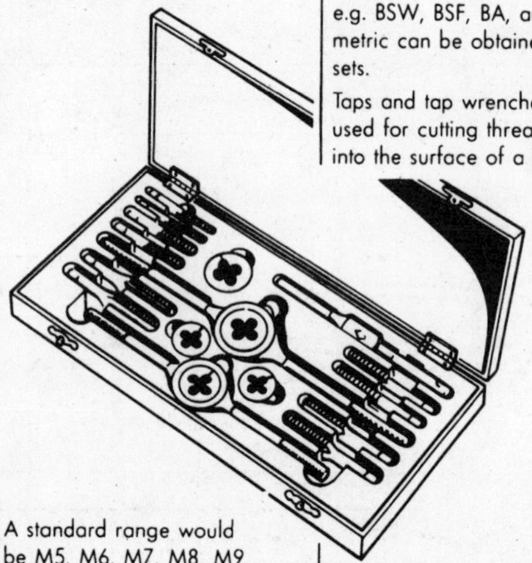 A standard range would be M5, M6, M7, M8, M9, M10, M11 and M12. There are small and larger ranges of sets.	A range of sizes and different cutting threads e.g. BSW, BSF, BA, and metric can be obtained in sets. Taps and tap wrenches are used for cutting threads into the surface of a hole. The dies and die holders are used for cutting threads on a round bar.		✓		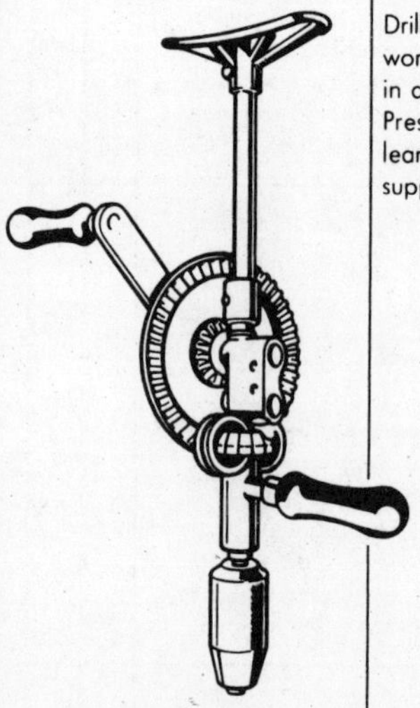 Breast drill	Drilling holes when the work to be drilled is fixed in a vertical position. Pressure is obtained by leaning against the curved support	✓		✓
Taper Tap	Starting a thread in a hole that has been drilled to the correct tapping size		✓		 Centre Auger bit	Boring holes in wood. Because of the length of the bit, deep holes can be bored	✓		
Second Intermediate Tap	Cutting a thread after a taper tap has been used. It deepens the partly threaded portion left by the taper		✓		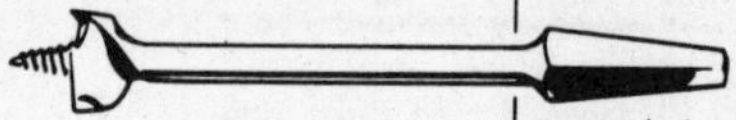 Centre bit	Boring holes in wood. Inclined to wander in the hole, not so accurate as an auger bit	✓		
Bottoming Plug Tap	Provided the final cut of a threaded through or blind hole		✓		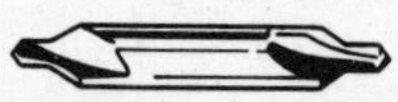 Combination Centre drill	Drilling a centre hole and countersink in the end of material to be used on a centre lathe		✓	✓

Fig. 9.4 Cutting Tools

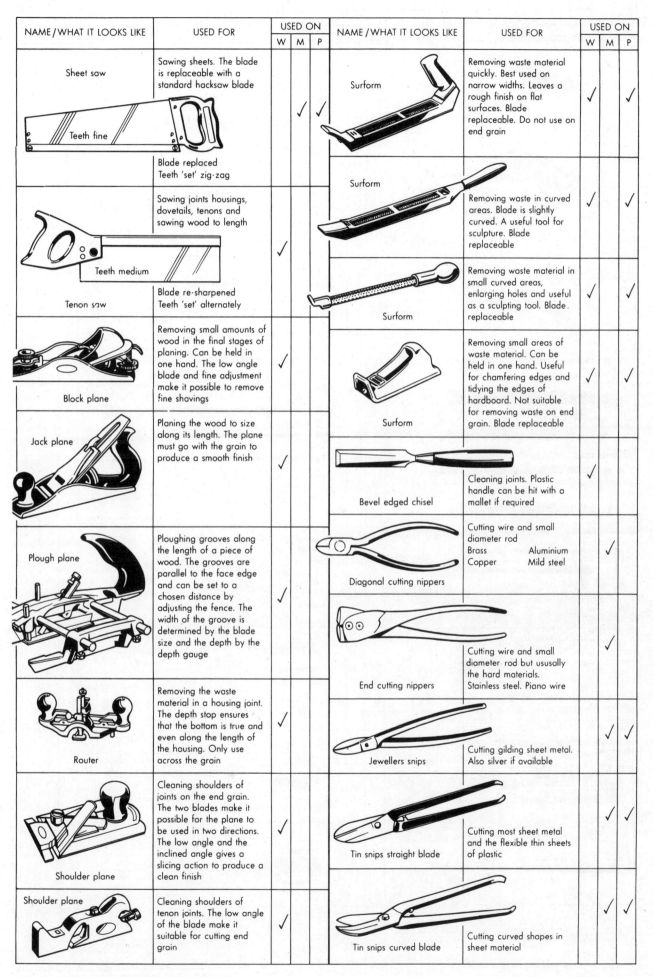

NAME/WHAT IT LOOKS LIKE	USED FOR	USED ON			NAME/WHAT IT LOOKS LIKE	USED FOR	USED ON		
		W	M	P			W	M	P
Sheet saw / Teeth fine	Sawing sheets. The blade is replaceable with a standard hacksaw blade		✓	✓	Surform	Removing waste material quickly. Best used on narrow widths. Leaves a rough finish on flat surfaces. Blade replaceable. Do not use on end grain	✓		✓
	Blade replaced Teeth 'set' zig-zag				Surform	Removing waste in curved areas. Blade is slightly curved. A useful tool for sculpture. Blade replaceable	✓		✓
Tenon saw / Teeth medium	Sawing joints housings, dovetails, tenons and sawing wood to length	✓			Surform	Removing waste material in small curved areas, enlarging holes and useful as a sculpting tool. Blade replaceable	✓		✓
	Blade re-sharpened Teeth 'set' alternately				Surform	Removing small areas of waste material. Can be held in one hand. Useful for chamfering edges and tidying the edges of hardboard. Not suitable for removing waste on end grain. Blade replaceable	✓		✓
Block plane	Removing small amounts of wood in the final stages of planing. Can be held in one hand. The low angle blade and fine adjustment make it possible to remove fine shavings	✓			Bevel edged chisel	Cleaning joints. Plastic handle can be hit with a mallet if required	✓		
Jack plane	Planing the wood to size along its length. The plane must go with the grain to produce a smooth finish	✓			Diagonal cutting nippers	Cutting wire and small diameter rod Brass Aluminium Copper Mild steel		✓	
Plough plane	Ploughing grooves along the length of a piece of wood. The grooves are parallel to the face edge and can be set to a chosen distance by adjusting the fence. The width of the groove is determined by the blade size and the depth by the depth gauge	✓			End cutting nippers	Cutting wire and small diameter rod but ususally the hard materials. Stainless steel. Piano wire		✓	
Router	Removing the waste material in a housing joint. The depth stop ensures that the bottom is true and even along the length of the housing. Only use across the grain	✓			Jewellers snips	Cutting gilding sheet metal. Also silver if available		✓	✓
Shoulder plane	Cleaning shoulders of joints on the end grain. The two blades make it possible for the plane to be used in two directions. The low angle and the inclined angle gives a slicing action to produce a clean finish	✓			Tin snips straight blade	Cutting most sheet metal and the flexible thin sheets of plastic		✓	✓
Shoulder plane	Cleaning shoulders of tenon joints. The low angle of the blade make it suitable for cutting end grain	✓			Tin snips curved blade	Cutting curved shapes in sheet material		✓	✓

Fig. 9.4 Cutting Tools (continued)

NAME / WHAT IT LOOKS LIKE	USED FOR	W	M	P	NAME / WHAT IT LOOKS LIKE	USED FOR	W	M	P
Retractable blade 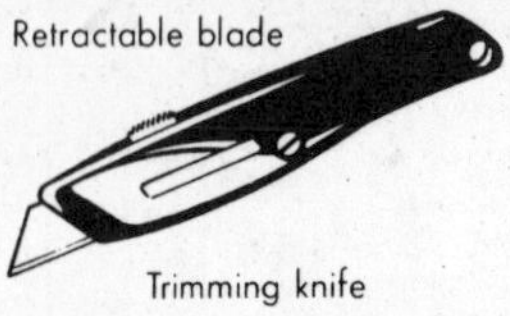 — Trimming knife	Trimming sheet material, scoring wood across grain. Blade slides back onto the handle when not in use. Good safety design	✓		✓	Warding / Pillar			✓	✓
Fixed blade 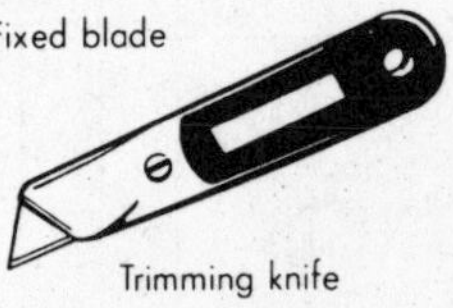 — Trimming knife	Blades are replaceable. Different shape blades are available for cutting a wide range of materials	✓		✓	Needle Files — Round, Square, Threesquare, Warding, Knife, Half round, Crossing, Barrette, Hand, Pippin, Slitting, Round-edge joint	Fine work mainly in jewellery		✓	✓
Files — Round, Half round, Square, Threesquare, Knife	Removing small amounts of material. Available in three grades of cutting. Bastard; second; smooth. The coarse cut is used to remove material quickly. The second more slowly and the smooth to produce a smooth finish		✓	✓	File handle	All files must have a handle. These are supplied separately and fitted when needed			
Groove punch	Setting a seam join of two sheets of thin metal Usually tin plate		✓		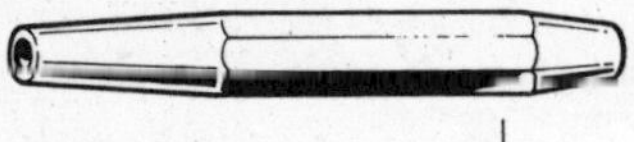  Rivet snap — Round head rivet		✓		
Hexagonal socket screw wrench — Socket screw			✓		  Ratchet spiral screwdriver — Slotted head screw		✓		
Pop rivet tool — Pop rivet	Jointing two sheets of metal or plastic sheet		✓	✓	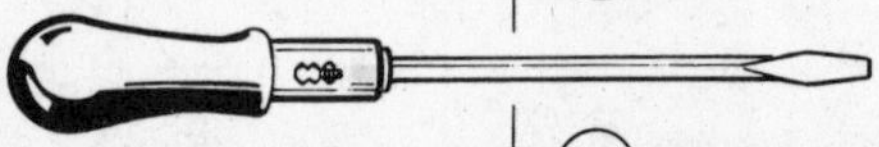  Ratchet screwdriver — Pozidrive head screw,  Slotted head screw			✓	✓
Rivet set — Round head rivet			✓		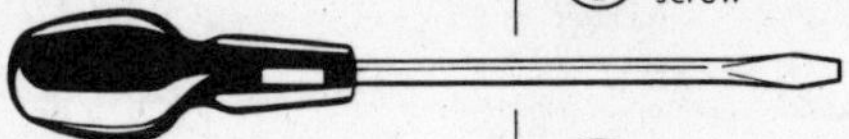  Screwdriver — Pozidrive head screw,  Slotted head screw			✓	✓

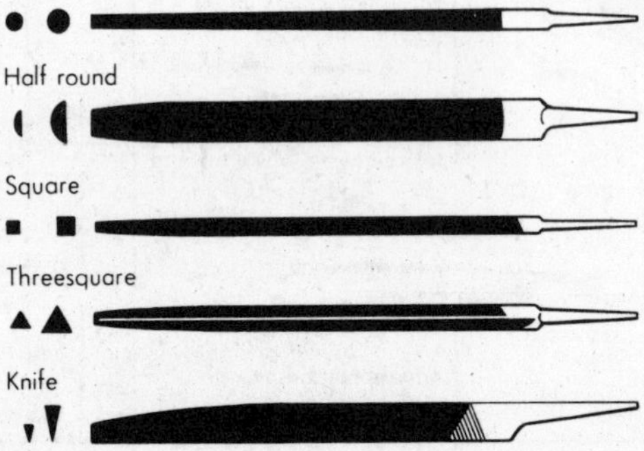

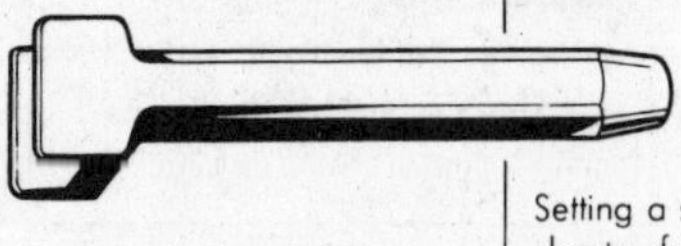

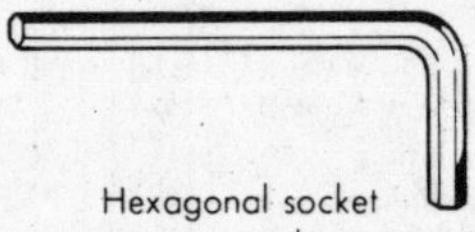

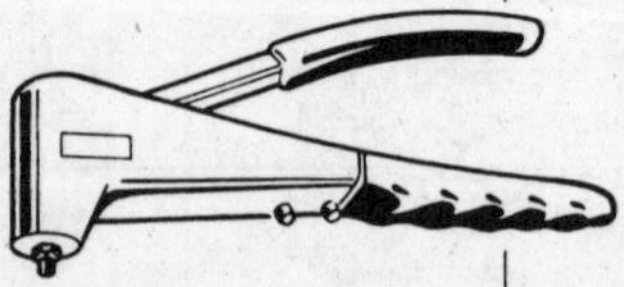

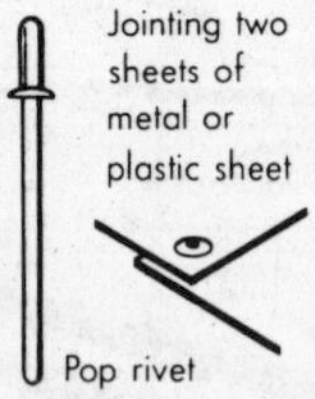

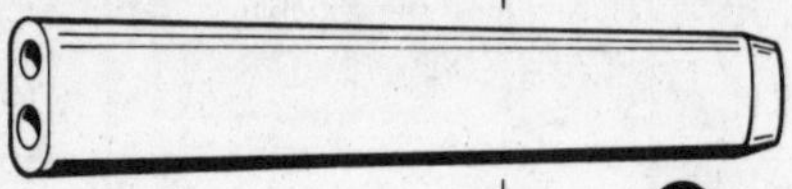

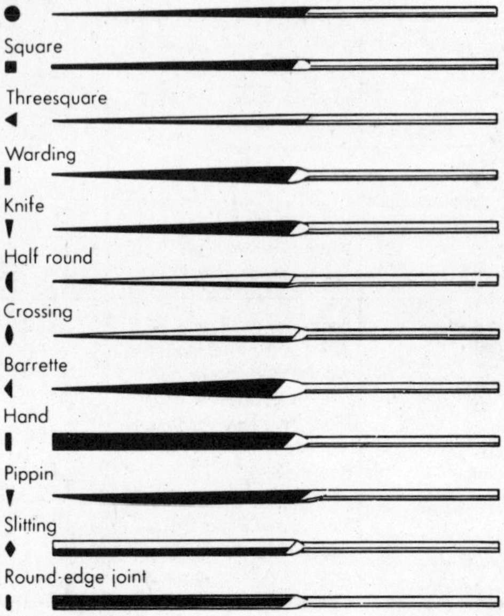

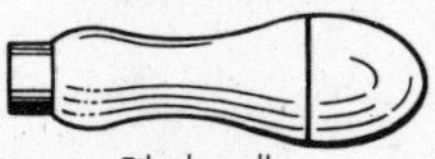

Fig. 9.4 Cutting Tools (continued)

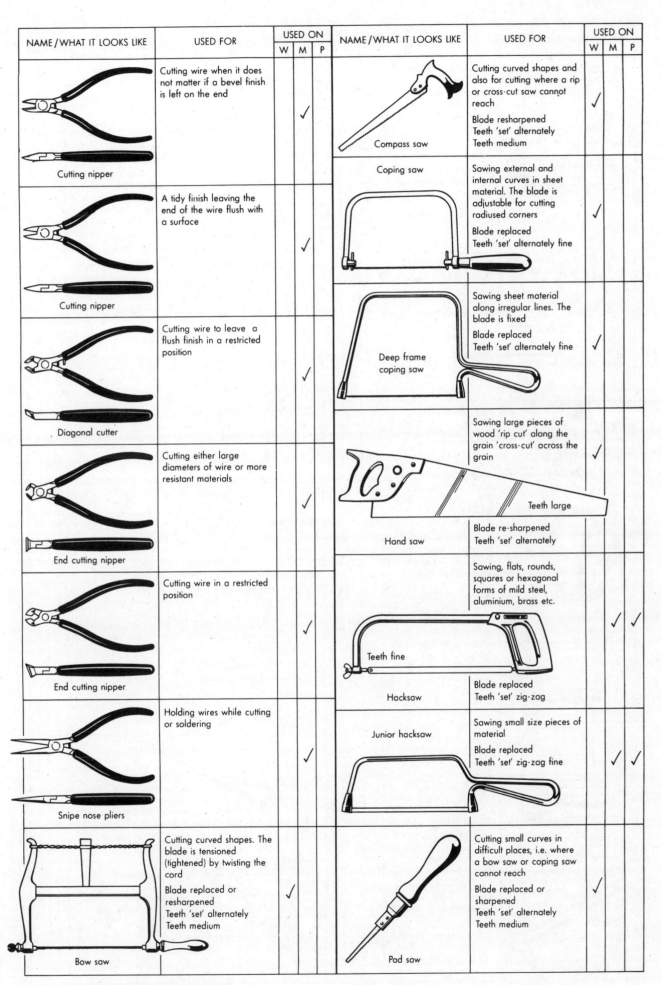

NAME/WHAT IT LOOKS LIKE	USED FOR	USED ON			NAME/WHAT IT LOOKS LIKE	USED FOR	USED ON		
		W	M	P			W	M	P
Cutting nipper	Cutting wire when it does not matter if a bevel finish is left on the end		✓		Compass saw	Cutting curved shapes and also for cutting where a rip or cross-cut saw cannot reach Blade resharpened Teeth 'set' alternately Teeth medium	✓		
Cutting nipper	A tidy finish leaving the end of the wire flush with a surface		✓		Coping saw	Sawing external and internal curves in sheet material. The blade is adjustable for cutting radiused corners Blade replaced Teeth 'set' alternately fine	✓		
Diagonal cutter	Cutting wire to leave a flush finish in a restricted position		✓		Deep frame coping saw	Sawing sheet material along irregular lines. The blade is fixed Blade replaced Teeth 'set' alternately fine	✓		
End cutting nipper	Cutting either large diameters of wire or more resistant materials		✓		Hand saw Teeth large	Sawing large pieces of wood 'rip cut' along the grain 'cross-cut' across the grain Blade re-sharpened Teeth 'set' alternately	✓		
End cutting nipper	Cutting wire in a restricted position		✓		Hacksaw Teeth fine	Sawing, flats, rounds, squares or hexagonal forms of mild steel, aluminium, brass etc. Blade replaced Teeth 'set' zig-zag		✓	✓
Snipe nose pliers	Holding wires while cutting or soldering		✓		Junior hacksaw	Sawing small size pieces of material Blade replaced Teeth 'set' zig-zag fine		✓	✓
Bow saw	Cutting curved shapes. The blade is tensioned (tightened) by twisting the cord Blade replaced or resharpened Teeth 'set' alternately Teeth medium	✓			Pad saw	Cutting small curves in difficult places, i.e. where a bow saw or coping saw cannot reach Blade replaced or sharpened Teeth 'set' alternately Teeth medium	✓		

Fig. 9.4 Cutting Tools (continued)

NAME / WHAT IT LOOKS LIKE	USED FOR	USED ON			NAME / WHAT IT LOOKS LIKE	USED FOR	USED ON		
		W	M	P			W	M	P
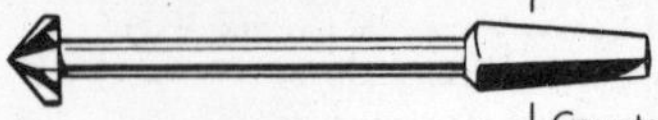 Countersunk rose bit	Countersinking holes so that a countersunk head screw can fit flush with the surface	✓			Slot drill	Cutting slots or precision grooves with a flat bottom. The threaded shank is for fitting into a vertical milling machine		✓	✓
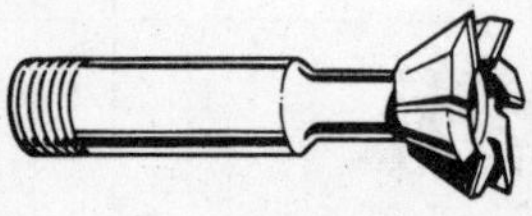 Dovetail slot cutter	Cutting dovetail slots. The threaded shank is for fitting into a vertical milling machine		✓	✓	Straight shank twist drill	Drilling holes, can be used in hand and powered drills. Max. size drill depends on the capacity of the drill chuck	✓	✓	✓
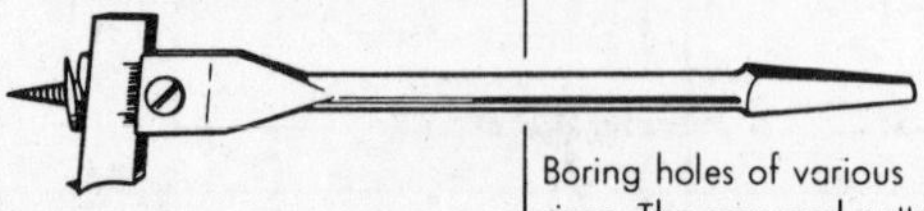 Expansive Centre bit	Boring holes of various sizes. The spur and cutter is adjusted to the diameter size hole required	✓			Taper shank twist drill	Drilling large holes. Used in drilling machine with a matching taper	✓	✓	✓
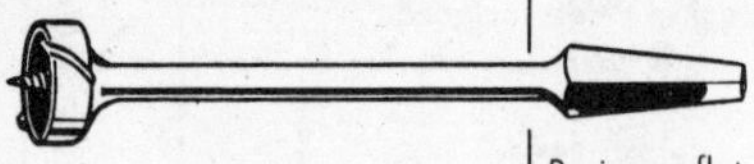 Forstner bit	Boring a flat bottomed hole	✓			Tank cutter	Cutting holes in sheet material. The size of the hole is governed by the setting of the cutter. Work must be firmly clamped when using this tool in a drilling machine. A slow speed is recommended	✓	✓	✓
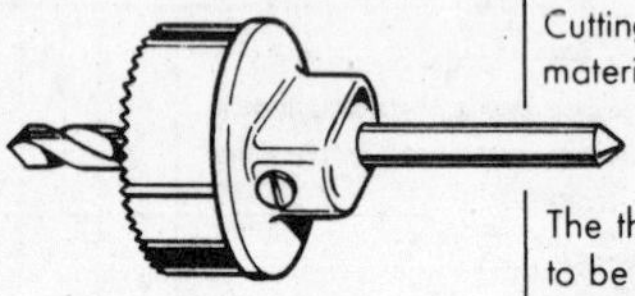 Hole cutter	Cutting holes in sheet material. The thickness of material to be cut is limited by the size of blade used. Maximum thickness for a standard blade is 4.8mm	✓	✓	✓	'T' slot cutter	Cutting 'T' slots. The threaded shank is for fitting into a vertical milling machine		✓	✓
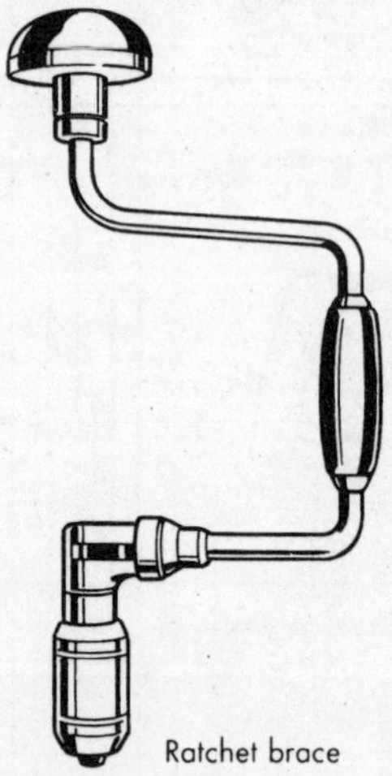 Ratchet brace	Holding centre bits. Designed to give leverage when cutting holes approximately 25mm diameter. The ratchet enables the handle to move through a complete circle or part of a circle and return while the bit only moves in a forward direction	✓			Twist drill, quick helix	Drilling thermoplastics e.g. nylon, polystyrene, polythene polyvinylchloride PVC			✓
					Twist drill slow helix	Drilling thermosetting plastics, e.g. urea formalehyde, melamine formaldehyde. Can also be used to drill acrylic and thermo-plastics material			✓
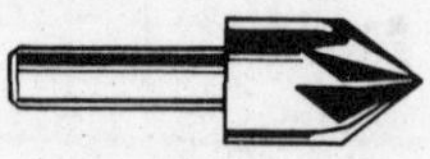 Rose bit countersunk	Drilling a countersink in a hole already drilled, so that a countersunk headerd screw or rivet will fit flush with the surface of the material		✓		Glass cutter	Scoring glass. When a pressure is applied the glass breaks along the scored line. Most score lines are straight but an expert can cut curved and circular shapes			
Rose bit countersunk	Drilling a countersink hole to receive a countersunk headed screw	✓			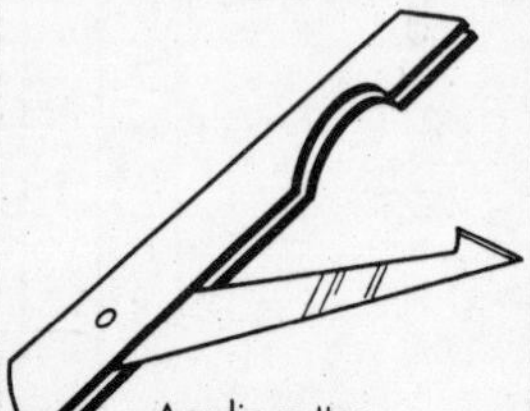 Acrylic cutter	Scoring a groove in acrylic sheet. when pressure is applied the acrylic breaks cleanly along the groove. The edge produced by this method is smooth			✓

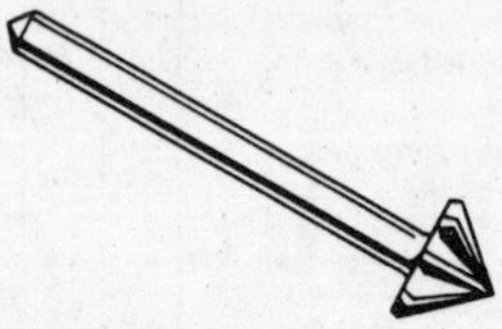

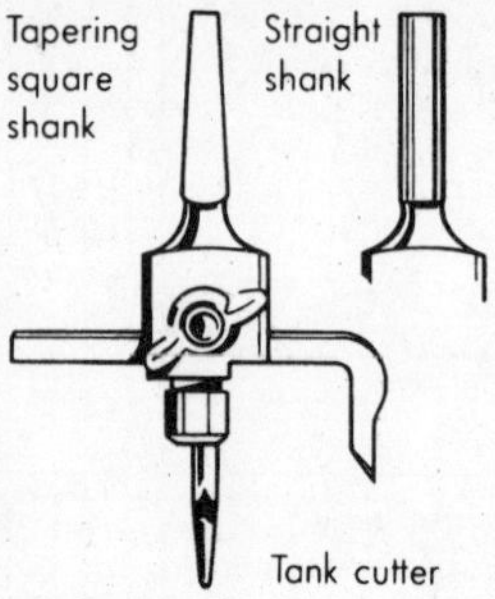

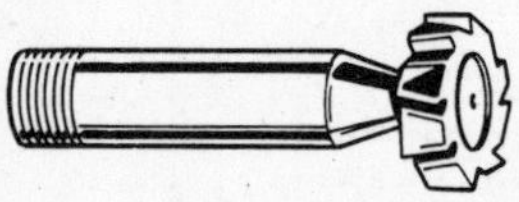

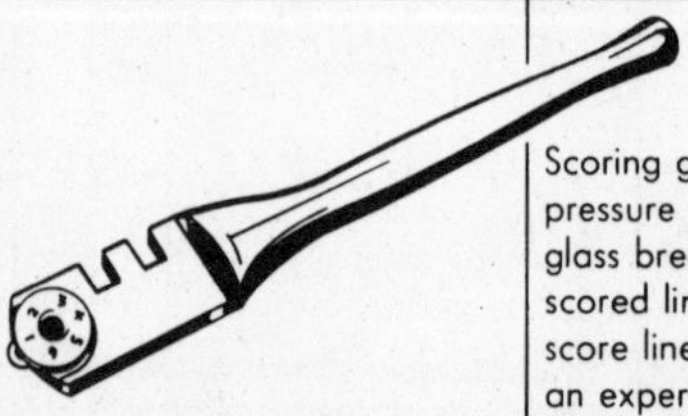

Fig. 9.4 Cutting Tools (continued)

NAME / WHAT IT LOOKS LIKE	USED FOR	W	M	P
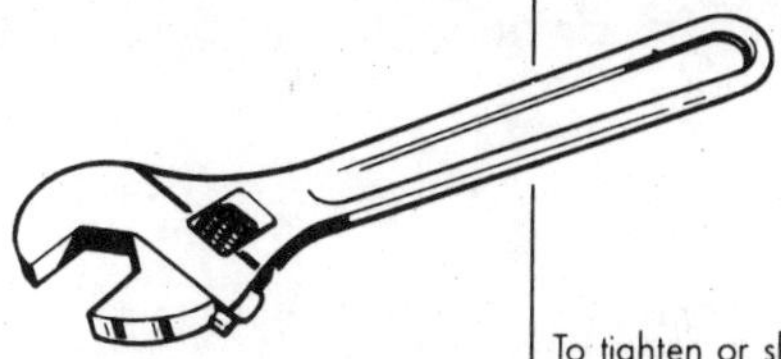 Adjustable spanner	To tighten or slacken square or hexagonal nuts		✓	
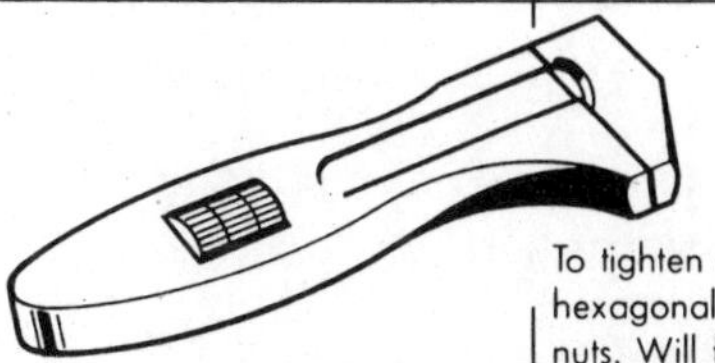 Adjustable spanner King Dick type	To tighten or slacken hexagonal and square nuts. Will function on a range of sizes of nut depending on the size of the spanner		✓	
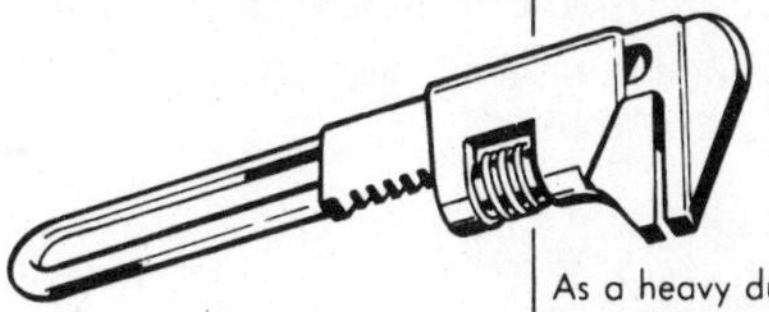 Adjustable wrench	As a heavy duty spanner for tightening or slackening large hexagonal or square nuts. Can be used to hold or twist square bar		✓	
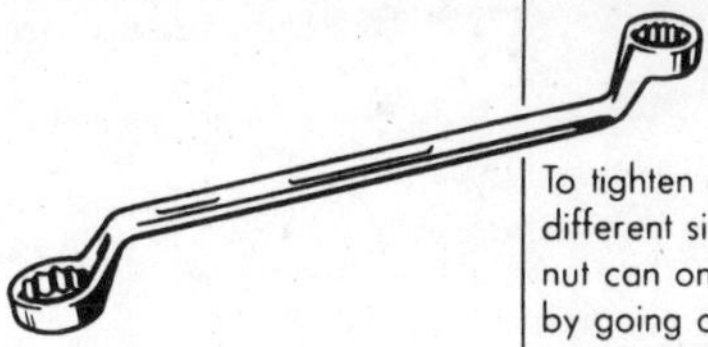 Double ended ring spanner	To tighten or slacken two different sizes of nut, the nut can only be engaged by going over the top. The 12 'V' Notches allows for a small movement and the spanner to be re-engaged		✓	
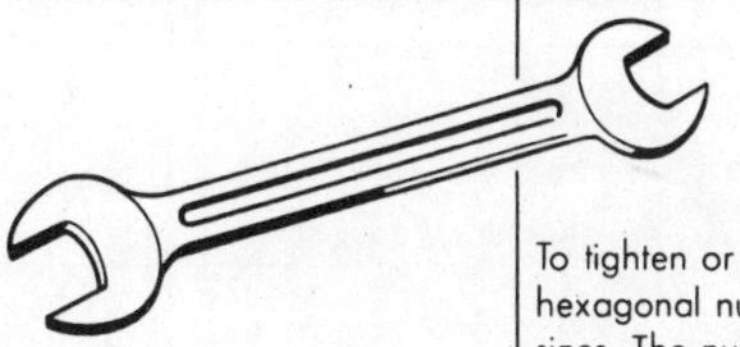 Double open ended spanner	To tighten or slacken two hexagonal nuts of different sizes. The nuts can be engaged from the side.		✓	
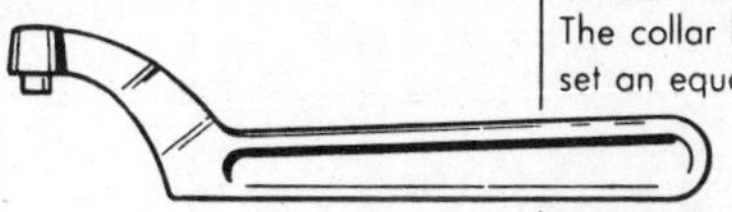 Pin spanner	To tighten or slacken circular threaded collars. The collar has four holes set an equal distance apart. The pin fits in one hole and leverage can be obtained by pressing on the arm		✓	
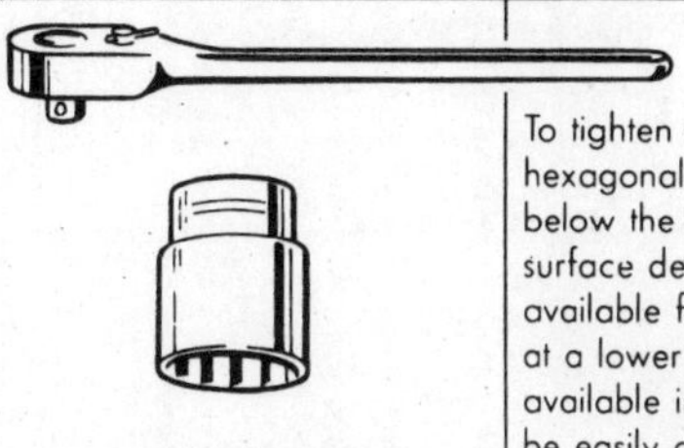 Ratchet and socket spanner	To tighten or slacken hexagonal nuts that are below the level of a surface deep sockets are available for nuts that are at a lower level. These are available in sets and can be easily attached to a ratchet lever		✓	

NAME / WHAT IT LOOKS LIKE	USED FOR	W	M	P
 Single open ended spanner	To tighten or slacken a hexagonal nut. The open jaw of the spanner enables the nut to be engaged from the side		✓	
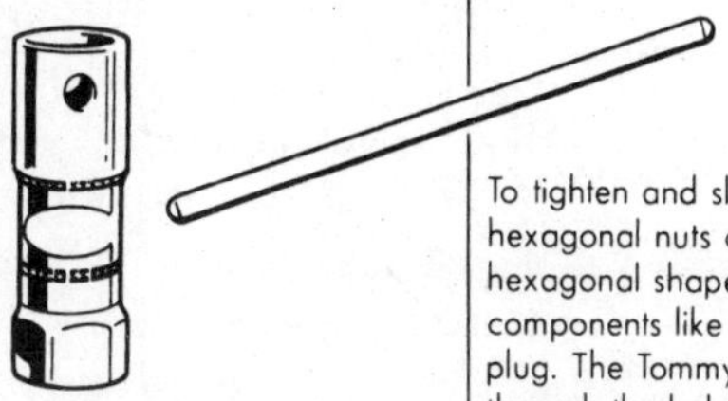 Tommy bar and box spanner single ended	To tighten and slacken hexagonal nuts or hexagonal shaped components like a sparking plug. The Tommy bar is put through the hole and used as a lever to rotate the spanner.		✓	
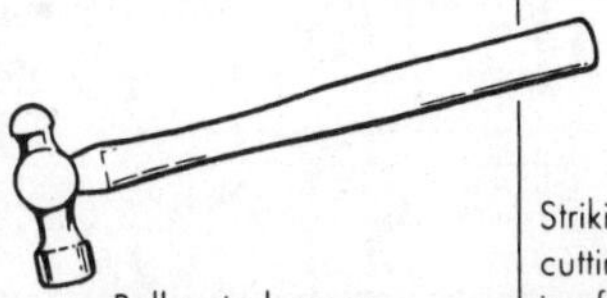 Ball pein hammer	Striking a cold chisel when cutting metal. The ball pein is often used in riveting		✓	
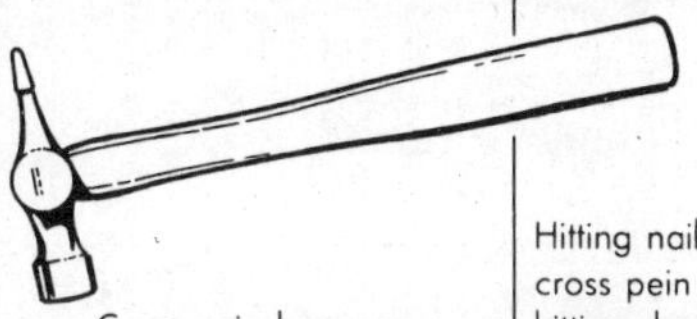 Cross pein hammer	Hitting nails in wood. The cross pein is used for hitting short panel pins		✓	
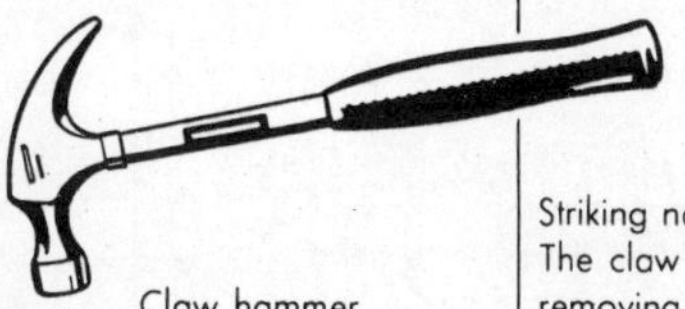 Claw hammer	Striking nails into wood. The claw is used for removing unwanted nails	✓		
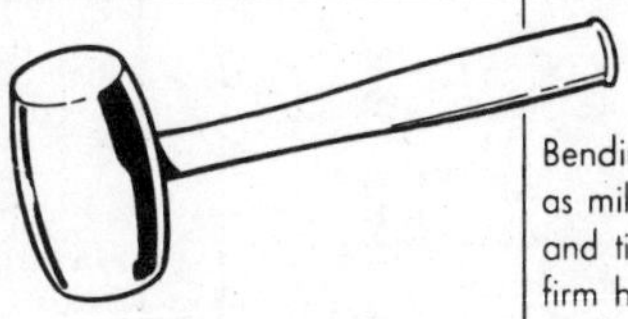 Composition mallet	Bending sheet metal such as mild steel aluminium and tin plate. The soft but firm head does not leave marks in the work		✓	
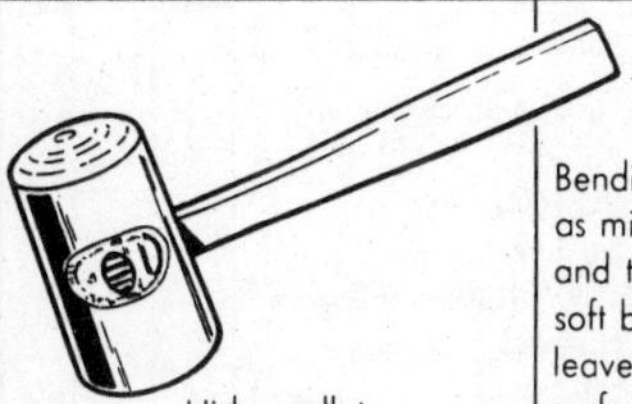 Hide mallet	Bending sheet metal such as mild steel, aluminium and tin plate. The hide is soft but firm and does not leave a mark on the surface of the work	✓	✓	
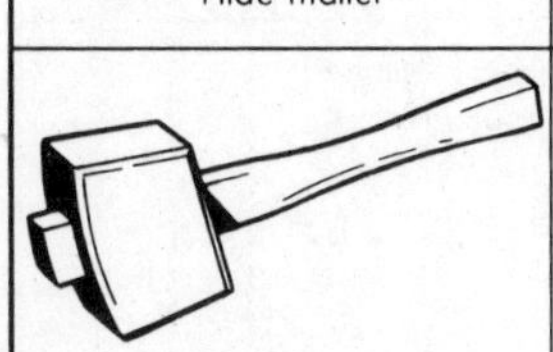 Woodworkers mallet	Striking the handle of chisels and gouges. The handles can be either made from wood or plastics	✓		✓

Fig. 9.5 Miscellaneous Tools

2⟩ POWER TOOLS

HAND POWER TOOLS

These are small portable powered machines, often much less powerful than non-portable machines that are fixed in a set position in a workshop.

Portable power machines have the *advantage* of:

a) They can be used where they are required which may be outdoors as well as indoors.
b) They perform a task more quickly than by hand.
c) They perform a task with far less human effort than the equivalent by hand.

Portable power machines have the *disadvantage* of:

a) They are more costly to buy.
b) They are more costly to run.
c) Because they work more quickly they remove more material more quickly and a mistake cannot be stopped as quickly as the equivalent hand tool operation.
d) The risk of having a serious accident is higher.
e) Protective breathing mask and eye goggles often need to be worn.
f) Trailing electric cables must be confined to those areas where they will not cause harm to anyone else.
g) An electrical cut out or trip should be plugged between the mains supply and the portable power tool being used.
h) A competent person should check the tool before it is used.

Fig. 9.6 gives information on the name, appearance and use of a variety of **portable power tools** and their **accessories**.

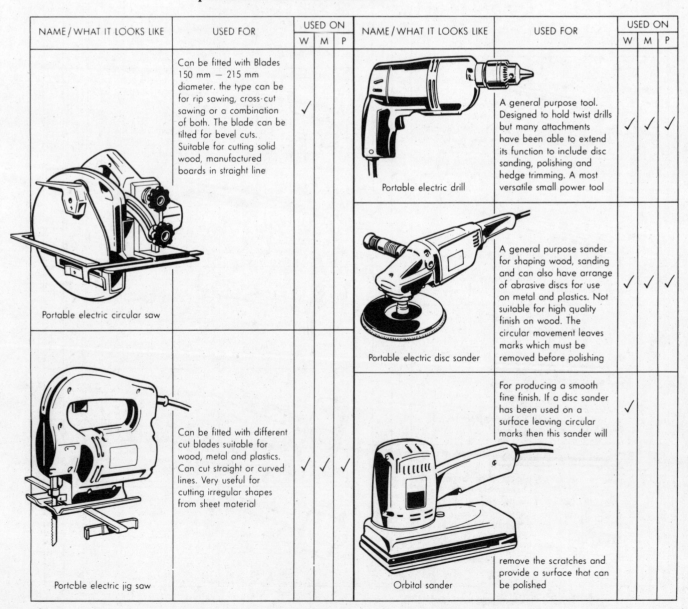

NAME / WHAT IT LOOKS LIKE	USED FOR	USED ON			NAME / WHAT IT LOOKS LIKE	USED FOR	USED ON		
		W	M	P			W	M	P
Portable electric circular saw	Can be fitted with Blades 150 mm – 215 mm diameter. the type can be for rip sawing, cross-cut sawing or a combination of both. The blade can be tilted for bevel cuts. Suitable for cutting solid wood, manufactured boards in straight line	✓			Portable electric drill	A general purpose tool. Designed to hold twist drills but many attachments have been able to extend its function to include disc sanding, polishing and hedge trimming. A most versatile small power tool	✓	✓	✓
					Portable electric disc sander	A general purpose sander for shaping wood, sanding and can also have arrange of abrasive discs for use on metal and plastics. Not suitable for high quality finish on wood. The circular movement leaves marks which must be removed before polishing	✓	✓	✓
Portable electric jig saw	Can be fitted with different cut blades suitable for wood, metal and plastics. Can cut straight or curved lines. Very useful for cutting irregular shapes from sheet material	✓	✓	✓	Orbital sander	For producing a smooth fine finish. If a disc sander has been used on a surface leaving circular marks then this sander will remove the scratches and provide a surface that can be polished	✓		

Fig. 9.6 Portable Power Tools

NAME / WHAT IT LOOKS LIKE	USED FOR	USED ON			NAME / WHAT IT LOOKS LIKE	USED FOR	USED ON		
		W	M	P			W	M	P
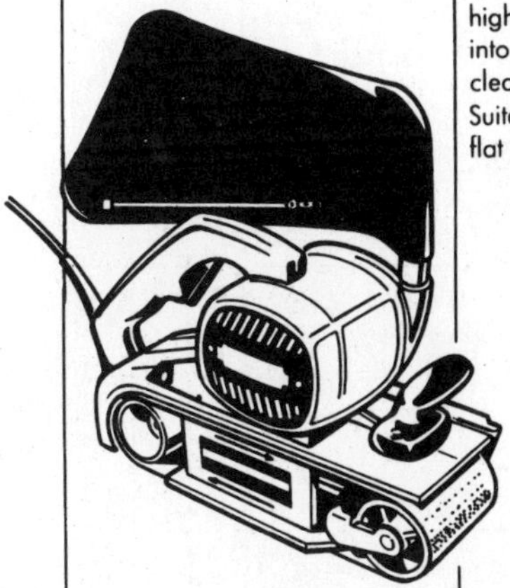 Belt sander	Suitable for removing large amounts of wood quickly. The belt rotates at high speed taking the dust into the bag like a vacuum cleaner. Suitable for use on large flat surfaces	✓			Dovetailer attachment	Cutters of the appropriate shape have to be used with the attachment. Only lap dovetails may be cut using this method, i.e. suitable for drawer fronts	✓		
 Plane	For removing wood quickly. Works on the same principle as the large planing machines by having a 2-blade cutter block	✓			Electric glue gun	To bond components quickly. The glue will run while it is hot and solidify as soon as it is cool. Surfaces receiving the glue should be warm. There is very little time for any adjustment	✓	✓	
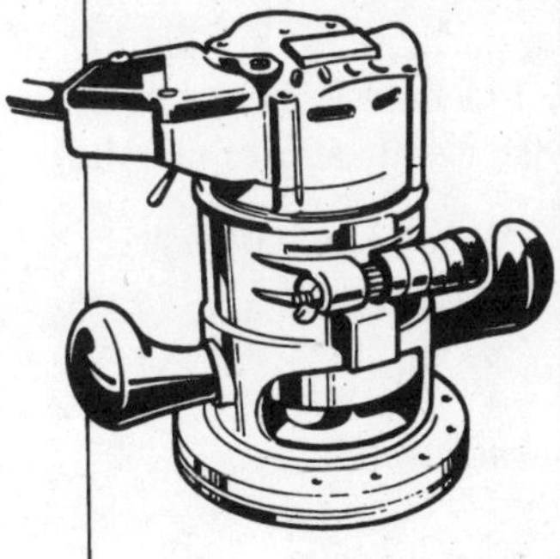 Router	This is a high-speed tool used for grooving, morticing, rebating, moulding edges and housing. With shaped cutters it can produce grooves with vertical sides or sloping sides similiar to a dovetail	✓			Electric engraver	The engraver has a variety of blades. Some pointed for engraving, rounded for embossing and others with a cutting edge for chiselling	✓	✓	✓
					Finishing sander attachment	To give a smooth fine finish	✓	✓	✓
 Circular rip saw attachment	Though its main function is to cut along the grain the 150mm diameter blade is a combination cross-cut and rip-cut blade. The ripping fence makes it possible for parallel straight cuts to be made. The accessory moves while the work remains still. Ideal for cutting large sheets of hardboard etc.	✓			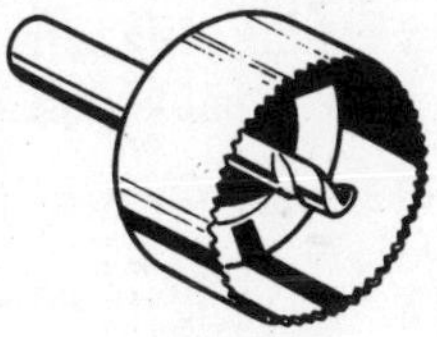 Hole saw	For cutting holes in sheet material that are larger than the standard range of twist bits. The piece removed may also be used as a wheel, washer, building a cylinder with a variety of colours and materials for turning on the lathe	✓	✓	✓
					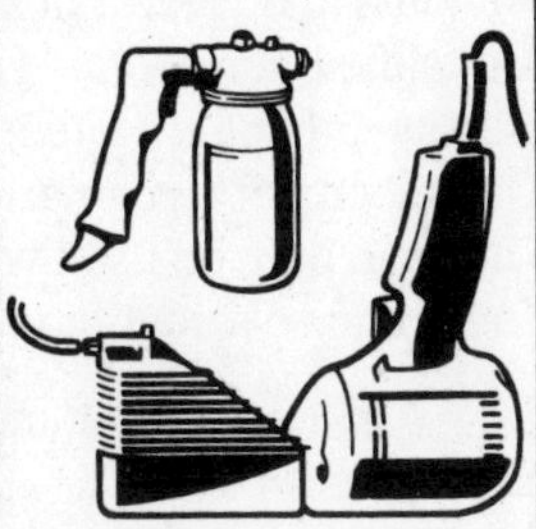 Light compressor attachment	The compressor produces approximately 80 PSI. The addition of a paint spray gun with an adjustable nozzle make it spray unit for a variety of fluids	✓	✓	✓

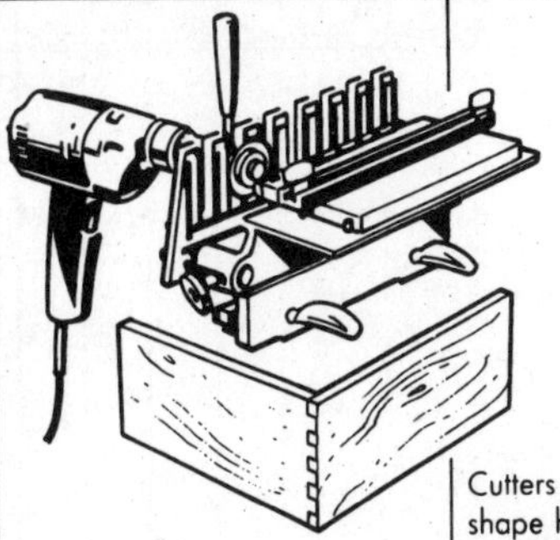

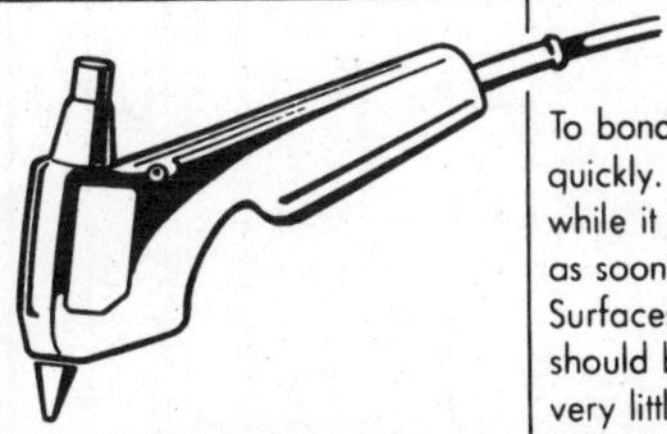

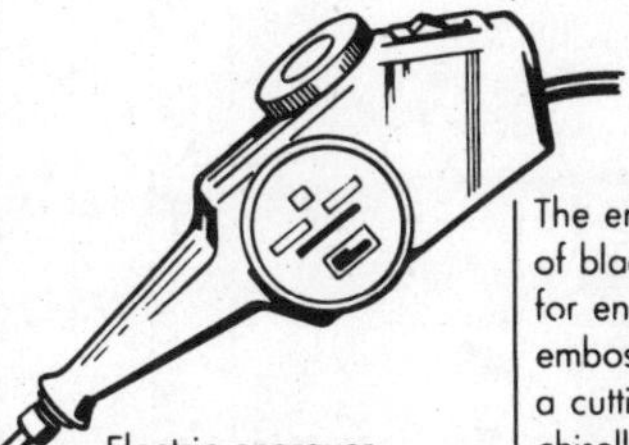

Fig. 9.6 Portable Power Tools (continued)

NAME/WHAT IT LOOKS LIKE	USED FOR	USED ON			NAME/WHAT IT LOOKS LIKE	USED FOR	USED ON		
		W	M	P			W	M	P
Portable power drill mounted in a bench stand	The bench stand provides a cradle for the drill to be firmly held. Using the drill in this situation means the drill is stationary and the work has to be moved		✓		Paint mixer	For mixing paint and varnish			
					Wire brush	For buffing and cleaning metal surfaces			✓
Saw table	The saw table converts the circular saw to a bench saw. The saw remains in position and the work moves. The guide-fence makes it suitable for cutting small boards and strips of timber. A calibrated mitreing protractor makes it possible for mitres and a range of angles to be cut	✓			Wire brush	For buffing and cleaning edges of strip square and round material			✓
					Wire brush	For buffing and cleaning broad surfaces			✓

Fig. 9.6 Portable Power Tools (continued)

3 > MACHINES

These are *not* usually portable and in the case of heavy machinery are bolted to the ground. The vibration from the movement of the mechanical parts, plus the loading required to cut through material, makes it necessary for the machine to be securely fixed in position. This will reduce the vibration and make it easier and safer to use the machine.

Fixed machines have the *advantage* of:

a) They are more powerful than portable hand power tools.
b) They are accurate and precision controlled.
c) They produce components or perform functions on material accurately.
d) They can be programmed to repeat operations.
e) They are capable of making identical parts.

Fixed machines have the *disadvantage* of:

a) They are costly to buy and run.
b) Protective masks, visors, etc., have to be worn.
c) Some machines need waste extraction systems.
d) A lot has to be learnt before they can be used.
e) A qualified person has to check that the machine has been set up correctly before the power can be switched on.
f) They need to be regularly maintained and cleaned.
g) They can only be used where they are situated.
h) They require a set of tools to change settings, gears, cutting tools, etc.

Fig. 9.7 gives information on the name, appearance and use of a variety of **power machines**.

4 > SAFETY EQUIPMENT

Fig. 9.8 provides information on the name, appearance and use of a range of **safety equipment** used when operating the various tools and machines.

Fig. 9.9 provides a useful summary of the various tools and machines which might be used for *particular* types of work.

NAME / WHAT IT LOOKS LIKE	USED FOR	USED ON			NAME / WHAT IT LOOKS LIKE	USED FOR	USED ON		
		W	M	P			W	M	P
Pedestal grinder	Grinding high speed steel cutting and marking out tools. Carbon steel tools can be ground on this type of grinder but care must be taken to not let the metal get too hot. If it does get too hot the tool will have to be hardened and tempered.		✓		Pillar drilling machine	General drilling. One of the most used machines in a workshop. The 5 step pulley drive gives a wide range of spindle speeds, that suits a range of sizes of drill bits and range of soft and hard materials to be drilled. The tilted table enables work to be drilled at different angles. The pillar makes it possible for large work to be positioned for drilling.	✓	✓	✓
Sharp edge grinder	Grinding most wood working edge tools. Chisels, marking knives, plane blades etc. A holding device sets the blade to the correct grinding angle and the constant supply of honing oil keeps the blade cool and clean.		✓		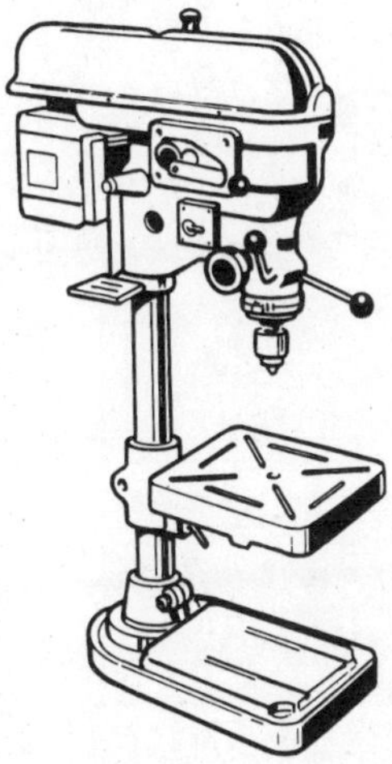 Bench drilling machine	Has the same facility for drilling except the shorter pillar means that large work would not be able to be drilled on this machine.	✓	✓	✓
Surface grinder	Grinding a true surface accurately. Only ferrous metals can be used. The means of holding the work is an electro magnet. A vice has to be used for other metals but aluminium must not be used because it cloggs the grinding wheel		✓		Universal milling machine 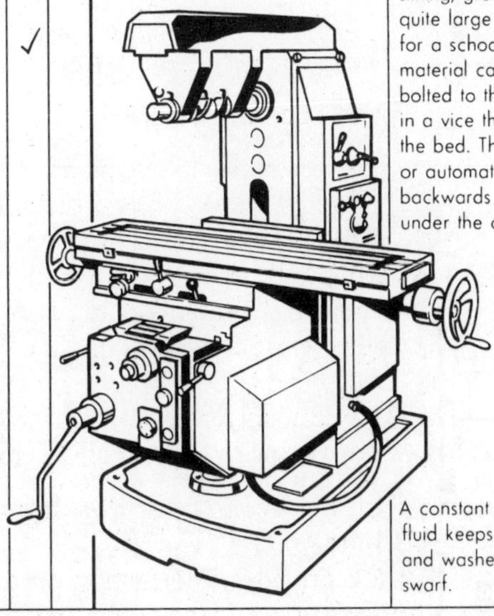	The milling machine is very much an engineering machine and is used for slitting, grooving, surfacing quite large pieces of metal for a school workshop. The material can either be bolted to the bed or held in a vice that is bolted to the bed. The bed is hand or automatically moved backwards and forward under the cutter. A constant supply of cutting fluid keeps the cutter cool and washes away the swarf.		✓	✓

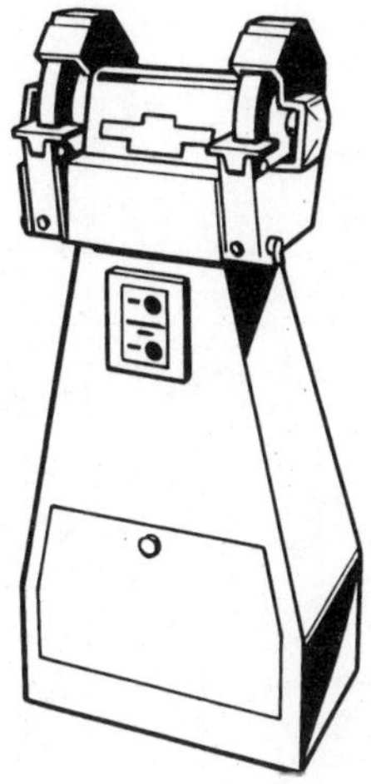

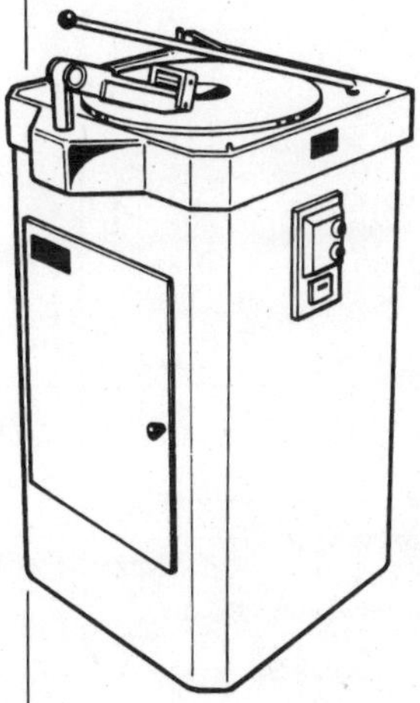

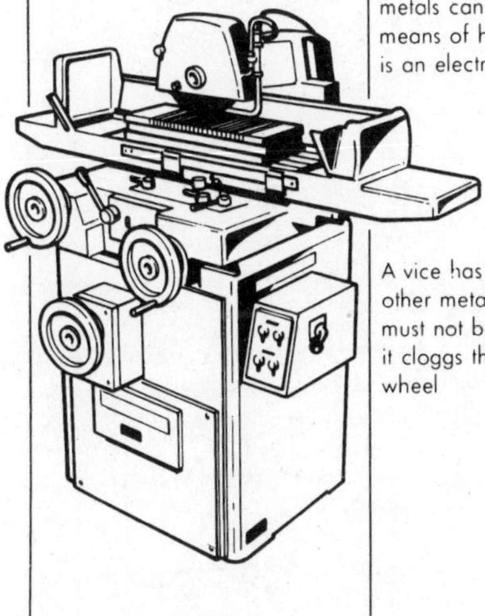

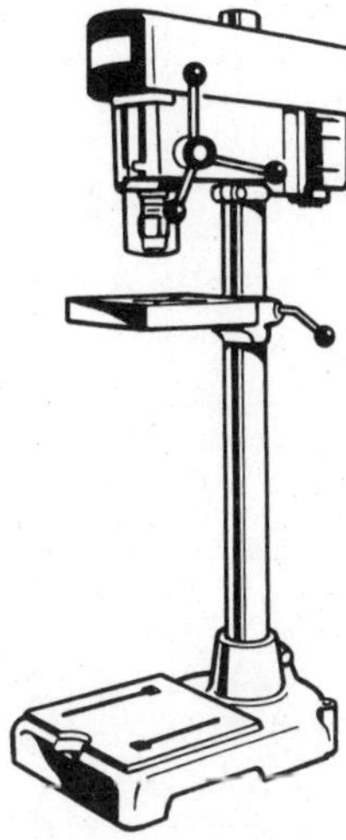

Fig. 9.7 Power Machines

NAME / WHAT IT LOOKS LIKE	USED FOR	USED ON			NAME / WHAT IT LOOKS LIKE	USED FOR	USED ON		
		W	M	P			W	M	P
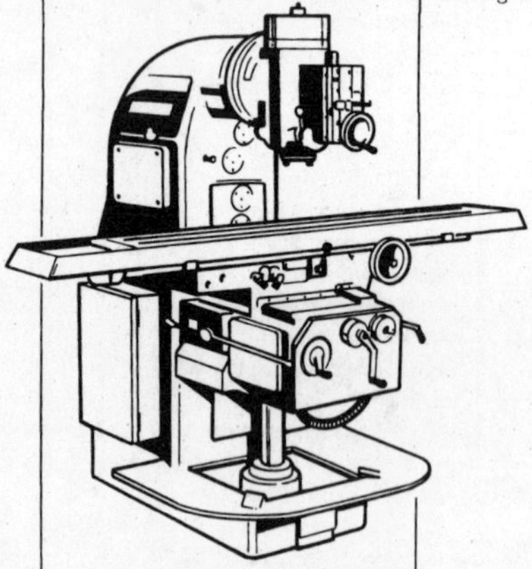 Vertical milling machine	Cutting slots		✓		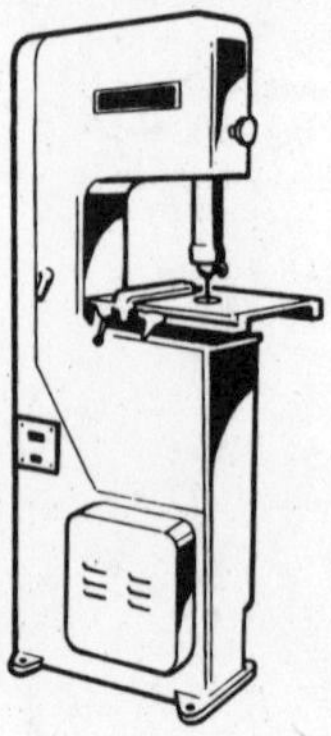 Band saw	For cutting sheet material along a straight or curved line. The appropriate blade and tension has to be used for the material being cut. The table can be tilted for bevel cuts. The maximum width of material that can be cut is determined by the distance between the blade and the throat	✓	✓	✓
Vertical milling attachment — Centre lathe with a vertical milling attachment			✓		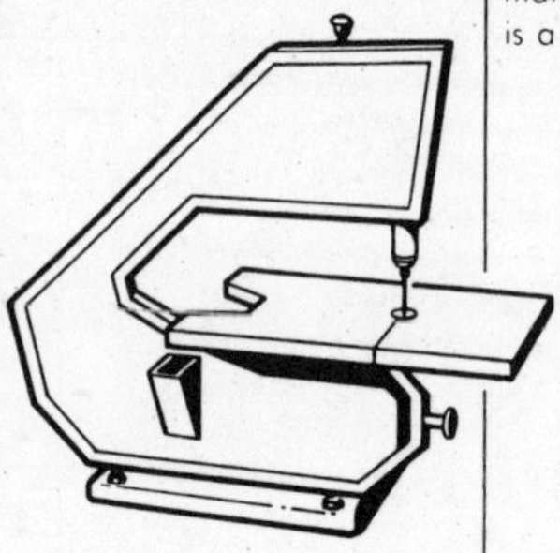 Bench band saw	For cutting thin sheet material or soft wood. This is a light duty saw	✓		✓
Metalturning lathe	For turning bar to produce parallel and taper shapes. Screw threading right hand and left hand threads. Knurling a surface to provide a grip on a component. Boring and centre drilling round bar		✓	✓	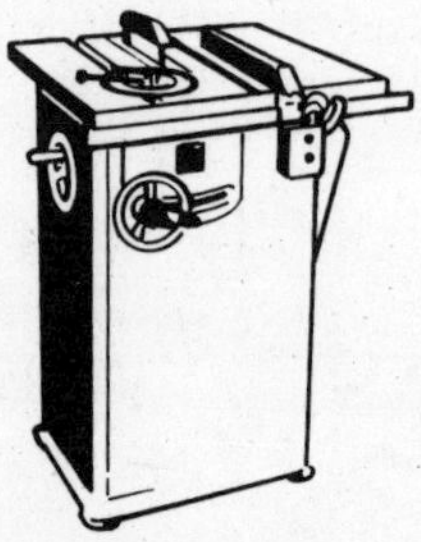 Circular saw	For sawing lengths of timber and manufactured board. The blade can be raised and lowered above and below the table. Grooves can be cut on a low setting of the blade. Edges can be bevelled by tilting the angle of the blade	✓		
Woodturning lathe	For turning between centres or on a face plate. This model has a tool rest on another arm which pivots radially and is suited for turning bowls. Sanding platforms or tables can also be mounted here for sanding the end grain of wood	✓			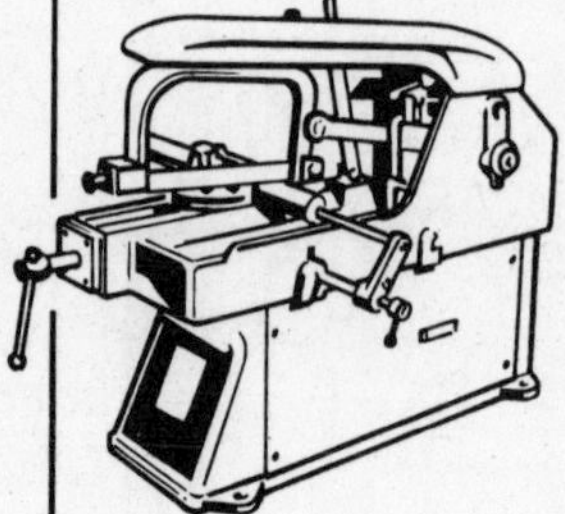 Mechanical hack saw	For cutting lengths of metal strip or bar off at 90° and 45° it has an automatic feed. The bow slide returns as soon as the metal has been cut off and switches off. The adjustable stop allows for many bars of the same length to be cut without the need for measuring the bar each time		✓	

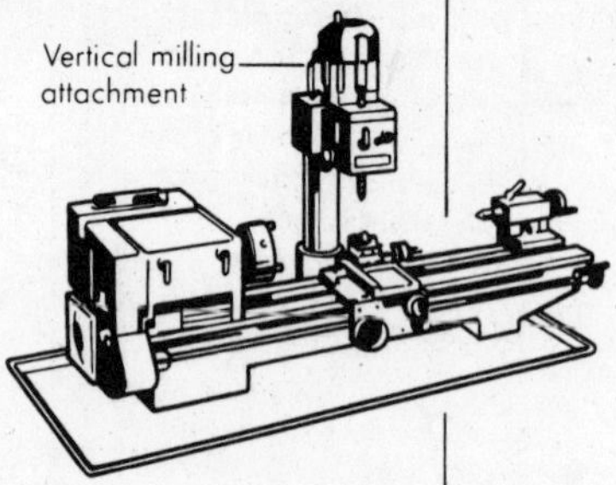

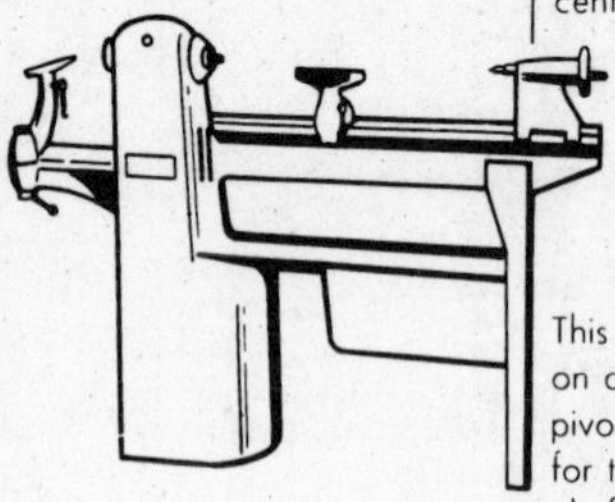

Fig. 9.7 Power Machines (continued)

NAME / WHAT IT LOOKS LIKE	USED FOR	USED ON			NAME / WHAT IT LOOKS LIKE	USED FOR	USED ON		
		W	M	P			W	M	P
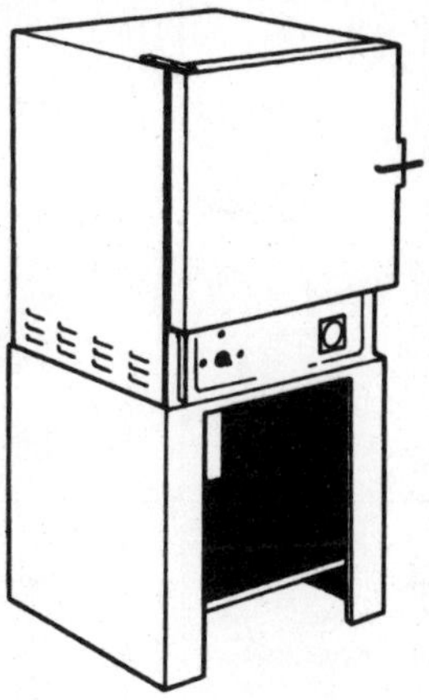 Convection oven	1. Plastic forming 2. Dip coating 3. Tempering 4. Annealing Aluminium		✓	✓	Hot wire sculptor tool	For sculpting expanded polystyrene			✓
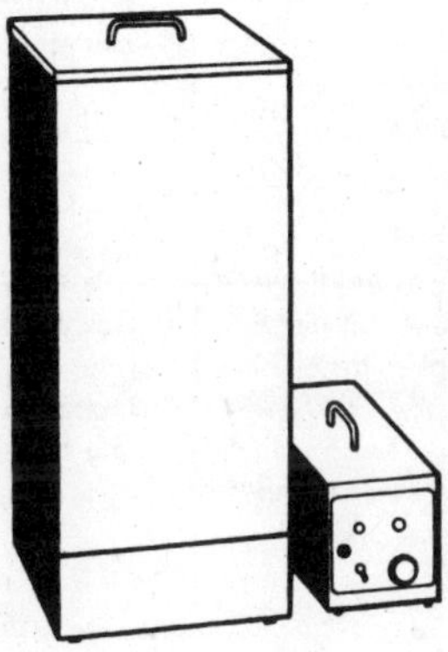 Dip coating unit Fluidised Bath	Dip coating. The bath is partially filled with a thermo plastic powder e.g. nylon or polythene and the blower forces air through the powder, making it behave like a fluid. Metal previously heated in the convection oven is lowered into the powder. The powder adheres to the surface of the metal. The heat from the metal causes the powder to melt. The metal is removed and allowed to cool. the coating can be colourful and protective			✓	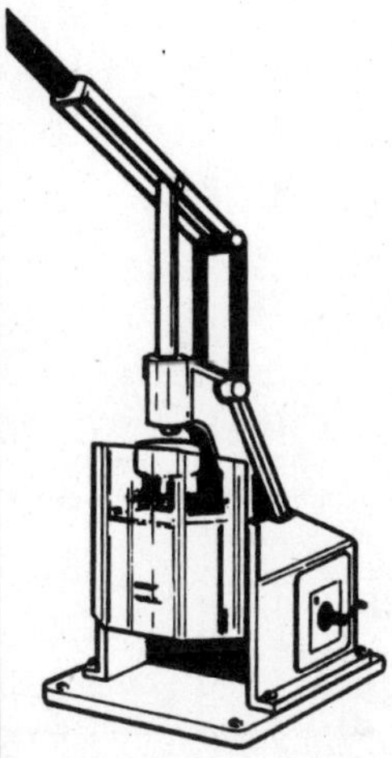 Injection moulding machine	Granules of a thermoplastics material such as:- Polyethylene L.D., Polyethylene H.D., Polypropylene, Polystyrene are heated until the material is soft enough to flow. The hand lever is pulled downwards and the plastics material is injected into a mould. This process is ideal for the production of such items as:- wheels, pulleys, small handles, dominoes, etc. The size of the product must not exceed the capacity of the machine. The mould must be filled in a single operation.			✓
Hot wire cutter	For cutting expanded polystyrene. The temperature of the hot wire is just sufficient to melt the expanded polystyrene and not too hot to cause the melted plastics to stick to the wire and give off fumes			✓	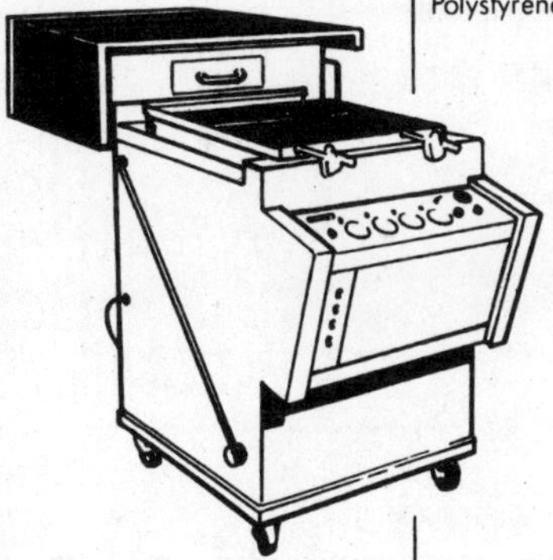 Vacuum forming machine	For heating and vacuum forming sheet thermo plastics eg. Polypropylene, Polystyrene, P.V.C.			✓

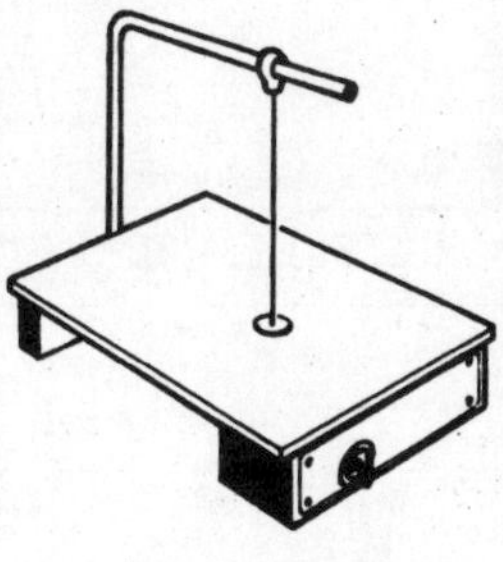

Fig. 9.7 Power Machines (continued)

NAME/ WHAT IT LOOKS LIKE	USED FOR	OPERATION	NAME/ WHAT IT LOOKS LIKE	USED FOR	OPERATION
 Goggles	To protect the eyes	1. Drilling 2. Filing 3. Sawing 4. Brazing 5. Sanding a surface	 Respirator	To prevent the breathing in of dusty air and unpleasant fumes	1. Casting hot metal 2. Laying up polyester resin 3. Sanding with a sanding machine 4. Routing with a machine
 Visor	To protect the face. Where there is likely to be chips of wood or plasics or metal swarf moving through the air	1. Drilling 2. Filing 3. Lathe turning 4. Casting			
 Welding helmet	To protect the face from hot sparks and to protect the eyes from ultra violet light which can cause temporary blindness and considerable discomfort	1. Arc welding	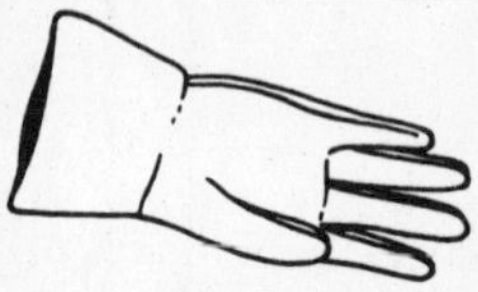 Gauntlet	To protect the hand and arm from heat and any splashes of hot metal. The gauntlets are made from leather	1. Casting aluminium or cast iron 2. Removing and casting from a mould
 Welders goggles	To protect the eyes and to improve vision of the flame and the work. The dark lenses cut down the glare. NOTE: they must not be worn for arc welding. They will not protect the eyes from ultra violet light	1. Oxyacetylene welding	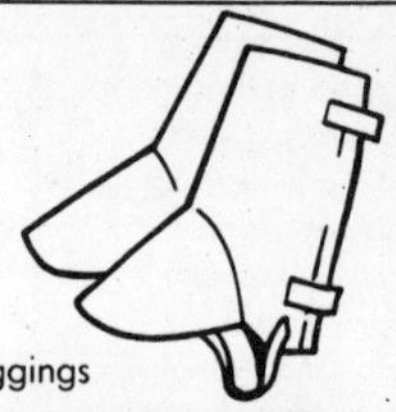 Leggings	To protect the legs from heat and any splashes of hot metal. The spat protect the shoes and prevents any hot material penetrating into the shoe	1. Casting and pouring molten metal into a mould
 Apron	To protect the body from heat and any splashes of hot metal. The heavy duty leather apron has a strap for going round the waist and one for going over the shoulders and round the back of the neck	1. Casting and pouring molten metal into a mould	 Shoes	To protect the feet from heat and hot splashes of metal that may have fallen on the floor. The shoes have thick leather uppers and soles	1. Casting and pouring molten metal into a mould

Fig. 9.8 Safety Equipment

WORK TO BE DONE	HAND TOOLS NEEDED	HELPFUL POWER TOOLS	HELPFUL MACHINES
Marking out on wood	Trysquare, rule, pencil, marking knife, marking gauge		
Marking out on metal	Engineers square, steel rule, engineers blue, scriber, dot punch, centre punch, oddleg calipers		
Marking out on plastics	Square, rule, felt pen		
Sawing along the grain of a piece of wood	Large pieces - rip saw Small pieces - tenon saw, dovetail saw	Jig saw, circular saw saw	Circular saw, band
Sawing metal cutting	Hack saw, junior hacksaw, snips, guillotine, nibbler	Power hacksaw, band saw (thin sheet)	Power hacksaw, band saw
Sawing plastics cutting rigid / flexible	Acrylic cutting tool, hacksaw, hot wire cutter / junior hacksaw, scissors, snips, trimming knife	Band saw	

Fig. 9.9 Summary

REVIEW SHEET

Using the correct tool for a specific task is important. Not only is it safer but you will also be able to get better results and the life of the tool will probably be extended.

Here are some illustrations of a range of tools. For each tool shown give its correct name, name the materials it can be used to mark, cut, measure etc. and say for what purpose it is used.

NAME	USE
_____ _____	
_____	
_____	
_____	
_____	
_____	
_____	
_____	

■ There are two classifications of tools, hand tools and hand powered tools. State how you would make the distinction between these two classes of tools giving examples.

_____

_____

_____

_____

■ Certain powered hand tools have **advantages** over hand tools. List **three** advantages.

1. _____

_____

2. _____

_____

3. _____

_____

■ Certain powered hand tools have **disadvantages** over hand tools. List **three** disadvantages.

1. _____

_____

2. _____

_____

3. _____

_____

■ When using hand tools you should always use good workshop practice i.e. use the tools correctly and safely. Select three different hand cutting tools and state what precautions should be taken to ensure that you do not have an accident.

1. Hand tool _____

Safety precaution _____

_____

_____

2. Hand tool _____

Safety precaution _____

_____

_____

3. Hand tool _____

Safety precaution _____

_____

_____

■ When using power hand tools safety precautions should be taken. List **three important safety precautions** you believe are necessary and state your reason why each is important.

1. _____

_____

2. _____

_____

3. _____

_____

STRUCTURES

GETTING STARTED

A structure is an arrangement of material or a combination of materials. Almost everything you see is a structure. This book is a structure. It is an arrangement of pages held together to enable you to read. It has a cover that protects the pages, making it a sound structure. The chair you are sitting on is an arrangement of materials held together to enable you to sit and be comfortable while you are reading. The parts of the chair are held together to support your weight, making it a sound structure.

If you set yourself the task of writing a list of things that are structures, you would find that the list would become endless. It would be of more value to limit your list to ten and to see if each structure is sound, i.e. are the pages held securely in this book? Is the chair you are sitting on supporting you safely?

Structures are either "man-made" or "natural". The book and the chair are two examples of "man-made" structures. A tree or a honeycomb are examples of a "natural" structure. The tree, in order to be a soundly growing tree, has to support its own weight and withstand external forces such as wind and rain. The honeycomb has to store the honey and to protect it from attack by other insects or animals.

You should by now understand that a *successful structure* is one that has strength. A *well-designed* structure is one that has *sufficient* strength to perform its task *without excessive use of material.*

Ever since Man began to make structures his main endeavour has been to use material to its fullest advantage. Sometimes the material has not been able to withstand the forces, because Man's calculations have taken it *beyond* its strength. A famous example of taking material beyond its strength was a suspension bridge in America that rippled like a snake whenever strong winds were blowing. The bridge became known as "Galloping Gerty" and car drivers would go across the bridge while it was snaking in the wind for a joy ride. Eventually the Tacoma Narrows Bridge collapsed, taking with it cars and people.

The sinking of the Titanic is another famous example where the material could *not* withstand the external forces caused by a collision with an iceberg. Such examples are classified as *Structural Failures.*

The reason why it is important for you to understand structures is so that you do not have a structural failure in what *you* design and make.

ESSENTIAL PRINCIPLES

1 > FORCES

A **sound structure** is dependent upon:

a) the strength of the material;
b) the form and arrangement of the parts;
c) the design and quality of the joining methods.

The **forces** that a structure may have to withstand are:

i)   **static:** a stationary force;
ii)   **dynamic:** a moving force;
iii)   **external:** a force applied to the surface;
iv)   **internal:** the force necessary to withstand the external force;
v)   **tension:** a pulling force;
vi)   **compression:** a pressing force;
vii)   **torsion:** turning or twisting force;
viii)   **shear:** two opposing pressing forces that are offset so that their paths do not meet.

A structure may have any number of forces acting upon it. They could be static or dynamic, and the structure has got to withstand the changing conditions without collapsing. The chair is an excellent example where the forces acting upon it are constantly changing. When you move about, you change your position and exert a force that has to be counterbalanced by another force. If the chair is unable to do this, it will collapse. When the internal forces and the external forces are *balanced*, the structure is said to be in a state of *equilibrium*.

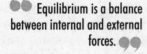
Equilibrium is a balance between internal and external forces.

If a structure is in a state of equilibrium, its *form* will not only be balanced but its *appearance* will "seem" to be right. In nature, the trunk of a tree is larger at its base than near the top, and so it has the bulk of material in the area where the major forces occur and less material where the forces are much smaller. This *form* not only helps the tree to withstand the forces but also give it an *appearance* of grace and beauty. Similarly in a man-made structure, such as the Severn Suspension Bridge or an aeroplane such as Concorde, the form helps to withstand the forces and the resulting structure is often beautiful (Fig. 10.1).

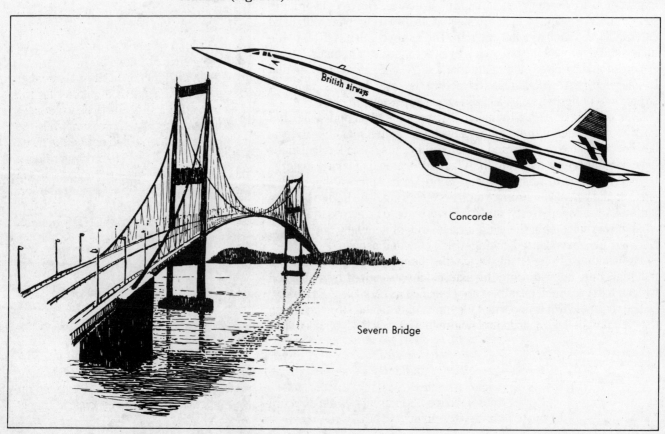

Concorde

Severn Bridge

Fig. 10.1

2> **BEAMS**

These are used to span gaps and to support loads. The gap to be spanned could be between two walls of a building and the load could be the weight of a roof, or it could be between two sides of a cabinet and the load a number of books (Fig. 10.2).

The *success* of a beam in being able to support a load can depend upon:

a) the material used;
b) the form of the material;
c) the position of the material.

Beams can be made from a *range of materials* and in a variety of forms. Metal beams are available in "I", "T", "U", "O", "L", "□", and "■" section. These sectional forms are lighter than a solid form and by being lighter reduce the load (Fig. 10.3).

Wooden beams cannot be produced in many of the sectional forms listed above. But, a piece of wood will be able to take a greater load in one position than another (Fig. 10.4).

When a beam is under a load it will bend. The top surface will be in compression and the *under surface* will be in tension. At the outer surfaces the compression and tension are at their greatest. These forces get less nearer the centre and reach a point where the beam is neither in compression nor tension. This position is called the "Neutral Axis" (Fig. 10.5).

Material can be removed from the neutral axis making very little difference to the strength of the beam and at the same time reducing the weight of the beam. The reduction of weight can be very important in aircraft construction.

3> **MAKING FLEXIBLE MATERIAL RIGID**

Paper is a very flexible material. Yet by making just a single fold, it can be made quite rigid. Increase the number of folds and the rigidity can be further improved (Fig. 10.6).

If *folding* improves the rigidity of paper, it will also improve the rigidity of more substantial materials. Thin sheet metal and sheet thermoplastics can be folded quite readily, which improves their rigidity. Thin veneers of wood and thin sheets of plywood can be laminated to improve the rigidity. The rigidity is much greater along an axis parallel to the fold than it is at right-angles to the fold. The rigidity in this direction can be improved by bonding a flat sheet to the top and undersides, so producing a form that is rigid along its length and its width (Fig. 10.7).

4> **FRAMES**

Many man-made structures are based on a frame construction. The frame is designed to counterbalance the external compression and tension forces. A good example is a stool (Fig. 10.8).

The load of a person sitting on the stool produces forces acting on the seat, legs and rails. These forces are not all the same. Some are in compression while others are in tension. It is important to *identify* these so that the appropriate design of frame can be selected and the members placed where they are most needed.

In the case of a frame that has a *splay* at the bottom, the function of the rail member will be to stop the leg members from splaying further. The splay is important for the stability of the stool in much the same way as the trunk of a tree needs to be wider near the base to withstand the greater forces. The top rail is mainly in compression while the bottom rail is in tension. This means that the bulk of the material will not be the same for both rails. To counter a compression force the material will need to be bigger than a rail that has to counter balance a tension force. If the two rails are the same form and dimension then one must be either too bulky or too small. The rail in tension can be less bulky than the one in compression.

> **66** The frame is used in many types of construction **99**

Frame construction in furniture is not confined to stools and chairs, etc. Many *cabinets* or *boxes* are designed around a frame construction often because:

a) They are lighter than those made from solid material.
b) They are more economic on the use of material.
c) They are less costly.

The *square* frame is strong when the forces are perfectly parallel to the axis of the material. As soon as the force is no longer parallel, then the structure is weak.

The *triangular* frame is a very rigid structure no matter what angle the force. A *combination* of the two frames helps to make a square or rectangular frame a much more rigid structure. Making use of this knowledge is referred to as "designing in triangulation". Many man-made structures use triangulation, e.g. gates, bicycle frame, bridges, cranes, roof structures, etc.

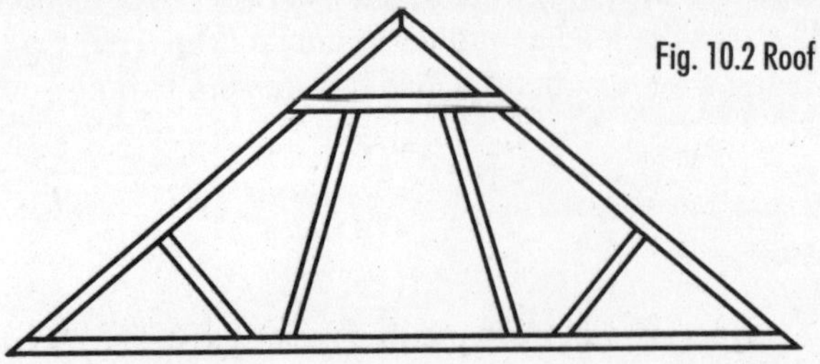

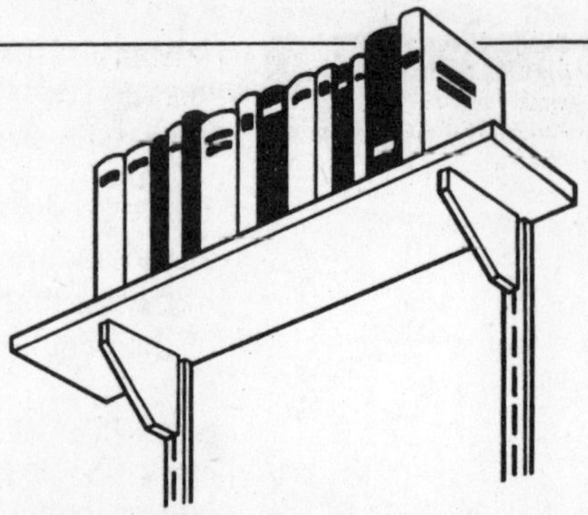

Fig. 10.2 Roof and books on a shelf.

Fig. 10.3 Sectional forms.

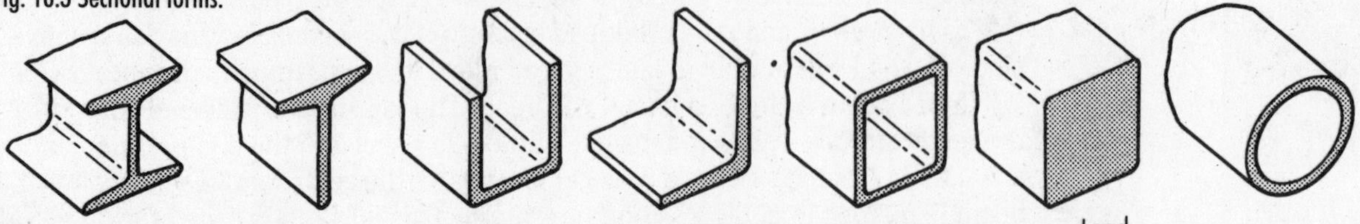

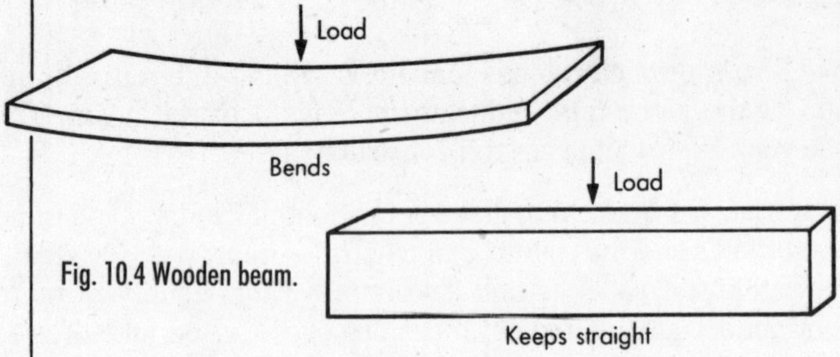

Load

Bends

Fig. 10.4 Wooden beam.

Load

Keeps straight

Load

Compression

Neutral Axis

Tension

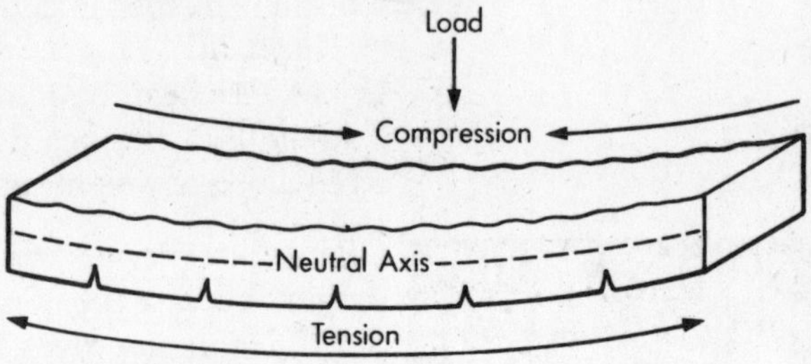

Fig. 10.5 Neutral axis.

Fig. 10.6

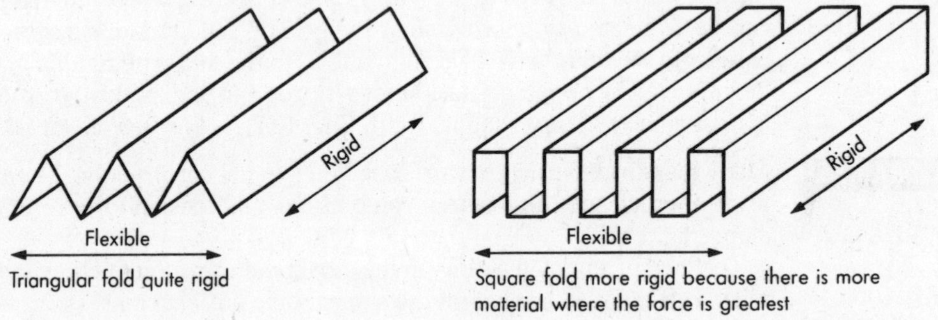

Rigid

Flexible

Triangular fold quite rigid

Rigid

Flexible

Square fold more rigid because there is more material where the force is greatest

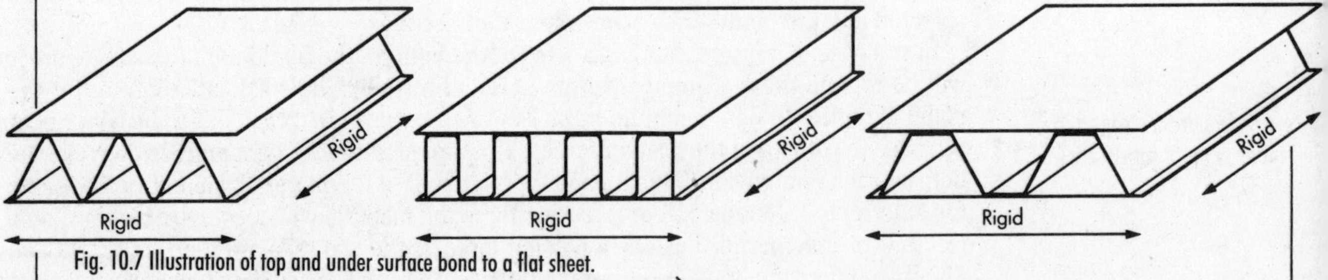

Rigid

Rigid

Rigid

Rigid

Rigid

Rigid

Fig. 10.7 Illustration of top and under surface bond to a flat sheet.

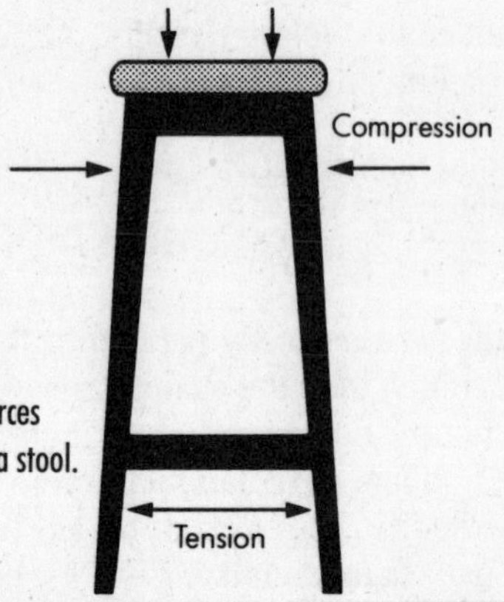

Compression

Tension

Fig. 10.8 Forces diagram of a stool.

Fig. 10.9

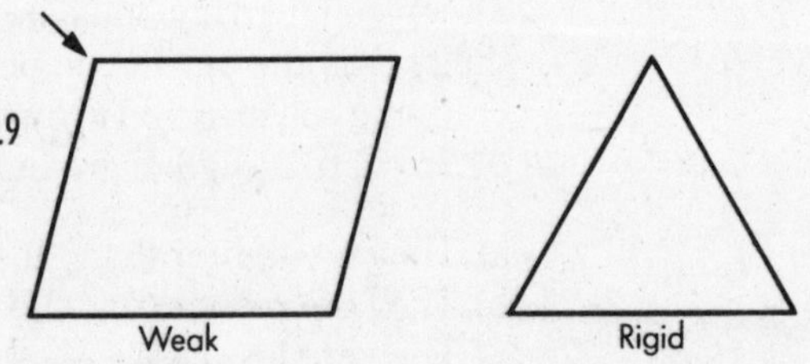

Weak

Rigid

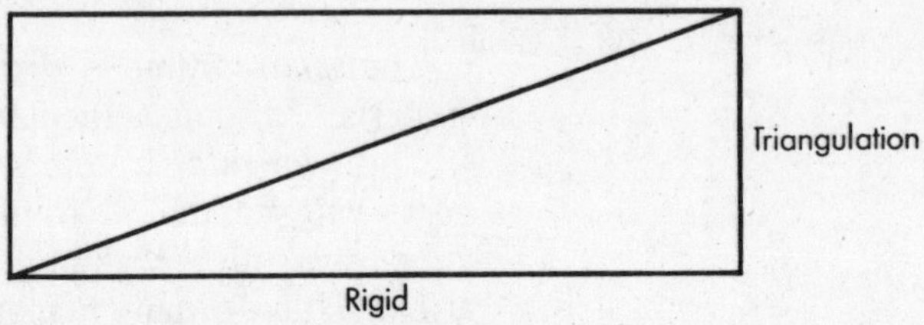

Fig. 10.10

Triangulation

Rigid

5 > TRIANGULATION IN PROJECTS

Many of the projects made in school do not require extra strengthening because the load they will have to support is very small. The projects in which triangulation may be important are:

1. the production of scale models using soft materials such as card, straws, balsa wood, string, etc;
2. gates, stools, wall-mounted shelves, folding chairs, folding desks, drawing tables, hanging basket brackets etc;
3. in the production of projects that carry weight and are designed for movement, e.g. go-carts, hovercraft, bicycle trailers;
4. in the production of large projects, e.g. stage flats and scenery, garden sheds, etc.

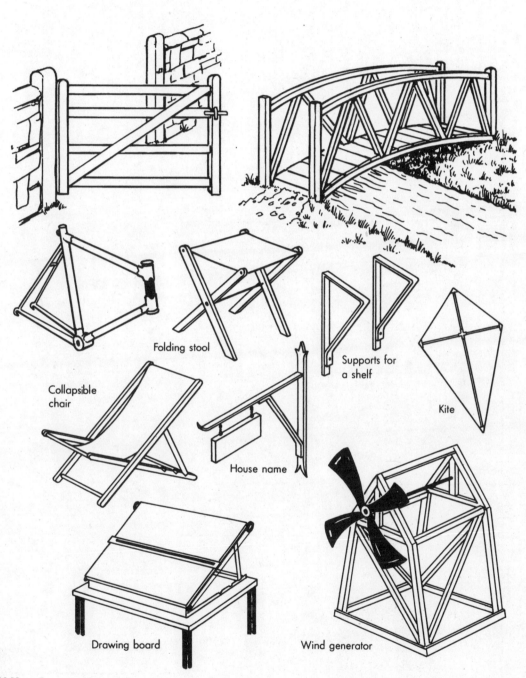

Folding stool

Supports for a shelf

Collapsible chair

Kite

House name

Drawing board

Wind generator

Fig. 10.11

REVIEW SHEET

■ A structure can be almost anything that is made by arranging and joining materials. The success of a structure depends upon its ability to withstand forces. A bridge that could not withstand the weight of vehicles would collapse and be regarded as not a sound structure. Look at a variety of bridge designs either in a book or ones that happen to be near where you live. Make a simple line drawing and put arrows on it to show the forces that are acting upon it. Name the forces against each arrow that you draw.

■ Identify the features that help to make the bridges you have drawn in a state of equilibrium.

_____

_____

_____

■ Explain how triangulation is used to provide added strength to a structure.

_____

_____

_____

■ The moulded cross section shape of metallic and plastic extrusions give lightness without sacrificing strength. Write a list of as many other advantages that can be gained from using extruded materials.

_____

_____

_____

■ Examine a product like a bicycle, which is made from a variety of materials. You will quickly find that some materials are hard and rigid and some that are soft and flexible. You will also be able to identify some section forms as being solid and others hollow. You can do this by tapping the part with a piece of metal and listen to the type of sound that will be emitted. Solid materials tend to give a short dull note, hollow materials tend to give a ringing and longer lasting note.

Using the table below, as a guide, list 4 different parts of the bicycle and complete the chart.

Part	Hard rigid material	Soft and flexible material	Solid section	Hollow section
1				
2				
3				
4				

■ Explain how the property of materials influence the form of a structure. You may wish to compare one structure that has been made using wood with a similar structure but made from metal or a fabric.

_____

_____

_____

_____

Materials are strengthened in a number of ways without changing the physical properties of the materials. For example the edge of a fabric is folded and stitched to form a hem. This stops the material from fraying and it slightly increases the rigidity of the fabric. There are a number of sectional forms illustrated in Figs 10.3, 10.4, 10.5, 10.6 and 10.7 that are employed in many of the everyday products that we use. Make a list of six products and illustrate the strengthening feature you have observed.

Product	Drawing of strengthening feature
1	
2	
3	
4	
5	
6	

If you have completed the tasks given on this review sheet you will have not only extracted information that has been given in this chapter but also broadened your knowledge, by reading other books, and by appreciating and understanding structures.

GETTING STARTED

THE SYSTEMS APPROACH

When you start to think about any control problem, it is good to try to think of it as a *system*, represented by a series of boxes in a block diagram, which are linked together. You will then need to think about what you are trying to do and to break this down into a block diagram form. Each part of the project will be represented by a box. At this stage you only need to know what inputs, processes and outputs you will require. Whilst a systems approach is useful for any type of design problem, this chapter will help you with electronic design specifically.

Systems that have feedback are called *closed loop* systems and those without feedback are called *open loop* systems. Feedback means taking an output signal or part of it and feeding it back into the input. A way of explaining it could be: when a driver turns the steering wheel (the input) of her car, the car will start to turn. By looking at how far the car is turning (the output) the driver can then readjust the steering to perform the required manoeuvre. The feedback element is looking at what the car is doing and adjusting the steering appropriately. Another example could be the thermostat on your central heating at home. This relays information about the temperature of the room back to your central heating boiler and adjusts it.

ELECTRONIC SYSTEMS AND COMPONENTS

ANALOGUE AND DIGITAL SIGNALS

DEVELOPING A SYSTEM

INPUT DEVICES

PROCESSING DEVICES

OUTPUT DEVICES

COMPONENTS

EQUATIONS AND CALCULATIONS

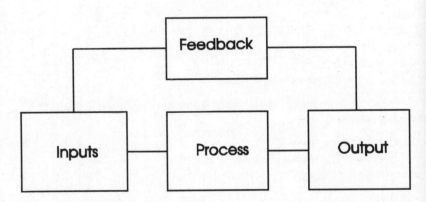

Fig. 11.1   The system

ESSENTIAL PRINCIPLES

1 > ANALOGUE AND DIGITAL SIGNALS

Electrical signals take two basic forms:

- *Analogue signals* which vary in amplitude over time.
- *Digital signals* which have only two states, *off* or *on* and these are usually denoted by 0 for off and 1 for on.

An analogue signal is fed to the loudspeaker of a radio; you hear the resulting signal as variations of frequency and loudness.

A typical digital signal could be said to be Morse code; the information is only carried in the on/off signal, not in the frequency, which should not change.

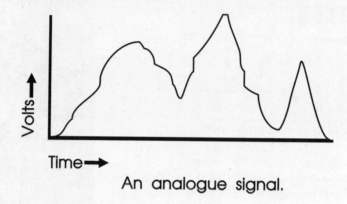

An analogue signal.

Fig. 11.2

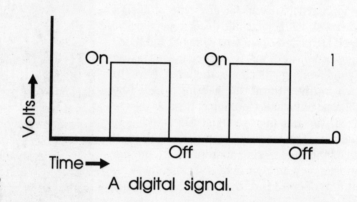

A digital signal.

2 > DEVELOPING A SYSTEM

These blocks of a system (often called black boxes) contain the elements to enable the project to work. However at first it is necessary to decide what each element is to do. You need to ask yourself:

"What is the system to do?"
"What do I need to measure?"
"What inputs do I need?"
"What processes do I want to happen?"
"What do I want to happen when these inputs occur?"

❝❝ Questions behind a systems approach ❞❞

For instance: the task may be to make an *automatic watering device* for use in a green house. The questions to ask are:

1. "How do I sense the dryness of the soil?"
2. "What is needed to control the output devices?"
3. "What are the output devices to do?"

The answers may be:

1. Use metal electrodes in the soil.
2. Measure their resistance and when it increases switch on the output.
3. Switch on the water supply to the sprinkler system.
4. Switch off the water when the soil is at the correct moisture level.
5. Perhaps sound a warning device or switch on an indicator light.

The next stage could be to discuss your system with someone who knows about gardening. They may tell you that plants should not be watered in bright sunlight, so how can you modify your system to cope with this? Perhaps other sensors are required to sense light and/or temperature.

Your plants will then be watered when both sensors tell the system that the soil is dry and the sun is not shining.

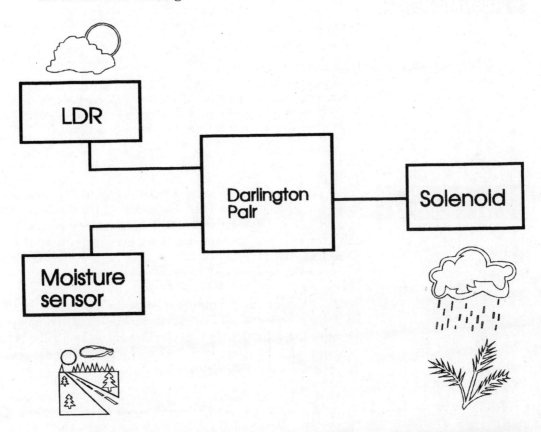

Fig. 11.3 A greenhouse watering device

It can be seen that you have already designed the system in outline without considering the electronics. There are a range of simple circuits which can be linked together based on what happens to their inputs and outputs. Indeed when designing using integrated circuits this is exactly what occurs. The designer is only interested in the signals which enter and leave the integrated circuit and not the electronics inside.

66 Bringing electronics into play 99

This decision-making process can be done either by writing out the steps or by using a flow chart and you are advised to use this method in your folio. You are also advised to draw a block diagram of your system.

The system has input devices called *sensors*, a circuit which processes these input signals and output devices which control the project. Sometimes feedback is used to make the control more precise. In this case, when the soil gets wet the sensor senses it and switches off the water source.

66 Input devices 99

Input devices can be:		
Light dependent resistors	senses	light
Phototransistors	senses	light
Thermocouples	senses	temperature
Thermistors	senses	temperature
Potentiometers	senses	movement
Electrodes	senses	humidity
Microphones	senses	sound
Strain gauges	senses	strain/bending
Switches	senses	manual/mechanical

❝ **Processing devices** ❞

Processing devices can be:
Amplifiers...amplifies small inputs
Electronic switches...switches at different levels
Timers ....switches after time delay
Gates..and/nand/or/nor...combines inputs
Counters...counts input pulses

❝ **Output devices** ❞

Output devices can be:
Relays ....controls higher voltages/currents
Lamps ....light
Buzzers/Bells..sound
Speakers..sound
Motors..movement (rotary)
Stepper motors ....movement (precise rotary)
Solenoids..movement (linear)
Linear actuators...movement (linear)
Indicators ....information.

③ INPUT DEVICES

Input devices are those sensors which respond to changes in temperature, light, moisture, humidity, sound etc. and provide a change in voltage, resistance or switch states which can then be applied to the processing element. The process element then amplifies, switches, times or counts and eventually causes the output states to change. This change could be to switch on a motor or pump, sound a buzzer, start a machine.

Light Dependent Resistor (LDR)

When light falls on a *light dependent resistor* its resistance falls: the brighter the light, the lower the resistance falls. To make it more selective, it is always a good idea to put it in a tube so that reflections are cut out. The circuit below shows how a LDR can be used to control a relay or motor. If the position of the LDR and the resistor are changed then the opposite action will happen.

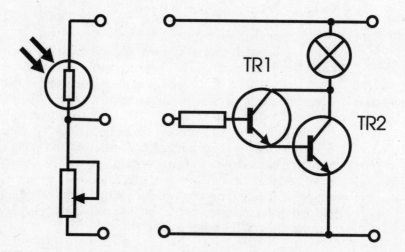

Fig. 11.4 Circuit switches on when
          light on LDR increases

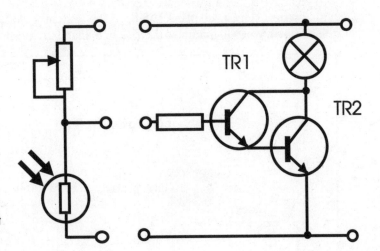

Fig. 11.4 (continued) Circuit switches off when light decreases

Phototransistor

Types of input device

LDRs are quite slow; if faster operation is required then a *phototransistor* can be used. The light falls on the junction of the transistor and causes a change in current which is then amplified. These will work up to many thousands of cycles per second, so could be used to measure the speed of the wheel of a bicycle for example.

Photo cells are devices which produce a voltage when light falls on them. The voltage and current produced are usually quite small and photocells are linked in series and parallel to provide higher voltages and currents.

To save time in accurately arranging a light source opposite to a phototransistor some manufacturers provide them in one package, usually called *opto-switches*. These have a small gap between an LED and phototransistor. If you arrange for something to cross the gap and prevent the light from reaching the phototransistor then a signal will occur. This can then be amplified.

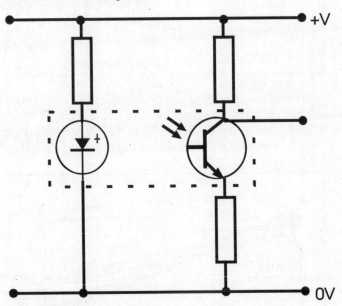

Fig. 11.5 A slotted opto-switch

Thermistors

Thermistors also change their resistance but this time with temperature. If, as the temperature increases the resistance decreases, then the thermistor is said to have a *negative temperature coefficient* (NTC). Thermistors which increase their resistance with an increase in temperature have a *positive temperature coefficient* (PTC).

Some thermistors are coated in resin and are colour coded, some are encapsulated in glass beads, so that they can be dipped into liquids without damage.

The smaller the thermistor the quicker that it responds to temperature change but these small bead types are easily damaged and expensive, so care is needed if you use them. Do not bend the wires near to the body of the component as either the glass or resin coating will crack.

If you have to bend the leads, then hold the lead near to the body of the component with a pair of snipe nose pliers and bend the lead on the other side of the pliers. Using this method, you will minimise the risk of damage to the component (Fig. 11.6).

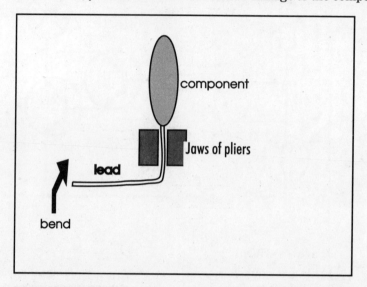

Fig. 11.6

Potentiometer

Potentiometers can be used to sense movement although they may be quite stiff to operate. Levers can be attached to the shaft to reduce this effect, then the resistance will change as the lever is moved (Fig. 11.7). Long levers or gears should overcome any stiffness of the control.

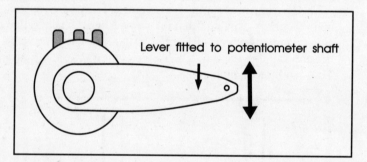

Fig. 11.7

If small movements are to be sensed, then a lever with a small card on it which cuts off the light to an LDR could be simply made (Fig. 11.8). This would result in a resistance change as more or less light falls on the LDR. For the best results the LDR and the light source should be fitted into tubes to prevent unwanted light interfering with the action.

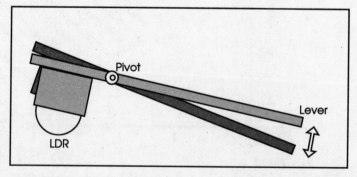

Fig. 11.8

To sense rotary movement or position, a magnet could be made to turn above a group of reed switches. As the magnet rotates then the reed switches will switch in sequence (Fig. 11.9).

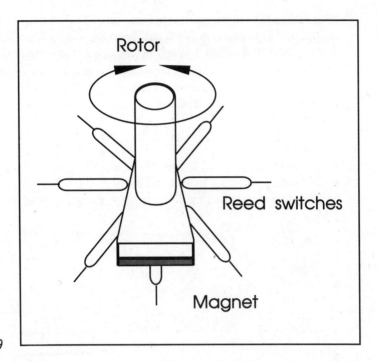

Fig. 11.9

Electrodes

If humidity, moisture, water level or rain needs to be sensed then this can be measured as a change of resistance across two *electrodes*. These electrodes could be just two metal rods pushed into the soil (Fig. 11.10). They need to be fitted into a holder which keeps them at a precise distance apart otherwise the resistance will change.

Various sensors can also be made by using printed circuit board or veroboard to provide metal strips which the moisture can bridge (Fig. 11.11).

Be careful when making sensors, to choose a glass fibre board or some type of plastic material as this will not absorb any moisture.

Self adhesive copper tapes are available which can be cut with scissors and attached to sheet material should you need to make a special type of sensor. These strips can be soldered just like printed circuit boards with a small soldering iron.

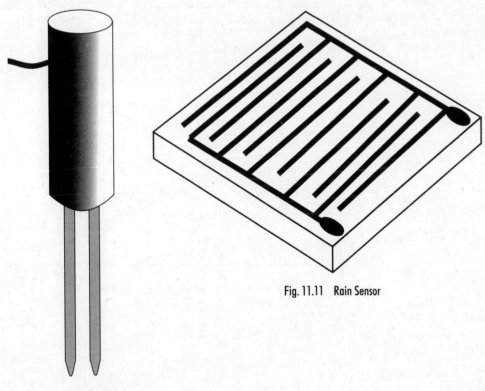

Fig. 11.10   Soil Probe

Fig. 11.11   Rain Sensor

Microphones

There are many types of *microphones* which can be used as sensors for systems. The main types are carbon, crystal and moving coil. This denotes either the material producing the signal when vibrated by the sound energy, or the type of construction. Some, like the carbon microphone, are very robust and produce large signals. Others, like the moving coil, are delicate and produce relatively small amplitude signals but of good quality.

Strain gauges

Strain gauges change their resistance when distorted, the changes are very small and need a circuit called a Wheatstone Bridge to provide a usable signal. They are expensive and need to be attached by glueing to the material being measured.

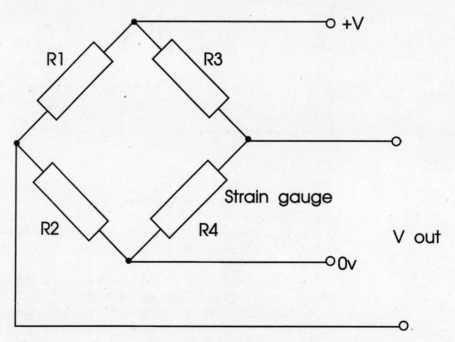

Fig. 11.12   Wheatstone
            Bridge Circuit

Switches

Switches make perhaps some of the most effective input devices. There are a large range of types all of which can be adapted in some way to fit your project needs.

S.P.S.T Single pole single throw. This will switch one circuit on and off.

 S.P.D.T Single pole double throw, this is a single pole change over.

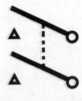 D.P.S.T Double pole single throw. This is most commonly used as a mains switch, where it switches two circuits ie the live and the neutral on or off at the same time.

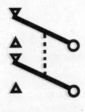 D.P.D.T Double pole double throw. This is a double pole change over switch, a common use is that of a reversing switch. See below.

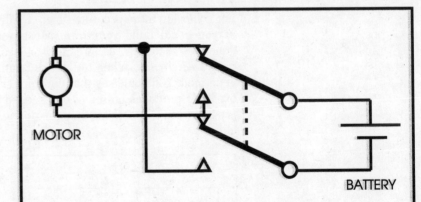

MOTOR

BATTERY

DPDT switch used as a reversing switch for a motor.

Fig. 11.13 Switches

4 ⟩   PROCESSING DEVICES

Gates

Gates will combine inputs to the *processing device* so that an output can be generated when two or more signals are present. This means that you can select a range of gates which will combine your inputs in any combination you wish to design. There is more about gates in the Electronic Components section below.

Amplifiers

Amplifiers take small changes in current or voltage and amplify them so that they can be used to drive output devices. The 741 operational amplifier is a useful integrated circuit for use in school. The LM308 is a much more powerful version. The amount the circuit amplifies can be accurately set by adjusting the feedback.

Amplifiers with very high gain switch over very rapidly; the darlington pair is a good example of this. Single transistors can be used but they are less sensitive than the darlington pair.

> ❝ Types of processing device ❞

Timers

Timers can be constructed using the 555 integrated circuit. It can be made up into:

- **Monostable** – one stable output state, it returns to original state after a timing period.
- **Bistable** – two stable states, it will change output state and remain in this state until triggered again. Often called a flip flop.
- **Astable** – Oscillates continually between its two states.

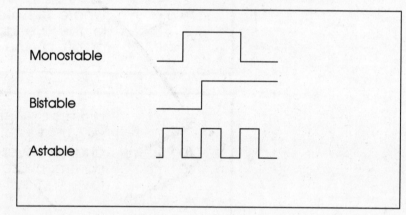

Fig. 11.14   Timers

Oscillators and counters

For achieving more accurate timer circuits, there are specific timer integrated circuits or you could build your own. Most work by having an *oscillator* (astable) which generates a continuous stream of pulses, these pulses are then counted by *counter integrated circuits*. When the desired number of pulses occur then an output pulse is generated. You could say that the counter is a "divide by" circuit. For example, if your oscillator produces pulses of one second length and your counter needs 1000 before producing an output pulse then the timing period will be 1000 seconds i.e. 16.6 minutes long.

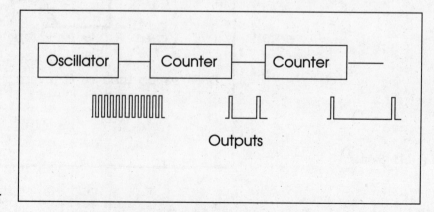

Fig. 11.15   Oscillator and counter

See the Electronic Components section for further details of amplifiers and timers.

5 > OUTPUT DEVICES

Output devices convert electrical signals to light, movement and sound and can, with the use of *relays*, switch high voltages and currents sometimes remotely.

Lamps

Lamps can provide either illumination or a warning signal and there is a wide range of types available. When ordering them you need to know:

- Working voltage, current, type, types of base.
- 12 volt, 0.5 Amps, round, MES (Miniature Edison Screw).
- 6 volt, .16 Amps, tubular, MBC (Miniature Bayonet Cap).

There are a range of holders for these small bulbs some of which have coloured lenses, and fit to panels.

Indicators such as *light emitting diodes* (LEDS) do not give out a great deal of light but can be found in a range of colours. They use low voltage, low current supplies and must always be used with a current limiting resistor. LEDs are very reliable and do not produce much heat. There is a wide range of fixings for LEDs.

LEDS are used in seven segment displays which can be made to represent numbers and letters, and bargraph arrays which can indicate the value of any electrical signal.

> " Types of output device "

Buzzers and bells

If you were making a burglar alarm then a sound will be required to warn people, this can be generated by buzzers, bells, sirens, speakers and sounders (piezo electric). Buzzers and bells are usually just ordered by stating the voltage at which they will work. There are two types of piezo electric sounders, ones that make a noise when a voltage is applied and ones which require an oscillator to make the sound. These sounders apply a voltage to a sheet of crystalline material which then vibrates. They are capable of making ear piercing noises.

Speakers

Speakers need an audio frequency to drive them. They are ordered by size in inches and by resistance usually 3, 5, 8, 16 or 35 ohms.

Solenoids, Linear Actuators and Motors

If your project requires movement then there are solenoids, linear actuators and motors which you can use. *Solenoids* are coils surrounding a metal rod. When a current is applied through the coil, the rod is forced out of the coil. The effect cannot be easily controlled, so it is usually either on or off. This is often used as the basis for locking mechanisms.

Linear actuators (Fig. 11.16) contain a motor which drives a rod in or out which can be used to open small hatches or doors. The motor can be stopped or reversed at any time. This is therefore capable of providing proportional control. There is usually an override device which prevents the actuator rod from jamming or stalling at the end of

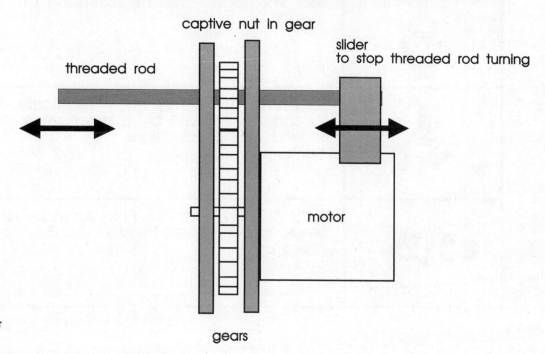

Fig. 11.16 The basis of a linear actuator

its travel.

There are a great range of DC motors available, from very small model motors through to large powerful ones. Most small model motors rotate at high speeds, and will need to be geared down to more usable speeds. This can also be done electronically using a 555 timer integrated circuit. This provides pulses which slow the motor down

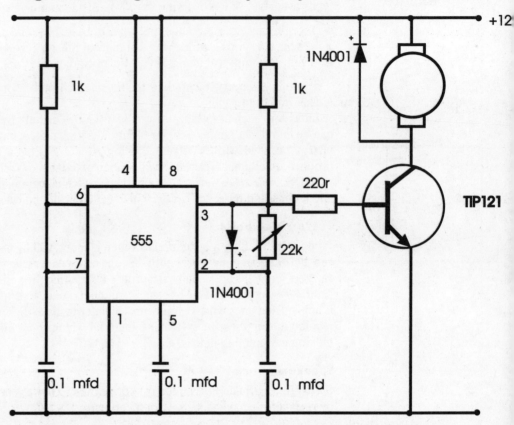

Fig. 11.17   Motor Speed Control

but with little loss of torque.

Stepper motors can be used with digital circuits. These turn a precise angle on the application of one pulse. This allows really accurate control of position. They need special circuits to drive them, but once again there are integrated circuits specially designed to make this easy.

A range of input devices is shown in Fig. 11.18.

	TOGGLE SWITCH:- available in miniature and standard sizes, the toggle can be extended and operated by a lever.
	SLIDE SWITCH:- usually quite electrically noisy, and stiff to operate if driven by a mechanism. Available in all SP and DP configurations.
	PUSH BUTTON:- can be Push to make or Push to break, also noisy electrically. Usually manually operated.

Fig. 11.18

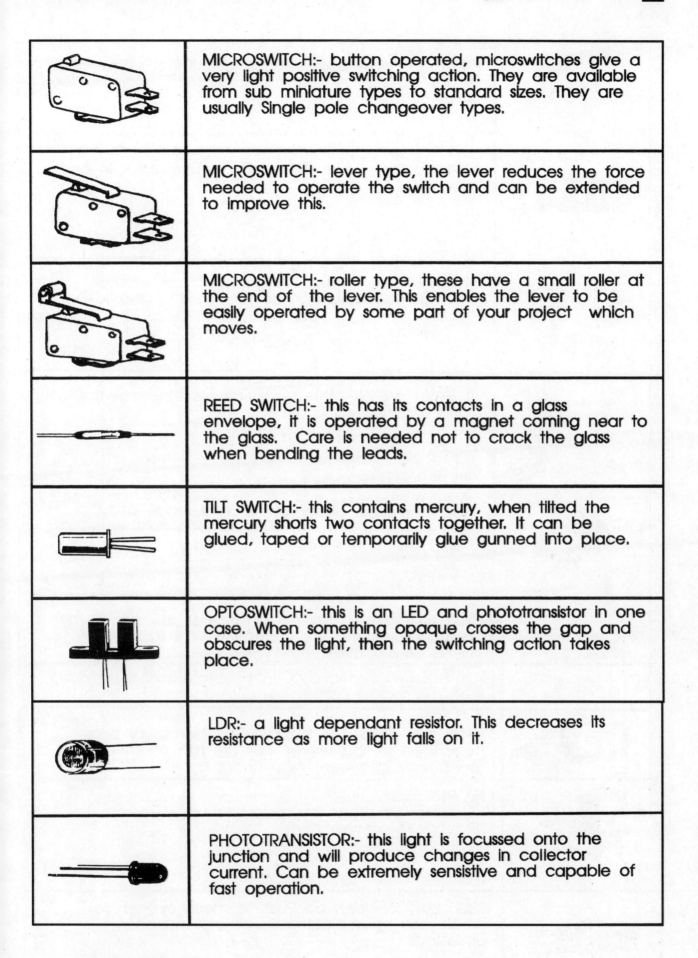

	MICROSWITCH:- button operated, microswitches give a very light positive switching action. They are available from sub miniature types to standard sizes. They are usually Single pole changeover types.
	MICROSWITCH:- lever type, the lever reduces the force needed to operate the switch and can be extended to improve this.
	MICROSWITCH:- roller type, these have a small roller at the end of the lever. This enables the lever to be easily operated by some part of your project which moves.
	REED SWITCH:- this has its contacts in a glass envelope, it is operated by a magnet coming near to the glass. Care is needed not to crack the glass when bending the leads.
	TILT SWITCH:- this contains mercury, when tilted the mercury shorts two contacts together. It can be glued, taped or temporarily glue gunned into place.
	OPTOSWITCH:- this is an LED and phototransistor in one case. When something opaque crosses the gap and obscures the light, then the switching action takes place.
	LDR:- a light dependant resistor. This decreases its resistance as more light falls on it.
	PHOTOTRANSISTOR:- this light is focussed onto the junction and will produce changes in collector current. Can be extremely sensistive and capable of fast operation.

Fig. 11.18 (continued)

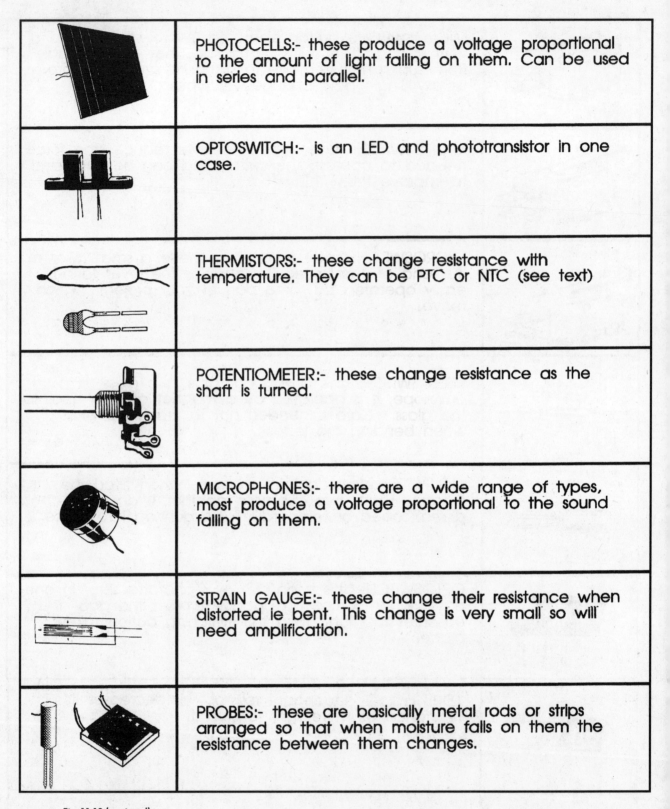

	PHOTOCELLS:- these produce a voltage proportional to the amount of light falling on them. Can be used in series and parallel.
	OPTOSWITCH:- is an LED and phototransistor in one case.
	THERMISTORS:- these change resistance with temperature. They can be PTC or NTC (see text)
	POTENTIOMETER:- these change resistance as the shaft is turned.
	MICROPHONES:- there are a wide range of types, most produce a voltage proportional to the sound falling on them.
	STRAIN GAUGE:- these change their resistance when distorted ie bent. This change is very small so will need amplification.
	PROBES:- these are basically metal rods or strips arranged so that when moisture falls on them the resistance between them changes.

Fig. 11.18 (continued)

A range of output devices is shown in Fig. 11.19.

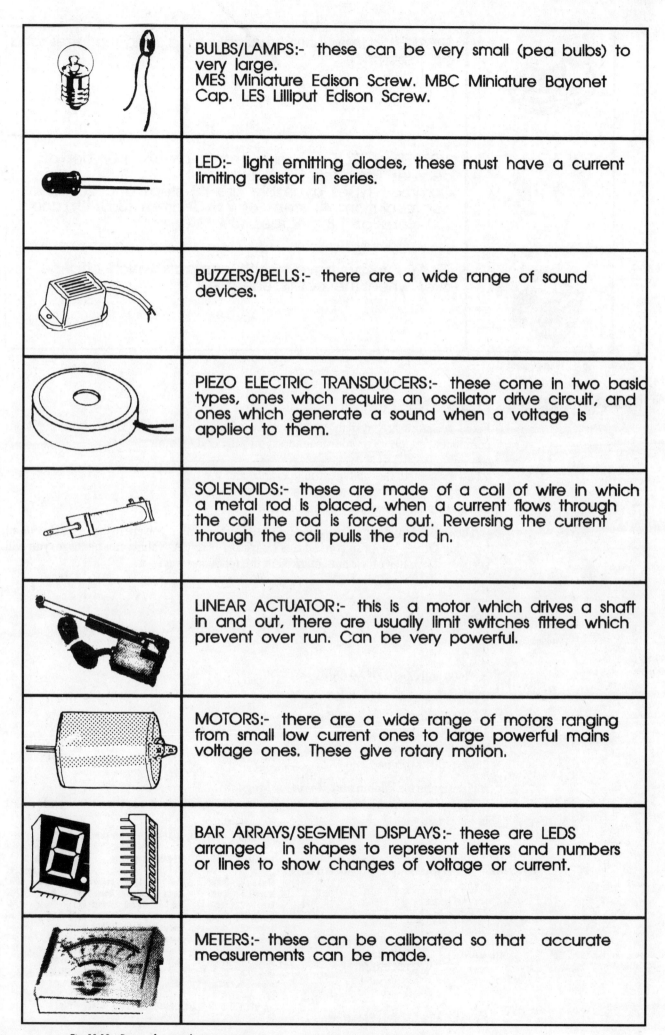

	BULBS/LAMPS:- these can be very small (pea bulbs) to very large. MES Miniature Edison Screw. MBC Miniature Bayonet Cap. LES Lilliput Edison Screw.
	LED:- light emitting diodes, these must have a current limiting resistor in series.
	BUZZERS/BELLS:- there are a wide range of sound devices.
	PIEZO ELECTRIC TRANSDUCERS:- these come in two basic types, ones whch require an oscillator drive circuit, and ones which generate a sound when a voltage is applied to them.
	SOLENOIDS:- these are made of a coil of wire in which a metal rod is placed, when a current flows through the coil the rod is forced out. Reversing the current through the coil pulls the rod in.
	LINEAR ACTUATOR:- this is a motor which drives a shaft in and out, there are usually limit switches fitted which prevent over run. Can be very powerful.
	MOTORS:- there are a wide range of motors ranging from small low current ones to large powerful mains voltage ones. These give rotary motion.
	BAR ARRAYS/SEGMENT DISPLAYS:- these are LEDS arranged in shapes to represent letters and numbers or lines to show changes of voltage or current.
	METERS:- these can be calibrated so that accurate measurements can be made.

Fig. 11.19   Range of output devices

	SPEAKER:- these are available in a range of sizes and coil resistances.
	STEPPER MOTOR:- these step a precise number of degrees for each input pulse. Common types available are 48 steps and 200 steps per revolution. 48 steps of 7.5 degrees (360/48) and 200 steps of 1.8 degrees (360/200)
	RELAY:- relays have switch contacts which change over when the coil is energised.

Fig. 11.19 (continued)

6 ▷ COMPONENTS

FIXED RESISTORS

Fixed resistors are available in a variety of types and sizes. When ordering from component suppliers or your teachers, you will need to know:

> The resistance, the wattage, the tolerance and the type.

e.g. 120 ohms, 1/4 watt, 10%, carbon film.

The *resistance* you require is usually stated on the circuit you are using or can be found by using Ohm's law or in some cases by trial or error. As values can be large, you will see resistor values on circuits marked in the following way:

66 Interpreting resistor values 99

R10
1K
1K2
2M
2M7

K =1000 and M=1000,000 ohms so:

R10=10 ohms
1K=1000 ohms
1k2=1200 ohms
2M=2000000 ohms
2M7=2700000 ohms

Kohm stands for kilohm and *Mohm* for Megohm.

The value is marked on the *component* by coloured bands; see the colour code chart in Fig. 11.20.

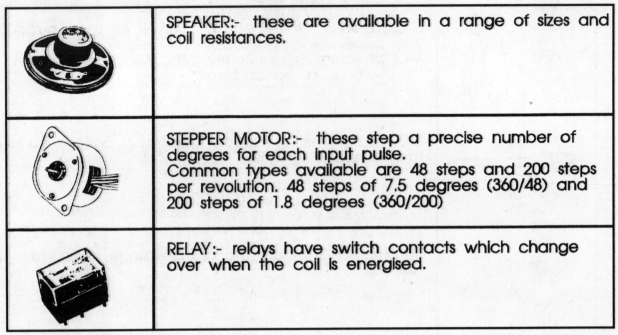

RESISTORS - COLOUR CODE: FIVE BAND TYPE

1st BAND		2nd BAND		3rd BAND		4th BAND		5th BAND (Tolerance)	
Black	0	Black	0	Black	0	Silver	Divide by 100	Brown	±1%
Brown	1	Brown	1	Brown	1	Gold	Divide by 10	Red	±2%
Red	2	Red	2	Red	2	Black	Multiply by 1	Gold	±5%
Orange	3	Orange	3	Orange	3	Brown	Multiply by 10	Silver	±10%
Yellow	4	Yellow	4	Yellow	4	Red	Multiply by 100		
Green	5	Green	5	Green	5	Orange	Multiply by 1,000		
Blue	6	Blue	6	Blue	6	Yellow	Multiply by 10,000		
Violet	7	Violet	7	Violet	7	Green	Multiply by 100,000		
Grey	8	Grey	8	Grey	8	Blue	Multiply by 1,000,000		
White	9	White	9	White	9				

e.g. WHITE, BROWN, BLACK, ORANGE, BROWN = 910KΩ ±1%

Fig. 11.20

(Colour code chart reproduced courtesy of Kelan Circuits Ltd.)

❝❝ Finding the wattage ❞❞

The *wattage* is found from the formula W=E x I

where W=watts
    E=voltage in volts (E stands for EMF Electromotive Force)
    I=current in Amps (Amperes)

In this type of circuit found in school most resistors will be 1/4 watt. The physical size is linked to the wattage, ie. a small resistor will usually be 0.125 or 0.25 watt.

❝❝ Finding the tolerance ❞❞

The *tolerance* is usually shown by a fourth band on the resistor and shows by how much the value of the resistor can be different to the measured value. A gold band shows that the resistor's value can be +– 5% of the stated value. A silver band +– 10% etc. Hence a 1000 ohm 10% tolerance resistor can be between 1100 ohms 900 ohms

1000+100=1100 ohms or 1000–100=900 ohms

The common range of resistors is between 1 ohm and 1 million ohms, this means that normally you would need to have to stock several of each value, however by taking advantage of the tolerances, one value can replace several fixed values. In the example above one resistor could replace many whose values would be between 900 and 1100 ohms.

This system is called *preferred values*. You will see in catalogues values such as 1.0, 1.2, 1.5, 1.8, 2.2, 2.7, 3.3, 3.9, 4.7, 5.6, 6.8 etc. These enable a limited range of values to be stocked for general use. For 10% tolerance there are multiples of 12 values and for 5% multiples of 24 values.

- **10% values** E12   10,12,15,18,22,27,33,39,47,56,68,82.
- **5% values** E24   10,11,12,13,15,16,18,20,22,24,27,30,
                    33,36,39,43,47,51,56,62,68,75,82,91.

Resistors can be multiples of these numbers, ie 15K, 3M3, 120R 4K7, 5M1. etc.

Should more accuracy be needed then higher tolerance resistors can be used although they are more expensive.

The main type in use is carbon film, however for lower noise, metal film is used and for higher wattage you will sometimes find wirewound resistors are used. When high wattage resistors are used they tend to get hot so you will see some which have metal cases which can be fixed to metal sheets to dissipate the heat.

VARIABLE RESISTORS

Variable Resistors are resistors which can be adjusted from zero to their stated values. You will have used them as the volume and tone controls on your cassette players and television sets. The correct name is a *potentiometer*. Most rotate through 300 degrees but some are multi-turn, i.e. capable of fine adjustment through up to 20 turns.

They are available in three main styles:-

- **Rotary:** these have a long shaft onto which a control knob will fit. The shaft is made of aluminium or plastic and can be easily cut to length with a junior hacksaw. There is a flat onto which the control knob locates when turned. They also have a threaded part and nut which can be fitted through a panel.

❝❝ Types of variable resistor ❞❞

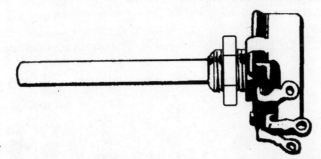

Fig. 11.21   Rotary potentiometer

- **Slide:** in these the control knob is designed to slide and not to rotate. These are often found on audio equipment.
- **Preset:** These are designed to be adjusted with a screwdriver, and are generally built into equipment, and are used to set up circuits but not for general use. They have legs which are designed to be fitted into printed circuit boards both to hold them and to

make electrical contact. The spacing of the legs will fit stripboard such as Veroboard. Some are made to stand vertically and others horizontally. Some have dust covers fitted and are called enclosed types, others are called open types.

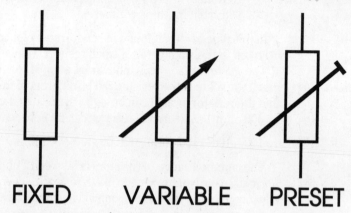

FIXED   VARIABLE   PRESET

Fig. 11.22

To order potentiometers you may need to quote:

| Resistance, size, style, type, wattage, type of track |

- 500K, miniature, volume control, carbon, 0.1 watt, linear.
- 200 ohm, vertical preset, miniature, cermet, logarithmic.
- 20K ohm, slider, carbon, logarithmic.

As with fixed resistors, they are made of different materials, the most common is carbon, but there are cermet types which are usually quite small and also wirewound for higher current applications.

There are three connections on potentiometers or variable resistors; one connection to each end of the track and one to a wiper which makes contact with the track along its length as the control knob or screwdriver slot is turned.

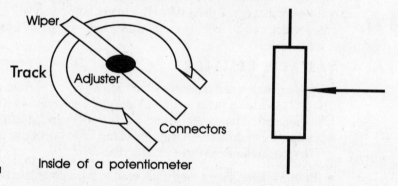

Inside of a potentiometer

Fig. 11.23   Connections on a potentiometer

If the track resistance changes evenly along its length, that is, if you turn the control to half way the resistance change is half the stated value, then the track is said to be linear. If the track's resistance increases towards the one end it is said to be logarithmic. The best way to understand this is to measure the value with a meter whilst turning the control. See Fig. 11.24. The most common use of logarithmic potentiometers is as a volume control on audio equipment. The words are often shortened to *Log* and *Lin*.

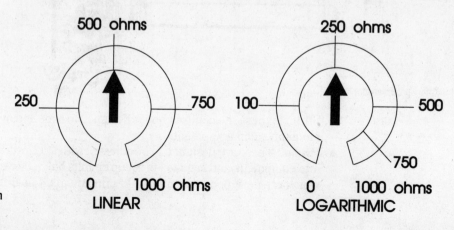

Fig. 11.24   The difference between linear and log tracks

Formulae for resistors in series and parallel

Resistors in Series

$R_{total} = R_1 + R_2 + R_3$

Resistors in Parallel

$$\frac{1}{R_{total}} = \frac{1}{R_1} + \frac{1}{R_2} + \frac{1}{R_3}$$

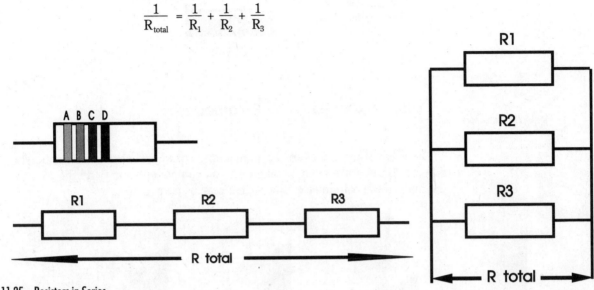

Fig. 11.25   Resistors in Series and Parallel

Capacitors

Sometimes *capacitors* are called "condensers" in older books; these devices store electrical charge and are often used in timer circuits. You will need to know the following to order these components:-

Capacity, type, working voltage, connection type.

e.g. ■ 100 mfd electrolytic, 25 volts, axial leads.
■ 10 pfd polyester, 100 volts, PCB mount.

The capacity is measured in *Farads* (after Faraday) although you will never see such a large value. They are normally much smaller than this and measured in picofarads(pfd), nanofarads(nfd), or microfarads(mfd).

1 pfd = 1/1000,000,000,000F
1 nfd = 1/1000,000,000F
1 mfd = 1/1000,000F

Values are mostly written on capacitors, although there are several colour codes similar to resistor ones, but it is best for you to look these up in the manufacturer's data.

There are many different types of capacitor all designed to do different tasks, but in school work on electronics you may only see a few types. Most of the names refer to the material from which they are made.

Types of capacitor

Paper	expensive, accurate, low loss
Polycarbon	cheap, general purpose
Tantalum	very small yet high capacity
Electrolytic	large values, high leakage, general purpose
Mica	small values used in radio, television circuits
Ceramic	high quality
Polystyrene	low loss, cheap, general purpose
Polyester	for printed circuits, high values in small space

If you need further details of the types of capacitor, you should refer to manufacturer's data or catalogues of suppliers such as RS Components of Maplin.

Both tantalum and electrolytic capacitors are polarised, that is they must be connected into your circuit in the correct polarity. The body of the capacitor is marked to show which lead is the positive one. The capacitor will be damaged if connected the wrong way round.

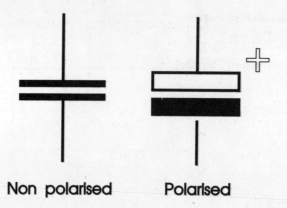

Fig. 11.26 Capacitors   Non polarised   Polarised

The leads of capacitors come out in a range of ways; below is a diagram showing the different types. Care must be taken with all components not bend the wire too close to the body of the component otherwise it may be damaged.

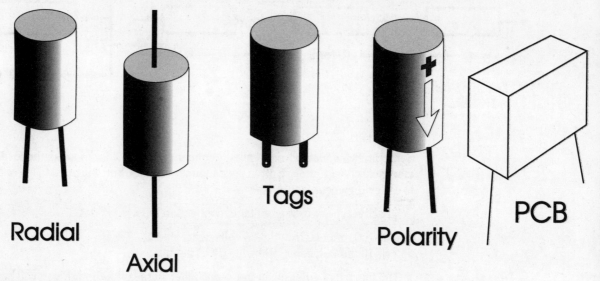

Radial   Axial   Tags   Polarity   PCB

Fig. 11.27 Different types of leads of capacitors

All capacitors have a working voltage that must not be exceeded. This is usually written on them. Providing you do not exceed the voltage you can use, for instance, a 200 volts DC capacitor in a 9 volt circuit but not vice versa. Tantalum capacitors are really sensitive to excessive voltage.

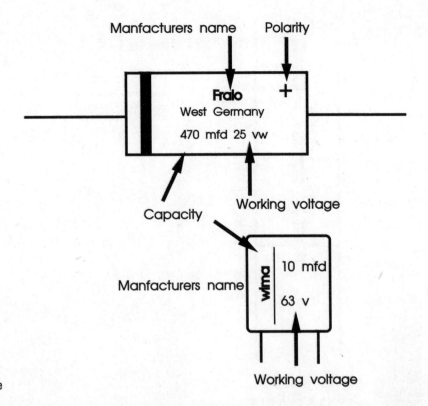

Fig.11.28 Capacitors and
working voltage

■ **Capacitors in Series** (Fig. 11.29)

$$\frac{1}{C_{tot}} = \frac{1}{C_1} + \frac{1}{C_2} + \frac{1}{C_3}$$

Working voltages add together.

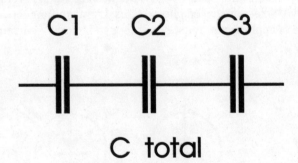

Fig. 11.29 Capacitors in
Series

■ **Capacitors in Parallel** (Fig 11.30)

$$\frac{1}{C_{tot}} = \frac{1}{C_1} + \frac{1}{C_2} + \frac{1}{C_3}$$

All the working voltages must be greater than the voltage applied.
This is the opposite for resistors, do you remember?
There are variable capacitors called *trimmer capacitors* usually only in very small
capacities.

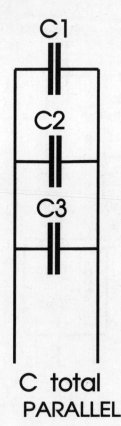

Fig. 11.30   Capacitors in Parallel

Diodes

Diodes pass current in one direction but not in the other. It has an anode and a cathode (sometimes spelt kathode). The cathode is shown by a bar both on the diode itself and on its circuit symbol. For it to conduct the anode must be positive. Zener diodes try to maintain a constant voltage across themselves when reverse biased. Diodes which are sensitive to light are called photodiodes. Light emitting diodes will produce a light when voltage is applied, you must remember to include a current limiting resistor in series with it.

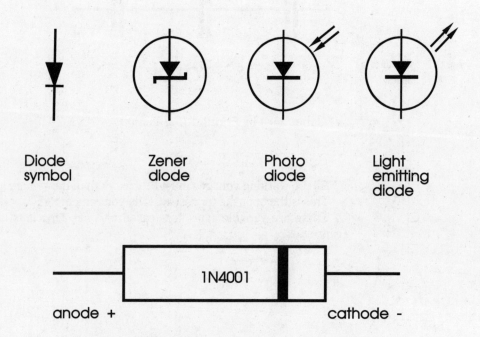

Fig. 11.31   Diodes

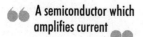

A semiconductor which amplifies current

Transistors

Transistors are *semiconductor* devices which amplify current. You can take a small current change and amplify it so that it will operate, for instance, a relay, which in turn can be used to control a powerful motor.

There are two main forms of transistor, PNP which has a negative voltage on its collector, and an NPN which requires a positive voltage. NPN and PNP refer to how the transistor is constructed internally. Commonly used transistors in school are BFY51, BC107, BC108, BC109.

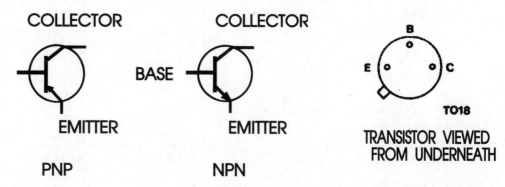

Fig. 11.32

Transistors have a variety of shapes and lead configurations. You must make sure that you connect them correctly. Fig. 11.33 is a data sheet which shows some of the bases of the various types.

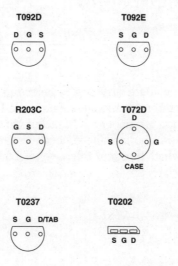

Fig. 11.33

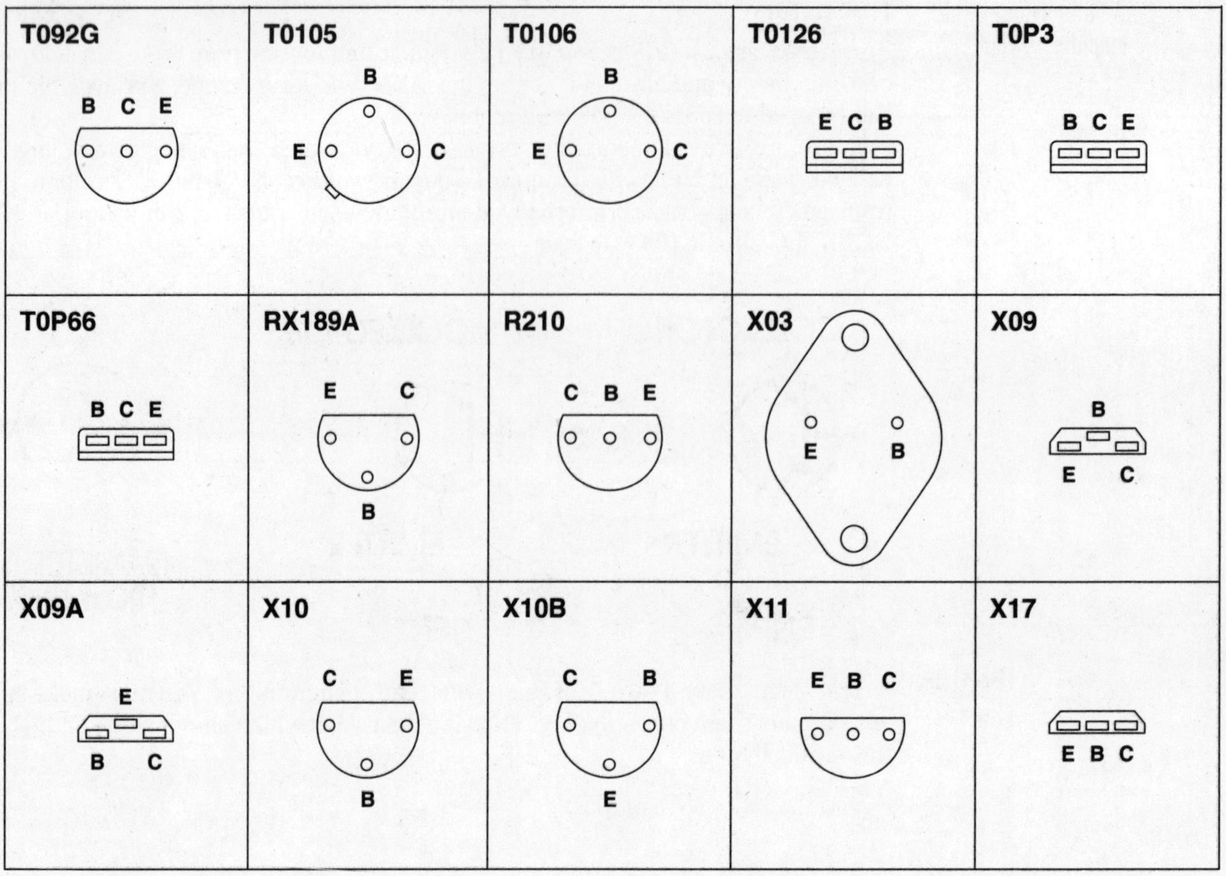

T092G	T0105	T0106	T0126	T0P3
B C E	B / E C	B / E C	E C B	B C E

T0P66	RX189A	R210	X03	X09
B C E	E C / B	C B E	E B	B / E C

X09A	X10	X10B	X11	X17
E / B C	C E / B	C B / E	E B C	E B C

Fig. 11.33 (continued)

When you are ordering or selecting transistors you will need to look them up in a manufacturers or suppliers data book. Fig 11.34 is a typical page from a supplier with a description of what each characteristic means. Some circuits will indicate that a general purpose PNP transistor is needed so selection is really easy, others will leave you to decide which type you will have to obtain.

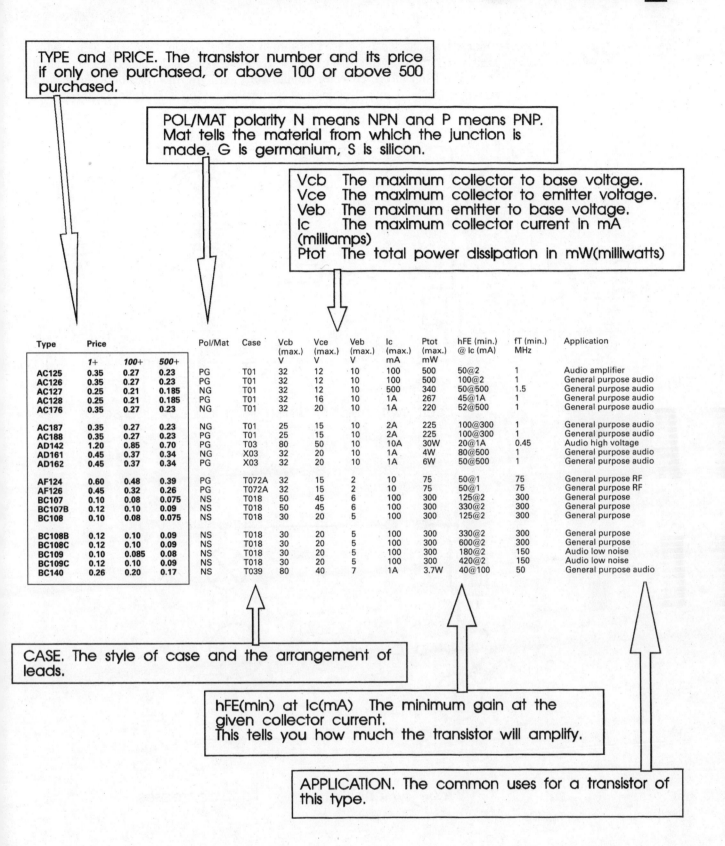

TYPE and PRICE. The transistor number and its price if only one purchased, or above 100 or above 500 purchased.

POL/MAT polarity N means NPN and P means PNP. Mat tells the material from which the junction is made. G is germanium, S is silicon.

Vcb The maximum collector to base voltage.
Vce The maximum collector to emitter voltage.
Veb The maximum emitter to base voltage.
Ic   The maximum collector current in mA (milliamps)
Ptot The total power dissipation in mW(milliwatts)

Type	Price			Pol/Mat	Case	Vcb (max.) V	Vce (max.) V	Veb (max.) V	Ic (max.) mA	Ptot (max.) mW	hFE (min.) @ Ic (mA)	fT (min.) MHz	Application
	1+	100+	500+										
AC125	0.35	0.27	0.23	PG	T01	32	12	10	100	500	50@2	1	Audio amplifier
AC126	0.35	0.27	0.23	PG	T01	32	12	10	100	500	100@2	1	General purpose audio
AC127	0.25	0.21	0.185	NG	T01	32	12	10	500	340	50@500	1.5	General purpose audio
AC128	0.25	0.21	0.185	PG	T01	32	16	10	1A	267	45@1A	1	General purpose audio
AC176	0.35	0.27	0.23	NG	T01	32	20	10	1A	220	52@500	1	General purpose audio
AC187	0.35	0.27	0.23	NG	T01	25	15	10	2A	225	100@300	1	General purpose audio
AC188	0.35	0.27	0.23	PG	T01	25	15	10	2A	225	100@300	1	General purpose audio
AD142	1.20	0.85	0.70	PG	T03	80	50	10	10A	30W	20@1A	0.45	Audio high voltage
AD161	0.45	0.37	0.34	NG	X03	32	20	10	1A	4W	80@500	1	General purpose audio
AD162	0.45	0.37	0.34	PG	X03	32	20	10	1A	6W	50@500	1	General purpose audio
AF124	0.60	0.48	0.39	PG	T072A	32	15	2	10	75	50@1	75	General purpose RF
AF126	0.45	0.32	0.26	PG	T072A	32	15	2	10	75	50@1	75	General purpose RF
BC107	0.10	0.08	0.075	NS	T018	50	45	6	100	300	125@2	300	General purpose
BC107B	0.12	0.10	0.09	NS	T018	50	45	6	100	300	330@2	300	General purpose
BC108	0.10	0.08	0.075	NS	T018	30	20	5	100	300	125@2	300	General purpose
BC108B	0.12	0.10	0.09	NS	T018	30	20	5	100	300	330@2	300	General purpose
BC108C	0.12	0.10	0.09	NS	T018	30	20	5	100	300	600@2	300	General purpose
BC109	0.10	0.085	0.08	NS	T018	30	20	5	100	300	180@2	150	Audio low noise
BC109C	0.12	0.10	0.09	NS	T018	30	20	5	100	300	420@2	150	Audio low noise
BC140	0.26	0.20	0.17	NS	T039	80	40	7	1A	3.7W	40@100	50	General purpose audio

CASE. The style of case and the arrangement of leads.

hFE(min) at Ic(mA) The minimum gain at the given collector current.
This tells you how much the transistor will amplify.

APPLICATION. The common uses for a transistor of this type.

Fig. 11.34 Transistor Characteristics (Reproduced by kind permission of Rapid Electronics Ltd.)

Single transistors can be used as simple amplifiers as in the circuit below, when a small current flows in the base circuit, a larger one flows in the collector circuit. In this circuit the lamp in the collector circuit will then light, the resistor R1 protects the transistor against damage and in most circuits can be approximately 1k ohm.

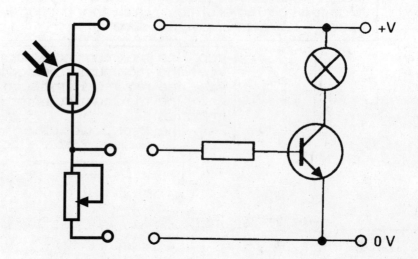

Circuit switches on when light on LDR increases

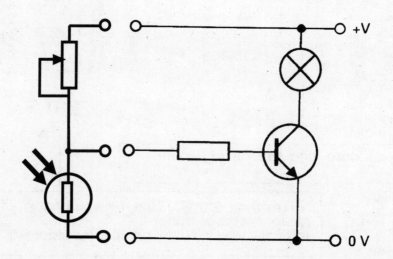

Circuit switches off when light decreases

Fig. 11.35

An even more useful circuit is the *Darlington Pair* which can be used for a range of switching purposes. This circuit, which is an improvement on the ones above, switches very positively due to the high gain of the two transistors TR1 and TR2.

A typical use is shown below, in the circuit when the light increases on the LDR its resistance drops and the circuit switches on, the point at which it switches can be set by the variable resistor R2.

If the opposite action is required, then the position of the LDR and resistor can be changed resulting in the circuit switching when less light falls on the LDR.

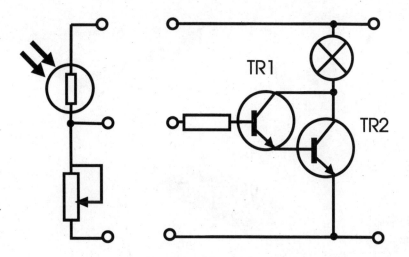

Circuit switches on when light on LDR increases

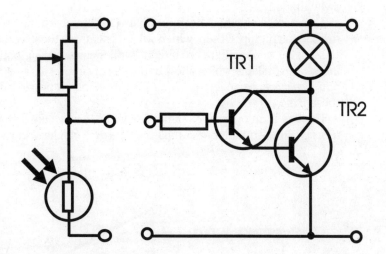

Fig. 11.36   Circuit switches off when light decreases

Integrated circuits

Integrated circuits (ICs) can be useful in building either quite simple or complicated circuits. Thousands of components and transistors can be etched onto a small silicon chip using photographic methods which is then protected by encapsulation in resin. As pointed out in the Systems chapter, you do not need to know what goes on inside of the chip, only how to connect it into your circuit.

Fig. 11.37 Integrated circuits and IC socket

The ICs can be soldered directly into printed circuit boards or plugged into sockets. It is a good idea to always use sockets as this makes fault finding easier, also ICs can be damaged by the heat from the soldering iron. Damage will also occur if you connect the power supply the wrong way around. These are semiconductor devices and are sensitive to over voltage and incorrect polarity so always carefully check your circuit prior to switching on.

The most likely ones that you will use in school are the 741 operational amplifier and the 555 timer chip. Others which will be useful are those containing gates and counters. In most DT books, there are circuits with ideas for using both of these chips. Specialist books are available which show hundreds of circuits for a particular chip, one being *The 555 Cookbook*. Suppliers such as RS Components provide data sheets on how to use these ICs.

The 741 is an operational amplifier which can be used as a single input inverting or non inverting amplifier or comparator. Its gain can be accurately set by using feedback.

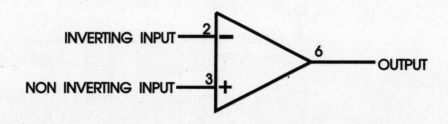

CIRCUIT SYMBOLS FOR IC WITH PIN NUMBERS

Fig. 11.38

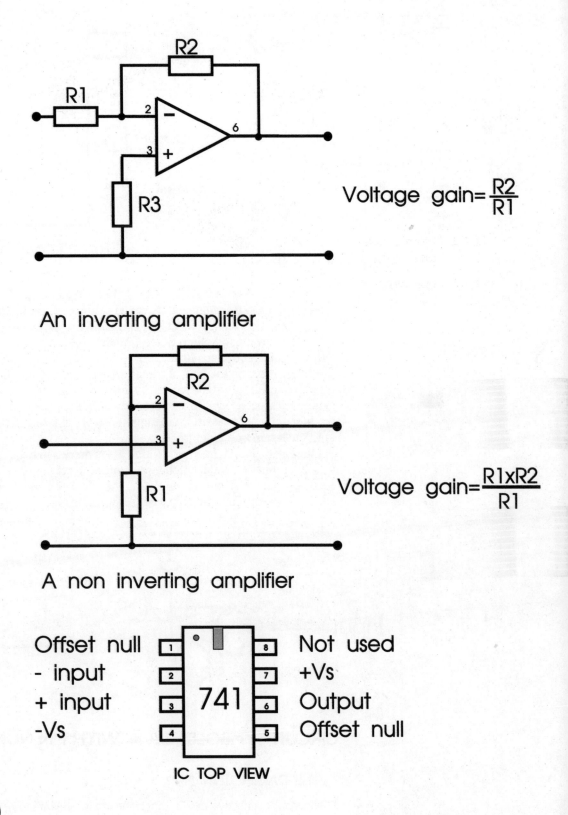

An inverting amplifier

$$\text{Voltage gain} = \frac{R2}{R1}$$

A non inverting amplifier

$$\text{Voltage gain} = \frac{R1 \times R2}{R1}$$

Offset null 1 ... 8 Not used
- input 2 ... 7 +Vs
+ input 3 ... 741 ... 6 Output
-Vs 4 ... 5 Offset null

IC TOP VIEW

Fig. 11.38 (continued)

The 555 is basically a timer chip and can be arranged as a monostable, bistable or astable oscillator. It can be triggered by pulses to provide time delays. The 556 is a dual version of this popular chip and there is a CMOS version which takes less current called 555C or 7555.

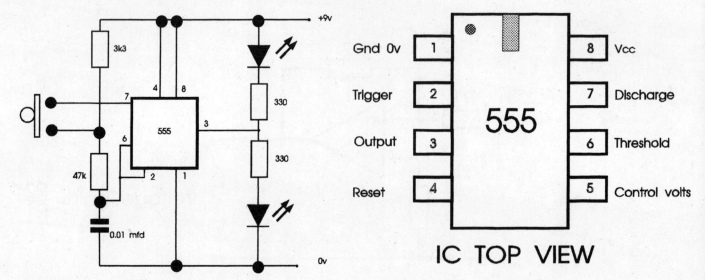

Fig. 11.39 A heads and tails circuit

IC TOP VIEW

The most common digital ICs likely to be used are either TTL (Transistor transistor logic) or CMOS (complementary metal oxide semiconductors) types.

TTL require a supply of 5 volts and CMOS a supply of 3–15 volts, both types have advantages over each other. Some CMOS types may be damaged by touching the pins, although the common 4000B series have built in protection. Static voltages can discharge through the pins of some ICs and can damage them. Your body can become highly charged with static electricity, caused by the clothes you wear also by walking on synthetic carpets. Usually the pins of these ICS are pushed into conducting foam plastic or aluminium foil to short them together to prevent this happening. Do not remove this until the last moment before use.

Integrated circuits have pins which are arranged in two rows usually called DIL (dual in line) and have a small notch to tell you which is pin one. Most common ones have 8, 12 or 16 pins. Pin one is always at the top left hand side and you count the pins anticlockwise around the chip, viewed from the top.

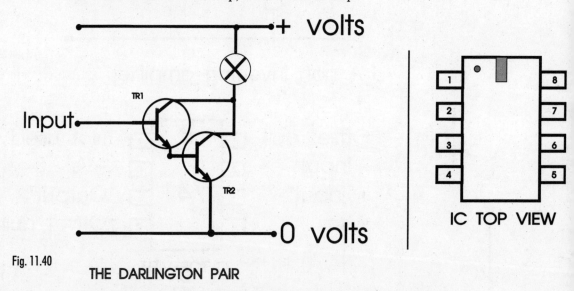

Fig. 11.40

THE DARLINGTON PAIR

IC TOP VIEW

The symbols used in circuit diagrams are as shown in Fig. 11.41.

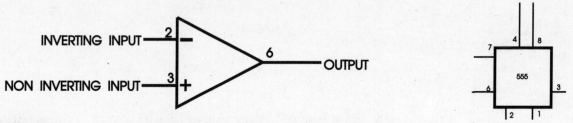

Fig. 11.41 Circuit symbols for 741 and 555 ICS with pin numbers

Gates and logic

Gates are digital circuits which are used to combine inputs. Imagine a machine which has some dangerous parts ie a mixing machine in a bakery, a guillotine in a paper factory. For instance, it may be necessary to ensure that both of the operator's hands are away from the dangerous part of the machine before it is started. This could be ensured by putting two start buttons on the machine so that the operator would have to press both of them before the machine would start. If either of the switches were released the machine would stop. The switches would have to be put apart so that both could not be pressed with one hand. The machine would only start if input A and input B are present, if either signal disappears the machine will stop. Similarly, if a door needed to be opened from either side then the output from two switches could be used as the inputs to an OR gate. An output would be available if either one or the other switch was operated.

There are NOT, AND, NAND, OR and NOR gates. Their states are described by Truth Tables. The input are usually named A, B, C etc and the output is usually shown as Q. The states of the inputs and output are 0 if off and 1 if on.

Fig. 11.42 shows symbols and the truth tables for the common gates.

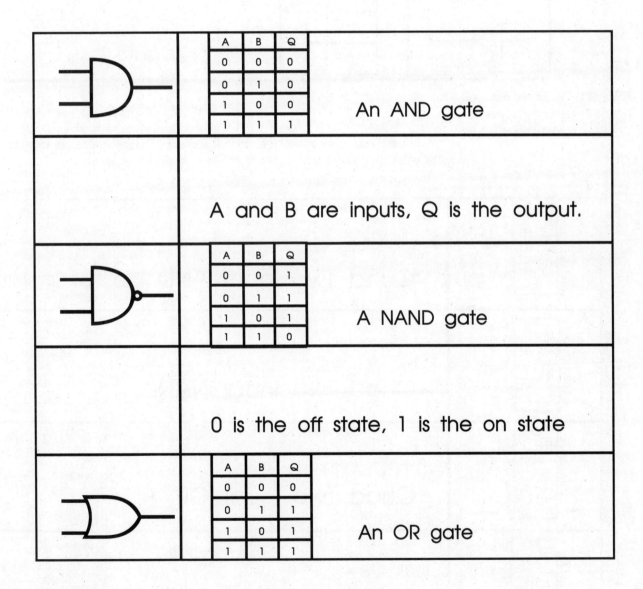

A	B	Q
0	0	0
0	1	0
1	0	0
1	1	1

An AND gate

A and B are inputs, Q is the output.

A	B	Q
0	0	1
0	1	1
1	0	1
1	1	0

A NAND gate

0 is the off state, 1 is the on state

A	B	Q
0	0	0
0	1	1
1	0	1
1	1	1

An OR gate

Fig. 11.42   Symbols and Truth Tables for Common Gates

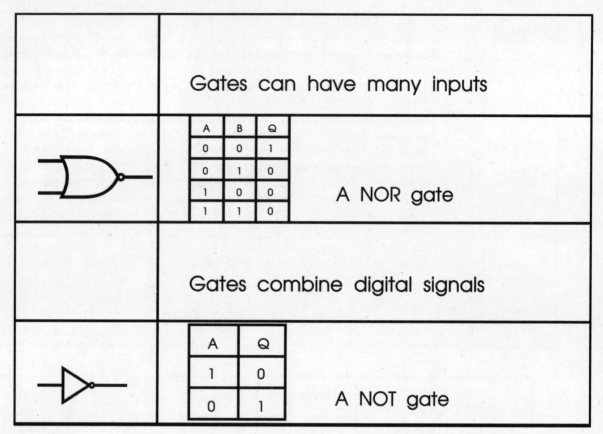

Gates can have many inputs		

A NOR gate

A	B	Q
0	0	1
0	1	0
1	0	0
1	1	0

Gates combine digital signals

A NOT gate

A	Q
1	0
0	1

Fig. 11.42   Symbols and Truth
Tables for Common
Gates (continued)

Some gates can have up to eight inputs, and common integrated circuits can have many gates in one package. Fig. 11.43 shows a range of logic gates.

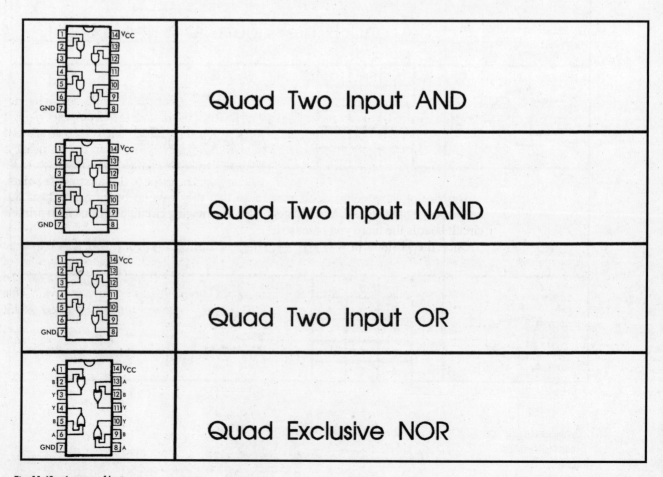

Quad Two Input AND

Quad Two Input NAND

Quad Two Input OR

Quad Exclusive NOR

Fig. 11.43   A range of logic gates

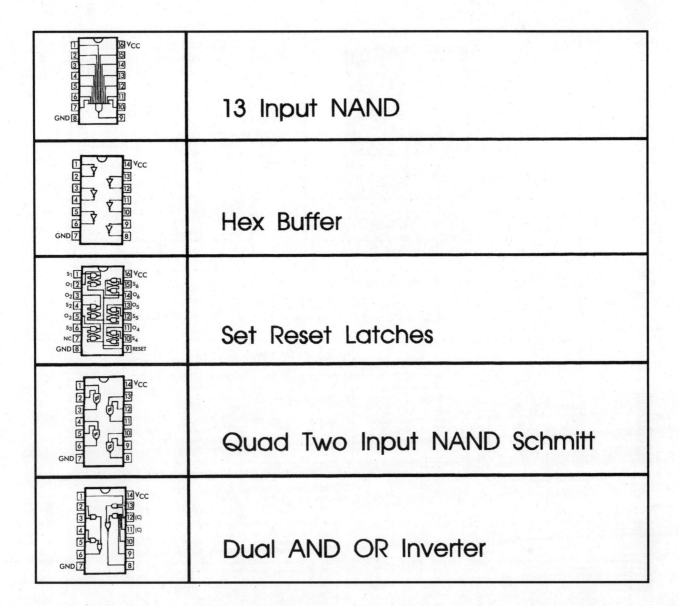

	13 Input NAND
	Hex Buffer
	Set Reset Latches
	Quad Two Input NAND Schmitt
	Dual AND OR Inverter

Fig. 11.43 A range of logic gates (continued)

Printed circuit boards

When you have designed and made sure that your electronic circuit works as you intend, you will need to tidy it up and make a *printed circuit board*. Printed circuits are good if you have a number of similar circuits to make; if you have only one then a stripboard such as Veroboard could be used. You may have prototyped your circuit using a breadboard, such as a SDec. You can then see that some components may have to be rearranged so that they fit neatly and connections can be made to the appropriate points.

The size of some components may mean that they have to be moved to near the outside edge of the board. You will get better at arranging circuit diagrams onto printed circuit boards the more you practise it.

Once the position of each component is settled, you will need to check that all connections are correct. Then the layout of your PCB can be started. There a number of different ways in which this can be done. You could transfer the layout of the components onto tracing paper and then turn it over and put in the track layout. This layout can then be transferred to the PCB. Fig. 11.44 shows a typical printed circuit board and a component overlay.

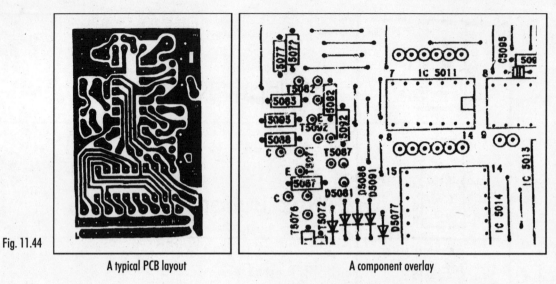

Fig. 11.44

A typical PCB layout   A component overlay

Fig. 11.45 contains a description of the most common methods of producing PCBs.

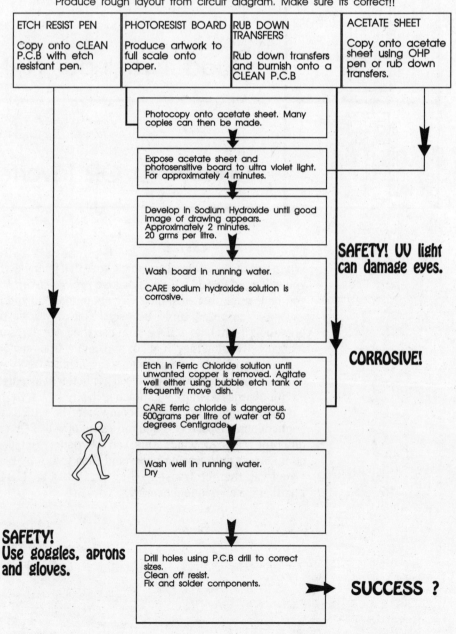

Making Printed Circuit Boards

Produce rough layout from circuit diagram. Make sure its correct!!

ETCH RESIST PEN	PHOTORESIST BOARD	RUB DOWN TRANSFERS	ACETATE SHEET
Copy onto CLEAN P.C.B with etch resistant pen.	Produce artwork to full scale onto paper.	Rub down transfers and burnish onto a CLEAN P.C.B	Copy onto acetate sheet using OHP pen or rub down transfers.

Photocopy onto acetate sheet. Many copies can then be made.

Expose acetate sheet and photosensitive board to ultra violet light. For approximately 4 minutes.

Develop in Sodium Hydroxide until good image of drawing appears. Approximately 2 minutes. 20 grms per litre.

Wash board in running water.

CARE sodium hydroxide solution is corrosive.

SAFETY! UV light can damage eyes.

Etch in Ferric Chloride solution until unwanted copper is removed. Agitate well either using bubble etch tank or frequently move dish.

CARE ferric chloride is dangerous. 500grams per litre of water at 50 degrees Centigrade.

CORROSIVE!

Wash well in running water. Dry

SAFETY! Use goggles, aprons and gloves.

Drill holes using P.C.B drill to correct sizes. Clean off resist. Fix and solder components.

SUCCESS ?

Fig. 11.45

There are computer programmes which make the design of the boards easy which also generate component overlays. Some will automatically join the various points of the circuit for you by the best routes, these are called *auto routing programmes*. All allow you to plot out the PCB design directly onto the clean copper face of the board using a plotter and a etch resistant pen, or to print out onto clear acetate sheet. This can then be transferred to the board by using photosensitive board.

All the methods put the track pattern onto the copper side of the board using a resist, this prevents the etchant (ferric chloride) from etching away those parts not covered with the resist.

You will need to keep checking that the process is working properly. If you leave the board in the etchant too long then some of your fine lines may be etched away by mistake.

When the board has been etched the holes for the components will need to be drilled.

The components can then be soldered into place. You must make sure that the solder does not bridge the tracks, if it does it can be carefully removed using a desoldering tool.

Soldering components

When *soldering components* several aspects are the same as for soldering any metal:

- The correct temperature
- The correct solder
- The correct flux
- Clean metal

When soldering electronic components there are a few more things to remember:

- Components are easily damaged by heat. Use a heat shunt. Do not allow the iron to stay on the joint for too long.

Useful hints when soldering

- Use electrical solder 60/40 Lead/Tin.
- Use a passive flux ie resin cored solder.
- Make sure that the solder does not bridge tracks on the PCB.
- Keep the bit of the soldering iron clean. Some plated bits just need wiping on a wet sponge. Plain copper bits may need filing.

Heat both component lead and copper strip equally otherwise a dry joint will result. Good soldered joints will look shiny and the solder will have flowed evenly. Dry joints will be frosted and usually the solder will be in a small ball.

If you intend to modify your circuit then it is a good idea not to bend over the component leads as this makes removal of the components difficult. If however, the circuit is to be built to last then make a good mechanical joint by bending over the leads before soldering.

7 > EQUATIONS AND CALCULATIONS

The following are examples of the electrical/electronic equations and calculations you need to be familiar with.

Candidates should use, where appropriate, the formulae given below when answering questions which include calculations.

1. Work done = force x distance moved in the direction of the force ($W = f \times d$)

2. Kinetic Energy = $\frac{1}{2}$ x mass x (velocity)^2 ($KE = \frac{1}{2} \times m \times v^2$)

3. Potential Energy = mass x gravitational field strength x height ($PE = mgh$)

4. Energy = potential difference x current x time ($E = VIt$)

5. Power = $\dfrac{\text{work done}}{\text{time taken}}$

6. Electrical Power = current x potential difference

7. Efficiency = $\dfrac{\text{work output}}{\text{work input}} \times 100\%$

    or = $\dfrac{\text{energy output}}{\text{energy input}} \times 100\%$

Fig 11.46 Formulae for calculations

8. Potential Difference = current x resistance ($V = IR$)

9. For potential divider

$$V_1 = \frac{R_1}{(R_1 + R_2)} \times V$$

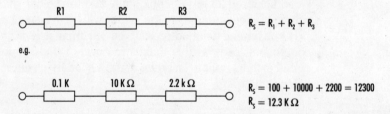

10. Series Resistors $R_{TOTAL} = R_1 + R_2 + R_3$ etc.

    Parallel Resistors $\dfrac{1}{R_{TOTAL}} = \dfrac{1}{R_1} + \dfrac{1}{R_2} + \dfrac{1}{R_3}$ etc.

11. Series batteries $V_{TOTAL} = V_1 + V_2 + V_3$

12. Moment of a force   = force x perpendicular distance from pivot

13. For equilibrium
    Sum of clockwise moments = Sum of anticlockwise moments
    Sum of coplanar forces = zero

14. Gear ratio of a simple gear train = $\dfrac{\text{number of teeth on driver gear}}{\text{number of teeth on driven gear}}$

(N.B. For a compound gear train

    Total Gear Ratio = the product of the gear ratios of all the sub-systems
    i.e. $G.R_T = G.R_1 \times G.R_2 \times G.R_3$ ... etc.)

Fig. 11.46 Formulae for calculations (continued)

▶ **Resistors in series**

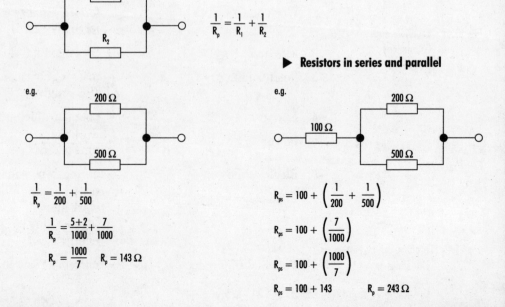

$R_s = R_1 + R_2 + R_3$

e.g.

$R_s = 100 + 10000 + 2200 = 12300$
$R_s = 12.3\,K\Omega$

▶ **Resistors in parallel**

$\dfrac{1}{R_p} = \dfrac{1}{R_1} + \dfrac{1}{R_2}$

▶ **Resistors in series and parallel**

e.g.

$\dfrac{1}{R_p} = \dfrac{1}{200} + \dfrac{1}{500}$

$\dfrac{1}{R_p} = \dfrac{5+2}{1000} + \dfrac{7}{1000}$

$R_p = \dfrac{1000}{7} \qquad R_p = 143\,\Omega$

e.g.

$R_{ps} = 100 + \left(\dfrac{1}{200} + \dfrac{1}{500} \right)$

$R_{ps} = 100 + \left(\dfrac{7}{1000} \right)$

$R_{ps} = 100 + \left(\dfrac{1000}{7} \right)$

$R_{ps} = 100 + 143 \qquad R_p = 243\,\Omega$

Fig. 11.47 Equations and Calculations

▶ **Capacitors in parallel**

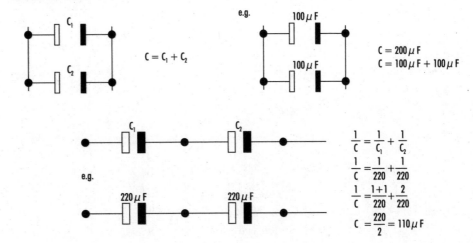

$C = C_1 + C_2$

e.g.

$C = 200\,\mu F$
$C = 100\,\mu F + 100\,\mu F$

$$\frac{1}{C} = \frac{1}{C_1} + \frac{1}{C_2}$$
$$\frac{1}{C} = \frac{1}{220} + \frac{1}{220}$$
$$\frac{1}{C} = \frac{1+1}{220} + \frac{2}{220}$$
$$C = \frac{220}{2} = 110\,\mu F$$

▶ **Ohm's Law**

voltage = current x resistance or $V = I \times R$

try to remember

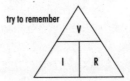

This can be used to calculate a potential divider

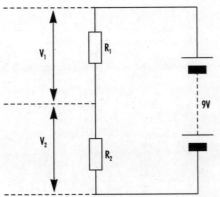

If we assume the current through the potential divider is to be 1m A (0.001 A). Using Ohm's Law we can calculate the total resistance of $R_1 + R_2$ where a current of 1mA flows as a result of applying 9 volts.

$$R = \frac{V}{I} = \frac{9}{0.001} = 9000\,\Omega = 9K\,\Omega$$

$$\therefore R = 9\,K\,\Omega$$

If 3 volts is to be produced across resistor R_2 and a current of 1mA is flowing through R_2 then

$$R_2 = \frac{V}{I} = \frac{3}{0.001} = 3000\,\Omega = 3K\,\Omega$$

$\therefore R_2 = 3\,K\,\Omega$

Since R_1 and R_2 are in series
$R_1 + R_2 = 9000\,\Omega$
$R_1 + 3000 = 9000$
$R_1 = 9000 - 3000 = 6000\,\Omega$
$\therefore R_1 = 6\,k\,\Omega$

The voltage drops across R_1 will be 6 volts since
$V_1 = IR$
$V_1 = 0.001 \times 6000$
$V_1 = 6$ volts
Note the ratio of $\dfrac{R_1}{R_2}$ is the same as $\dfrac{V_1}{V_2}$

Fig. 11.47 Equations and Calculations (continued)

REVIEW SHEET

SYSTEMS

■ Why is the systems approach a good way of designing electronic systems?

_____

_____

_____

■ What are the main building blocks of a system?

_____

_____

_____

■ Explain the difference between analogue and digital systems.

_____

_____

_____

■ Name three input devices.

_____

_____

_____

■ Describe the action of one processing device.

_____

_____

_____

■ Light dependent resistors respond quite slowly to changes of light. What other types of light sensors are faster?

_____

_____

_____

■ What precautions do you have to take when bending the leads of components?

_____

_____

■ Using a LDR, how could you make it sense movement?

_____

_____

■ How could you make a sensor which would respond to rain?

_____

_____

■ If you required an electrical component to open a door in a project, what could you use?

_____

_____

COMPONENTS

■ Describe how the values of resistors and capacitors are shown on them.

_____
_____
_____

■ What does the term tolerance mean?

_____
_____
_____

■ Explain the term preferred values.

_____
_____
_____

■ List three types of capacitor and the main advantage of using the type.

_____
_____
_____

■ What is the main difference between PNP and NPN transistors?

_____
_____
_____

■ What precautions need to be taken when soldering semiconductors?

_____
_____
_____

■ For what could a darlington pair circuit be used?

_____
_____
_____

■ What are the advantages of using integrated circuits?

_____
_____
_____

■ What does TTL and CMOS stand for?

_____
_____
_____

■ Describe why gates are used in electronic systems.

_____
_____
_____

■ Describe the stages for producing a printed circuit board from the circuit diagram.

_____
_____

MECHANISMS

GETTING STARTED

Machines, such as those illustrated on pages 155–157, are examples of a family of mechanical devices. The car, bus, train or bicycle are all examples of mechanical devices. Many of them appear to be quite complicated and so advanced in their design that an understanding of how they work is going to be extremely difficult to follow. This need not be the case if one mechanism is studied at a time.

A **mechanism** is a device for changing one kind of force into another, and for transferring it from one place to another. For example if you use a bottle-top opener, you apply a lifting force with the handle and a *more powerful* force is *transferred* to the bottle-top, making it possible for the top to be removed. Try to remove the top by pressing with your thumbs and the top will not move because you are unable to apply sufficient force to the point where it is needed. A screwdriver is another mechanism where the transference of a force is essential for it to be able to turn a screw. These are not as complicated as the examples given earlier and yet they are examples of mechanisms.

The examples given all have one thing in common: *movement*. In reading other books you may come across such headings as, "The way things move", or "How to produce movement". Such titles are referring to *Mechanisms*.

The different *types* of mechanism include levers, pulleys, gears, cams and cranks.

LEVERS

MOMENTS

CHANGING DIRECTION OF MOVEMENT

PULLEYS

BELT AND CHAIN DRIVES

GEARS

SCREWS

CAMS AND CRANKS

RATCHET AND PAWL

ESSENTIAL PRINCIPLES

1 LEVERS

This is a simple mechanism, the principle of which was discovered and applied many thousands of years ago. It is believed that the heavy boulders of rock in ancient monuments could have only been moved by people who knew something about levers.

Levers consist of a *beam*, and a *pivot*. The beam can be placed on the pivot and remain balanced in a horizontal position. As soon as a weight or load is placed on one end, that end of the beam will lower itself until it meets the floor or ground. To raise the load into the horizontal position again, a force that is *equal* to the load has to be applied at the *opposite* end of the beam. The beam will then return to the horizontal position. If the force is *greater*, then the load will be raised to a *higher* position until the beam can no longer pivot. The advantage is gained when the pivoting point of the beam is nearer to one end.

The three classes of lever can be seen in Fig. 12.1.

It is important for you to know an example of each so that you can show that you really understand the differences.

EXAMPLES

1st class lever
Crowbar, claw hammer, pincers (two 1st class levers working together).
2nd class levers
Wheel barrow, bottle-top opener, nut crackers.
3rd class levers
Fishing rod, instrument tweezers, spade.

2 MOMENTS

The forces acting on a lever cause it to rotate. This effect is dependent upon the *distance* the *force* is away from the *pivot* (or *fulcrum*). If you imagine a 1st class lever such as a see-saw, with the pivot in the centre and children of equal weight at either end, then the see-saw will be balanced. The forces acting at either end of the pivot are equal and opposite and are said to be in a state of *equilibrium*. If the children were not of equal weight, or the pivoting point was not in the centre, then the see-saw would rotate and this turning force is known as a **MOMENT**.

Moments can be calculated so that the effort required to move a load can be worked out. The ratio between the load to be moved and the effort required is known as **MECHANICAL ADVANTAGE** (Fig. 12.2).

The formula used is:

$$\text{Mechanical Advantage} = \frac{\text{Load}}{\text{Effort}}$$

Moments can be used to work out an unknown load or distance on a beam. The example has a load missing. To keep the beam in equilibrium what must be the effort made or load (Fig. 12.3)?

When you are applying a force on a spanner you can work out the force that is applied to the nut by multiplying the distance from the fulcrum (pivot) by the force (Fig. 12.4).

3 CHANGING DIRECTION OF MOVEMENT

- The movement of a simple lever can make a forward input motion go in the reverse direction as an output motion, as shown in Fig. 12.5 (a).
- Or the same action can change a small input motion into a large output motion by changing the position of the fulcrum, as shown in Fig. 12.5 (b).
- To make the input motion and the output motion the same, then two levers are needed, as shown in Fig. 12. 5 (c).
- To change an input motion into an output motion at 90°, the device known as a "Bell crank" is used. A common example of this movement is used in the braking system of a bicycle (Fig. 12.6).

A **pulley**, which is a rotating wheel, can perform similar mechanical functions to that of a lever. It can:

a) move a load by exerting a force in the opposite direction to which the load will move;

b) have a mechanical advantage that allows a heavy load to be lifted easily;

c) by having different diameters of pulleys, vary the mechanical advantage.

FIXED PULLEYS

With this type there is no mechanical advantage. The force down, i.e. the effort, is equal to the load. It allows a change of direction only.

A FIXED PULLEY AND A MOVING PULLEY

This is known as a "Block and Tackle", and it has a mechanical advantage, in that the load raised can be *greater* than the effort needed to make it move. In the example shown in Fig. 12.7, where the moving pulley is half the diameter of the fixed pulley, the mechanical advantage is 2, i.e. only *half the effort* is needed to raise the load: or the load raised is *twice the effort*. The only disadvantage is that the rope has to be pulled twice the distance that is needed to raise the load.

''WHEEL AND AXLE''

Two pulleys of different diameter can share the same axle. This is sometimes known as a "wheel and axle" and is shown in Fig. 12.8.

The mechanical advantage is calculated by dividing the radius of the smaller pulley into the radius of the larger pulley. It will also give the *Velocity Ratio*, i.e. the ratio of the effort distance and the load distance. For a wheel and axle that has a large radius of 150 mm and a small radius of 50 mm, the velocity ratio is 1: 3. This means that the *effort needed* to raise a load of 90 N will be 30 N, and the *effort distance* will be 3 m for 1 m distance of the load raised or lowered.

A belt is a continuous loop and runs in a pulley. The belts must fit the size and form of the pulley. There are two commonly used pulley and belt systems.

The belts are made from a flexible material and rely upon their surface contact with the pulley to transmit loads. Because the Vee belt (Fig. 12.9) has a larger surface contact with the pulley wheel, it will transmit larger loads. Belts will slip if the load is too great, which can be thought of as a safety factor. Most of the machines in the workshops are fitted with pulleys, e.g. drilling machines, lathes, circular saws, etc.

STEPPED CONE PULLEYS

These enable the machine to operate at a variety of speeds.

In Fig. 12.10 you can see two *cone pulleys*: a Driver pulley and a Driven pulley. The *driver pulley* is attached to the spindle of an electric motor. The *driven pulley* is attached to the spindle of the drilling machine. The cone pulleys are arranged so that the driver pulley has the largest diameter pulley at the top and the driven pulley has its smallest pulley at the top. The motion is transmitted via a belt from the driver to the driven pulley. The belt can only be used when the belt is fitted in the pulleys that are directly opposite each other. The spindle speed of the drilling machine can be changed by fitting the belt in the top pulleys for a high speed and in the bottom pulleys for a slow speed.

CHAIN DRIVE

This is another method of transmitting motion from a driver wheel to a driven wheel (see Fig. 12.11). They do not slip but if they are overloaded they will break. An excellent application of the chain drive is seen in the bicycle.

Chains have to be fitted on to *sprocket wheels* for maximum efficiency (Fig. 12.12). Calculating speeds is important if you want to know how fast a driven wheel will rotate on a child's toy, a robot, or a mechanical system (Fig. 12.13).

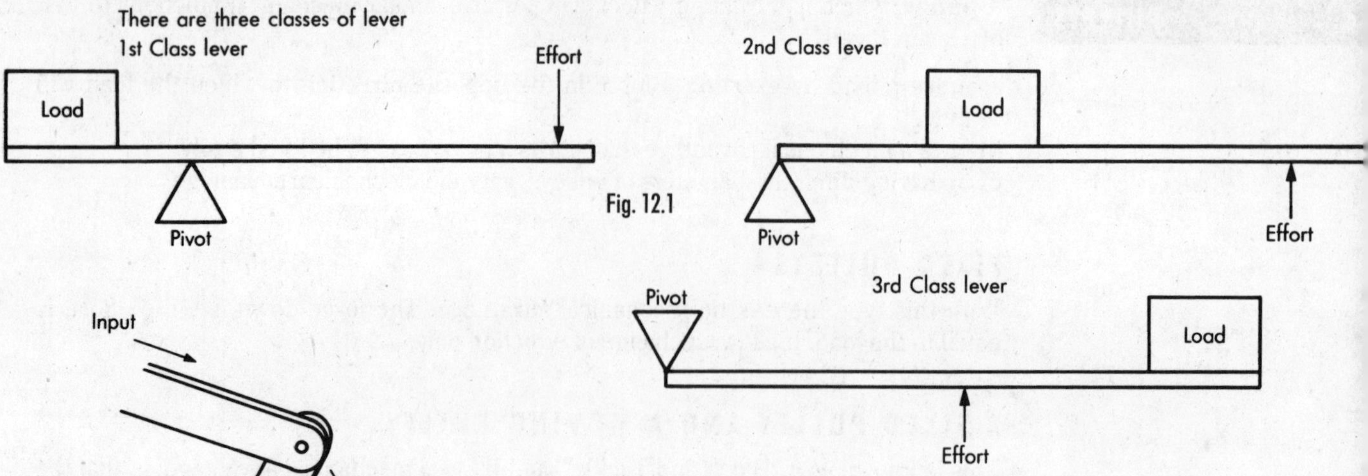

There are three classes of lever
1st Class lever

Load

Effort

Pivot

Fig. 12.1

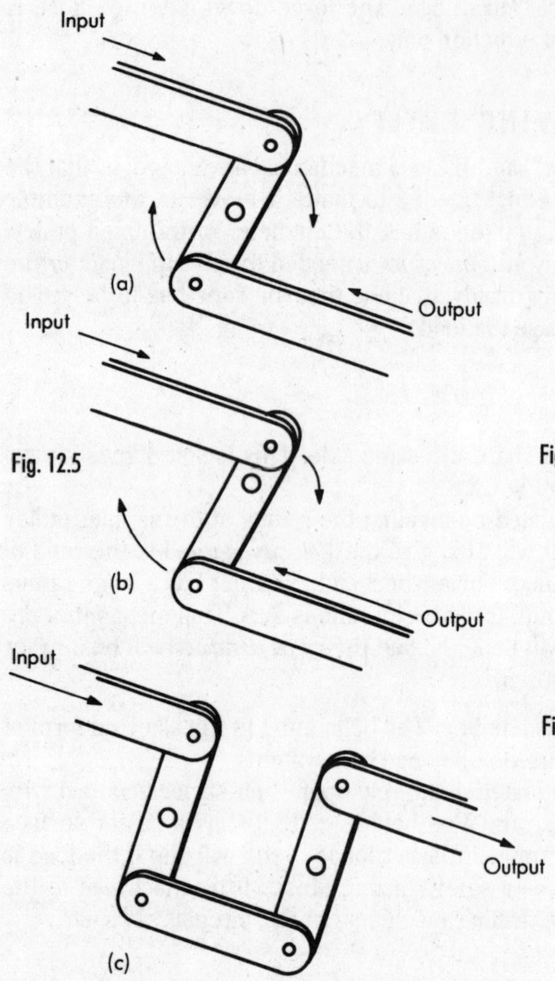

2nd Class lever

Load

Pivot

Effort

3rd Class lever

Pivot

Load

Effort

Input

(a)

Output

Fig. 12.5

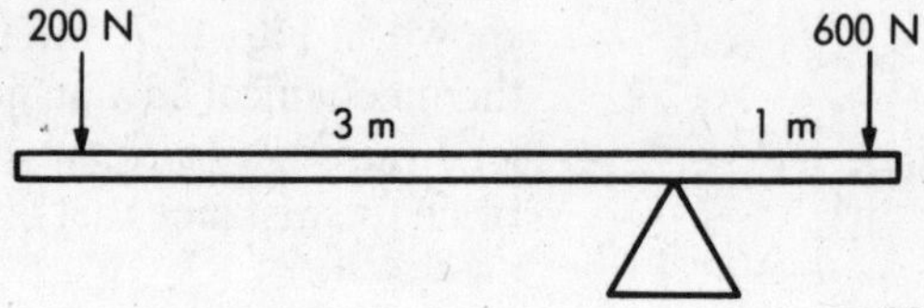

Input

(b)

Output

Input

(c)

Output

Fig. 12.2

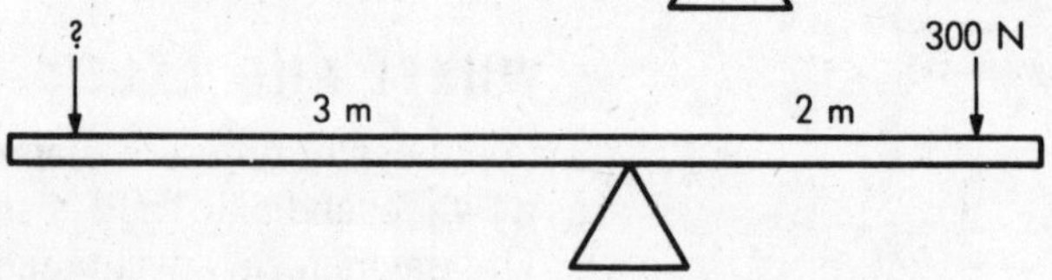

200 N   600 N

3 m   1 m

Fig. 12.3

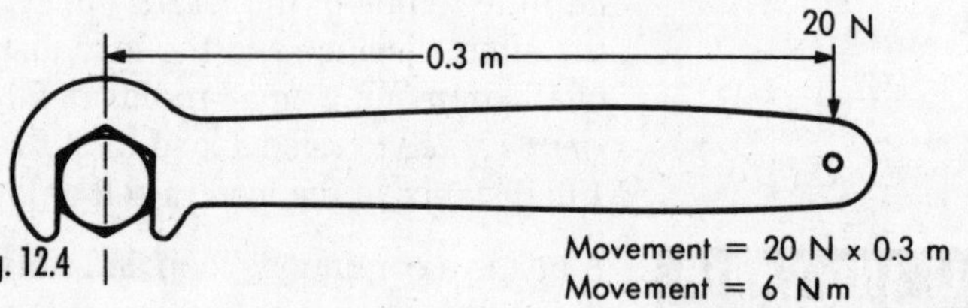

?   300 N

3 m   2 m

Fig. 12.4

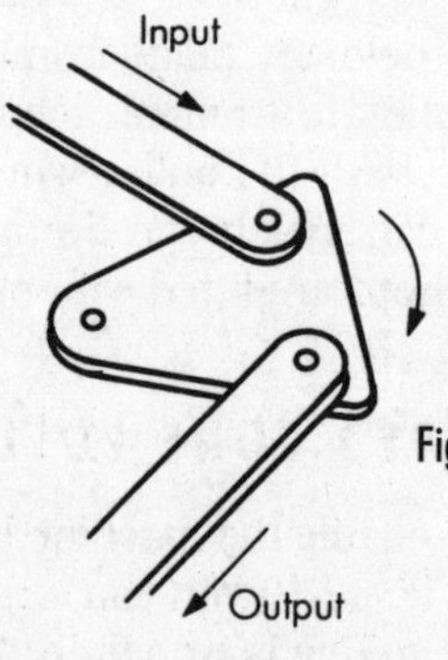

0.3 m   20 N

Movement = 20 N x 0.3 m
Movement = 6 N m

Input

Fig. 12.6

Output

Fig. 12.7

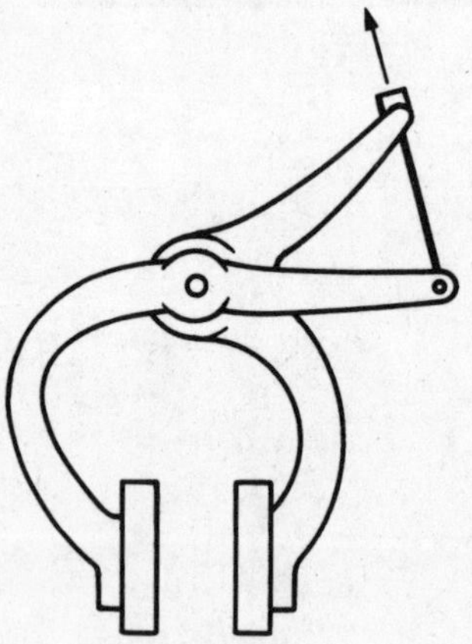

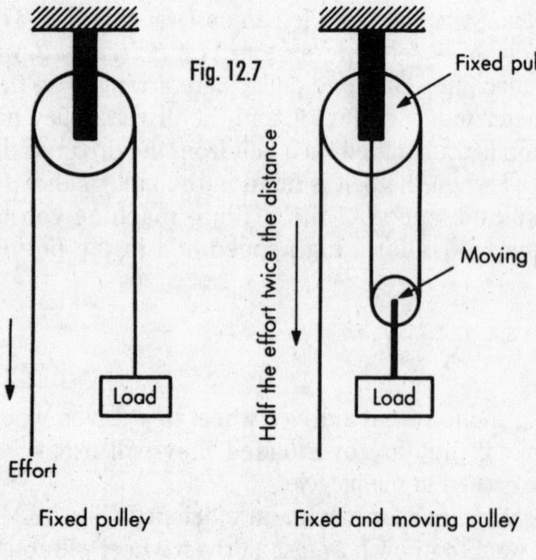

Fixed pulley

Moving pulley

Half the effort twice the distance

Load

Load

Effort

Fixed pulley

Fixed and moving pulley

Wheel and axle

Fig. 12.8

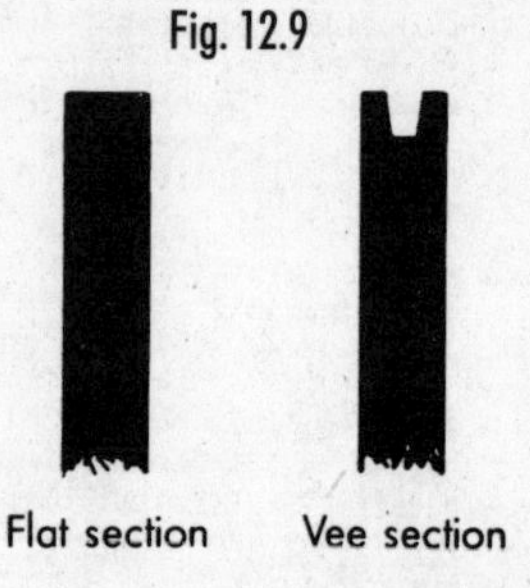

Fig. 12.9

Flat section   Vee section

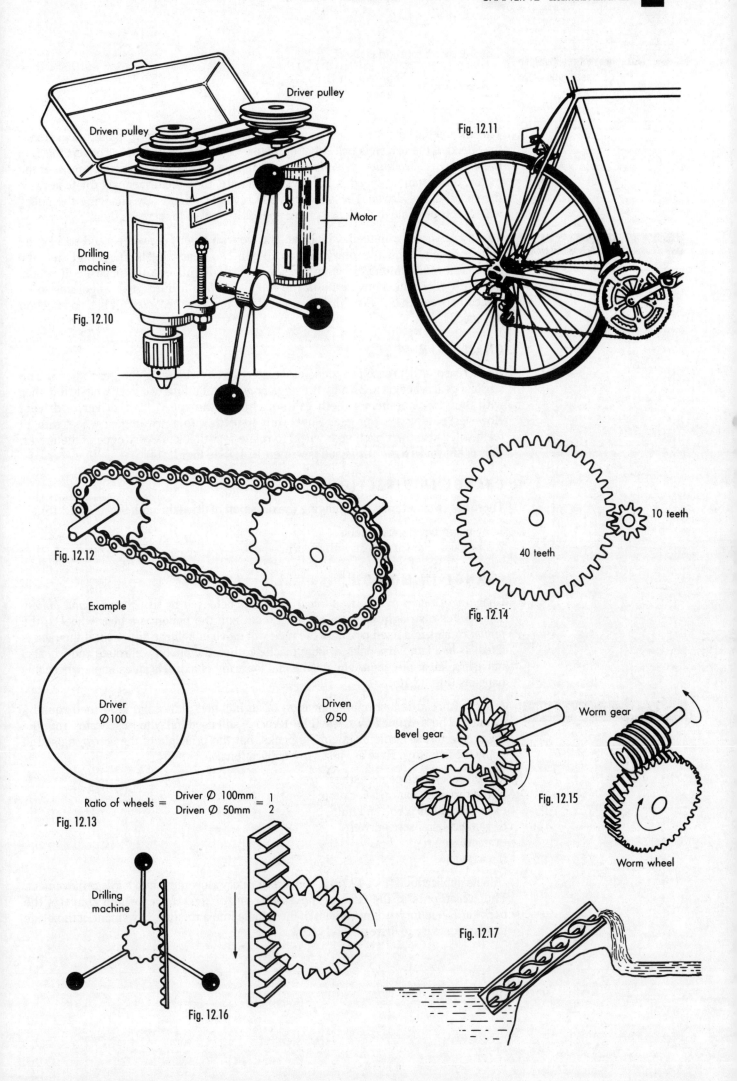

Driven pulley

Driver pulley

Motor

Drilling
machine

Fig. 12.10

Fig. 12.11

Fig. 12.12

10 teeth

40 teeth

Fig. 12.14

Example

Driver
Ø 100

Driven
Ø 50

Ratio of wheels = $\dfrac{\text{Driver } \varnothing \ 100\text{mm}}{\text{Driven } \varnothing \ 50\text{mm}} = \dfrac{1}{2}$

Fig. 12.13

Bevel gear

Worm gear

Fig. 12.15

Worm wheel

Drilling
machine

Fig. 12.16

Fig. 12.17

❝ Make sure that you know the speed ratio ❞

The following method is used:

$$\text{Speed Ratio} = \frac{\text{Diameter of Driver}}{\text{Diameter of Driven}}$$

This means that the *driver* has to rotate once to make the *driven* rotate twice. Hence the speed of the driven is twice that of the driver. If you then want to convert this into the *number of revolutions per minute*, you will need to find out the *spindle speed* of the motor. If the spindle speed is 100 revs per minute, then the driven will rotate at twice the speed of the driver. The answer is 200 revs per minute. By changing the pulley wheels it is possible to decrease driven speeds as well as to increase them.

6 ⟩ GEARS

These are wheels with teeth which can engage with other gear wheels and so, like the pulley wheels, transmit rotary motion. When two gear wheels mesh together, the driver will rotate in one direction and the driven will rotate in the opposite direction. For both gear wheels to rotate in the *same* direction a third gear wheel has to be placed between them. The third gear wheel is known as the "*idler*". It has no effect on the speed.

CHANGE IN SPEED

An increase or decrease in speed can be achieved by changing the gear wheels. The *size* of a gear wheel is known by the *number of teeth*. Putting two gear wheels together with the *same* number of teeth will not change the speed from driver to driven. However, putting a driver gear wheel with 40 teeth with a driven gear wheel with 10 teeth will cause the driven gear wheel to rotate four times to every once of the driver. This is known as a *gear ratio* and is written 1 : 4. (See Fig. 12.14)

CHANGE IN DIRECTION

There are two methods for changing the direction of drive through 90° (Fig. 12.15):

1. by using bevel gear wheels;
2. or by using a worm gear with a worm wheel.

CHANGE IN MOTION

Changing a *rotary* motion to a *linear* motion is achieved by using a *rack and pinion*. The *rack* is a straight piece of bar with teeth and the pinion is a gear wheel. If the *pinion* rotates in a fixed position, the rack will move in a linear direction. If the rack is fixed, as in a lathe or a pillar drilling machine, then the pinion will rotate and will also move in a linear direction. The raising and lowering of a drill is an example where this happens (Fig. 12.16).

7 ⟩ SCREWS

A screw thread is just one application of an inclined plane that is formed round a cylinder. The *Archimedian screw* (Fig. 12.17) is still used today to raise water from the River Nile to the fertile plains on its banks, but the principle of the screw is used in many mechanisms. Here are just a few applications:

a) feed screw on a centre lathe;
b) the threaded bar on a G-clamp;
c) the thread on a bolt and nut;
d) yankee spiral screwdriver;
e) micrometer;
f) car jack.

In its applications (Fig. 12.18) it converts a *rotary* movement into a *linear* movement. The *exception* is in the case of the *Yankee spiral screwdriver* which converts the backwards and forward movement of the handle into a rotating movement of the blade that is necessary to drive a wood screw.

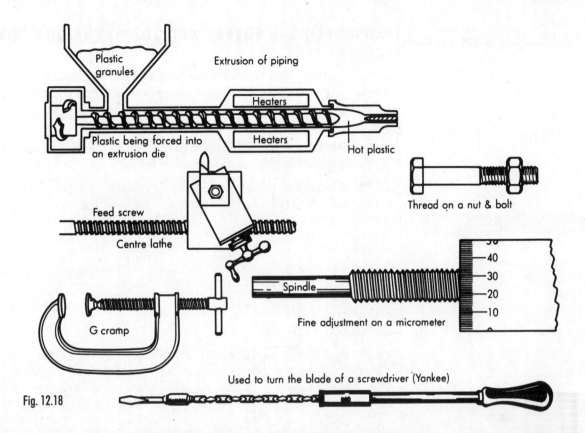

Fig. 12.18

8 > CAMS AND CRANKS

A mechanism that can change a *rotary* movement into a *reciprocating movement*, i.e. a round and round movement into a backward and forward movement, is mostly used in the design of car engines. The movement is achieved by three methods (Fig. 12.19):

1. a cam and follower;
2. a flywheel and connecting rod;
3. a crank and slider.

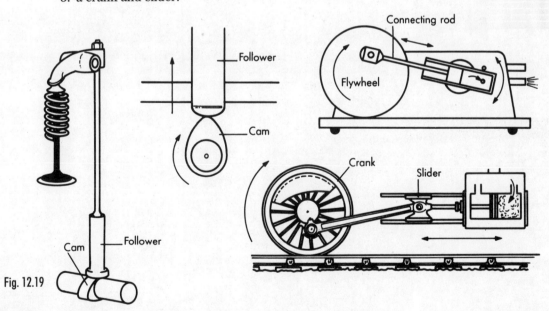

Fig. 12.19

9 > RATCHET AND PAWL

Many of the movements created in children's toys use these mechanisms. Other mechanisms that you may find helpful include the following.

The *ratchet* is a wheel that has teeth. The front edge of the tooth has a surface that has a steep slope, and the back edge has a gradual slope. The gradual slope allows the *pawl* to slide over the surface but the steep slope prevents it from moving and so stops the ratchet wheel rotating backwards. Examples are ratchet screwdriver, freewheel in a bicycle and the opening system for lock gates. You may find it useful in a winding mechanism for a crane to keep a load in a raised position.

TRANSMITTING A ROTARY ACTION THAT IS NOT IN A STRAIGHT LINE

This is necessary when the axle of the engine or motor and the part to be driven are not in line. This often happens in the case of car and lorry transmission systems. This can be overcome by using a "Universal Joint". The same can happen in mechanical projects and may be overcome by two methods (Fig. 12.20):

1. using a model universal joint, the type that can be obtained in constructional kits;
2. using a piece of flexible plastic or rubber tubing.

Much of what has been covered in this chapter can be demonstrated by using constructional kits, e.g. Lego Technical, Meccano "M" Sets, Polymek or Fischer Technic.

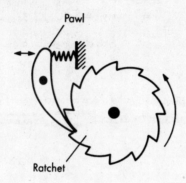

Fig. 12.20

REVIEW SHEET

■ Explain in no more than five sentences, the meaning of mechanisms.

_____

_____

_____

_____

_____

_____

_____

_____

■ Name and illustrate five different types of mechanisms.

1. _____   2. _____

3. _____   4. _____

5. _____

■ For each of the types of mechanism you have named and illustrated above, give an example where this mechanism is in common use.

	Mechanism	Use
1.	_____	_____
2.	_____	_____
3.	_____	_____
4.	_____	_____
5.	_____	_____

■ Mechanisms not only transfer movement but make some parts move more quickly or slowly than other parts. Explain how this is achieved and give three examples of where changes of speed are used in hand operated devices and three examples in more sophisticated devices such as power operated machines.

Hand operated devices.

1. _____

_____

2. _____

_____

3. _____

_____

■ Power operated machines.

1. _____

_____

2. _____

_____

3. _____

_____

■ Explain why it is important to be able to increase or decrease the rotary speed of a cutting tool such as a drill bit or the reciprocating movement of a needle in a sewing machine.

_____

_____

_____

_____

_____

■ The forces acting upon a mechanism or part of a mechanism enable a mechanical advantage to be obtained. Explain what is meant by 'mechanical advantage'.

_____

_____

_____

_____

■ Mechanical advantage can be measured. Write down the formula that you would use to calculate the 'mechanical advantage' of a 1st, 2nd and 3rd class lever.

Formula _____

Give an example of its application.

Describe and illustrate how rotary movement is converted into reciprocating movement.

_____

_____

_____

13

PNEUMATICS

SAFETY

CYLINDERS AND VALVES

**REGULATORS, RESTRICTORS
AND RESERVOIRS**

SOME BASIC CIRCUITS

GETTING STARTED

Pneumatics use compressed air to produce both linear and rotary motion. If the air is replaced with a liquid such as oil then this is called *hydraulics*. The air can be compressed by an electric pump called a compressor or for certain purposes by pumping by hand. For instance, in school, a car inner tube can be pumped up using a foot or hand pump, the stored air then being used to power a very simple mechanism or project. Similarly syringes can represent very simple systems.

You will probably have seen pneumatics used in buses and trains for closing the doors and operating the brakes on large vehicles. You can tell that air is being used by the loud hissing sound when the system is in use. Hydraulics are commonly seen on bulldozers and diggers. The main use for pneumatics is to provide economical power with reliability. It is used in industry to operate machines. Its main advantage over electronic solutions is that it can provide short bursts of high power which can be difficult to achieve by electronic means. Pneumatics can be used in conjunction with electronics to provide complex, efficient machines.

In school, you are likely to find pneumatic boards containing a range of cylinders and valves which can be easily connected together by plastic tubing. The tubing locks into the connectors and is easily removed and reused. Some school pneumatics systems are made from translucent plastic so that internal working parts can be easily seen and understood. In the same way that electronic components have circuit symbols to represent them and allow easy drawing, there are symbols for pneumatic components. Your school may have a set of magnetic BS symbols which will enable you to produce a diagram of your proposed project. If not, you could photocopy and cut up the symbols in this book and assemble them, making any connections by drawing lines.

ESSENTIAL PRINCIPLES

1 ⟩   SAFETY

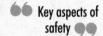

66 Key aspects of safety 99

- You must wear eye protection whilst using pneumatics, as compressed air can easily blow dirt and dust into the eye.
- If tubing comes adrift under pressure it can flick about and may hit the eye.
- You must disconnect the supply before making alterations to the system.
- Never allow air at pressure to touch your skin, it can force oil and particles under your skin.
- Keep the pressure as low as possible (1–2 bar).

2 ⟩   CYLINDERS AND VALVES

The components which give movement are called *cylinders* and those which switch them on or off are called *valves*.

Both have movable pistons incorporated in them, the air is prevented from moving past the piston by plastic seals. The inside of the cylinder is very smooth so that a close fit between the piston seal and cylinder is made preventing a loss of air.

The points where air is fed in to and out of valves and cylinders, are called *ports*, and the valves are named by the number of ports which they have, i.e. a 3 port valve. In this valve there is an air inlet port, an exhaust port and an outlet port which connects to a cylinder. A 5 port valve has an air inlet port, two exhaust ports, and two ports for connection to a double acting cylinder. The diagram shows 3 and 5 port manually operated and mechanically operated valves. The different types of operators are shown in Fig 13.1 and can be fitted to any type of valve.

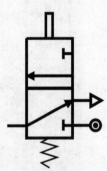 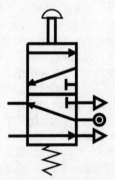

Plunger operated 3 port valve
Mechanically operated plunger.

Push button operated 5 port valve
Manually operated button.

Fig. 13.1   Types of operators.

You can see from Fig 13.2 that both states of the valve are shown in the one diagram. The symbol comprises two blocks, the top block shows the ON state, when the air supply is connected to the cylinder, the lower block shows the normal OFF state when the air supply is prevented from connection to the cylinder, but any air in the cylinder is allowed to exhaust. The symbols for the exhaust and air inlet ports are shown.

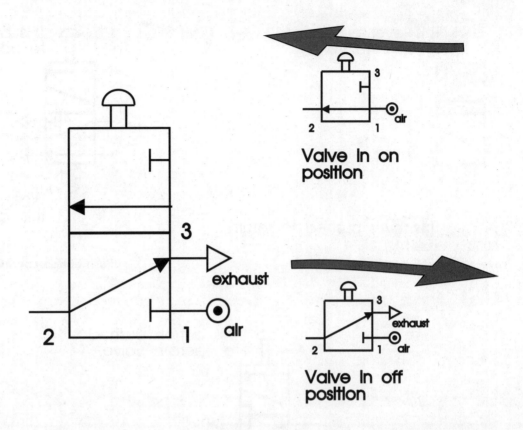

Fig. 13.2 On the left, the symbol for a push button 3-port value. On the right are the on and off states of the valve.

Operating Valves

Valves can be operated by keys, levers, rollers and push buttons and can also be operated electrically by built in solenoids. Some valves use air pressure to move the piston. This is done by an extension to the piston which is called the spool. Air is fed to the spool which causes the valve to operate. If a spring symbol is shown beneath the valve then the valve is returned to its original position by this spring. If another symbol is shown, ie a lever, then the valve will be returned to its original position by operating this lever. Similarly any valve could be returned by air pressure. The symbols above and below each valve denote by which method the valve is set and reset.

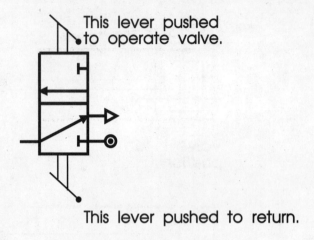

This lever pushed to operate valve.

This lever pushed to return.

Lever set reset 3 port valve

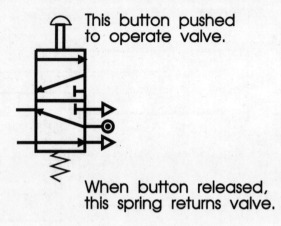

This button pushed to operate valve.

When button released, this spring returns valve.

Push button operated 5 port valve

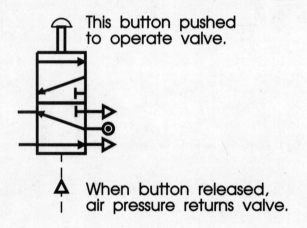

This button pushed to operate valve.

When button released, air pressure returns valve.

Push button air return (pilot) 5 port valve

Fig. 13.3 Methods used to set and reset valves.

Single and Double Acting Cylinders

Single Acting cylinders are those in which the air supply pushed the piston against a spring; when the air pressure is released the spring pushes the piston back to its original position. The cylinder can have the spring on either side of the piston, so that the normal state can be with the piston fully out or fully in.

Double acting cylinders have two ports, one on each side of the piston, when air pressure is applied to one port the piston moves forward. If the air pressure is removed the piston will stay in that position. Only if air pressure is applied to the other port will the piston return to this original position. (This assumes that there is no mechanical force pushing the piston back in.) Some cylinders can be cushioned to stop the piston from slamming into each end on heavy loading.

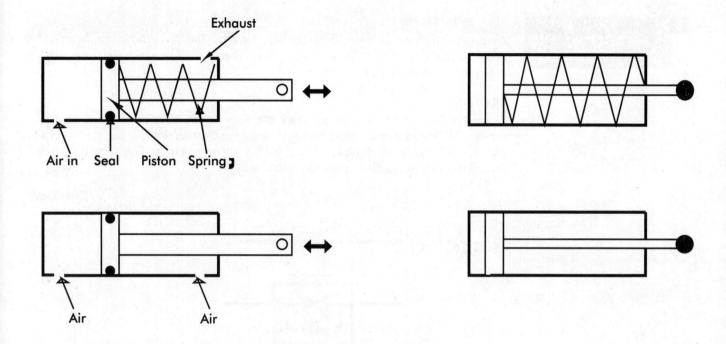

Fig. 13.4 Cross sections of cylinders.

Shuttle Valves

Shuttle valves have three ports in the shape of a T and allow air to flow from each direction to an output port but not straight through. These are useful in controlling double acting cylinders. In the diagram below you can see that the shuttle valve acts as an OR gate. Air pressure from either A or B will produce an output.

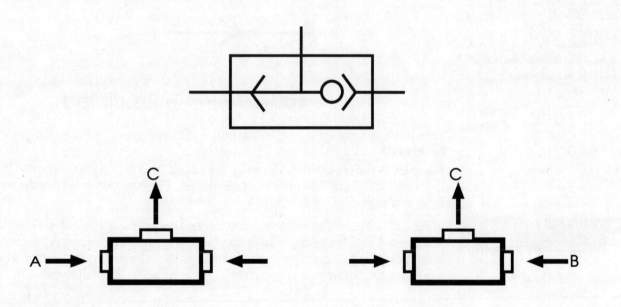

Fig. 13.5 The shuttle valve. Input A or Input B gives an output at C.

3 **REGULATORS, RESTRICTORS AND RESERVOIRS**

Flow regulators

Unidirectional flow regulators (flow regulators) control the flow of air in one direction but allow the free flow of air in the other direction. These could be said to be the equivalent of diodes in the electronic circuit.

Restrictors

These are basically a coupling in which the flow can be obstructed by an adjustable screw. The flow rate is therefore reduced equally in both directions. The screw consists of a tapered needle which obstructs the air flow through a hole. The more the screw is turned the less air is able to pass the restriction.

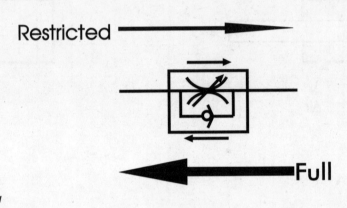

Fig. 13.6a A unidirectional flow regulator.

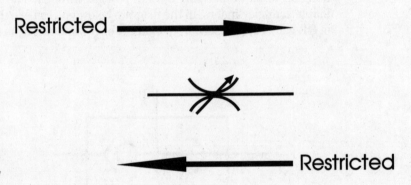

Fig. 13.6b A bidirectional flow restrictor.

Reservoirs

These are cylinders in which air can be stored and used to provide delays, and in fact are the equivalent of capacitors in electronic circuits. The larger the reservoir the longer the delay available.

4 **SOME BASIC CIRCUITS**

In Fig 13.7, a 3 port lever set reset valve controls a single acting cylinder. When the lever A is pressed air is fed to the cylinder and the piston out strokes. The cylinder will remain in this position until lever B is pressed returning the valve to its original state. The spring will return the piston to its original position, air being fed through to exhaust.

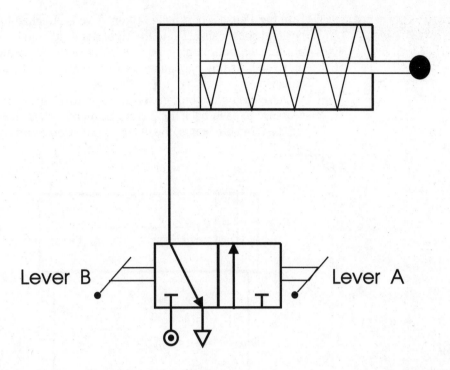

Fig. 13.7   A 3 port valve controlling a single acting cylinder.

In Fig 13.8, two 3 port roller trip operated valves are used to control a double acting cylinder. When the left hand valve is operated the piston will outstroke, as soon as the valve is released it will return to its original position, the piston will stay in the out position. When the right hand valve is operated the piston will then return to its original position. The cylinder is only under pressure when one or other of the valves is operated and held on. In all other conditions the piston could be pushed back as there is no pressure on the piston.

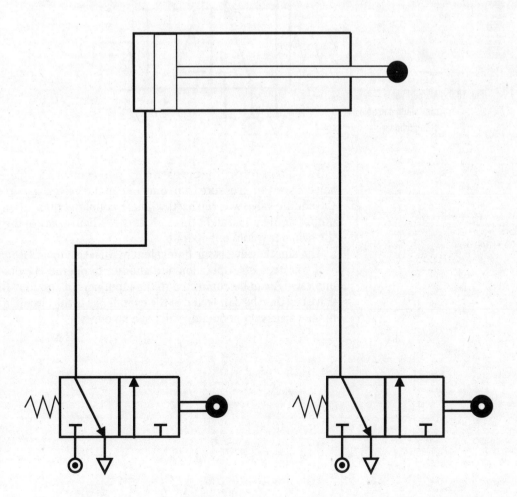

Fig. 13.8   Two 3 port valves controlling a double acting cylinder.

In Fig 13.9, a 5 port push button valve is attached to a double acting cylinder. In the position shown air is fed to the right hand side of the piston holding it in. On operation of the push button, air pressure is fed to the lefthand side of the piston causing it to outstroke. As this happens pressure on the right hand side of the piston is allowed to exhaust.

On releasing the button, the spring returns the valve to its first position, allowing air pressure to push back the piston, air on the other side of the piston once again goes to exhaust. In both states, the piston is under pressure.

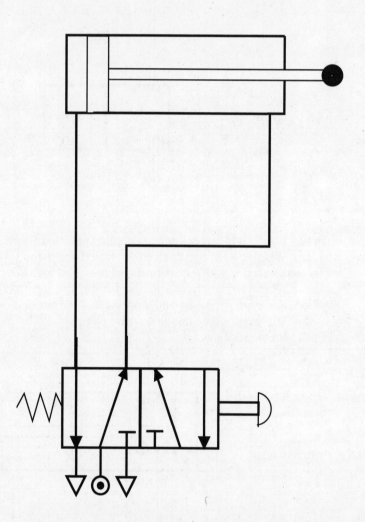

Fig. 13.9   A 5 port valve controlling a double acting cylinder.

Two 3 port roller trip valves are used to control a single acting cylinder. The shuttle valve allows air pressure from only one of the valves at a time to operate the cylinder. If the shuttle valve was replaced with a T coupling, then when one valve was operated its output would go straight through to the exhaust port of the other valve and, of course, the cylinder would not operate.

The shuttle valve is the equivalent in this case to an OR gate.

If you need one operation and another to operate a cylinder then the output port of one valve A can be connected to the input port of another, B. The output of this second valve can then be connected to the cylinder as in the circuit in Fig 13.11. Operating either of the valves independently will have no effect.

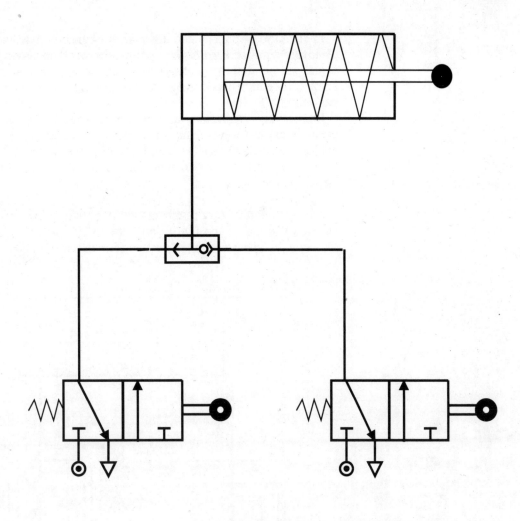

Fig. 13.10 Two 3 port valves
controlling a single
acting cylinder using a
shuttle valve. Valve A or
valve B will operate the
cylinder.

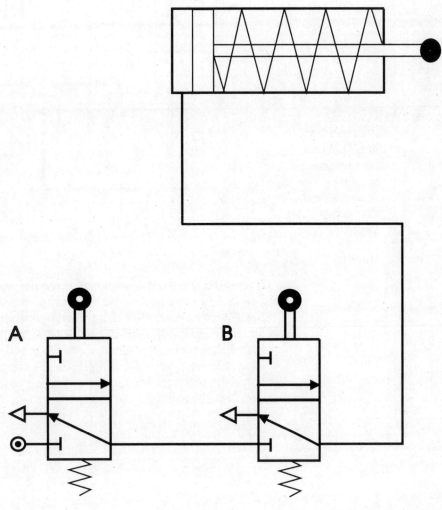

Fig. 13.11 Two 3 port valves
controlling a single
acting cylinder. Valve A
and valve B will operate
the cylinder.

In all of the circuits looked at so far, the cylinders have been operated at full speed. There are many occasions when a slow controlled operation of a cylinder is required. It would not be good to have the doors on buses, for example, crashing forwards and backwards at high speed, they would not last very long and there would be many injured passengers. We therefore need a method of controlling piston speed.

It is not a good idea to restrict the air flow into the cylinder as this results in a jerky action. We can however restrict the exhaust. If you imagine putting your finger over the end of a cycle pump and pushing the piston, you will know that this exhaust pressure resists your push. If you now allow some of the air to escape, the piston moves. Similarly by restricting the exhaust from one side of the piston you can slow the speed of the piston down.

If you remember, flow regulators allow air to flow freely in one direction, in this case when driving the piston (Direction A and A1 in Fig 13.12), and slowly in the opposite direction. In this direction the piston is forcing air from the cylinder to the exhaust port (Direction B and B1). The flow restrictor is adjustable and so gives good control over piston speed.

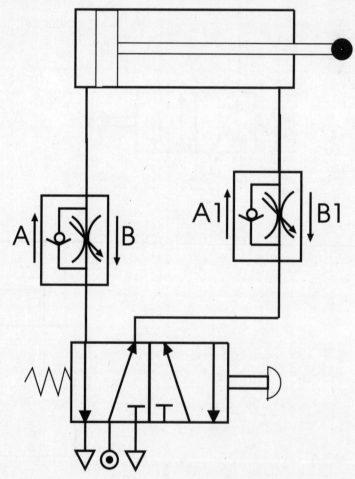

Fig. 13.12 A 5 port valve controlling a double acting cylinder, with piston speed control in both directions. Flow regulators are used in the exhaust side of the cylinder.

If time delays are required then flow regulators and reservoirs can be used. They are the equivalent to variable resistors and capacitors in electronic timing circuits.

In the circuit below, when the set lever is operated the flow regulator restricts the flow of air into the reservoir, after a time the pressure builds up sufficiently to operate the air operated 3 port valve, this allows air to the cylinder causing the piston to outstroke.

When the set/reset valve is reset, the air operated valve returns to its original state and the piston returns (due to the spring) air passing freely through the reservoir and the regulator to exhaust.

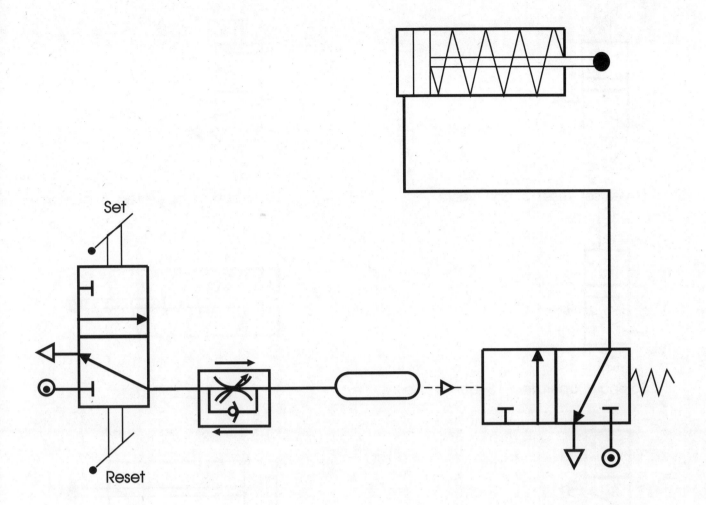

Set

Reset

Fig. 13.13 Using a reservoir and flow regulator to delay the stroke of a single acting cylinder.

When designing your pneumatic system, you must decide what inputs, processes and outputs are required then you can decide which type of valves and cylinders to use; are they to be manually operated, or mechanically? If mechanically, what type and direction of movement is to be sensed? The output must also be considered, what length of the movement is needed, what direction of movement, what speed, what force is required? If the pneumatics are to be linked to electronics, how is this to be achieved?

You should try to use the school's pneumatics boards to prototype your ideas, as this will make fault finding and quick changes to the design much easier than construction using discrete components. Once the system works in principle, the components can be ordered and plans can be made to make the project box or container.

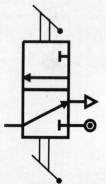

Lever set reset 3 port valve

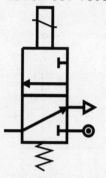

Solenoid operated 3 port valve

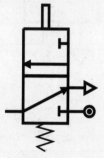

Plunger operated 3 port valve

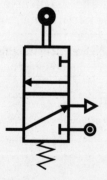

Roller trip operated 3 port valve

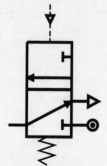

Air operated 3 port valve

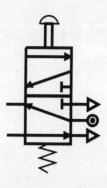

Push button operated 5 port valve

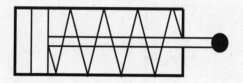

Single acting cylinder

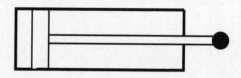

Double acting cylinder

Pneumatic reservoir

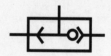

Shuttle Valve

Bidirectional restrictor

Unidirectional flow regulator

Fig. 13.14 BS symbols for a range of
pneumatic components.

REVIEW SHEET

■ Give two reasons why pneumatics are used in industry.

_____

_____

_____

■ Explain the difference between pneumatics and hydraulics.

_____

_____

_____

■ Give two examples of everyday use of pneumatics with which the general public would come into contact.

_____

_____

_____

■ Give three safety precautions when using pneumatics in the school situation.

_____

_____

_____

■ What are the connections to valves and cylinders called?

_____

_____

■ Explain how valves are described.

_____

_____

_____

_____

■ What are the differences between single acting cylinders and double acting cylinders?

_____

_____

_____

■ Valves have different types of operators, why?

_____

_____

_____

■ How are these operators shown on the BS symbols?

_____

_____

_____

_____

■ Describe why you would use a shuttle valve.

_____

_____

_____

_____

■ If you needed to reduce the flow of air in your system, which two components could you use and explain the difference between them.

_____

_____

_____

■ How could you slow down the speed of operation of a cylinder?

_____

_____

_____

■ How could you delay the action of a valve or cylinder?

_____

_____

_____

■ In designing your pneumatic system what factors do you need to consider?

_____

_____

_____

_____

_____

■ When would you use pneumatics, in preference to electronics?

_____

_____

_____

_____

■ What is a safe pressure to use in school pneumatics?

_____

_____

14

INFORMATION TECHNOLOGY

GETTING STARTED

Information Technology is a tool which you can use to enhance your coursework both in its production and its final appearance. If you use a word processor to write a report, then you can start to note down ideas and comments from an early stage of your work. This can be saved to disc and retrieved at a later date. Be sure to make backups of important work always and to save frequently whilst working. You can then sort, move around and improve your writing gradually as your project progresses. Finally as the time for submission gets nearer, you will only have a small task to go through the document to improve its readability. Another advantage is that you are able, on most word processors, to check spelling. You are likely to have marks deducted for poor spelling in most examinations.

Similarly being able to cut and paste text and graphics into your folio can improve the overall effect. If you need to find out the preferences of the potential users of your artefact, then questionnaires can be generated and the results easily put into charts. Data can be analysed and modelled from within spreadsheets and printed out in more easily understood forms such as barcharts, piecharts and graphs.

Included in this chapter are introductions to the uses of the various types of computer package and it is suggested that you ask your teachers what is available in your school or college. At all times, you must make the decision as to which is the best and most efficient, least time consuming method to use. It is your ideas and thinking which examiners wish to see, not necessarily perfectly produced graphics. If you can manage to do both tasks well then you are to be congratulated.

Note: words printed in capitals (e.g. MOUSE) are defined on p.244.

WHAT COMPUTER PACKAGES DO

WORD PROCESSING

COMPUTER AIDED DESIGN (CAD)

COMPUTER AIDED MANUFACTURE (CAM)

DATABASES

SPREADSHEETS

COMPACT DISC READ ONLY MEMORY (CD ROMS)

SCANNERS

OUTPUT DEVICES

CONTROL

SOME USEFUL WORDS

ESSENTIAL PRINCIPLES

1 > WHAT COMPUTER PACKAGES DO

Information Technology is concerned with the storage, retrieval and manipulation of data using computers. In Design and Technology all of these can be used in a wide variety of ways. The National Curriculum at present includes IT capability and the strands are handling information, communicating information, modelling, measurement and control. Whilst it must be remembered that learning to use any IT *package* can be time consuming, time is saved once the drawing or document is stored on disc, as changes and alterations are easily done. It is advised that you become proficient in the use of a relatively few packages and use these regularly; in this way you will work most efficiently. At all times you must decide on the most effective way to work, perhaps using a computer to draw one simple diagram could waste a lot of time. Most modern packages have extensive help menus that are context sensitive which means that if you ask for on screen help, the help screens shown will correspond to the function being used at the time.

Table 14.1 Computer Packages and their uses

PACKAGE	POSSIBLE USES IN TECHNOLOGY
WORDPROCESSOR	Writing and editing reports. Writing and editing letters. Producing tables. Cut and paste into folio.
DATABASE	Referencing materials. Suppliers. Educational resources. Energy/Food etc. On line research.
SPREADSHEET	Materials cutting lists. Components lists. Pricing materials. Ingredient lists. Modelling. Financial etc.
CONTROL	Animating projects. Controlling processes. Industrial simulation.
GRAPHICS (PAINT)	Pictorial representations. Folio covers. Packaging design.
CAD	Isometric drawing. Orthographic drawing. Modelling.
CAM	Knitting. Weaving. Embroidery. Milling. Turning. Modelling. Production.
DTP	Folio production. Presentation materials. Lettering. Letter writing. Report writing.
OTHER	Specific textile design packages. Specific food/nutrition packages. Learning packages.

With the advent of packages to work within WINDOWS, most packages will look similar, which will reduce the time needed to become familiar with them. Similarly the use of a MOUSE and pull down menus can speed up usage.

Integrated packages are available which contain a word processor, a database and a spreadsheet, these are useful because the three are designed to work easily together, therefore the interchange of data can be quickly achieved.

Fig. 14.1 shows a WINDOWS screen, by clicking onto ICONS, programmes can be loaded simply. Icons are small pictures which denote the various programmes on your system. This is much easier than typing complicated lists to load a programme.

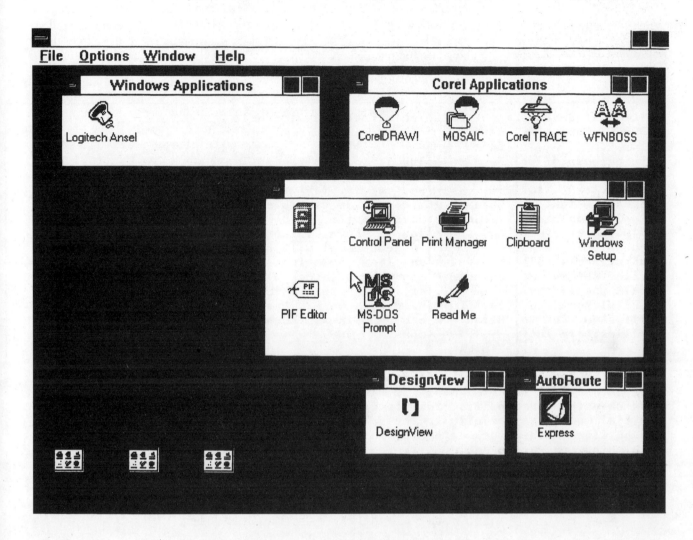

Fig. 14.1 A Windows Introduction Screen

Table 14.2 presents some useful programmes, but individual manufacturers make similar ranges for all makes of computer.

Table 14.2 Specific packages

TYPE	NAME
INTEGRATED PACKAGES	LotusWorks, ClarisWorks, Works for Windows, MicroSoftWorks
WORDPROCESSORS	WordPerfect, Write, AmiPro, WordStar
DATABASES	DBase, DataEase
SPREADSHEETS	AsEasyAs, Excel, Lotus123
GRAPHICS	PaintBrush, Corel Draw, Harvard Graphics, Drawmouse
CAD	AutoSketch, AutoCad, EasyCad, Designer, SignDesign
CAM	AutoCad, Drawmill, Plotmill, CNC Designer, Arc Embroidery
CONTROL	TinyBits, Nimbits, ControlIT, Contact
DTP	PageMaker, PagePlus, QuarkXPress Publisher
OTHER	Fastrax, PCB

2 > WORD PROCESSING

Nowadays most *word processing* programmes (WP) will accept graphics, draw lines and boxes and are therefore more often like Desktop Publishing Packages (DTP).

There is a wide range of word processing packages ranging from very simple to complex commercial standard ones. All enable the composition of documents in a wide variety of forms. Text will flow onto the next line or page automatically, words can be corrected, inserted or deleted and the whole document is automatically adjusted. The documents can be saved to disc and printed easily. Some word processors are advertised as WYSIWYG which means – What You See Is What You Get. This means that if you change the size of type or font this will be shown on the screen. Some do not do this, but allow you to see how the document will look, when printed, in a preview screen but not as you are typing.

An important aspect to remember when using the computer is that you must regularly save your work to disc, otherwise in the event of a power failure or computer fault all of your work will be lost. Keep these backup discs safely and away from sources of heat, humidity, dust and magnetism.

```
File Edit Search Layout Mark Tools Font Graphics Help
PRODUCT MODELLING   Line
                    Page
The purpose of pr   Document    ing is to give the designer or a
prospective clien   Other       imensional representation of an
artefact. At its                pe, colour, texture, feel and
perhaps weight ar   Columns ▶    reality as possible, sometimes very
simple models are   Tables  ▶   stablish the basic form. Generally
only the external   Maths   ▶   ion is shown, internal parts and
mechanisms are no                A good model will be
indistinguishable   Footnote▶   ual item. Sometimes these models are
called concept mo   Endnote  ▶  lly when related to vehicles. Full
scale models show               actly what the vehicle will look
like without the    Justify ▶   uilding a working prototype. Models
will show, for in   Align   ▶   ery containers, keyboards, displays,
grilles, air inta               ches.
                    Styles
MATERIALS: These                om styrofoam, plastics (ie vacuum
forms), MDF- medium density fibreboard, wood, and metal.
MDF is an ideal material as it is easy to work and takes a good
finish using spray paints. Foam is extremely easy to work up into
initial models, especially in the school situation. Wood needs
to be fine grained such as beech, so that both cutting and
finishing are easily achieved.
B:\MODELLIN\MODEL                      Doc 1 Pg 1 Ln 1" POS 1"
```

Fig. 14.2 A typical Word Perfect Screen

A range of type styles and fonts are usually available in most packages. A variety of ways of manipulating the text are also available, including:

- **Cut and paste:** Where blocks of text can be selected (cut) and then moved (paste).
- **Copy:** Where text can be copied to new locations leaving the original in place.
- **Spell:** The document can be checked for spelling mistakes against a dictionary. Your own specific dictionary can be generated to include specialist terms.
- **Thesaurus:** A range of words with similar meanings as the word at the cursor can be put on screen. If you wish to change then you select the word and it will be changed.

Some ways of manipulating text

- **Charts and columns:** Charts can be designed easily and drawn on screen. Text will flow in the boxes and the size of the box will adjust automatically.
- **Date:** Prints the date at the point of the cursor.
- **Search and replace:** Specified words can be searched for and replaced with another.
- **Merge:** Standard documents can be written with codes included, then information stored in databases can be input into these documents. For example, if a standard letter has to be sent to many people then each copy of the letter can have the name and address included automatically.
- **Save and retrieve:** The documents can be saved to disc and retrieved at a later date.
- **Graphics:** Graphics can be imported from other programmes and text can be adjusted to fit around these pictures. There is a wide range of CLIPART available on disc for this use.
- **Font:** A wide range of lettering styles are available in a range of sizes to enable the selection of the most appropriate style to be used. Remember that the style is often linked to the product and that designers are aware that the image of a product or company can be enhanced or transmitted by the typeface used on their literature.

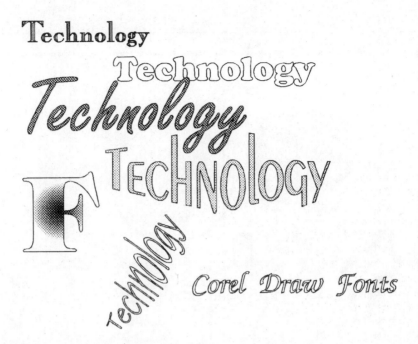

Fig. 14.3   Some font styles

DESK TOP PUBLISHING

This enables pages containing graphics and text to be generated, text can be flowed around text and put in boxes. Text can be arranged in columns and different fonts used as well. These packages are used to create newspaper and magazine type pages as well as posters. They are generally similar to the methods that printers use to make up pages for newspapers. The blocks of text and graphics can be pasted into position easily.

GRAPHICS AND PAINT PACKAGES

These allow the user to paint and draw, using brushes, fills and spray gun effects. The size of the brushes and sprays can be adjusted both for shape and size. Some are designed to retouch images which have been scanned in. Background textures and fills can be accurately matched to the originals. If you require a pictorial representation of your project then this is the package to use. A simple one is usually included in Windows called Paintbrush, there are many complex ones; even ones which allow you to paint using the styles and texture effects of the famous old masters.

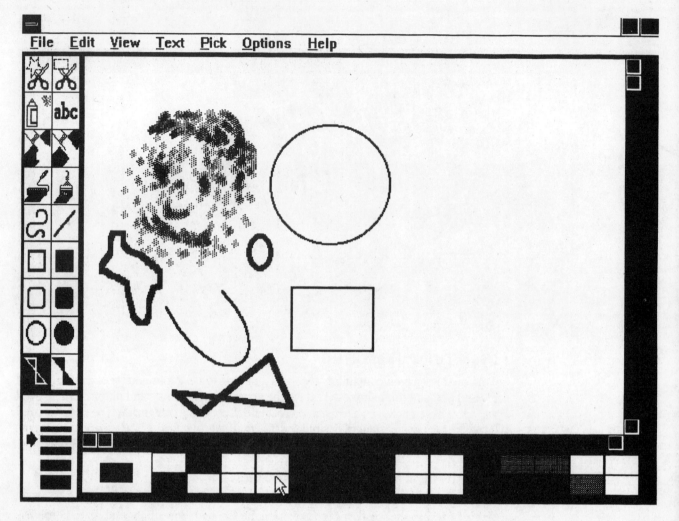

Fig. 14.4 Paintbrush

<table>
<tr><td>3></td><td>COMPUTER AIDED DESIGN (CAD)</td></tr>
</table>

These packages offer the possibility of drawing, sizing and moving objects around the screen. Lines, circles, ellipses and rectangles can be easily drawn and joined to represent complex parts of a project. These elements of the drawing can be adjusted for size, rotated or inverted and combined with others, this can be achieved by using different layers, in effect the drawing can be viewed as individual layers or through other layers, enabling complex drawings to be more readily understood.

Dimensions can be added sometimes automatically.

Usually there is an on screen TOOLBOX from which the various tools can be easily selected. Output can be made to printers, plotters and cutters.

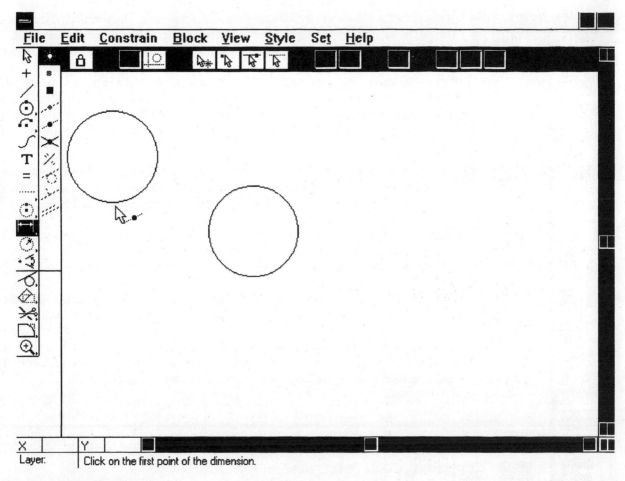

Fig. 14.5   A typical Design View Screen

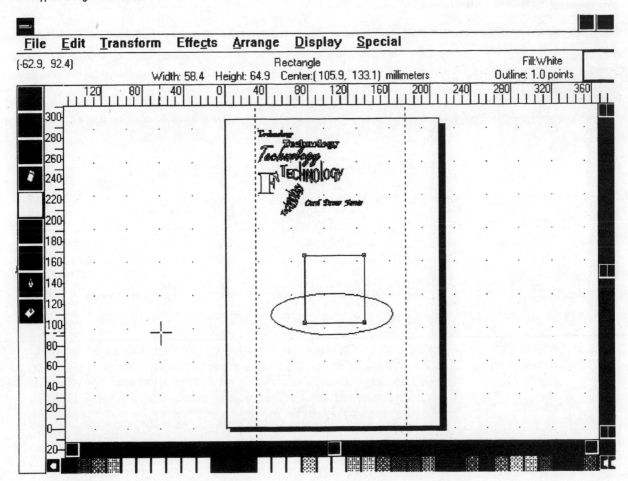

Fig. 14.6   Corel Draw

4 COMPUTER AIDED MANUFACTURE (CAM)

If the drawings made using CAD are output to a machine which cuts or shapes resistant materials or manipulates textiles then the process is said to involve CAM. Some machines have their own specific software which generates the codes (G Codes) to operate the machine, others generate the codes but they are not available for the user to see. Packages which are designed for use in school or college have software designed to work with custom built small machines perhaps simplified for the school situation. These machines include lathes, milling machines, profile cutters, sewing, knitting and embroidery machines. Those designed for textile use are usually made for specific machines.

5 DATABASES

These are used to store data and to allow its retrieval in a variety of ways. The most important aspect of the construction of a database is to understand what you wish to do with the data and how you wish to retrieve it. For example, you could design a database for your project work, it may contain the titles, author's name, Dewey number and pages of interest of the books you have used for your research. This means that you could find them in the library and that you could search this database each time you needed information about the books. However, it is most likely that you will use an existing database to retrieve data.

The name of your book, author etc. are stored in FIELDS, and each RECORD comprises a number of fields. A range of records are stored as a file. You can have many files which can be imported into the same database. So you could have a book database and files of Textiles or Technology or Electronics books.

By using a modem coupled to the computer there is a range of databases available for use over telephone lines, these are called online databases. (Ecctis)

```
Index:RECORD #                     BOOK                    Record:231
  Searching for:
  1 TITLE       CDT Design and Realisation
  2 AUTHOR      Rees David
  3 PUBLISHER   Longman
  4 PRICE       8.99
  5 ISBN        058201882x
  6 AGE
  7 TOPIC       CDT
  8 KEYSTAGE    3,4
  9 PUBDATE     1988
 10 RATING      vg
 11 LOCATION    Lib
 12 MODULE
 13 DEWEYNO
```

```
<F>wrd <B>ack <N>ext <P>rev <E>dit <D>elete <S>earch <I>ndex <T>ag <Z>oom  <Esc>
```

Fig. 14.7   A File Express Screen showing one record

In Fig. 14.7 can be seen one record (Number 231) with 13 fields, ie Title, Author, Publisher. You can search all of your records for any field or combination of fields. Indeed this database could be searched for all the books David Rees had published and all of those concerned with CDT. Look at field 2 Author, and field 7 Topic.

The database would then list the result of the search.

```
Index:RECORD #                    Quick Scan                    File:BOOK
√ Rec|TITLE                                            |AUTHOR
     |                                                 |
    1|Foundrywork for the Amateur                      |Aspin B. T
    2|Artistic Woodturning                             |Nish D.
    3|A Craft Approach to Technology                   |Barnes R W.
    4|A Craft Approach to Technology Teachers' Book    |Barnes R.W
    5|Advanced Design and Technology                   |Norman Eddie
    6|Alec Issigonis                                   |Nahum A.
    7|All about Creative Textiles                      |Holland
    8|An Introduction to CAD                           |Maycock B.
    9|An Introduction to CDT in the National Curriculum|Coventry City Council ::
   10|An Introduction to Craft Design and Technology   |Dunn Stewart
   11|Basic Electronics: Books 1-5                     |Plant M.
   12|Book of Gifts from the Pantry                    |
   13|CDT - Past, Present and Future                   |Penfold J.
   14|CDT - a Resource for Teachers and Students       |Webb Glynn
   15|CDT Design and Communication                     |Bland Stuart
   16|CDT-Technology                                   |Simmonds Keith
   17|Information Technology for C.D.T                  |MESU
   18|CDT for GCSE Projects                            |Shipley + Webster
   19|CDT in Context                                   |Williamson David
   20|CDT in Schools - some successful examples        |DES
F1:TITLE
Alt: <E>dit:OFF <D>elete <Z>oom <W>idth <T>ag <I>ndex <S>earch <A>dd        <Esc:
```

Fig. 14.8 Two views of File Express Database

A File Express Screen showing the Quickscan Mode can be seen in Fig 14.8. All databases have this method of quickly looking at, and accessing your records. You can see on this screen the record number, the title of the book, and the author's name. At the bottom of the screen are the commands to use for different functions. By pressing the "Alt" key and E, you can edit any record.

6 > SPREADSHEETS

A *spreadsheet* is a table of columns and rows, containing numbers. The content of rows and columns can be sorted and manipulated i.e. calculated and the results put into other columns or rows. The place where each number resides is called a CELL. Each cell is located in the spreadsheet by being referenced from the top left hand corner, horizontally by letter and vertically by number i.e. D3. Formulae can be put into cells which use the values in other cells to calculate the value for another cell. Cells can also be used as labels for the various columns and rows.

These are very useful for modelling and generating material cutting lists and costings of your project work. For example, a list of components and their prices could be entered, you could then type in the numbers of each type required for your electronics project, and the spreadsheet could calculate the total price.

A spreadsheet can be used to model or test any group of related numbers and to see how changing one or two affects the others. Cells can have formulae in them and will put the result of this calculation in another cell. If cell A1 had the length of the material in it and A2, the width, and A3 the thickness, then in another cell could be the formula $A1*A2*A3= A4$. The volume of your material would then appear in cell A4. Similarly if the price of the material per cubic metre is put in another cell, it is easy to see that the actual price of your small piece could be automatically worked out.

The dimensions of an artefact could be entered and changes could be made to see how others are affected.

A Spreadsheet screen showing part of a cutting list is found in Fig 14.9

```
     |   A    ||   B   ||   C   ||   D   ||   E    ||   F   ||   G   ||   H    |
1    NUMBER              MATERIAL          LENGTH            WIDTH                   HODI
2         5              MAHOGANY              12                1                   ▲▲
3                                                                                    ◀ ||
4        60              OAK                    1                1             1      ▼▼
5                                                                                    ENY
6         1              PINE                  12                2                    CEE
7                                                                                    ───
8        10              STEEL                  1                1                    ??
9                                                                                    !!
10                                                                                   ΣΕ
11                                                                                   F((
12                                                                                   ───
13
14
15                                                                                   ───
16                                                                                   GPPI
17                                                                                   PUUI
18                                                                                   AUI
19                                                                                   ───
20                                                                                   //
→ TEMP1!H8
Width:  9  Memory:    74  Last Col/Row:H8
   1>
READY F1:Help   F3:Names   Ctrl-Backspace:Undo   Ctrl-Break:Cancel   CAPS NUM
```

Fig. 14.9 Spreadsheet
CA SuperCalc

7 ⟩ CD ROMS. COMPACT DISC READ ONLY MEMORY (CD ROMS)

Your school may have computers capable of using *CD Roms*. These look like regular compact discs which you can buy for playing music. These have both sound, moving film and pictures recorded on them. Most are in the form of encyclopedia or reference works and contain thousands of pictures and text. There are many available which could be useful for both your research and as a source of drawings and pictures for your folio. Stored text and pictures can be retrieved into most graphics and DTP packages and then adjusted in size to fit your particular need. A recent addition is called The Design Image Bank available from the Design Council which has over 1800 picture images of furniture, graphics, textiles and exhibitions. Included are text files and details of the entry such as its history and designers.

8 ⟩ SCANNERS

Scanners enable graphics and text to be saved to disc and then imported into your graphics programmes to be printed. If you wish to import text and alter it into a word processor, then you will need Optical Character Recognition software (OCR) to do this, otherwise the text will be treated as a graphic. In this case the text can only be adjusted for size and not for content. There are two types of scanners, one which is pulled across the page to be scanned and the other in which the book or drawing is laid on the machine for copying. When copying from large books it is often difficult to copy part of a page with a flat bed scanner especially if the part to be copied is near to the inside edge of the page. Generally hand scanners are much cheaper but it can be difficult to move the scanner slowly and evenly over a document.

They are available both for black and white and colour. The files can be saved to disc in a variety of formats such as GIFF, PCX, WPG and then imported in your documents. The software supplied with most scanners enable you to edit and size graphics and also erase and crop areas. Some allow you to retouch and change colours and fills.

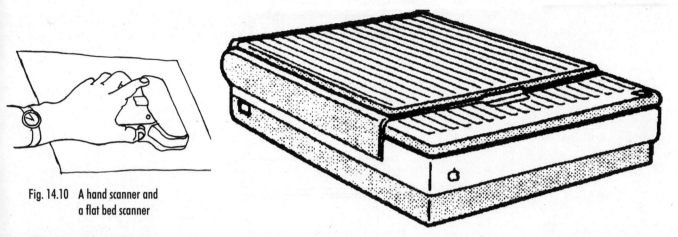

Fig. 14.10   A hand scanner and
a flat bed scanner

9 > OUTPUT DEVICES

There is a wide range of *output devices* (Table 14.3) available to print out your text and graphics once you have finished them. Generally the higher the price you pay the better definition you get. They output in colour and black and white.

Table 14.3   Output Devices

TYPE	ADVANTAGES	DISADVANTAGES
Dot Matrix Printer	Cheap to purchase and run. Lowest definition of all printers.	Better definition the higher the number of pins in the print head. Usually from 9 to 24 pins. Can be noisy.
Inkjet Printer	Relatively cheap to purchase. Higher definition. Colour very good.	Expensive to run. Can be slow on graphics.
Laser Printer	Excellent definition. Fast to print. Medium cost.	Expensive to buy. Not ozone friendly.
Plotters	Good for technical graphics i.e. line drawings.	Slow, can be costly to purchase.
Stencil Cutters	Can cut thin sheet plastic materials such as vinyls.	

10 > CONTROL

Computer *control* is an important area of Technology for several reasons. One, it can be used to replicate industrial control on a small scale; two, it provides a stimulating area of work for pupils taking static projects and providing movement and interaction; thirdly it gives an insight into the careful planning needed for the control of logical operations.

If looked at through a systems approach, then control is achieved through the operation of input devices i.e. sensors and switches which are manipulated by a programme to provide a range of output changes. The changes can be used to control lights, motors and actuators which in turn provide the power to move or illuminate the project.

The computer needs to be protected from accidental damage due to external voltages being applied incorrectly. This is called *buffering*. Commercially available interfaces called buffer boxes enable easy and safe connection to be made to the computer without the possibility of damage.

There are specific control programmes such as Control Logo, Contact, Control IT and Tiny Bits available which will allow you to programme in easily understood terms such as Switchon, Switchoff, Ifinputon. These programmes provide an easy to understand introduction to control. They enable the user to see on the computer monitor a diagrammatic view of the stages of the inputs and outputs, some allow the control programme to be stepped through slowly to enable faults to be readily identified. The use of these control languages allow quite complex linear programming to be done albeit at the expense of speed of operation. If speed is necessary then you could use Machine Code. Indeed one successful method of using these languages is to prove that the programme operates as intended. Once this is successfully achieved, its stages can then easily be converted to Machine code assembler. The buffer box will operate under any language.

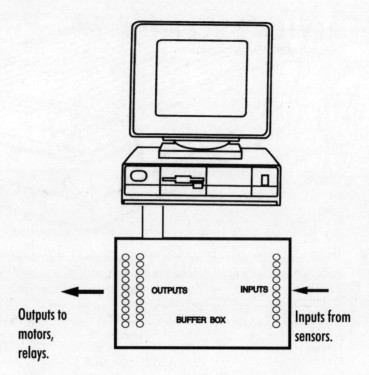

OUTPUTS   INPUTS

BUFFER BOX

Outputs to motors, relays.

Inputs from sensors.

Fig. 14.11 A typical computer control system

Example of typical (CONTACT) programme

SWITCHON 1	switch on output 1
WAIT 26	wait 2.6 seconds
SWITCHON 2	switch on output 2
WAIT 24	wait 2.4 seconds
SWITCHOFF 1 2	switch off outputs 1 and 2
WAIT UNTIL INPUTON?1	wait until input 1 is on then
SWITCHON 3 4	switch on outputs 3 and 4
WAIT 40	wait 4 seconds
SWITCHOFF 3 4	switch off outputs 3 4

The buffer box usually provides eight inputs and eight outputs. The outputs will enable eight lights or indicators to be switched on or off or four motors to be switched on or off and reversed. There is also a DC power supply built in which will supply up to one ampere of current. This is sometimes preset to six or twelve volts.

Buffering circuits can be constructed to control projects and be built in to projects but extreme care should be exercised so that damage to computers is avoided. For safety reasons, on no account should mains voltages be used.

11 SOME USEFUL WORDS

CAD	computer aided design
CAM	computer aided manufacture
Cell	a box into which values are put in a spreadsheet
Clipart	graphics on certain themes for your use
Cursor	small flashing mark on computer screen
Directory	a section of a computer disc
Fields	parts of a database
Filename	the name of a computer file
Font	a style of type
Graphics	drawings
G codes	used by machines for control
Icons	small pictures/logos in computer packages
Mouse	a desk top device that guides a pointer on the screen
Point	the height of type
Menus	instructions or tools in computer programmes
Records	a group of fields on a database
Toolbox	a group of commonly used icons
Windows	a method of accessing computer programmes

REVIEW SHEET

■ Give three reasons for using Information Technology in your coursework.

_____

_____

_____

_____

■ Give two reasons for not using Information Technology.

_____

_____

_____

■ You have just taken an hour to produce a drawing of your project using a computer, what do you need to do next?

_____

_____

_____

■ Describe a situation when you would use a spreadsheet.

_____

_____

_____

_____

■ Describe a situation when you would use a database.

_____

_____

_____

_____

■ What are the advantages of using computer control programmes?

_____

_____

_____

_____

■ Name three CAM textile processes.

_____

_____

_____

_____

■ List some sources of information which are available for use with computers.

_____

_____

_____

_____

_____

_____

■ When sending a drawing to printers and plotters, how do you choose which one to use?

_____

_____

_____

_____

_____

■ What advantages do desk top publishing packages have over most word processing packages?

_____

_____

_____

_____

_____

■ When would you use a paint type package? What type of activity would you be involved in?

_____

_____

_____

_____

_____

GETTING STARTED

It is important that you consider if the textile materials which you are going to use are fit for the purpose for which they are intended. Also you should have thought about the environmental, social and moral implications for using them.

- **Environmental:** – Are the materials made at the expense of using natural resources?
  –Do they biodegrade or can they be recycled when they are finished with?
  – Does their production/use/disposal cause pollution?
- **Social:** – What are the effects upon employees in the industry?
  – Are we exploiting Third World peoples?
- **Moral:** – Are we using animal products, furs etc?
  – Are we subjecting people to dangerous manufacturing processes?

Have you also considered the aesthetic areas of your design?

CHAPTER 15

TEXTILES

FIBRE CONTENT

CONSTRUCTION OF FABRICS

COLOUR

DYEING AND PRINTING

EQUIPMENT

ESTIMATION

AFTERCARE

CONSUMER AWARENESS

DESIGN AND FASHION

CREATIVE USE OF TEXTILES

PROJECT PLANNING

ESSENTIAL PRINCIPLES

Originally people would have used *natural* materials such as animal pelts, fur and plant fibres to make clothes. These have largely been superseded by *chemically produced* fibres which in some cases yield similar materials.

Natural Fibres

- **Cotton.** This is the most common *natural fibre*, this comes from a plant and is found around the seeds of the plant. The cotton bolls are picked and then separated from the seed, once done by hand, but now mechanised.
- **Linen.** This is another *natural fibre*, comes from stem of the flax plant. Both cotton and linen are composed of cellulose, a polymer.

❝ Types of natural fibre ❞

- **Wool.** This is a natural fibre but this comes from animals such as sheep, rabbits and goats. Particular breeds have certain advantages over others, for example the wool of the Angora goat can be spun into a really soft yarn.
  These are known as staple fibres and need to be twisted together to make a long yarn.
- **Silk.** This is produced by the silkworm, a caterpillar, in long filaments from spinnerets on their bodies. As they start to pupate they spin this filament around themselves into a cocoon. The cocoon is unravelled in water and produces a long continuous filament of protein.

Man-made fibres

The first *man-made fibres* were produced from cellulose from trees. Wood was broken down by chemical action into a sticky solution which was injected into acid where a filament was produced. This fibre was called *viscose* or *rayon* and belongs to the regenerated group of fibres.

Mostly the new fibres are made from plastics which are derived from oil. They are manufactured from a liquid by being forced through small holes called spinnerets. This imitates the action of the silkworm. These fibres are called *synthetics* and include *nylon, polyester, acrylic* and *polyester*. You will recognise these names as those of the common plastics used in Design and Technology.

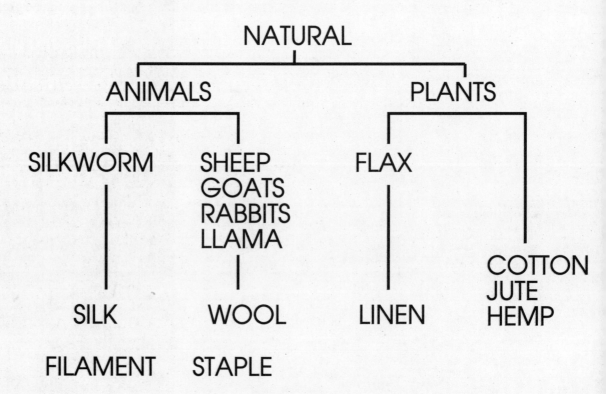

Fig. 15.1   Types of textile material

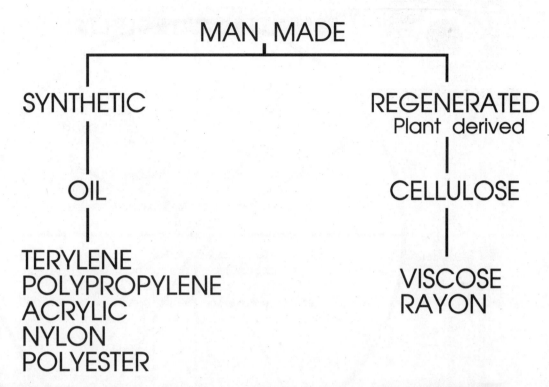

MAN MADE

SYNTHETIC

OIL

TERYLENE
POLYPROPYLENE
ACRYLIC
NYLON
POLYESTER

REGENERATED
Plant derived

CELLULOSE

VISCOSE
RAYON

Fig. 15.1 Types of textile material
(continued)

2 **CONSTRUCTION OF FABRICS**

All of these fibres have to be *spun* into yarns before they can be used. In the staple (short fibre) ones the strands are pulled out of the ball of tangle fibres and twisted together until a yarn is produced. This can be done by hand, or by using a spinning wheel or, in industry, by machine.

Filaments, such as silk, could be used straight away but they are often too thin for this and need bulking up. They could be chopped into short lengths and spun. They are often processed to increase their bulk, which puts tiny curls and loops or twists into them, which gives the effect of a much thicker, more springy yarn. Once a long length of yarn is produced it can be woven or knitted into fabric.

In *weaving*, lengths of yarn called the warp are put onto a loom and other yarns are interwoven across the warp, this is called the weft. Simple patterns can be produced by threading the weft alternately over and under the warp. More complex patterns can be produced by missing out certain parts of the warp ie perhaps every second warp. The interlacing provides a range of effects with names such as hopsack, satin and twill. The looms can be hand operated or very large complex fast electrically powered ones.

In *knitting*, threads are interlocked either by hand or machine and there are a range of different ways of achieving this. Also the texture of knitting can be changed by using thick or textured threads and large needles. There is plenty of scope for you to experiment in this area.

There is a wide range of other techniques and methods to produce fabrics which include sticking, and melting the fibres together. Once the fabric is produced, it is cleaned and stentered, which flattens and pulls it into shape. Processes are then given to improve the characteristics such as waterproofing and making it flame retardant.

Methods of producing
fabrics

3 **COLOUR**

Colour is very important, both from the point of view of the psychological effects of colour upon people and from a fashion sense; colours go in and out of favour. Another important aspect of colour is how they interact with each other and you must consider this when designing.

The colour wheel or circle shows a range of 12 hues (Fig. 15.2).

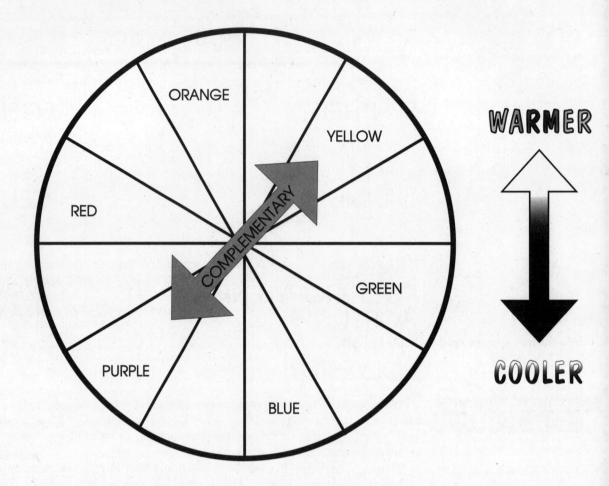

The 12 colours are called HUES

A Hue mixed with **BLACK** is a TINT

A Hue mixed with WHITE is a SHADE

COMPLEMENTARY colours are opposite each other.

Fig. 15.2 Colourwheel

- **Primary colours** are those which cannot be achieved by mixing i.e. red, yellow and blue.
- **Secondary colours** are made by mixing two primary colours together ie orange, green and violet.
- **Tertiary colours** are derived by mixing a primary colour and a secondary colour.

❝ Colours and their uses ❞
- **Complementary colours** are those opposite each other on the colour wheel, if mixed together a grey results.
- By putting two complementary colours together on a garment we may have achieved contrasting and startling effects.
- Shades are made by mixing white to the colour.
- Tints are made by adding black.
- Colour can be light or dark, this is said to be their "value".

4 ▷ DYEING AND PRINTING

Types of dye

Natural dyes come from plants, animals or minerals. The Romans used crushed shellfish to provide a dye for wool, and the cochineal beetle is used to provide red dyes. There are many plants which provide dyes, there are obvious ones such as beetroot and blackberry, all of which have to be boiled to extract the dye. Others such as the bark from trees may not be so obvious, it may be worth collecting various plants and materials and trying them. Dyed fabrics are said to be "colour fast" if the dye remains when the material is washed and "not fast" if it washes out. Different materials respond to dyeing in different ways and there are commercially available dyes for synthetic materials. Chemicals called mordants are used to fix dyes to materials.

Different fabrics will need the appropriate dyes, fabrics containing natural fibres will dye well as the fibres will absorb the dyes, synthetic fibres often do not accept dyes so readily.

Synthetic dyes are chemicals which reproduce a wide range of colours, which can resist fading and are fast.

It is a good idea to wet the fabric before dyeing as this allows the dye to penetrate the fibres of the material more easily and evenly. After dyeing the material will need to be rinsed to remove excess dye and then dried.

Techniques of dyeing

There are many different dyeing techniques which can be achieved in school or college, combining some of the processes can be used to provide exciting techniques.

- **Tie dyeing:** where cloth is tied tightly with string into bundles or knotted around pebbles and then dyed, the string can then be retied and the material redyed. A wide range of interesting patterns can result. Different types of string can be tried, as can paper clips, rubber bands or, indeed anything which will prevent the dye from reaching the fabric.
- **Batik:** this is where a wax is painted onto the material which is then dyed. The wax prevents the dye from soaking into the fibres. Traditionally the wax is dribbled onto the material using a tjanting tool, which is a small funnel-like tool made of metal into which the hot wax is poured. The wax is removed by ironing between absorbent sheets of paper. The process is repeated until a satisfactory design has been achieved. As the wax would be melted by using hot water only cold water dyes should be used in this process.

Fig. 15.3 A tjanting

Printing

Before any form of *printing* the fabric needs to be washed and ironed to firstly remove any proofing from the manufactured cloth and to make it flat so that the printing will be successful.

Block printing involves making a block (Fig. 15.4) onto which the paints can be put, the pattern or design then being transferred to the fabric by pressing the block onto it. The block can then be moved and repeats achieved. At the simplest level, blocks can be made from potatoes by cutting in half and then cutting the pattern into the surface. Many vegetables when cut have their own intricate patterns which can be used i.e. onions, cabbages, and celery for example.

Blocks can be made by cutting out shapes from card, foam rubber, polystyrene tiles and gluing them onto a block of wood.

In fact anything which has an interesting surface can be used to transfer the paint onto the fabric.

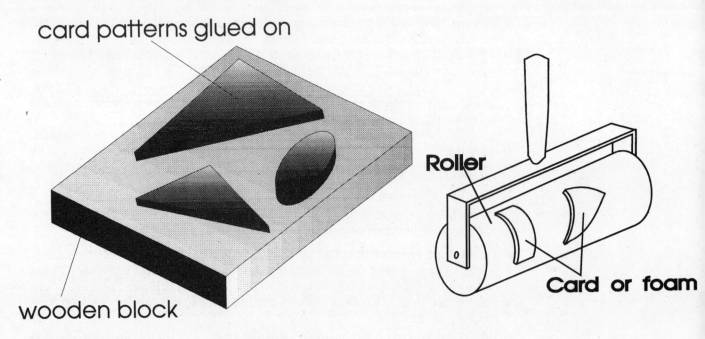

Fig. 15.4 A printing block

Fig. 15.5 Roller

If this method is used to put patterns onto a roller (Fig. 15.5) then the pattern can be easily repeated along the fabric. Lino cuts can also be used.

Stencilling involves cutting out designs in card and then laying the card over the fabric, then paint is applied by sponging, spattering with an old toothbrush or with an airbrush. The paint will only meet the fabric where there are holes in the stencil. Airbrushes can be simple mouth blown devices consisting of a paint container into which a paint tube is fitted, a piece of tube then allows air to be blown over the end of this tube causing the paint to be sucked up and atomised. Also they can be more expensive and driven by a compressor and be capable of drawing very fine lines.

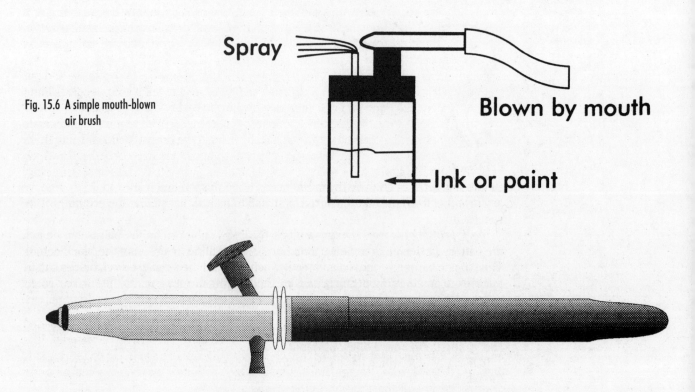

Fig. 15.6 A simple mouth-blown air brush

Fig. 15.7 A compressor driven air brush

Screen printing (Fig. 15.8) has a wooden frame onto which a polyester mesh is fitted. Paint is applied over the screen using a squeegee, a stencil allows the paint to be applied to the fabric. There are methods of applying the design directly onto the screen and not using a stencil.

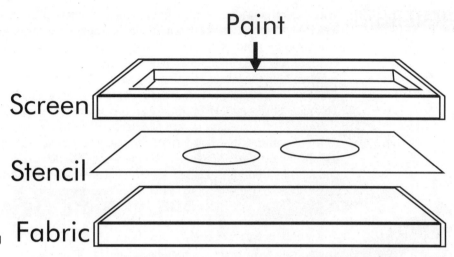

Fig. 15.8 The screen printing process

There are a range of pens and crayons which can be applied directly to washed fabric, to make them fast they are then ironed on the reverse side of the fabric usually through two sheets of clean paper. Some can be applied to paper and then ironed onto the fabric, but you must remember that your design will be reversed.

Texture effects can be achieved by using commercially available tubes or squeezy bottles of very thick paints which dry as raised lines on the fabric. These can be purchased in exciting colours and effects such as silver, gold and speckled. When applied to old clothes and trainers, they can give a futuristic space-like look, and are interesting for making younger children's play clothes.

If you have a computer and printer capable of using sublimatic inks then you can make your design using a graphics package such as Drawmouse and then print onto paper. The paper is then put ink side down onto the material and using an iron, the pattern or design can be transferred to the cloth. Drawmouse allows complex patterns and colour ways to be produced with variable drops.

5 > EQUIPMENT

In the school situation, you may well be required to use a wide range of tools/machines in the production of artefacts. It will be necessary to find out how to use these safely and properly. This can be done, firstly by your teacher showing you how to use them, or it could be by you reading a manufacturer's handbook or following a familiarisation course. You should not attempt to use equipment with which you are unfamiliar as damage can be expensive to put right.

When using sewing machines, for example, you should be able to recognise and put right faults. By looking at your stitching you should be able to tell if your needle is blunt or if the tension is wrong and you should know how to rectify these problems.

Sewing, embroidery, overlockers and knitting machines will all require maintenance to keep them working correctly; you can help by using them properly and cleaning them when you have finished your work. Many of these machines have accessories which must be carefully stored after use, they are usually expensive to replace and, if missing, may well prevent you or someone else from finishing their project.

Once you are familiar with a range of equipment you will need perhaps to buy something for your own use. You should be able to compare different machines in the shops and select the best one for your needs. It will be useful to be able to devise tests to evaluate one machine or tool against another. The things which you want the machine to do should be written as a list. Aspects which may be useful could be written next, then each machine could be compared on your list together with its price. Decisions could then be taken once you have compared the machines.

6 > ESTIMATION

As with any Design and Technology topic, it is necessary to list all the materials needed for a project and to *estimate* accurately the quantities, sizes and type of material. It is important to realise that as well as the fabric for textiles, there are likely to be patterns, buttons, threads, zips, linings and trimmings to buy. Often these items can be quite expensive and add considerably to the overall price.

When estimating fabrics, the pattern on it, the surface finish and the stretch will each have a significant effect on the area required, as the fabric pattern will have to be matched where pieces join, similarly where the fabric has a pile or nap, care has to be taken.

When working with commercial patterns it is a good rule to buy a larger size than you need if you are between two sizes, as you can always take the garment in.

7 ⟩ AFTERCARE

Washing removes any soiling in the fabric, water on its own will not remove soiling, we need to add soap. Soaps are made mainly from vegetable oils and caustic soda. They are often coloured and perfumed to make them more attractive to use. Detergents are made synthetically and contain molecules which bond with grease and dirt and assist in their removal from the fabric. Heating and agitating the clothes in a washing machine aids the process. Some detergents contain biological agents called enzymes to help digest stains. To make fabrics appear brighter or more white, chemicals which fluoresce are added.

Ironing is the process of removing creases from washed fabrics; the iron must be set to the recommended temperature for that fabric and manufacturer's instructions are usually included on the label of the garment. If in doubt choose the lowest temperature and start by ironing a small area of the garment which does not show.

Caring for all your fabrics

Today most people have clothes made from a wide variety of materials ranging from traditional fabrics like cotton, silk and wool to man made fabrics such as viscose, nylon, lycra and polyester. Because of this your wash needs special attention.

Full washing, drying and ironing instructions are usually provided on the labels of most garments. By following these instructions and by using **novon**, you can be sure that your clothes will be as clean and bright as possible – wash after wash.

Washing temperatures: To achieve the best quality results from **novon**, it is important to wash your clothes at the right temperature. When in doubt always refer to the garment label.

Fig. 15.9

Fabric care guide

TEXTILE/MACHINE CODE OLD	TEXTILE/MACHINE CODE NEW	MACHINE	HANDWASH	EXAMPLES OF APPLICATION
1/95° 9/95°	95°	MAXIMUM wash in cotton cycle	Hand hot (50°C). or boil. Spin or wring.	White cotton and linen articles without special finishes.
2/60°	60°	MAXIMUM wash in cotton cycle	Hand hot (50°C). Spin or wring.	Cotton, linen or viscose articles without special finishes where colours are fast at 60°C.
3/50° 4/50°	50°	MEDIUM wash in synthetics cycle	Hand hot. Cold rinse, short spin or damp dry.	Polyester/cotton mixtures, nylon, polyester; cotton and viscose articles with special finishes. Cotton/arcylic mixtures.
5/40°	40°	MAXIMUM wash in cotton cycle	Warm Spin or wring.	Cotton, Linen or Viscose articles where colours are fast at 40°C but not 60°C.
6/40°	40°	MEDIUM wash in synthetics cycle	Warm, cold rinse, short spin. Do not hand wring.	Acrylics, acetate and triaceatate; including mixtures with wool; polyester/wool blends.
7/40°	40°	MINIMUM wash in wool cycle	Warm. Do not rub. Spin. Do not hand wring.	Wool. Wool mixed with other fibres; silk.
8/30°		Articles labelled 8/30° or 30°		should be washed in the appropriate MEDIUM or MINIMUM cycle or hand washed.
(handwash)	(handwash)		Handwash only, (see garment label).	
(do not wash)			Do not machine or handwash	

The terms 'MINIMUM', 'MEDIUM', and 'MAXIMUM' wash refer to the washing time and agitation required.
Follow the manufacturer's instructions.

Ingredient	Function
Detergents	Dissolve grease
Optical Brighteners	Add fluorescent brightness to fabrics
Carboxy Methyl Cellulose	Keeps soil in suspension
Phosphonate	Reduces deposition of hard water salts
Silicone	Reduces foam level
Sodium Carbonate	Softens hard water
Sodium Bicarbonate	Softens hard water
Sodium Disilicate	Alkaline cleaning agent
Sodium Perborate	Oxidises and removes stains
Sodium Tripolyphosphate	Softens hard water and keeps soil in suspension
Tetra Acetyl Ethylene Diamine	Activates sodium perborate

Garment care labels

HANDWASH	BLEACHING	IRONING	DRY CLEANING
Handwash only	Chlorine bleach may be used	Cool iron	May be dry cleaned. Other letters and/or a bar beneath the circle will indicate the required process to the dry cleaner.
A cross through any symbol means "DO NOT"	TUMBLE DRYING — May be tumble dried	Warm iron	
		Hot iron	

Pressing is the process of deliberately putting creases into a garment, such as the pleats in a skirt or creases in trousers. Some synthetic materials are made from thermoplastics and can therefore have pleats heat set into them during manufacture. These keep their creases better after being washed.

Most fabrics when made up into finished articles have labels fixed into them which tell you how to look after the fabric. These include the temperatures at which they should be washed and ironed, and details of the washing and drying cycles. It is important to follow these instructions carefully so that you do not damage or shorten the life of your fabrics. These are shown in Fig. 15.9.

8 CONSUMER
AWARENESS

When making any artefact to sell there are many aspects which need considering.

- Is there a need? In marketing your work you must find out if there is a need for it; how many people are likely to want to buy?
- What is the competition? Are there others doing the same thing?
- How are you going to promote your work? Will it be by selling to friends initially and then building up by people telling others or will you advertise?
- If you advertise, who will be your target customers?
- Will you go to the top end of the market and make a few expensive items, or will you make thousands of items for the lower end?
- If you then decide to sell to the top end, how will you sell? Will it be through an established business or will you open your own shop?
- How will you convince an established outlet to sell your work? What is special about your work?

Once you have started you will need to set a realistic price for your goods. This means that you have to find out your costs.

Costings

These are likely to include:

- **Time:** How much do you and your workers' time cost?
- **People:** How much does a good machinist cost?
- **Skills:** What employees do you need?
- **Equipment:** What equipment do you need? Do you rent or buy the equipment? How much is depreciation? How much is maintenance?
- **Materials:** How much do the materials cost? How much can you afford to keep in stock? How quickly can you obtain stock? How much will be wasted? How do you control the amount of stock needed?
- How much will heating, lighting, rent and rates cost?
- **Marketing:** How much will it cost to market the goods? You will have to visit suppliers and customers, how much will this cost? You will have to advertise in papers, journals and magazines.
- **Distribution:** The cost of delivery will have to be included in your prices. You will have to pack your goods and have to buy paper, string, tape, postage stamps etc.

Quality control

Ultimately, when the business is running well, how do you make sure that the items you are selling are made to the correct standards; if they are not then future orders will not come. This aspect is called *quality control* and once the business starts to grow it is increasingly difficult to achieve. This is because as your business grows you will have to delegate responsibilities to others, and they may not be so conscientious as you were.

Other factors

You will need to know what your customers want, and be aware that their needs are likely to *change* quite rapidly especially in the area of fashion. This can be done by market research, by questioning the general public or the section at which you are aiming your sales and then analysing the results. A sample of your goods could be sent to selected groups to ask their opinion or for them to test.

You must also be aware of *legislation*, that is any law concerning the design and production of your work. This is likely to be in the areas of Consumer Protection, Health and Safety, British Standards and The Sale of Goods Act.

On the *financial side*, any business will be subject to general influences such as recession, inflation, changes in the market. Good business practice attempts to predict and change quickly to respond to these factors.

When beginning to *raise money* to start your business, your bank manager will want to see a Business plan, to see what you are going to do, how and where you are to do it and whether you have identified a market for your goods.

In the school situation, this can be tried out on a small scale by Young or Mini Enterprise. This includes the setting up of a company with directors, managers and production staff with capital being raised and shares issued. Local business people will give advice and it enables students to have an insight into all of the challenges listed above. Whilst these schemes give an insight, they can only give limited experience of what running a business is really like because of their small scale.

Most enterprise schemes make and sell things for school fetes, parent's evenings and charity events.

9 DESIGN AND FASHION

Fashion is the art of wearing clothes that are thought to be "in" at any particular time. Your image is the personality which you present to the public. People can project an image through what they wear. This can show their importance or status or which social, political or economic groups to which they belong. With young people this can be very important and can decide how well you fit in with your friends. Obviously as a group of people become more wealthy, they have more money to spend on clothing and so it may become less functional, i.e. not just to keep warm, but move towards more extreme *fashions* which have little to do with functionality. If you think back to the hot pants and flared trousers of the 1960's, these are fashions in which functionality is reduced and image is all important.

Some fashion changes and innovation are led by the great designers and fashion houses, others come from within the general public.

The availability of new fabrics allow clothes to develop with colours, fixings and designs which would have been quite impossible to achieve with older fabrics. Modern ski wear is one example where new materials have allowed vast improvements in design.

With a large number of people now being able to travel to other countries then the influences of other cultures will affect fashion.

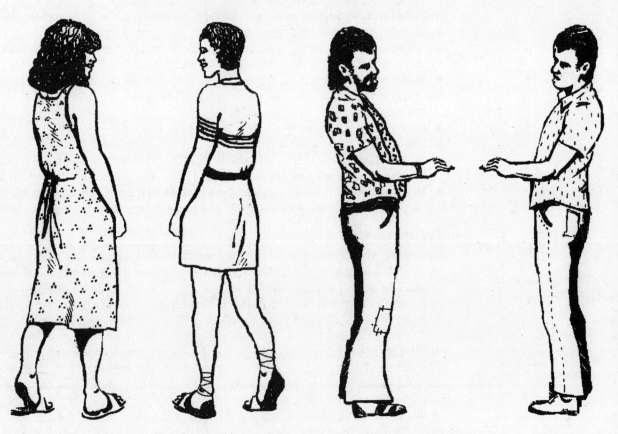

Fig. 15.10 Changes in fashion?

Corporate Image

Companies must advertise themselves and one way of successfully achieving this is to often dress their employees in similar clothes. The clothes often have badges or logos of the company on them or sometimes this is more subtly achieved by just using the colours associated with the company. Airlines such as BA and Virgin have a range of uniforms for all of their staff from baggage handlers through to pilots and cabin staff. This advertises and projects the appearance which the company wishes to have as its own image.

In examinations, there are often questions asking you to design clothes for the employees of a large company. Sometimes you are asked to choose a business, on other occasions you are given a choice of several different types of occupation. If, for example you are asked to design for a supermarket:

1. What are the needs?
2. How many different jobs can you think of?
3. What are the requirements of the clothes of all these jobs?
4. How do you link all of the people together?
5. How do you ensure that the staff will be happy to wear them?
6. What image is the company trying to project?
7. Are there cultural aspects likely to affect the design?

The answers may be:–

1. The designs must be capable of being adapted for a range of needs.
2. Drivers, Shelf Stackers, Checkout Staff, Food Handlers, Butchers, Security, Office Staff, Managers.
3. Some of these clothes need to be hard wearing, some hygienic, some easy to bend and stretch in, some frequently washed, some easy to sit in at a till for long periods, some to look business like.
4. Links can be made by a common colour range or stripe or style. Distinctive shape or hats etc.
5. Staff could initially be given the choice of the design or be involved with the design. The design should be fashionable and make staff pleased to wear it.
6. In the case of airlines perhaps efficiency, authority and yet a friendly image. Perhaps a fast food outlet may want to project a young, dynamic, fun image.
7. It may be against employees' culture or belief to wear certain types of clothing. Do the designs address these aspects and allow for diversity?

Your first line of enquiry should be about the image of the company and then the requirements of the clothes. You then need to find out how many different jobs need to be done and what are the requirements of the clothes.

10 CREATIVE USE OF TEXTILES

Quilting. This is the technique of placing polyester wadding between two layers of fabric, it provides a decorative raised effect but is especially used to trap air and make clothes or quilts very warm.

Appliqué. This is applying, by sewing, fabric shapes onto other fabrics usually for decorative effect.

Macramé. This is the decorative use of knotted cords, string or rope. This can be used to make belts, plant holders etc.

Embroidery. This uses coloured threads to produce a decorative effect on fabric, the stitches can also give pleasing textures to the fabric.

Patchwork. This is the sewing together of small pieces of fabric to make larger pieces. The shapes are often geometric patterns which tesselate together. Traditionally the shapes were frequently hexagons.

Many of these techniques can be combined to produce interesting effects. Experiment!

11 PROJECT PLANNING

Fig. 15.11a shows you how a project planning sheet might be devised for the assignment "Clothes for Outdoor Activity" Fig. 15.11b provides one for you to fill in as you undertake your project in this area.

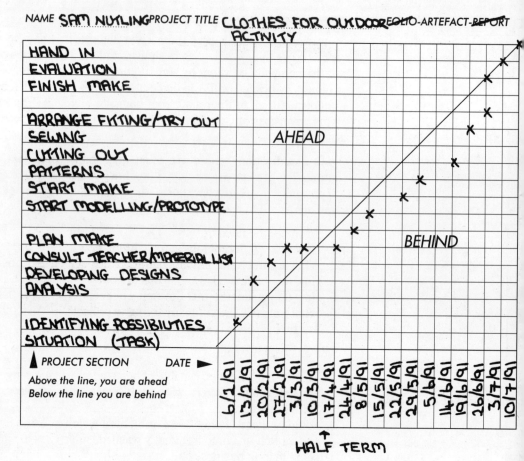

Fig. 15.11a   Project planning sheet

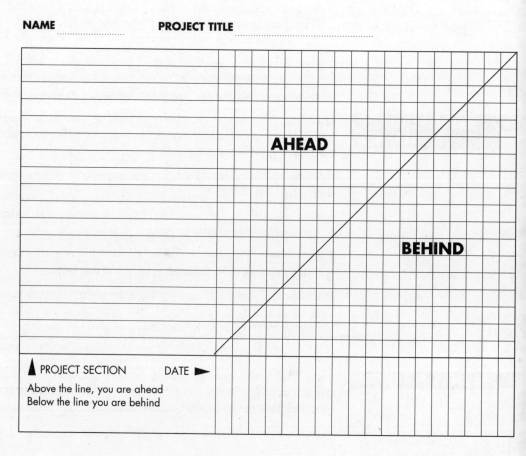

Fig. 15.11b   Project planning sheet

REVIEW SHEET

■ Give some examples of natural fibres.

_____

_____

_____

_____

■ Give some examples of synthetic fibres.

_____

_____

_____

_____

■ How are viscose or rayon fibres made, and from what source does the raw material come?

_____

_____

_____

_____

_____

■ List some important environmental facts when considering the use of particular fabrics.

_____

_____

_____

_____

_____

■ Explain the terms staple and filament.

_____

_____

_____

_____

_____

■ If filaments are too thin for use, how can they be increased in effective size to be more useful?

_____

_____

_____

_____

■ Why is colour so important?

_____

_____

_____

_____

■ When dyeing fabrics, what do you need to know about the fabric?

_____

_____

_____

_____

■ Describe two methods of colouring fabrics.

_____

_____

_____

_____

_____

■ Explain with examples, the reasons for ironing fabrics.

_____

_____

_____

_____

_____

■ What does marketing mean?

_____

_____

_____

_____

_____

■ Give some examples of things which would influence a fashion designer.

_____

_____

_____

_____

■ Describe a local company's use of clothes for enhancing its corporate image.

_____

_____

_____

_____

_____

ERGONOMICS AND ANTHROPOMETRICS

COLOUR

SHAPE

FORM

SIZE

SOUND

THE NATURE OF "ERGONOMICS"

GETTING STARTED

Ergonomics is the study of those aspects that improve the quality of the environment and in turn improve the efficiency of human beings. If you accept that you can do things *better* in some situations than others, it may be because the environment was more suitable. In an environment where you are happy, comfortable, and have the use of well-designed equipment, you are most likely to do well at whatever task you have to tackle.

The efficiency with which you are able to *perform* a task will depend on many factors, and these may include any combination of the following:

1. colour;
2. shape;
3. form;
4. size;
5. sound.

We start by considering the influence these factors have on behaviour and performance.

Anthropometrics ("man" measurement) is an important part of ergonomics.

ESSENTIAL PRINCIPLES

1 ▷   COLOUR

Colour plays an important part in our lives. Colour can be associated with having an effect upon human moods. Bright colours such as yellow, orange or red tend to make us feel bright and cheerful. Warm colours such as brown or orange tend to make us feel comfortable and warm. Blue and white colours give a feeling of coolness. Black and grey colours are dark and dull and in some situations make us feel sad and mournful. The colour of things around us is important if a particular mood is to be created, from the clothes we wear to the colour of the wall in a room.

2 ▷   SHAPE

Shape is concerned with a two-dimensional arrangement of lines. A dot is a line that has approximately equal length and thickness. A line can be straight, wavy, or curved. When it joins up with itself it is called an *outline*. An outline encloses an area that can be described as a *shape*. When areas are shaped and combine in something solid they are then presenting *a form*.

Shape is concerned with pattern. Lines can be arranged to make a plain surface interesting, or to draw your attention to a detail. Line can be used to deceive the eye e.g. optical illusion. It can be used to create a feeling of height or a feeling of movement, rhythm, depth, etc. (Fig. 16.1).

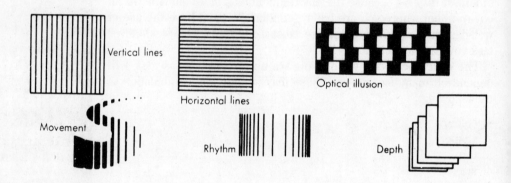

Fig. 16.1

All these feelings are a natural response to shape. Combine shape with colour and the impressions or feelings can be made stronger.

3 ▷   FORM

This is still concerned with shape, but this time it is concerned with three dimensions – solid **forms**. Most of our environment is in three dimensions. There are two groups:

a) natural forms;
b) man-made forms.

Natural forms include: trees, animals, birds, insects, nests, e.g. bees-nest, mountains, rivers, pebbles, rocks, etc.

Man-made forms include: buildings, bridges, roads, cars, aeroplanes, chairs, cups, knives, computers, etc.

The natural forms, large or small, have influenced man in the shaping of the environment.

The "Crab" cramp is an example of a design that was not intended to look like a crab's pincer. It so happened that working out the movements that were required to give an efficient grip on materials, plus a study and an investigation of pincer movements in animals, resulted in the final design resembling a crab's pincer.

4 ▷   SIZE

It is important that man-made products to be used by Man are made to a size that is comfortable. In order to arrive at the correct sizes an area of study has been developed and is known by the name "Anthropometrics" (derived from two words Anthropod, meaning *man*, and Metrics, meaning *measurement*) – Man measurement. This study is an important part of ergonomics.

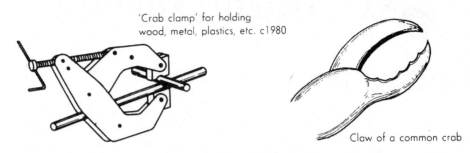

'Crab clamp' for holding
wood, metal, plastics, etc. c1980

Claw of a common crab

Fig. 16.2

A study of *human measurements* is necessary if the things you use are going to fit. A chair is an excellent product to examine to see how the height and width match your needs. This has nothing to do with comfort yet, only sitting positions. If you are sitting in front of a computer screen operating a keyboard or mouse control it is important for you to be able to see the screen and operate the controls from a comfortable position. To be able to do this, the measurements of you and the measurements of the movements you have to make to operate the controls need to be known.

At the drawing board stage, scale model (one-tenth full size) "Manikins" can be used. These are cardboard cut-out shapes of human-beings with pivoting joints for arms, legs and neck, etc. Front or side profiles can be made. Once the sizes have been established, a "manikin" can be made and used to establish preliminary dimensions of possible designs.

5 ▷ SOUND

Just as we live in an environment of colour, shape and form, so we also live in a world of **sound**. Some sounds such as the blast from a car horn give us a warning and we respond to that warning by making sure we are not going to be involved in an accident. The sound is not pleasant and to be blasted at by a horn often makes us feel annoyed. The important thing is that it is an efficient way of making us respond quickly. Where there is a greater sense of urgency, high-pitched continuous sounds are used. These are used by the emergency services on vehicles such as those used by the police, fire crews, and ambulance crews.

Sound is also used for far less urgent reasons. The ring of a telephone, the buzz from the oven timer, the bleep from the open door of the freezer, the noise from an alarm clock, etc., are all sounds calling our attention to the fact that we need to respond with an action. The bleep on a computer tells us that a wrong key has been pressed and we need to check what should be done to get the correct action from the computer.

6 ▷ THE NATURE OF "ERGONOMICS"

Ergonomics is a study of the five areas just covered, all *brought together* under one heading, since they all relate to the way in which people respond. An understanding of causes and effects in each of the five areas helps designers to produce products that are:

1. easy to use;
2. very difficult to use wrongly;
3. able to produce the appropriate human response.

If the human factors are resolved the product will be used efficiently.

PUTTING "ERGONOMICS" INTO PRACTICE

It is said that the study of ergonomics arose from a real-life situation. During World War 2, many British bomber planes crashed on the runways after returning from bombing missions over Germany. A returning crew had avoided all the enormous risks of being shot down by enemy aircraft and military gun fire, yet in landing the aircraft crashed. Because there were so many crashes of this kind, a team of experts was appointed to resolve the problem. Calling it "pilot error" was clearly only part of the answer.

The team was composed of:

1. engineers, who covered mechanisms, electrics, hydraulics, aerodynamics and production;
2. doctors, who specialised in physical and mental behaviour.

After considerable research, which included going on bombing missions, the team resolved the problem. The answer was very simple. When a pilot was exhausted, his mental and physical responses were *not* at their best. To land an aeroplane required many instruments to be observed, and switches, levers and knobs to be operated. Two controls that were side by side operated two *different functions*, but the *handles were identical*. The tired pilot depended, in the very dim light, on his sense of *touch* to find and to operate them. In doing this, the pilots would regularly move the *wrong* handle, which unfortunately would result in the aeroplane crashing. Since touch was the sense being relied upon by an exhausted pilot, the design of the handles was changed. One remained as a *smooth* sphere, and the other as *rough* grip, similar in shape to that of a handle bar grip on a bicycle. The change of *form* and *surface texture* of one control made the identity of each *unmistakable* to the pilot. The number of aeroplanes crashing on return from a bombing mission was greatly reduced. The success of solving such a problem highlighted the need to look at the following:

a) the way we respond to shape and form;
b) the need for considering the importance of texture.

You may now wish to consider the importance of ergonomics in relation to operating a machine in the workshop.

CASE STUDY: OPERATING A DRILLING MACHINE

EASY TO USE?

If the machine is easy to operate it may be because of:

a) the size and position of the controls;
b) the use of colour, which makes it easy to identify press buttons, safety bars, control handles;
c) the use of form, which gives a clear indication that some things are pressed, some are turned, and others are pulled;
d) the use of texture on surfaces, which helps to ensure that a firm grip is possible. Or the use of a smooth surface where a sliding grip is necessary.

VERY DIFFICULT TO USE WRONGLY?

The drilling machine is a very efficient machine. However, like landing the aeroplane, *human error is possible*, which might include any of the following:

1. leaving the pulley cover partially open so exposing moving parts;
2. leaving the chuck key in the drill chuck;
3. not putting the guard over the drill chuck and bit;
4. having the wrong speed for the size of drill being used;
5. not having the work securely fastened to the table.

Of the five errors, only the first two might result in stoppage of the machine being used.

1. There is a small spring loaded switch which is pressed down by the pulley cover. Only when the cover is *properly down* will the machine be able to be operated.
2. Some, but very few, machines are supplied with a spring loaded chuck. The key will only stay in the chuck while it is held by hand. If the hand pressure is *released*, the key will gently come out of the hole *before* there is any chance of switching on the machine. If the key is attached to a chain, the key will hang where it will do no harm.
3. The large majority of machines do *not* have a safety device to give a warning signal, either audio or visual, to the user or to prevent it from being switched on.
4. Indicating drill speed in relation to drill diameter should not be too difficult. To link it with tank cutters that have a drill shank very much smaller than the diameter of

the blade makes the problem much more complicated. A further complication would be to have the correct drill speed for specific materials.

5. Since the holding device does not form part of the drilling machine, it may mean that a warning device should be incorporated in the machine vice.

There are very few accidents on a drilling machine, the credit for which may be due more to the careful user rather than to the designer.

PRODUCE THE APPROPRIATE HUMAN RESPONSE?

The function of a machine is to perform an activity of work. If the machine is used for the purpose it is intended, then it must by its appearance produce the correct responses. Many pupils are introduced to a drilling machine as one of the first machines they ever use. At the age of 11, many pupils are quite small, and a full-size drilling machine is big and rather frightening for them to use. Apart from their fear they also find it difficult to reach and operate some of the controls. This is not because the drilling machine is poorly designed but because the machine was designed mainly for use by adults. The sizes are therefore based upon the size of people who have finished growing rather than those who are still growing.

The colour of the machine is often grey, a colour that suggests seriousness and work. A pink and yellow machine might suggest it is a toy and promote the response that it is something to be played with rather than to be used for a serious purpose.

The green buttons are recessed so that they cannot be knocked accidentally and indicate a point where power can be brought to the machine. The red button stands out from the casing to ensure that it can be easily operated for switching off the electric supply quickly. Also, the red emergency stop bar that can be operated with the foot is large and difficult to miss. The red in contrast to the grey helps these devices to show up clearly.

The small switch at the side is for setting the drill in a forward or reverse motion; being grey it does not stand out. The black knob handle on a short lever does indicate that it is a control mechanism. It can often be left in the forward position and not be touched by the user of the machine. Its lack of prominence is reflected in its infrequent use. The user has therefore not got to be made aware of it during most drilling operations.

SUMMARY

Anthropometrics is concerned with measurement and movement.
Efficiency is concerned with a) the human response; and
                                  b) the device that is used by a human.
Ergonomics is concerned with efficiency.

You will read in some books that Ergonomics is to do with measurement. It would be more helpful to think of measurement as an important part of ergonomics. If things are the right size then efficiency will be that much easier.

REVIEW SHEET

■ Briefly explain what the study of ergonomics includes and describe how this influences the design of a working environment.

_____
_____
_____
_____
_____
_____
_____
_____
_____
_____
_____
_____

■ Ergonomics also includes the study of anthropometrics. Define the term anthropometric and explain and illustrate to show how the design of:
a) a battery torch,
b) a domestic kitchen, is influenced by the data obtained from this study.

Definition _____
_____
_____
_____

Battery torch

Domestic kitchen

■ Describe the effects that colour can have upon a person's mood. Give examples where different colours may be used to create a feeling of coolness.

_____

_____

_____

■ Describe and show how the use of line and pattern can have a visual effect upon an object.

_____

_____

_____

_____

_____

_____

_____

_____

■ In the commercial and industrial world putting ergonomics into practice is very important. Briefly explain why this is deemed to be so necessary.

_____

_____

_____

_____

_____

_____

_____

_____

_____

_____

_____

_____

CHAPTER 17

ENERGY

NON-FOSSIL FUEL ENERGY

FORMS OF ENERGY

CONVERSION OF ENERGY

GETTING STARTED

Without energy there would be no life. The most basic storage of energy comes from *plants*. Plants depend on light to grow and the light to make growth possible comes from the sun. Plants that grew millions of years ago died and were buried beneath the earth's crust but they did not lose that energy. Today those plants are mined in the form of *coal*. A similar example is *peat*. The plants that lived many thousands of years ago and became covered by water and silt are now being dug out, allowed to dry and used as a fuel for heating.

Animals live by eating plants, and by eating other animals who also eat plants. Many millions of such animals lived in the water. They were *crustaceans*, i.e. they had a hard shell to protect them, and included crabs, lobsters, shrimps, etc. When these died, they formed a layer of *shell* at the bottom of the ocean. In time (over many millions of years), as the earth cooled and its own crust crumbled and twisted, these layers of shell became trapped underneath rock. Today those crustaceans are being extracted in the form of *crude oil* and *natural gas*. Oil is used to supply heat and mechanical energy. Gas is used to supply heat energy. These types of fuel are known as **fossil fuels**.

Coal, gas and oil are referred to as fuels that come from **natural resources**. Since the process that produces them takes millions of years, there will come a time when these natural resources will run out, perhaps sometime during the next century. Other sources of energy are available but as yet are insufficiently developed to meet with today's demands.

ESSENTIAL PRINCIPLES

1 NON-FOSSIL FUEL ENERGY

WIND

Wind as a source of energy has been used for thousands of years. It has been a major source of energy for sailing craft of all kinds and more recently, but very much underdeveloped, for the generation of electricity.

WATER

Water has provided a direct source of energy to drive machinery for many hundreds of years. Water wheels have turned the gears and pulleys of grinding wheels, hammers and milling machines, etc. Now water turns the turbines of electricity generating machines to provide an indirect source of energy. Electricity produced by this means is known as "hydroelectricity".

Tidal waves have been lashing and eating away our shores for millions of years and are likely to continue doing so for many millions of years to come. This energy is being tapped in France where tidal waves are used to generate electricity. The geographical conditions for this to be possible are not common, but research into such a scheme for Britain is taking place at the mouth of the River Severn. Here the rise and fall of the tide is one of the largest in the world and it is possible that a tidal electricity generating station will be built before the end of this century.

GEOTHERMAL

Geothermal energy is evident in Britain and perhaps the best-known source is at the Roman Baths in Bath. Here there is a constant supply of warm water. The quantity of warm water is insufficient to be of real benefit as a source of energy, so it remains a tourist attraction, though it was used at one time as a health centre for people suffering from arthritis. In New Zealand, however, the temperature of the water is much higher and warm water is available in much larger quantities. Some development and progress has been made to tap this energy source.

SOLAR

Solar energy makes use of the Sun's rays. One way of tapping the Sun's energy is to heat water under glass, and this method has been used for a number of years. Some homes and large buildings have systems attached to their roofs, which certainly raise the temperature of the water but *another* source of energy is still needed to drive the electric pumps to make the water circulate. The *net* advantage gained is currently minimal, so until further developments take place, the use of this source of energy is unlikely to increase.

Another method of tapping solar energy is in the use of *solar cells*. The energy output is small, but light aircraft can fly using solar energy when they carry large numbers of these cells. Some pocket calculators and watches are able to function on this source of energy since their energy requirements are very low.

NUCLEAR

Nuclear energy is a very powerful source of energy. It has grown and replaced many coal and oil-fuelled electricity power stations all over the world. The natural supply of uranium is so abundant that it was thought at one time that this would be the source of energy that would replace coal, oil and gas. However the accidents that have occurred in America and Russia have been so serious that the non-nuclear sources of energy have received increased support in recent times.

It is important for you to be *aware* of the world's resources and the way in which energy is trapped, but it will do little to help you solve *design problems* in a project in which energy plays an important role. You will probably find this information more helpful when you are answering questions in a Technology Examination or as part of an answer on conservation.

HUMAN ENERGY

It is very easy to forget that before electrical and mechanical energy was available, the only readily available energy was human. The Great Pyramids and temples of Egypt are the result of the expenditure of considerable amounts of human energy. On a smaller scale, the bicycle would not be able to move without human energy. The problems you are about to solve could not take place without *you* using your energy!

FORMS OF ENERGY

MECHANICAL ENERGY

There are two forms of **mechanical** energy:

1. *Potential Energy.* This is where energy is "at rest" and only becomes evident when *movement* occurs. An elastic band that is stretched will remain stretched until released, then it will move as *Kinetic Energy*. This knowledge is employed on the moving head of the toy in Chapter 21.
2. *Kinetic Energy.* This is energy related to movement. It is often linked with *Potential Energy*. The return of the elastic band to its original size after being stretched is an example of kinetic energy. A ball that has been hit with a bat or kicked by a foot are other examples of kinetic energy.

A ball thrown into the air appears to be moving all the time, in which case it can be said to have kinetic energy; but at the point at which it is not going up and it is not yet falling, it must be *stationary*. Therefore if the ball is *not* moving it must be in a position of potential energy. When it falls, it is moving again and the potential energy has turned into kinetic energy.

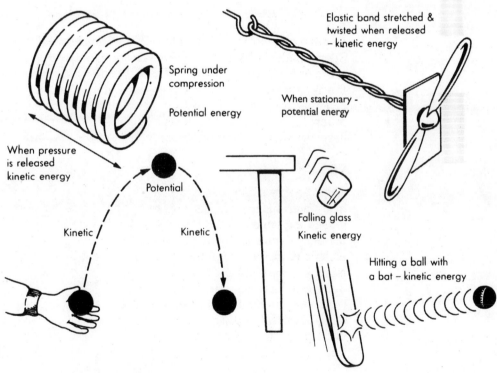

Fig. 17.1

ELECTRICAL ENERGY

An electrical charge can be obtained in two ways:

1. chemically, as in a battery;
2. mechanically, as with a dynamo.

Batteries are classified as wet or dry.

Wet batteries require distilled water and constant "charging". They are mainly used in cars and lawn mowers.

Dry batteries are sealed and cannot normally be recharged. Once the battery has lost its charge it is no longer of any use and has to be replaced with a new battery. There are, however, batteries that are rechargeable but these are more expensive and have to be put "on charge" when not in use. Dry batteries are essentially designed for use in small items that require a low level of energy supply, e.g. torches, portable radios, electrical clocks, childrens toys, calculators and gas lighters, etc. For really low-level energy supply such as deaf aids, watches, etc., a small disc-type battery is available. Again this is not rechargeable and has to be replaced when flat.

3 > CONVERSION OF ENERGY

Wind, running water in a stream, potential energy in a stretched elastic band, and chemical energy in a battery, are all of little value unless that energy can be *used*. Wind can be used to turn a propeller that is attached to a shaft, which in turn is connected to a dynamo to produce electricity. A water wheel can also be used to convert the *kinetic* energy of the water in the stream to electricity. The *potential* energy in a stretched elastic band can be used to drive a small toy or to fly a model aeroplane. The battery can be used to drive an electric motor. These *energy conversions* offer tremendous opportunities for projects.

Many examination problems have included an understanding of energy conversion.

A design problem set by ULEAC gave as the theme for study "SIMPLE ENERGY CONVERSIONS". Further details can be seen on page 354 and examples of students' response on pages 355–358.

Because movement is very much a part of energy, Chapter 12 should be given close attention.

REVIEW SHEET

It is important that you have a good understanding of the meaning of the term **"energy"**. You need to know how energy can be used without damaging the environment and appreciate that sources need to be available for future generations of animals, plants and humans. So what is energy? Where does it come from? Where does it go when it has been used?

■ Write down a list of five different everyday items that use energy.

1. _____

2. _____

3. _____

4. _____

5. _____

■ Briefly describe three possible natural sources of that energy, explaining how that natural source is converted into usable energy.

Natural Source No 1 _____

_____

_____

_____

Natural Source No 2 _____

_____

_____

_____

Natural Source No 3 _____

_____

_____

_____

■ List two different products that you would expect to find in the home. Briefly describe how each product was manufactured and draw a *flow chart* to show the stages the product went through from manufacture to being in your home.

Product No 1 _____

_____

_____

_____

Product No 2 _____

_____

_____

_____

■ Fossil fuel is classified as *non-renewable*. Give three examples of fossil fuel and explain why they are non- renewable.

1. Example _____

_____

_____

2. Example _____

_____

_____

3. Example _____

_____

_____

■ Non- Fossil fuel is classified as *renewable*. Give three examples of non-fossil fuel and explain why they are renewable.

1. Example _____

_____

_____

2. Example _____

_____

_____

3. Example _____

_____

_____

■ Our supply of Electrical energy comes from both renewable and non-renewable sources. Explain the advantages and disadvantages of using each type of energy source.

Renewable sources

Advantages_____

_____

_____

_____

Disadvantages_____

_____

_____

_____

Non-renewable sources

Advantages_____

_____

_____

_____

Disadvantages _____

_____

_____

_____

18

JOINING
MATERIALS

GETTING STARTED

Most things that are made involve the need to **join materials together**. There are many different ways that materials may be held together and as part of your role as a designer you have to *select* the method that is most appropriate.

When choosing a joint or a method of joining you need to consider the following:

1. Has the joint to be a permanent one?
2. Can the joint be a semi-permanent one?
3. Can the joint be temporary?
4. Does the joining method have to allow for movement?
5. Will the joint be used for similar materials?
6. Will the joint be used for dissimilar materials?

To be able to answer these questions, it is necessary to know the *joining methods* that fall into these six categories. Also it would be helpful to distinguish between a joint and a joining method.

A **joint** involves the *shaping of material* so that two or more pieces may be held together: e.g. mortice and tenon, dovetail, halving, tapping and threading, rivetting, dowelling, etc.

A **joining method** involves the bonding of a single or more pieces of material together *without changing the shape*, e.g. soldering, gluing, nailing, etc. It may also involve the use of a fitting, e.g. bracket, nut and bolt, hinge, etc.

PERMANENT JOINTS

USES OF MATERIALS IN BONDING

TERMS USED

TECHNIQUES IN WELDING

SELECTING A SOLDERING OR WELDING PROCESS

TYPES OF JOINT

JOINING MATERIALS AND ALLOWING FOR MOVEMENT

JOINING SIMILAR MATERIALS

JOINING UNLIKE MATERIALS

ESSENTIAL PRINCIPLES

1 ▷ PERMANENT JOINTS

Any surface that is bonded together with an adhesive must be considered as *permanent*. The only way in which the surfaces can be parted must cause damage. Therefore a decision to join materials by this method must be final. Adhesives are used to bond joints, e.g. mortice and tenon, etc., and to bond flat surfaces, such as laminates, veneers, etc. The choice of adhesive will depend on:

a) the materials to be bonded;

b) whether indoor or outdoor use;

c) whether the surface area is large or small;

d) the need to slide one surface over another, e.g. when assembling a mortice and tenon joint;

e) whether cramps can be used or not, e.g. when bonding a plastic laminate to a work top of a desk or table;

f) the length of time for the adhesive to set or harden.

2 ▷ USES OF MATERIALS IN BONDING

To help you make your decision quickly a chart (Fig. 18.1) has been drawn.

SITUATION	MATERIAL							
	Wood/wood	Wood/metal	Acrylic/acrylic	PVC rigid/PVC rigid	PVC flex/PVC flex	Fabric/fabric	Paper card/paper card	Balsa
Contact (allows adjustment by sliding the joint)	PVA	Epoxy	Tensol Nos 12 and 70				Copydex, PVA	Cement
Contact made directly (adjustment cannot be made)	Epoxy contact	Epoxy contact		Contact cement			Copydex contact	
Construction of modes	PVA	Epoxy	Tensol No. 12	PVC Contact cement Glue Gun PVC	Contact cement	PVA Plastisol	Copydex	Cement
Hand pressure	Epoxy rapid	Epoxy rapid	Tensol No. 12 Super Glue	Contact cement		PVA	Copydex	Cement
Jewellery	PVA	Epoxy	Tensol No. 12	Contact cement				
Long setting time (more than 5 mins)	PVA	Synthetic	Tensol No. 70 1 hr Tensol No. 12 3 hrs	Contact cement		PVA	PVA	
Quick setting time (less than 5 mins)	Epoxy rapid 3–5 mins Glue gun 20–60 secs	Epoxy rapid	Super Glue	Glue gun, PVC Grey 80–90 secs		Glue Gun, black	Copydex contact	Cement
Strength	Synthetic	Epoxy	Tensol No. 12 Super Glue	Contact cement		Plastisol		
Sustained pressure, vice clamp, etc.	PVA	Synthetic						
Temporary	Masking tape	Masking tape	Masking tape	Masking tape	Masking tape	Masking tape	Masking tape, Blue Tack	Masking tape, Blue Tack
Units storage	PVA	Epoxy	Tensol No. 12	Contact cement				
Wet	Synthetic	Epoxy, synthetic	Tensol No. 70	Contact cement		Plastisol		Cement

Table 18.1

Here are a few details of the adhesives that you might find in the school workshop.

PVA POLYVINYL ACETATE

A good general purpose wood glue. Easy to use and leaves ample time for getting the work together before "going off". Not suitable for outdoor use or where conditions are wet because the glue will soften and lose its bonding strength. The glue can be thinned slightly by adding water when used with paper or card. The setting time is between two and three hours and the work should be held under pressure in cramps, vice or by a heavy weight. It is suitable for veneering work when a vacuum press is available.

GLUE GUN

The gun is purely a means of heating an adhesive until it melts. A trigger then enables you to apply the glue to a surface. The gun is fed with a glue stick which is heated electrically. The glue gun requires up to 10 minutes to melt the glue before it can be used. Remember that the glue sets on cooling and does not give you very much time to apply it and assemble the parts. Because of this, large surfaces cannot be bonded using this method. It is ideal for bonding small work where the joining surface is small and a quick process is required, e.g. making models of your designs from off-cuts of wood. A little extra time for assembling can be achieved if the surfaces are warm. The cold surface can chill the glue and prevent a successful bonding.

TENSOL CEMENT

This is only suitable for bonding acrylic. It is a solvent as well as a filler, therefore it is important that the cement is applied only to the surface that is to be bonded. Cement that comes into contact with the shiny surface where it is not wanted will leave a mark no matter how much care is taken. The protective paper that normally covers the acrylic should remain in position as long as possible. Masking tape can be used if a surface needs protection. The cement hardens quickly so assembling has to be done without delay. The work can be hand held while working.

EPOXY RESIN

This is a two-part adhesive that is available in two tubes: one contains the adhesive and the other the hardener. An estimate is made of the quantity required and half the amount is squeezed from each tube onto a clean surface of non-absorbant material for mixing. Once the two parts are thoroughly mixed a chemical reaction starts the adhesive to set. The working time, i.e. for you to apply the mixture and to assemble the parts, is 10–15 minutes for the "ordinary" but 2–5 minutes for the "rapid". The "ordinary" takes 2–3 hours to cure (set firmly) and requires holding in position with a holding device. The "rapid" takes only 4–5 minutes to set firmly enough for the parts to stay together and a holding device is not required. The adhesive bonds metal to wood or metal to metal, and is commonly used in cheap jewellery.

SYNTHETIC ADHESIVE

This is a two-part adhesive that needs preparing before it can be used. It is available in a powder with the two parts already mixed. Water has to be added to the powder before a chemical reaction can take place. The mixture has to be made into a creamy paste that can be smoothly applied to both surfaces with a thin piece of wood. Do not use a brush because the adhesive will set hard and it will be impossible to remove. It is water resistant and excellent for bonding wood that is to be used outside or is in contact with water such as on a model boat or a bathroom fitting.

CONTACT ADHESIVE

This is sometimes referred to as an impact adhesive because as soon as the two surfaces to be bonded come into contact they cannot be moved for adjustment. Assembling parts has to be done precisely and the parts must be brought into direct contact to each other without sliding. It is an excellent adhesive for bonding plastics laminates to wood.

The two surfaces are given a thin coat with a clean spreader and allowed to go tacky. After about 15 minutes the two surfaces can be brought together, pressed firmly by hand and left to bond completely. Though trimming can be done almost straightaway, it is advisable to leave the work for a while. If the work is small and can be put in a cramp or cramps for a minute, then work can continue.

SUPER GLUES

These are glues with exceptional bonding strength and a high speed of setting. They bond almost on contact and are mainly used on small surfaces. Because of their quick setting times, some people have been unfortunate to have fingers stuck together. Some manufacturers now sell this adhesive with a "skin release agent", e.g. Bostik 12.

BALSA CEMENT

This is a quick setting cement ideally suited for the bonding of balsa wood. The pieces being joined can be hand held or held by a pin while the cement sets. It is available in a tube and ready for immediate use. A pin should be placed in the exit hole to prevent the glue from setting in the tube.

POLYSTYRENE ADHESIVE

This is specially suited for the bonding of solid polystyrene but not expanded polystyrene. Many models of transport are made in kit form and the numerous parts are bonded with this adhesive. The quick setting time allows for the work to be hand held while the parts are joined.

POLYVINYL CHLORIDE ADHESIVE

This is used mainly for joining pipes and fittings made from PVC and not always available in a school workshop.

There are many adhesives available for bonding materials for all types of conditions. Those mentioned should be adequate to cover most needs. It is important that you should be aware of the differences and be able to select the most suitable adhesive for a particular need and to be able to give a reason for your selection.

3 > TERMS USED

The correct use of the **terms** is also important, especially when you make reference to the use of an adhesive in your Design Folder and answer questions in a Technology examination.

An adhesive either "bonds" or "adheres" to a surface. Be very careful if you use the word "stick". Though what you mean may be understood, it is not so precise as the terms "bond" and "adhere".

SOLDERING AND WELDING

These are broad terms that cover a range of techniques used mainly to join metals, but some thermoplastics also respond to a welding technique.

SOLDERING TECHNIQUES

In general these are techniques that employ the use of heat and an alloy to join two similar metals.

SOFT SOLDERING

This process is used to join tinplate – a thin sheet of steel coated with tin. The tin protects the steel but also makes soft soldering easier. The solder is available as a "stick" or as a paste. It is an alloy of tin and lead. In the paste form, a flux (a cleaning fluid) gives the paste consistency and makes it possible to paint the surface before it is heated. The flux is a corrosive liquid which should be washed off after the soldering process has been completed. Soft solder is also used to join sheet copper and wire. For use in electrical circuits, the solder is available in a coil and has a non-corrosive core of flux. This means that there is no need for the work to be washed.

SILVER SOLDERING

There are two grades of silver solder in common use. "Easy Running" and "Hard Running". The easy running melts at a lower temperature than the hard running silver solder. This means that two joins may be soldered at different stages. The first join can be made using the hard running solder and the second join using the easy running solder without fear of melting the first join. Silver solder is an alloy of copper, zinc and silver. It is available in strip or wire, and has to be used with a suitable flux. This method is used to join gilding metal and copper.

BRAZING

Brazing is very similar to silver soldering except that the solder is an alloy of copper and zinc, which melts at a much higher temperature, approximately 870°C. This means that only metals with higher melting points can be brazed. Because brass has a melting point only a little higher than 870°C there is a danger of melting the brass as well as the solder. Brazing is commonly used to join mild steel. The solder is available as rods and is applied to the metal when it is red hot. A flux is also used to prevent oxidisation (the formation of a skin that prevents the solder reaching the clean steel).

ALUMINIUM BRAZING

This process is possible using an aluminium alloy brazing rod and appropriate flux. It is more difficult to perform than the other soldering and brazing techniques. It is also desirable to use oxy-acetylene welding equipment to get the correct control of flame. It is used for joining aluminium sheet and tube.

WELDING

This is achieved by fusing the two surfaces to be joined. It is different from soldering in that a solder is not required. When the metal is heated to a temperature that allows the molecules to move, the molecules will link together. At this point the heat source is removed and the metal begins to solidify. The molecules are now joined by fusion. The rod that is used in welding is the same type of metal as that being joined and acts as a "filler".

There are two techniques commonly used in the workshop:

1. oxy-acetylene welding;
2. arc welding.

OXY-ACETYLENE WELDING

A cylinder of Oxygen and a cylinder of Acetylene plus an Oxy-acetylene torch is essential equipment for carrying out this process. Special goggles are also required to protect the eyes from the bright light of the flame. A set of different size nozzles is needed to produce the size of flame required. The temperature is controlled by setting the valves at the head of the cylinders to the correct pressure and adjusting the supply of oxygen and acetylene gas at the controls on the torch. It is commonly used to join sheet or tube mild steel or repair castings made from cast iron.

ELECTRIC ARC WELDING

The heat for this process is obtained by an electric arc. To create this arc a transformer is used. One lead from the transformer is attached to the work and one through an insulated handle to a small spring-loaded grip holding a welding rod. When the free end of the welding rod is brought near the work an electrical arc is formed. The heat melts the rod and heats the surface of the metal being joined. The rod is moved along the joining area in a stirring action. The rod is coated with a flux which ensures that oxidisation does not take place to prevent the operation being successful.

PLASTICS WELDING

Heat can be used to fuse polythene and is used in industry for making plastic bags. Very carefully controlled heat from both sides is needed for success. This is not a process that is commonly used in schools.

Though it is possible to take components apart after they have been soldered by re-heating them, these joining methods are permanent. The welding processes are impossible to take apart without causing damage to the work.

A chart has been drawn (Fig. 18.2 below) which should help to guide you in the best direction.
First make a list of the available **facilities**, e.g:

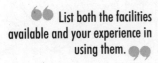

List both the facilities available and your experience in using them.

1. Brazing hearth with a natural gas and air supply, plus a range of silver solders and brazing rod.
2. Electric soldering irons and a supply of tinmans solder and electricians multi-core solder.
3. Gas heated soldering irons and tinmans solder.
4. Gas ring. A paste soft solder.
5. Propane bottled gas and propane torch.
6. Oxy-acetylene equipment.
7. Arc welding equipment and an arc welding bay. Note: arc welding must not be done in a workshop where other pupils are working. The ultra-violet light is harmful. The working area should be completely enclosed by suitable screens.

Now make a list of your **experience** in using these processes. This may include, 1, 2, 4 and 7. Read the chart (Fig. 18.2) to see if they are *suitable* for joining the materials you are using. This may reduce your list further so that you are left with 1 and 4. Now see if you are going to solder more than once. If the answer is yes then the method you need is the one that will be suitable for two- or three-stage soldering and that leaves you with 1. Check with your teacher before commencing.

SITUATION	METALS						
	Mild steel/mild steel	Aluminium/aluminium	Copper/copper	Gilding/gilding	Cast iron/cast iron	Tin plate/tin plate	Brass/brass
General	Brazing spelter 870°C	Ali brazing	Soft solder Silver solder, Sil fos	Silver solder	Cast iron gas arc	Soft solder B	
Low melting range	Soft solder A 183–185°C	Silver solder No. 2 Soft solder A	Easy Flo No. 2 608°–617°C			Soft solder A	
High melting range	Soft solder V 183°–276°C Brazing spelter		Soft solder V Silver solder C4 740°–780°C				
Strength important	Oxy-acetylene welding						
Tack together	Arc welding		Silver solder		Arc welding		
Electrical circuits			Multi core resin flux				Multi core
Sweating	Soft solder A Tinmans 183°–185°C		Soft Solder A Tinmans 183°–185°C			Soft solder A Tinmans 183°C–185°C	

Table 18.2

6 > TYPES OF JOINT

PERMANENT JOINTS IN WOOD

Most joints require an *adhesive*. So if an adhesive is used this will automatically ensure that the joint is unable to be taken apart and it is therefore permanent. The following joints (Fig. 18.3) are commonly used in frame construction:

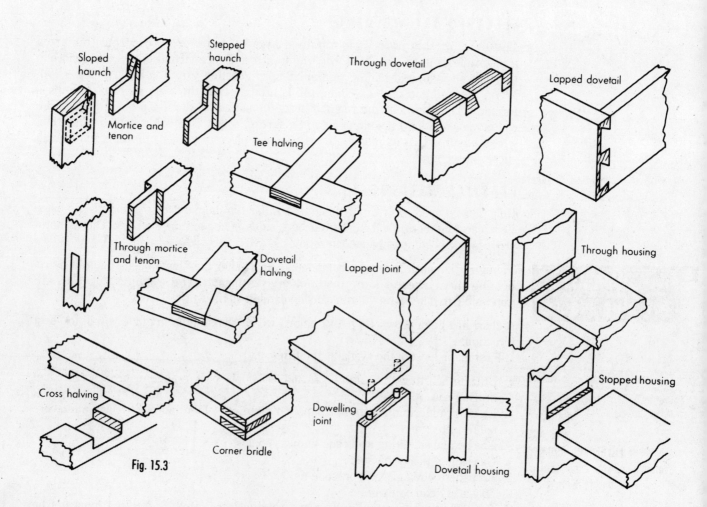

Fig. 15.3

Fig. 18.3

a) mortice and tenon; through mortice and tenon, stepped haunched mortice and tenon, sloping haunched mortice and tenon, tee halving, dovetail halving, corner bridle.

The following joints are commonly used in box or carcase construction:

b) through dovetail; lapped dovetail, lapped joint, through housing, stopped housing, dovetail housing, dowelling.

Some joints do not need an adhesive, thus falling into the next class of joints, and will be included in the temporary type of joint.

PERMANENT JOINTS IN METAL

If two or more components are soldered or welded together, it is obviously intended they should not be taken apart for inspection or during the maintenance of other components. Metal adhesives have also made it possible for metal components to be bonded together permanently without the need of heat.

Riveting, using soft iron, aluminium or copper rivets, is another method of joining in which the components are expected to remain joined permanently. There are two methods of riveting:

1. the conventional method using snap head, countersunk and flat head rivets that are hammered and shaped with a snap head tool, set or dolly;
2. pop rivets that are fitted in position with a "pop riveting tool".

Round headed rivets are commonly used where strength is required and the finished surface does not have to be flat or smooth. This method is suitable for joining sheet material. It is also suitable for a pivoting or swivel joint as used on scissors, snips, door or gate latches, etc.

Countersunk head rivets are used for strength where a smooth flush surface is required. The metal must be thick enough to allow the head of the rivet to fit flush with the surface.

Pop riveting does not require the use of a hammer as in the case of the first method. Instead a "pop riveting tool" has to be used. This method is used for joining sheet material, metal, plastics and some manufactured boards. The controlled pressure applied by the riveting tool means that the work is unlikely to be damaged and that less resistant materials such as hardboard, acrylic sheet, PVC sheet, etc., can be safely joined. A combination of different materials can be joined as well as like materials. It is a very quick method, and access to one side only is required.

There are two commonly used **riveting joints** (Fig. 18.4).

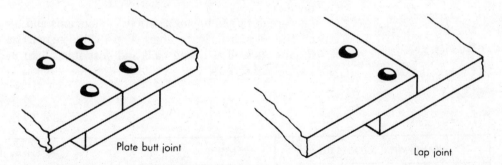

Plate butt joint

Lap joint

Fig. 18.4

- The **plate butt joint** is strong and requires an extra piece of material for the join to be made. It has the added advantage that one side of the join has a flush finish.
- The **lap joint** has the advantage that no extra material is required and the disadvantage that both sides have a step.

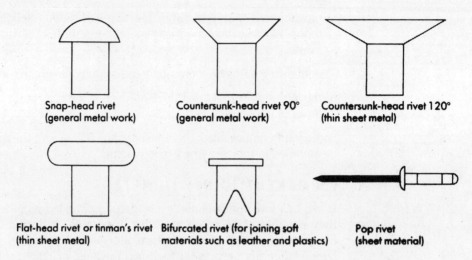

Snap-head rivet
(general metal work)

Countersunk-head rivet 90°
(general metal work)

Countersunk-head rivet 120°
(thin sheet metal)

Flat-head rivet or tinman's rivet
(thin sheet metal)

Bifurcated rivet (for joining soft
materials such as leather and plastics)

Pop rivet
(sheet material)

Fig. 18.5

SEMI-PERMANENT JOINTS

Nailing a joint or fastening a board to another can be as permanent as is required, but a nail *can* be removed. Pincers, claw hammers, and claw wrenches are tools designed for removing nails. Unfortunately this operation cannot be done without damage to the nail or the material.

TEMPORARY JOINTS

Using a screw to fasten boards, panels, and fittings such as hinges, brackets, etc., can result in assembly for as long or as little as required but the means of taking the pieces apart can be done without damage to the panel or fitting and these can be reassembled when required. e.g. a hinge on the lid of a box. Screwdrivers of different sizes and shape of blade are designed to tighten and undo this type of fitting.

Metal and plastic strips can be held together using metal screws, nuts and bolts, or threaded bar and hole, etc. There are numerous designs of spanners to cope with square-headed, hexagonal headed, nuts and bolts and keys for socket screws so their use must be for situations where the nut, bolt, etc., has to be removed for inspection or maintenance from time to time, e.g. car engine, electrical switch or plug, back of a television set, etc.

These fittings are for holding together parts that are not taken apart frequently. They often provide a security or safety factor in that they may be holding a cover over moving or electrical parts. Because the cover cannot be removed quickly and a special tool has to be used to remove them it is unlikely that the cover will be removed by accident.

Nails are designed to suit a variety of situations and there is a correct way of using them. The list of nails in the chart (Fig. 18.6) is just an example of the most commonly used nails. As well as listing nails and describing their uses, Fig. 18.6 does the same for a variety of screws.

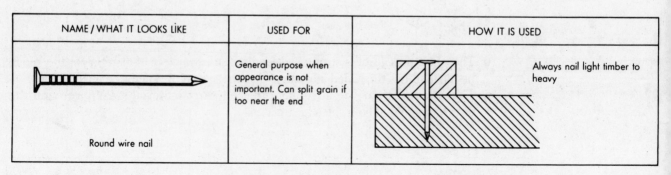

NAME / WHAT IT LOOKS LIKE	USED FOR	HOW IT IS USED
Round wire nail	General purpose when appearance is not important. Can split grain if too near the end	Always nail light timber to heavy

Fig. 18.6 Nails, screws and their uses

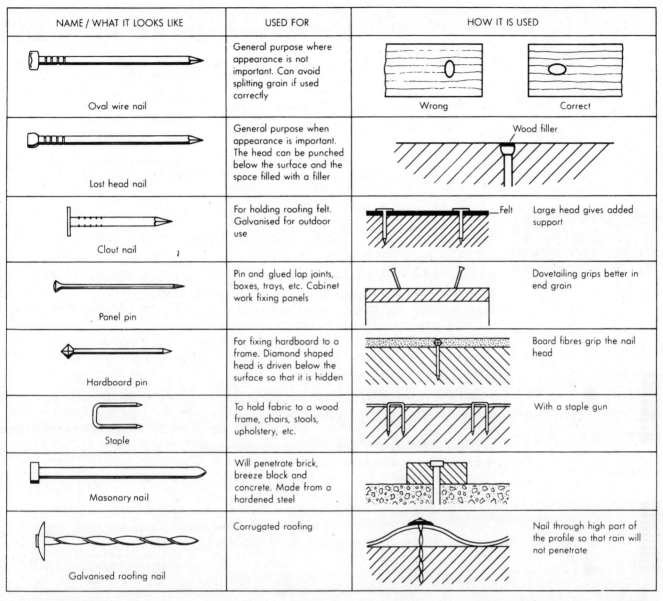

NAME / WHAT IT LOOKS LIKE	USED FOR	HOW IT IS USED
Oval wire nail	General purpose where appearance is not important. Can avoid splitting grain if used correctly	Wrong — Correct
Lost head nail	General purpose when appearance is important. The head can be punched below the surface and the space filled with a filler	Wood filler
Clout nail	For holding roofing felt. Galvanised for outdoor use	Felt — Large head gives added support
Panel pin	Pin and glued lap joints, boxes, trays, etc. Cabinet work fixing panels	Dovetailing grips better in end grain
Hardboard pin	For fixing hardboard to a frame. Diamond shaped head is driven below the surface so that it is hidden	Board fibres grip the nail head
Staple	To hold fabric to a wood frame, chairs, stools, upholstery, etc.	With a staple gun
Masonary nail	Will penetrate brick, breeze block and concrete. Made from a hardened steel	
Galvanised roofing nail	Corrugated roofing	Nail through high part of the profile so that rain will not penetrate

NAME / WHAT IT LOOKS LIKE	USED FOR	USED ON		
		W	M	P
Countersunk wood screw	General woodworking, fitting hinges etc. Pozidrive head or slot head. Clearance and pilot hole needed	✓		
Countersunk self tapping screw	Generally used to cut a thread in soft metal and some plastics and manufactured boards. Much used in self assembly furniture. A countersunk clearance and tapping hole needed	✓	✓	✓
Mushroom head self tapping screw	Holding panels made in soft or thin material. The large diameter head gives added support. A clearance hole in the panel and a tapping hole in the frame needed	✓	✓	✓
Nut and bolt	For holding two components together. Two clearance holes required		✓	

NAME / WHAT IT LOOKS LIKE	USED FOR	USED ON		
		W	M	P
Roundhead wood screw	General woodworking and fittings that do not have a countersunk holes. Clearance and pilot hole needed	✓		
Raised countersunk self tapping screw	Generally used to cut a thread in soft sheet metal and some plastics and manufactured boards. Used to secure panels. A plastic cap is used to hide the head if required	✓	✓	✓
Hexagonal head self tapping screw	Provides a strong fixing in frame construction work in models, carts, furniture, etc. A clearance hole and a tapping hole needed		✓	✓
Cap head, hexagon socket screw	For holding an inspection cover on a piece of machinery eg lathe, milling machine. A counter bore, clearance and threaded hole required		✓	✓

Fig. 18.6 Nails, screws and their uses (continued)

NAME / WHAT IT LOOKS LIKE	USED FOR	USED ON			NAME / WHAT IT LOOKS LIKE	USED FOR	USED ON		
		W	M	P			W	M	P
 Hexagon socket set screw (Grub screw)	For adjusting a sliding jib on a lathe; holding a die in a holder		✓	✓	Split cotter pin	For holding two components but allows freedom of rotation. Often used to prevent a nut from coming undone		✓	

Fig. 18.6 Nails, screws and their uses (continued)

7> **JOINING MATERIALS AND ALLOWING FOR MOVEMENT**

HINGES

There are many types of **hinges** available. The important thing is to be able to choose the correct type. There are three main designs:

1. those that are suitable for cabinet quality work such as domestic or office furniture and small jewellery boxes, where appearance is important;
2. those that are suitable for carpentry quality work such as garden gates, shed doors, etc., where appearance is not as important as function.
3. those that are suitable for "Flat Pack Furniture" such as domestic and office furniture that has to be assembled by a non-skilled person with very limited tools, and yet appearance is important.

For *indoor use*, brass, nylon, or plated hinges should be used. They are more expensive than the same designs made from mild steel. The hinges designed for use with "Flat Pack Furniture" are most suitable for doors and cabinets that have the necessary holes already drilled by the manufacturer.

For *outdoor use*, mild steel hinges can be used. They must be painted to protect them from rusting.

The three most common *types* of hinge are:

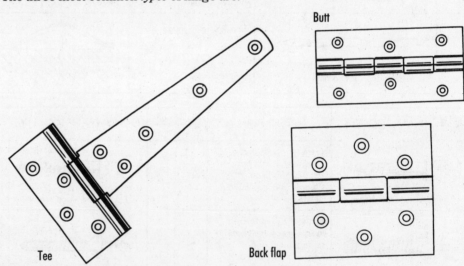

Fig. 18.7   Tee   Butt   Back flap

8> **JOINING SIMILAR MATERIALS**

JOINING WOOD TO WOOD

There are two groups of "wood":

1. **natural timber**, which is seasoned timber ready to use;
2. **man-made board**, which is a product made from timber.

Joining natural timber

The important points to remember when joining natural timber are:

a) The direction of the grain.
b) It will split along the length of its grain.
c) It expands and contracts in its width and thickness according to the amount of moisture in the air. (It expands when the air is moist because it absorbs the moisture and swells slightly. It contracts when dry because it loses some of its moisture.)

The design of joints is greatly influenced by (a) and (b). Hence there is variation in shape, form and proportion of each design of joint to suit all circumstances. Much of the design of the joints has evolved over the centuries and the test of time has resulted in a number of joints being suitable for frame or carcase construction. These are drawn on page 284 of this chapter.

Joining man-made boards

The important points to remember when joining man-made boards are:

a) There is no single direction of grain.
b) Plywood, laminboard, chipboard have equal strength in all directions.
c) There is no movement, expansion or contraction. Most man-made boards are not affected by changes of moisture in the air.
d) The design of joints for natural timber are not suitable for man-made boards. Pins, nails, screws, adhesives and fittings are most suitable because there is no need to allow for more strength in one direction than another and there is no need to consider the effects of moisture in the air.

Joining natural timber and man-made boards

To avoid problems it is often better to join like with like. There are only a few occasions where success is possible:

1. plywood panels in a frame construction;
2. the bottom of a drawer;
3. the back panel of a carcase construction.

In each case some allowance must be made for movement of the natural timber. Panels fitted in grooves are not glued and the depth of the groove is not completely filled with the panel.

JOINING METAL TO METAL

Like man-made boards metal has equal strength in all directions.
    Metals are joined using the following methods:

a) heat treatment, e.g. soldering, brazing, welding;
b) cold treatment, e.g. riveting, threading;
c) using fittings, e.g. screws, nuts and bolts;
d) adhesives, e.g. epoxy resin.

JOINING WOOD TO METAL

The important points to remember are:

a) Natural timber must have some allowance for movement. This is often achieved by having screw slots instead of screw holes. See the drawing of a bracket opposite. If the bracket is to be attached to a metal frame, heat treatment may be used. If it is to be attached to a wooden frame, then it may be secured by wood screws. Note the direction of the slots. Movement of wood is mainly in its width and very little in its length.
b) Man-made boards are stable and do not need allowance for movement. There is no need for a bracket to have slotted holes.
c) Adhesives, e.g. epoxy resin, may be used to bond man-made board with metal, but only small sizes of natural timber may be used in this method, e.g. pendants, rings, etc.

Fig. 18.8

JOINING ANY MATERIAL WITH ANY OTHER MATERIAL

Most materials will respond to adhesives. Selecting the appropriate adhesive is all that is necessary. For guidance see the chart on page 280.

REVIEW SHEET

■ Most artefacts are made from a number of components or parts. Examine a household product to see how all the parts are held together. Then using the following chart tick the methods you have identified to keep the product complete.

Product	Number of parts	Permanent joins	Temporary joins	Moving joins
Electric plug				
Pair of scissors				
Comb				
Folding chair				
Jewellery box				
Brooch				

■ Materials are permanently joined together using adhesives. Because there are a variety of materials it is necessary to have an adhesive which suits the material.

Name a suitable adhesive for the following situations when bonding:

Wood to wood _____

Wood to metal _____

Fabric to Fabric _____

Card to card_____

Acrylic to acrylic _____

Rigid PVC to Rigid PVC _____

Polystyrene to polystyrene _____

Aluminium to aluminium _____

■ Metals are also bonded together by either soldering, brazing or welding. Explain the difference between these processes.

_____

_____

_____

_____

_____

_____

■ Traditional methods of joining wood are still commonly used by craftsmen. Make a *free hand drawing* of the following joints.

Stepped haunch mortice and tenon

Through dovetail

Cross halving

Stopped housing

■ Two pieces of metal can be held together using rivets. Illustrate the process by showing a sequence of stage by stage drawings.

Stage 1   Stage 2   Stage 3

Stage 4   Stage 5

■ Wood screws are identified by four details. Assume that you want 10 screws, write down an order that would ensure you get exactly what you require.

_____
_____
_____
_____

■ Describe and illustrate how to prepare two pieces of wood that are to be fixed together using a countersunk wood screw.

_____
_____
_____
_____
_____

■ Describe and illustrate how to prepare two pieces of metal that are to be fixed together using a raised countersunk head self tapping screw.

_____
_____
_____
_____

PROCESSES

GETTING STARTED

Products are produced using a variety of ways of shaping material. Materials can change their **form** by:

1. cutting and removing the unwanted parts;
2. bending, beating, casting, moulding;
3. heating, bending, casting, moulding.

The **appearance** of materials can be changed by two methods:

1. application of a surface treatment, e.g. paint, varnish, polish or a plastics coating;
2. sanding, scraping, buffing, using "wet and dry" or a metal polish such as Brasso.

A finished product may be made from a number of components, each having been made using different processes. This means that joining processes will also have been used, such as those included in the previous chapter.

CUTTING AND REMOVAL OF UNWANTED MATERIAL

SAWING

FILING

PLANING

DRILLING

TURNING ON A LATHE

REMOVING MATERIAL BY ABRASION

CHISELLING

BENDING

HARDENING AND TEMPERING

CASTING & MOULDING

SURFACE TREATMENT

SUMMARY CHART–FINISHES

ESSENTIAL PRINCIPLES

1 ▷ **CUTTING AND REMOVAL OF UNWANTED MATERIAL**

This is the most commonly used method of changing the form of material. The cutting processes include:

- sawing
- filing
- planing
- drilling
- turning on a lathe
- abrading
- chiselling

2 ▷ **SAWING**

Though most materials can be sawn, saws have been designed to suit the material to be cut and the type of cut to be achieved, i.e. straight or curved. You can find the commonly used saws illustrated in Chapter 9 and you can see the type of cut they will achieve and the material for which they are best suited.

Saws can be put into two groups:

1. those that require sharpening;
2. those that require a replacement blade.

- Saws that require *sharpening* are designed to cut natural timber and man-made boards.

They can be identified by:

a) The blade and handle are permanently attached.
b) The "set" of the teeth is alternate, i.e. one to the left and one to the right all along the length of the blade (Fig. 19.1).

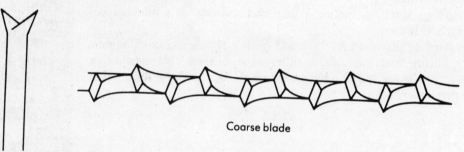

Coarse blade

Fig. 19.1

- Saws that require a *replacement blade* are designed mainly to cut metals. They can be identified by:

   a) The blade can be easily taken out of the handle and frame.
   b) The teeth are fine and the "set" of the teeth is wavy or zig-zag (Fig. 19.2).

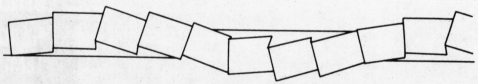

Fig. 19.2

Fine blade   (enlarged to show detail)

As a guide you can say that saws that are suitable for cutting metals are also suitable for cutting plastics materials.

If a saw has to cut through a *combination* of materials, such as a plastics laminated board, then a saw with a replacement blade that has the teeth set in a wavy or zig-zag pattern should be used.

A *rule of thumb* to remember is:

- Saws with teeth set alternately are designed to cut wood and man-made boards only.
- Saws with a zig-zag set are designed to cut metal and plastics.

HOW TO CHOOSE THE CORRECT SAW FOR THE JOB

You should by now be able to *select* a saw that is suitable for the material to be cut. Here then is another guideline:

■ "Use a fine toothed blade for thin material."

The next decision you have to make is the *type of cut*, i.e. curved or straight. Here then is another guideline:

■ "Straight cut wide blade."
■ "Curved cut narrow blade."

What type of saw blade would you use to cut a 250-mm diameter hole in a 6-mm thick piece of plywood?

The answer to such a question would be:

"The *blade* should:

a) be narrow;
b) have fine teeth;
c) have teeth with each tooth set alternately."

If you were then asked to *identify* such a saw you could look at the chart in Fig. 9.4 and see which saw or saws fitted a), b) and c). You would first look *down the column* for *material* and read off those in the *wood section*.

Your list for a) will then include:

1. hacksaw;
2. junior hacksaw;
3. coping saw;
4. deep frame coping saw;
5. bow saw;
6. pad saw;
7. compass saw.

The next feature b) is that *fine teeth* are required for cutting *thin sheet* material. This will reduce your list to the two hacksaws and the two coping saws. The others have medium size teeth.

Finally, because the material to be cut is *wood*, and saws with teeth *alternately set* cut wood efficiently, only those with alternately set teeth are required. This feature c) reduces the list to the two *coping saws*. The *deep frame* coping saw has the advantage that it can be used on a larger piece of plywood than the *standard* coping saw. But it has the disadvantage that the blade is set at a fixed angle. The blade in the standard coping saw can be adjusted so that the frame does not come into contact with the outside edge of the piece of plywood. The *standard coping saw* is the most suitable saw to cut the hole successfully.

WHY ARE SOME SAWS RE-SHARPENED?

The saws that are *re-sharpened* are often quite expensive and have a broad blade. To throw away this type of saw when the teeth were no longer sharp would be a very wasteful use of materials and expensive to replace. They are designed so that they can be re-set and re-sharpened many times before coming to the end of their useful life. The teeth are often large enough for them to be reset and re-sharpened by the user. Since this is quite a skilful operation, saws can be sent away to be done properly.

WHY ARE SOME SAWS DESIGNED TO HAVE REPLACEMENT BLADES?

These saws use *narrow blades* and they are mainly intended for cutting *relatively hard materials* such as aluminium, steel, copper, etc. This means that the teeth become "dull" (not sharp) more quickly than teeth cutting softer materials such as wood. Hence the need to have a saw that cuts efficiently means that a frequent change of blade is necessary. The blades cannot be re-sharpened using the method employed to re-sharpen the broad blades because the teeth are set in a zig-zag pattern and they are often too fine to be sharpened with a three-square file.

3 > FILING

Files were originally designed for removing unwanted material on metal. Now they can be used for removing unwanted material on most plastics. The teeth are quite fine and the process of removing unwanted material by filing is slow. This has the advantage of being able to produce an accurate surface and finish on a material.

Files can be re-sharpened. They have to be sent away because the process requires specialised equipment. This process cannot be repeated many times and the files have to be replaced. Small files such as "Needle files", see Fig. 9.4, are not re-sharpened because the teeth are so fine and the cost of the process is similar to the price of a new file.

HANDLES

Most files are bought without a handle. The end of a file has a square-sectioned tapering tang which makes it possible to fit a handle.

The **advantages** of this are:

> 66 Plastic handles are now available and do not split. 99

1. A single handle may be used many times on different files when they need to be replaced.
2. It is not necessary to buy a new handle every time you buy a new file.

The **disadvantages** are:

1. The wooden handles are forced on the tang and with overtightening they split. A split handle is very dangerous and must be replaced with a new one before the file can be used again.
2. The handles do have to be regularly checked for tightness and splits.

Needle files do not require a handle to be fitted. They are suitably designed so that they can be held by hand. See Fig. 9.4.

FILES ARE IDENTIFIED BY THREE FEATURES

1. cross-sectional shape;
2. length;
3. cut.

Cross-sectional shape

The **cross-sectional shapes** are: Round, Half-round, Square, Three square, Knife, Warding and Pillar. See Fig. 9.4.

Length

The length of a file is the measurement of the blade only. The lengths are given in even numbers and the most commonly used lengths are 6, 8, and 10 inches.

Cut

The **cut** refers to two features:

a) **Coarseness**. This refers to the size of the teeth. Teeth are measured by the number per inch. The three most commonly used sizes are:

1. bastard   25 teeth per inch ⎫
2. second-cut   30 teeth per inch   ⎬ The more teeth to the inch,
3. smooth   45 teeth per inch ⎭ the smoother the cut.

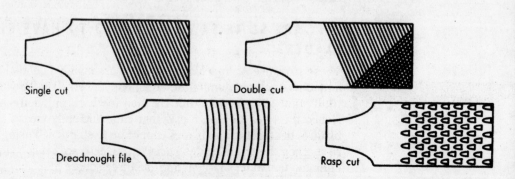

Single cut   Double cut

Fig. 19.3   Dreadnought file   Rasp cut

b) **The shape of the teeth**. They are usually diamond-shaped and are formed by the crossing of two sets of grooves. This is known as a "second cut". A single set of straight grooves is known as a "single-cut" or "float". A single set of curved grooves is known as a "dreadnought". (See Fig. 19.3.)

HOW DO I KNOW WHICH FILE TO USE?

Files have traditionally been designed for cutting metals such as mild steel, aluminium, copper and brass, etc., but many of the rigid plastics can be shaped and edges finished using a file. Though a file can be used to shape wood it is not the best tool for the job and there are surform files which are wood files and these are dealt with below:

- For removing material "quickly" and where the surface finish is "rough" use a file with large teeth.
- For removing material "slowly" and where the surface finish is "smooth" use a file with small teeth.
- Use a long file on large work.
- Use a short file on small work.

These are common-sense ways of selecting a file and can be used to help you choose a file. The next factor that needs to be considered is the *shape* of the material:

- For an external round shape use a flat file.
- For an internal or hollow shape use a half-round file.
- For a hole or small radius curve use a round file.

HOW TO USE A FILE

Filing is done in two stages:

1. **Cross-filing**, where the file moves forward and across the surface in a single stroke and leaves diagonal scratches.
2. **Draw filing**, where the file, held at right-angles to the surface, moves parallel to the work and leaves a smooth finish with only very fine scratches.

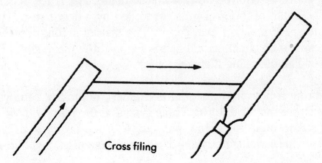

Fig. 19.4   Cross filing

Rasps

These are designed to be used on *soft metals*, e.g. aluminium, but are most commonly used on natural timber, man-made boards and plastics. The finish they produce is dependent upon the fineness of the teeth. Wood has to be finished with glass paper for a really smooth finish.

Surforms

These are good shaping tools that have replaceable blades with open rasp-like teeth see Fig. 9.4). They have three forms of blade: flat, round, and half round. They can be used to shape wood and plastics, but give a rough finish. Rubbing down with glass paper to provide a smooth finish may be necessary as a final stage.

4 > PLANING

These tools are designed to cut *natural timber*. The blades have to be re-sharpened and set in a plane very carefully.

JACK PLANE

The most commonly used plane is the **Jack Plane**. It removes shavings of wood along the length of a piece of timber in the direction of the grain. Going against the grain produces a rough finish. The blade can be adjusted to cut a thick shaving to remove wood quickly, or a thin shaving to produce a good-quality finish. See Fig. 9.4.

SMOOTHING PLANE

The **Smoothing Plane** is very similar to the jack plane but it is shorter and sometimes wider. It is used as a final stage of planing to produce an excellent quality finish.

SHOULDER PLANE

The **Shoulder Plane** is a specialised plane suitable for planing the end-grain shoulders of joints. There is no cap iron to crack the shaving since shavings do not occur on end-grain. Instead the grinding angle is set uppermost and it is this that lifts the unwanted wood after it has been cut. The low angle of the blade in the plane also provides for an easy cutting action. The vertical side of the plane runs along the surface of the tenon to produce a shoulder at right-angles. Because the blade is cutting end-grain it is necessary for the plane to be used in both directions, i.e. from the outside edge to the centre so that the wood does not split.

BLOCK PLANE

The **Block Plane** is a useful little plane that can be held in one hand and is used to remove fine and small amounts of wood. Like the shoulder plane it does not have a cap iron and the blade is set at a low angle with the grinding angle uppermost. A low angle and a fine setting produces a good finish.

PLOUGH PLANE

The **Plough Plane** cuts a groove along the length of a piece of wood. These planes have a set of blades of different widths. You choose the blades by the width of the groove you want to cut, very much in the same way as you would select a drill bit to produce a hole. The distance of the groove away from the edge of the wood is controlled by a fence. The fence moves along two guides and can be set whatever distance is required away from the blade. The fence is held in position by two screws. The depth of the groove is controlled by a depth stop. This can be raised or lowered and set in position by a screw. The task of setting a plane is important. Each setting needs to be checked and as a safeguard the plane should be tried on a spare piece of wood before using it on your work.

Boring a hole into material is a quick method of removing unwanted material. The main reason for **drilling** a hole is so that the *space may be occupied by a fitting*, such as a screw, bolt, dowel rod, pin, etc. A group of holes, or a line of holes, can also be a stage in *changing the shape* of a piece of material. See Fig. 19.5.

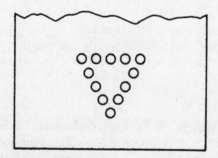 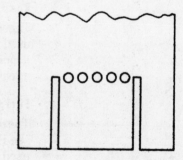

Fig. 19.5

5 > DRILLING

DRILL BITS

Drill bits are designed to suit the material they cut. It is thus important to select the correct drill bit.

There are three different metal alloys used in the manufacturing of drills; each is intended to be harder than the material to be drilled and they are listed in Table 19.1.

METAL ALLOY	MATERIAL TO BE DRILLED
Carbon steel	Wood, plastics and soft metals, e.g. aluminium
High-speed steel	Mild steel, tool steel
Carbide tipped	Stone, brick, concrete block

Table 19.1

Table 19. 2 lists the advantages and disadvantages of metal alloys in drill bits.

METAL ALLOY	ADVANTAGES	DISADVANTAGES
Carbon steel	■ Cheaper than HSS ■ Excellent for drilling wood and plastics	■ Only suitable for wood and plastics ■ Requires more frequent sharpening ■ Loses its "temper" if over heated ■ A coolant must be used when drilling metals
High-speed steel	■ Suitable for drilling metal as well as wood and plastics ■ Requires little maintenance ■ Can be used at high speed without the need of a coolant	■ More expensive than CS
Carbide tipped	■ Drills stone, brick and concrete ■ Requires little maintenance	■ Very expensive ■ Specially hard grinding wheel is required to re-sharpen the drill bit ■ Not suitable for drilling wood, metal on plastics

Table 19.2

Jobbers drill bit

The "**Standard**" or "**Jobbers**" drill bit may be used for drilling plastics, but chipping or tearing may occur. The chipping or tearing is caused by the cutting angle, and the grinding angle of the drill bit. The cutting angle is determined by the helix, and the grinding angle by the angle at which the drill bit is held to the grinding wheel. If you compare the three drill bits you will see a jobber's drill bit with a standard head of helix. The drill bit for thermosetting plastics has a "Slow Helix" (less number of twists) and the drill bit for thermoplastics has a "Quick Helix" (more number of twists). The grinding angle is also different from the "jobber's twist drill bit" in that the thermosetting drill bit has a very pointed cutting end and the thermoplastics has a much flatter cutting end.

Thermosetting plastics drill bit

The **Thermosetting Plastics** drill bit is used to drill such plastics as polyester and epoxy resin and plastics laminate materials such as Formica. There is an exception to the rule. This drill bit is ideally suited for drilling acrylic which is a thermoplastics material.

Thermoplastics drill bit

The **Thermoplastics** drill bit is suited for drilling such material as; nylon, polystyrene, polythene and polyvinyl chloride (PVC), etc.

Twist drill bits

Twist drill bits are the most commonly used drill bits. They are made from either carbon steel or high-speed steel. The carbon steel drills can be easily identified from the high-speed drills by their colour. Carbon steel drill bits are black; high-speed drill bits are silver. You should be able to read the letters CS or HSS on the shank of the drill bit where you can also find the size. There are different lengths of drill bits and the most commonly used is the *"Jobbers"*. A shorter drill, which is not so commonly used, is the *"Stub"* drill bit.

Twist drill bits with a straight or parallel shank are suitable for drilling the small range of holes, e.g. 0.50 mm diameter-12 mm diameter. Larger holes have to be drilled with twist bits that have a tapered shank which fits directly into the spindle column of a drilling machine and not into a chuck. The sizes range from 12 mm diameter to 50 mm depending on the size of the taper.

To drill a hole in the larger range of sizes on a drilling machine it is necessary to do two things:

1. Drill with small-size drill bits, gradually increasing the sizes until the final size is reached. For a 25-mm diameter hole you may use as many as four drill bits before finally drilling with the 25-mm diameter drill bit. Doing it this way ensures an accurate and cleanly cut hole.
2. Decrease the drill speed with the increase of the size of the drill bit used.

Carpenter's ratchet brace

The large range of hole sizes can be achieved by using hand tools such as a **"Carpenter's Ratchet Brace"** (see Fig. 9.4). Because of the leverage that has to be applied when drilling, the bit has a tapering square shank. This prevents it from rotating in the four-jaw chuck. The screw centre draws the bit into the wood and the outer spur cuts the edge of the hole while the cutter removes the unwanted material. It is a single operation and drilling with smaller bits is not necessary. If a small hole has been drilled it will be necessary for it to be plugged before a centre bit can be used.

To obtain a cleanly cut through hole on both sides of the material it is necessary to drill from both sides.

Tank and washer cutter

Drilling a large-diameter hole, e.g. 25 mm–125 mm, can be achieved by using a **"Tank and Washer Cutter"**. The type illustrated in Fig. 9.4 has a square shank that is suitable for use with a carpenter's brace. A straight-sided round shank is needed for use in a drilling machine. The cutter is adjusted to the radius of the hole required, i.e. for a hole 84 mm diameter, set the cutter 42 mm away from the centre of the drill. The thumb screw is then tightened to secure the cutter. The tank and washer cutter is only suitable for producing holes in sheet material. When a hole has been cut, the material from the centre comes away complete like a washer. Because the cutter was essentially used to produce holes in water tanks the name "tank and washer" became a commonly used name.

This tool can be used to produce wheels in acrylic and plywood very quickly. The large-diameter holes should be cut at the lowest speed possible on a drilling machine because the cutter travels faster the further away it is set from the centre.

Hole cutters are also available for use in either a drilling machine or a portable power drill (see Fig. 9.4). They are not adjustable and in order to be able to cut a range of hole sizes a set of 4–6 cutters may be necessary. The cutters are a saw blade held on a circular casting by two screws and can be attached by a third screw to a 6mm twist drill bit.

Drills used for cutting slots

Slot drills: can be used in vertical milling machines for cutting slots in mild steel, aluminium, and plastics. The drills are similar to twist drill bits in that they are fluted and are made from high-speed steel. They differ in that the shank has a thread and the end is not pointed. The cutting takes place on the edge of the two spiral flutes. The slot is cut in stages. Only a shallow cut is made during each stage of the cutting operation. The work is securely fixed to a moving table. It is then put on automatic feed for the work to move beneath the slot drill. This work can be done on a *Vertical Milling Machine* or a *Vertical Milling Attachment* on a centre lathe. See Fig. 9.7.

"T" Slot Cutter: made from high-speed steel, it can cut mild steel and nylon. It is useful for cutting slots in a table or base for fixtures that need adjustments of position. It is commonly seen on milling machines, shaping machines and surface grinding machines.

Dovetail slot cutter: made from high-speed steel it can be used on metal and plastics. These slots are useful for allowing a sliding movement in a straight line in two directions only, e.g. the controlled movement of an adjustable jaw in a machine vice. See Fig. 9.4. The cutter can also be used to cut the slope of the dovetail. This ensures a good fit.

TURNING ON A LATHE

Most materials are able to be **turned** on either a wood turning lathe or a metalworker's centre turning lathe. Plastics are best turned on a metalworker's centre lathe.

In both situations the work rotates and the cutting tool moves in a line at approximately right-angles to the work surface.

WOOD TURNING LATHE

There are two types of turning:

1. turning between centres to produce cylindrical shapes such as legs for stools or chairs;
2. turning on a face plate to produce discs or bowls.

Turning between centres

The work is *held in position* by two centres. The driving centre, known as the "Head Stock Centre", is located at the head stock of the lathe and is the one that rotates. It is forked-shaped to grip the wood. The centre at the opposite end of the work is known as the "Tail Stock Centre" and fits into the tail stock of the lathe. It is cone-shaped and does not rotate. The work rotates freely on the tail stock centre. A little smear of grease helps to ensure the smooth running and prevents the wood from getting too hot.

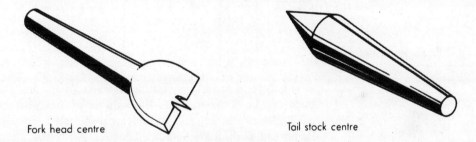

Fig. 19.6   Fork head centre   Tail stock centre

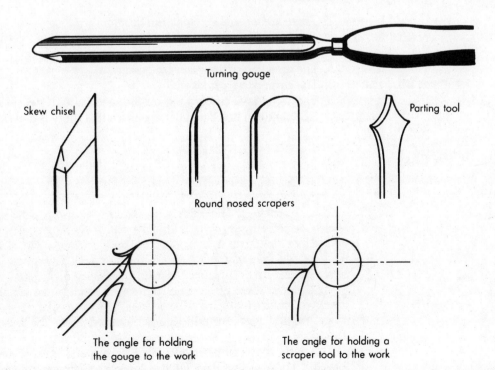

Fig. 19.7

Turning gouge

Skew chisel   Round nosed scrapers   Parting tool

The angle for holding the gouge to the work   The angle for holding a scraper tool to the work

The wood is *shaped* using turning gouges. These are held in position on a tool rest. With the gouge held at a suitable angle it is moved gradually towards the rotating wood until it just makes contact and is then moved along the tool rest. This process is repeated until the wood has been turned to the desired shape and size. The surface will be slightly rough from the gouge and can be smoothed by using a skew chisel.

- The gouge removes material quickly and leaves a rough finish. The skew chisel removes material slowly and produces a smooth finish.
- For hollow work, round nose scraper tools can be used to produce a smooth finish.
- For cleaning off the work to length, a parting tool can be used.

If the work is to be glass papered, only fine grades should be used and the tool rest must be removed.

Turning speed: start the turning process on the slowest speed. The surface of the work will be rough but the aim is to get the work running true. Once the work is true the speed can be increased by moving the pulley on to the next pulley. The skew chisel can be used on the next speed up and the surface of the work made smooth. The top speed can be used for the final stages, i.e. glass papering with a fine grade glass paper and polishing with Carnauba wax.

Turning on a face plate

The disc of wood is fastened to a face plate by countersunk wood screws.

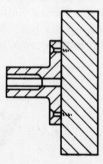

Fig. 19.8 Illustration of wood and face plate

This type of turning is commonly used for turning bowls, lamp bases, etc. The face plate can be screwed on to the spindle of the head stock on either side. For small work, the side facing the tail stock can be used. For large work, i.e. that which has a larger radius than the distance between the centre and the lathe bed, the open end of the tail stock can be used.

The important points to note when *selecting and preparing wood* for *fixing to the face plate* are:

1. There are no shakes (splits) in the wood.
2. The wood is thick enough to accept screws without getting in the way of the gouge when turning.
3. The direction of the grain (see diagram).
4. The corners are removed.
5. The wood is securely held on the face plate. If necessary the surface against the face plate can be planed flat to ensure that there is a perfect contact.

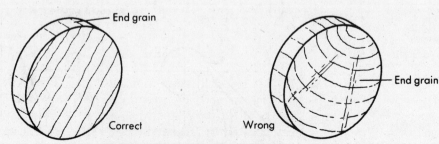

Fig. 19.9

Direction of grain of wood to be turned

When the face plate and work is to be *mounted on the lathe* the following points should be observed:

1. The face plate should be screwed onto the lathe spindle until it can go no further.
2. There is no need to tighten the face plate by applying pressure.
3. The cutting action of the gouge will have the effect of tightening the face plate.

When *putting the tool rest in position* the following points should be observed:

1. That it does not come into contact with the work. This is checked by rotating the work by hand. Do not switch the lathe on to do this check.
2. Check the height of the tool rest with the gouge in position so that you can check that the cutting edge is horizontal with the centre.
3. That the tool rest arm is long enough to reach the centre of the work.

Before switching on, check the lathe to make sure that it is set on the slowest speed. Also ensure that you are wearing goggles and that you have no loose clothing or long hair dangling near the lathe.

TURNING ON A METALWORKER'S CENTRE LATHE

The **Metalworker's Centre Lathe** is much more complex than the wood turning lathe and Fig. 19.10 illustrates this.

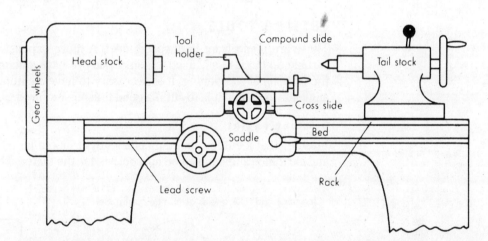

Fig. 19.10   Metalworker's centre lathe

Because metal is a harder material than wood the cutting tool has to be fitted into a compound slide and the movement controlled by turning handles. This means that greater precision can be acquired and that identical objects can be produced. The control can be by hand, automatic or computer aided.

Though the computer aided lathe is the most recent type of lathe to be developed you are not expected to be able to answer questions on it in a Technology Examination. However, if you are fortunate to have the opportunity to use one during the course, you would be advised to do so. Understanding the conventional lathe will help you to understand the principles of lathe turning.

The basic principles of all lathe turning are:

1. The work has to be held but be free to rotate.
2. A cutting tool has to be held and its movements must be under control.

The Metalworker's centre lathe has four main components:

1. A bed;
2. Head stock;
3. Tail stock;
4. Saddle.

- The **Bed** is usually made from cast iron and is sturdy enough to take the weight of the other components. It also has to be firm and not vibrate when in use.
- The **Head Stock** is the driving end of the lathe. It contains the electric motor, the gear wheels that transmit the power to the spindle and the automatic feeds and the controls for switching on or off.

- The **Tail Stock** helps to hold the work in position while it is being turned. It can be moved along the bed of the lathe and locked in any position. Fine adjustment can be made by winding a handle that is attached to the barrel and tail stock centre.
- The **Saddle** contains the controls for the movement of the cutting tool. A cutting tool is held in a tool holder. A commonly used pattern is illustrated in Fig. 19.11.

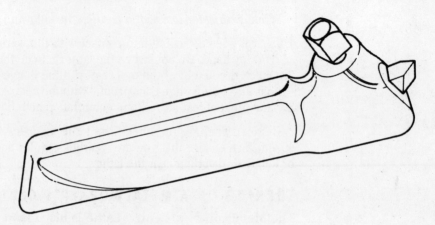

Fig. 19.11   Cutting tool and holder

The tool holder is fitted in the tool post.

CUTTING TOOLS

These are made from high-speed steel. A more expensive tool can have a tungsten carbide tip but if this is used it is necessary to have a diamond grit grinding wheel for the occasional sharpening. It is necessary to have a cutting tool ground to the correct angle for the metal it is to cut if a good finish is required.

Grinding angles

In order that a cutting tool cuts efficiently it has to be more than just sharp. Its rake and clearance angle has to be appropriate for the material being cut.

Clearance and rake angles of a lathe cutting tool

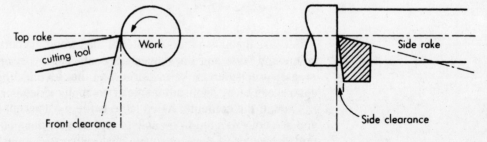

Fig. 19.12

For each cutting tool there are two rake angles and two clearance angles (Fig. 19.12). The two *clearance angles* are the same for all metals i.e.

Front Clearance   8 degrees
Side Clearance   6 degrees

See Table 19.3 for the *rake angles*.

The most commonly shaped cutting tool is the *Round Nose*. It can be used in most turning operations (Fig. 19.13). There is often a set of tools available and they include:

- A *left- and right-hand knife tool* for producing a clean finish and a clean internal right-angle corner (Fig. 19.14).
- A *parting off tool* for cutting a bar to length (Fig. 19.15).
- A *boring bar* used for enlarging an internal hole (Fig. 19.16).

METAL	TOP RAKE	SIDE RAKE
Aluminium	30°	15°
Mild steel	20°	15°
Carbon steel	10°	5°
Brass	0°	0°

Table 19.3

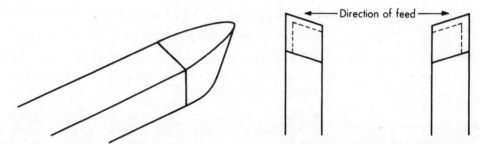

Fig. 19.13 Round nose

Fig. 19.14 Left and right hand knife tool

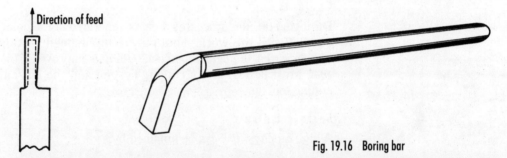

Fig. 19.15 Parting off tool

Fig. 19.16 Boring bar

Turning between centres means that the work is held by two centres: a head stock centre and a tail stock centre. Before this can be done the ends of the work need to be drilled with a centre drill (Fig. 9.4). The angle produced by the larger diameter of the centre drill matches the angle of the centre. The pilot hole drilled by the smaller diameter part of the drill provides a clearance for the point of the centre and, at the tail stock end, a space for a lubricant. This drilling operation is best done on the lathe. The work is held in a three-jaw self-centring chuck fitted at the head stock end. The drill is also held in a three-jaw chuck but at the tail stock end.

The drilling operation is done by the work rotating and the drill moving forward. The lock nut holding the barrel is slackened and the rotation of the handle allows the drill to move forward or backwards. With both ends of the work done the work can be mounted between centres, setting the cutting tool in the correct position (Fig. 19.17).

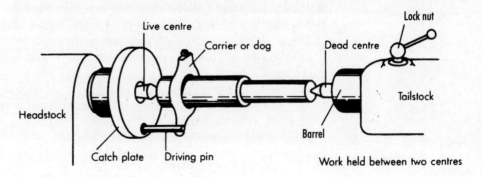

Fig. 19.17

Work held between two centres

The cutting edge of the tool must be set to the horizontal central height of the work. The front horizontal clearance angle can be achieved by adjusting the swivelling and tool post and locking it in the correct position or by rotating the compound slide (Fig. 19.18).

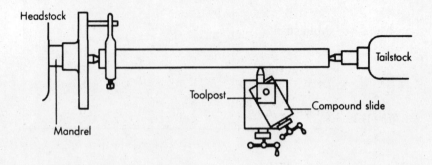

Fig. 19.18

Selecting turning speed of work

The important points to remember are:

a) The mandrel speed is constant and measured in revolutions per minute.
b) The peripheral speed of the work increases with the size of the diameter of the work.

- For deep cuts to remove a lot of material quickly, select a slow mandrel speed.
- For light cuts on a small diameter piece of work, select a medium mandrel speed.
- For light cuts on a large diameter piece of work, select a slow mandrel speed.
- High mandrel speeds should be selected for light cuts and high-quality finish.

Coolants

During all turning processes, heat is generated at the point where the cutting tool is in contact with the work. Though the high-speed cutting tool can withstand high temperatures, the performance of cutting is improved if the tool and the work are kept *cool*. Most lathes have a cooling system and the coolant can be directed onto the cutting tool tip.

Surface finish

A high-quality *finish* can be obtained by:

1. Taking a light cut;
2. Using a high mandrel speed;
3. Using a coolant;
4. Setting the cutting tool on automatic feed;
5. Using a sharp cutting tool that has the appropriate rake and clearance angles for the material being turned;
6. Setting the cutting tool to the correct height.

Knurling is a surface treatment that provides a better grip. This can be done using a knurling tool in the tool post. In order to produce a good quality finish the following must take place:

a) The work must turn at the slowest speed possible. This can be achieved by using a "back gear" which is easily engaged by using a lever.
b) The knurling tool must be clean and free from any metal bits.
c) The knurling wheels must be at right-angles to the work.
d) The work must be securely mounted in the lathe to withstand the pressure of the knurling tool. This tool does not cut the surface, it makes an indentation by pressure.
e) The tool must traverse the work slowly.
f) The knurling tool must not be taken off the work until the knurling process is finished. It is impossible to re-engage the knurling wheels in exactly the same position and the previous work will be spoilt.

There are three knurling patterns:

1. Checkered;
2. Spiral;
3. Straight.

They are produced by using:

1. A single knurling wheel with a checkered cut, or two knurling wheels in a two-wheeled holder with a checkered pattern wheel (Fig. 19.19).

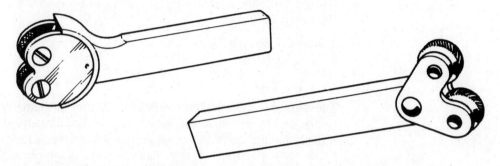

Fig. 19.19

2. A single knurling wheel with either a left- or right-hand spiral (Fig. 19.20).

Fig. 19.20

3. A single knurling wheel holder with a straight pattern wheel (Fig. 19.21).

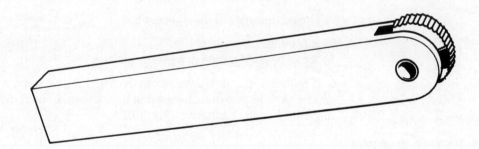

Fig. 19.21

Abrasion uses a hard material to wear down another material that is softer. It should not be confused with using such materials as glass or sand paper, emery cloth, or wet and dry paper. These are used to improve the *quality* of finish of a surface rather than for the removal of unwanted material.

Removing material by abrasion often leaves the surface with a lot of scratches and a "finishing" treatment has to follow. Most abrading processes are done either with a *portable electric tool* or an *electric powered machine*.

PORTABLE ELECTRIC TOOLS

Using a portable electric drill a number of accessories can be used. The two most commonly used are:

1. Abrasive discs;
2. Abrasive belts.

Abrasive disc

The **abrasive disc** is approximately 150 mm in diameter and is fixed to a flexible rubber pad by a dished washer and screw. The abrasive disc is a strong card coated with aluminium oxide. It can be replaced whenever a new one is needed. With a drill set on its highest speed, soft material such as wood can be removed quite quickly (Fig. 19.22).

Fig. 19.22

The **disadvantages** of this process are:

a) It makes a lot of dust.
b) The marks left are circular and the scratches show.

The **advantages** of this process are:

a) It is quick.
b) It can be used on wood, metal or plastics.

If required, the disc sander can be fitted into a stand and converted into a bench sander. A rigid disc must be used in this situation. An abrasive paper is attached to the disc with a contact adhesive (Fig. 19.23).

66 Safety note: air extraction units are required for this process. Face masks to cover the mouth and nose should be worn. 99

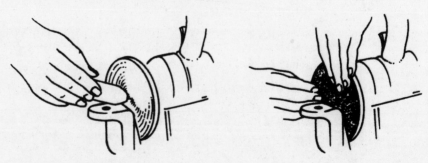

Fig. 19.23

The adhesive is spread evenly on to the surface of the disc and the back of the abrasive paper, allowed to go tacky and then brought together and pressed down firmly (Fig. 19.24).

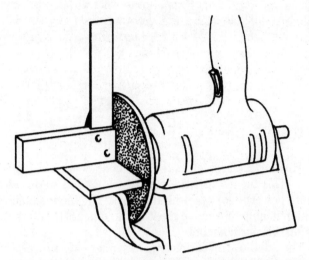

Fig. 19.24

The table must also be checked for squareness to the disc before use.

Using the fixed sander and table

The working half of the disc is from the centre to the outer edge that is on the downward movement. The work must be held firmly on the table and moved along the surface of the disc while applying a gentle pressure. Too much pressure will cause burning. Remember that the disc is travelling much faster near the outer edge and it is here where burning is likely to take place.

Properly used, the disc will remove material from end-grain or edges of man-made boards such as plywood and hardboard. It can be set to abrade at right-angles or, with an adjustable fence, any angle between 0° and 180°. Curved shapes can also be achieved by moving the material in an arc while keeping it in complete contact with the surface of the table. With the appropriate abrading disc, wood, metal and plastics may be used.

The **advantages** of using this method of removing material are:

a) It is quick and easy to operate.
b) Accurate surface angles can be achieved.
c) There is very little chance of splitting the end-grain of natural timber.

The **disadvantages** are:

a) The process can be very dusty if there is no means of extracting the dust.
b) Goggles and a mask should be worn.
c) Wood has a tendency to get scorched very easily.
d) The scratch marks show.
e) It is only really suitable for trueing up edges and cleaning surfaces that have been left from the saw.

Abrading machines

Abrading machines are designed to remove material. These are much larger than the "drill attachment" type and work on the same principle.

The **advantages** are:

1. They are more robust and capable of doing more work.
2. They can cope with larger pieces of material.
3. A dust extraction unit is often fitted.
4. There is sometimes a combination of a disc sander and a belt sander incorporated in a single machine.

The **disadvantages** are:

1. They are in a fixed position and the work has to be brought to the machine.
2. They are more costly to buy and the discs more costly to replace.
3. They are not suitable for small delicate work.

Belt sanders

These are most suited for flat surfaces. Though there are attachments for portable drills, the most efficient designs are purpose made (Fig. 19.25).

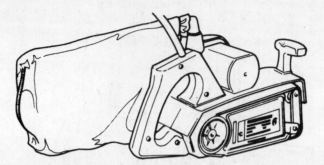

Fig. 19.25

The surface area of material in contact with a belt is much larger than that with a disc. This means that the electric motor has to do a lot more work and needs to be more powerful to cope with the work. The model illustrated above has a dust extractor which is able to remove most of the dust. It is advisable for a mask to be worn when using this portable tool.

The **advantages** of this type of sander over a disc sander are:

1. The scratch marks are in a straight line and not an arc so by working the belt sander along the length of the grain the scratches can hardly be seen.
2. A much larger surface area can be sanded.

Belt sanding machines

These are fixed in position and often fitted with a dust extraction system. The working area is uppermost and the material is brought down on top of the revolving belt (Fig. 19.26). The belt moves away from the worker. This prevents work from being thrown into the worker should it be let free. A fence which extends across the width of the belt is placed at the end of the table to enable work to be under control.

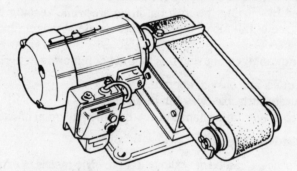

Fig. 19.26

GRINDING WHEELS

Grinding Wheels are mainly associated with the sharpening of sharp edge tools. But there are machines designed for removing unwanted metal in the production of a component or product. These are surface grinders, which are precision machines able to grind the surface of mild steel alloys. The work is held by an electromagnet on a moveable bed. The bed can be raised or lowered to control the depth of grinding. It can be moved horizontally in a line parallel with the grinding wheel and also horizontally in a line at right-angles to the grinding wheel (Fig. 19.27).

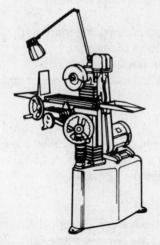

Fig. 19.27

The **advantages** of such a machine are:

1. It can produce an accurately ground surface;
2. The quality of finish is excellent.

The **disadvantage** is:

It is only suitable for grinding ferrous metals.

CHISELLING

This was perhaps the earliest means known of removing unwanted material. It is still an important and much used process that can be employed on a variety of materials.

There are three commonly used designs of chisel used for cutting wood: the Firmer Chisel, the Bevelled Edge Chisel and the Mortice Chisel.

THE FIRMER CHISEL

This is used for general work. It is sturdy and can be used for removing material in most situations. The older version has a wooden handle and the newer version has a plastic handle. Both are equally good but the plastic handle is less likely to split if hit with a hammer instead of a mallet (Fig. 19.28).

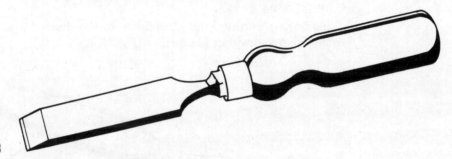

Fig. 19.28

THE BEVELLED EDGE CHISEL

This is particularly useful for cutting in corners that are less than 90°, e.g. in between dovetails (Fig. 19.29).

Fig. 19.29

THE MORTICE CHISEL

This is designed to cut mortices. It is a much thicker chisel than the firmer or bevelled edge and is shaped to withstand the blows of a mallet and leverage. The wooden handled version has a leather washer and a steel ferrule. The London pattern has a leather washer but no steel ferrule. It acquires its resistance to splitting by being rounded at the striking end and slightly bigger (Fig. 19.30).

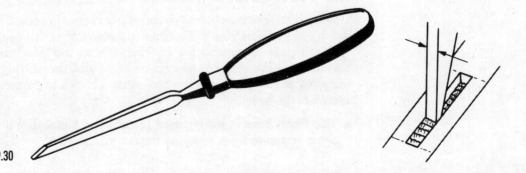

Fig. 19.30

GOUGES

Gouges are a curved form of chisel. There are four types of gouge; a firmer gouge, a scribing gouge, a carving gouge and a woodturner's gouge.

The firmer gouge

This has its cutting edge ground from the outside. It is mainly used for hollowing out work, e.g. a carved wooden bowl (Fig. 19.31).

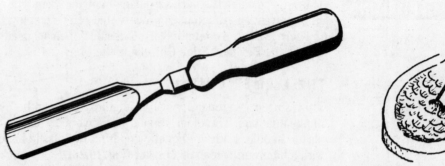

Fig. 19.31

The scribing gouge

This has its cutting edge ground from the inside. It is mainly used for cutting mouldings so that they fit together (Fig. 19.32).

Fig. 19.32

The carving gouge

This is very similar to the firmer gouge. It has its cutting edge ground from the outside. There is a greater variation of curvatures and sizes available to cope with the wide range of forms that the woodcarver needs (Fig. 19.33).

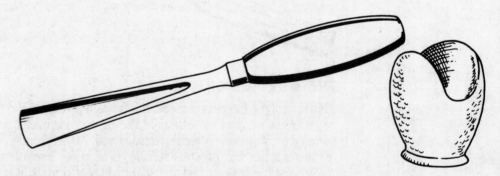

Fig. 19.33

THE COLD CHISEL

This is a metal cutting chisel. It is called a cold chisel because it cuts metal that is cold, and to distinguish it from a blacksmith's hot set chisel that cuts metal while it is hot.

The two most commonly used cold chisels are the "Flat" chisel and the "Cross-cut" chisel. They are made from carbon steel and the cutting end is hardened and tempered at 280°C. (It is quenched when a brown to purple oxide is formed on the surface of the metal.)

■ The **Flat Chisel** is mainly used to cut sheet metal. The metal to be cut has to be firmly supported. For reducing the size of a piece of metal it is held in an engineers vice along the line that is to be cut. The cold chisel is held at an angle to the line and struck with a hammer. The metal is sheared as the chisel travels along the line (Fig. 19.34).

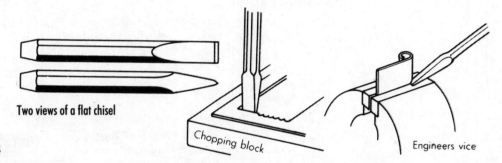

Two views of a flat chisel

Fig. 19.34

Chopping block

Engineers vice

To remove metal from a middle portion the work has to be supported on a chopping block.

■ The **Cross-cut Chisel** is used for cutting a groove or "Keyway", and again the chisel has to be struck with a hammer (Fig. 19.35).

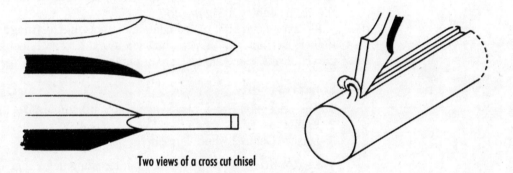

Fig. 19.35

Two views of a cross cut chisel

9 BENDING

Most materials will **bend**. Some will stay in the bent position, others will spring back to their original shape. Some materials will not respond to bending at all.

BENDING WOOD

Wood in general is a springy material and will bend under pressure.

Because not all timbers have identical characteristics, some respond to bending better than others. Yew is a naturally springy timber and in the early days of bow-making was the most commonly used timber for making bows.

The main reason for bending a material is that it should keep the bent form after all pressure has been released. Methods have been developed so that this can be achieved.

1 Steam bending

When timber is heated in a steam bath it is much more pliable and will bend without splitting. If the timber is cramped in a former and left to cool and dry out, the timber will keep its new bent form. This process is suitable for making coat hangers, coat hooks, and decorative forms of jewellery, etc.

The efficiency of this process is greatly improved if the timber is cut into laminations. The steam can get to all parts of the timber more quickly and the laminations can be bonded with an adhesive at the stage of cramping if a thicker form is required (Fig. 19.36).

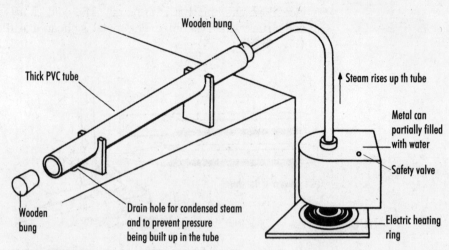

Wooden bung

Thick PVC tube

Steam rises up th tube

Metal can partially filled with water

Safety valve

Wooden bung

Drain hole for condensed steam and to prevent pressure being built up in the tube

Electric heating ring

Fig. 19.36

2 Laminating

Thin strips of wood are bonded together by an adhesive. They are cramped in a former that has been prepared to the desired form and when the adhesive has set, the cramps are released and the laminations remain in their bent form. The laminations all have the grain running in one direction, unlike plywood that has alternate plies with the grain running at right-angles.

A curved form built up from laminations is much stronger than one made from solid timber. Examples of this can be seen in modern architecture. The support beams are curved forms, e. g. elliptical, arc or parabolic and form a major feature of the building.

Examples

1. The Reception Hall for passengers at Southampton Docks.
2. Exhibition Halls.
3. Leisure Centres where large open spaces are required.

The extra strength has permitted an interesting new range of forms to be developed in furniture. Chairs made from laminations are noted for their strength and are used in public places including many schools.

Process

The lamina (a thin sheet of material 2 mm–4 mm thick) must be cut accurately. The thickness must be constant throughout the length and this is best achieved by using either a circular saw or a thickness planing machine.

■ A *former* is cut from a thick piece of solid timber to the exact form of the inside curve. If the former is for small work it may be possible to cut a profile of the outer curve. Doing it this way makes cramping much easier.
■ A *synthetic resin* is applied to one surface of the lamina that are to form the external surfaces and to both surfaces of the internal lamina. The lamina are placed together with a piece of paper covering the outside surfaces. This is to prevent the lamina from adhering to the former. When the lamina are placed in the former and squeezed together there is always a chance that some adhesive will come into contact with the former.
■ The *lamina* are squeezed together by applying pressure to the former. This can be done in a vice if the work is small enough, or "G" cramps or short sash cramps.
■ The work is left cramped until the adhesive has set.
■ When the laminated form is removed from the former it will retain its bent form and is ready for cleaning up (Fig. 19.37).

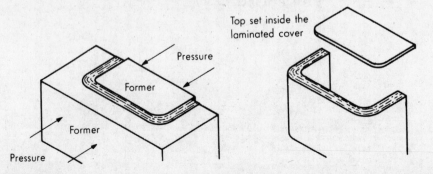

Top set inside the laminated cover

Pressure

Former

Former

Pressure

Fig. 19.37 Pressure

The **advantages** of using this process are:

1. The finished piece of work is light and strong.
2. It is suitable for batch production, i.e. making a small number of identical objects.
3. Curved forms can be achieved which may add to the aesthetic appeal.

The **disadvantages** of using this process are:

1. A former has to be made.
2. It is expensive on time and materials if only one product is made.
3. It is only suitable for the production of curved forms.

BENDING METAL

Most metals used in a school workshop are suitable for bending. Aluminium, copper and mild steel will bend quite easily when cold and in sheet, wire, small-diameter rod or thin strip form. When metal is bigger it is sometimes necessary to anneal (soften) the material before attempting to bend cold. Much larger thicknesses may only successfully bend when hot.

Bending a piece of material has the effect of squeezing the material on the inside curve and stretching on the outside of the curve. The thicker the material the greater the effect on the squeezing and stretching (Fig. 19.38).

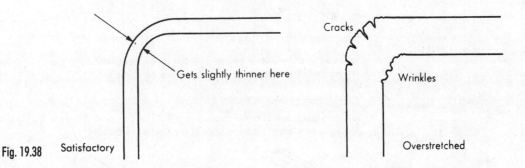

Fig. 19.38

BENDING COLD

Most materials are available in an annealed state. If this is not so for the material you wish to bend, then it will be necessary for *you* to do the annealing. The material needs to be securely held along the line of the bend. This can be achieved by a variety of methods.

PREPARING MATERIALS FOR BENDING

- **Annealing metals**. Small-section and sheet material will normally bend quite easily and no preparation is necessary. Where there is a danger that the metal may weaken or even fracture by bending cold it should first be annealed.
- **Annealing mild steel**. Heat to cherry-red and allow to cool slowly in a hearth.
- **Annealing copper**. Heat to cherry-red and allow to cool slowly or it may be quenched in water to cool it quickly.
- **Annealing aluminium**. Smear the surface with a liquid soap. Heat gently until the soap turns brown. Quench the metal in water. Remember aluminium has a much lower melting point than steel or copper and must not be allowed to reach the high temperature that causes steel and copper to turn cherry-red. The soap will turn brown when the correct temperature for annealing aluminium has been reached, 350 °C.
- **Annealing brass.** Brass is an alloy of copper and zinc. While copper is an easy metal to anneal, zinc is not. Great care is needed to anneal any alloy that contains zinc. Heat to dull red and allow to cool slowly in air. Do not quench. Small cracks will appear.

Large-section mild steel, cast steel and wrought iron will bend more readily when heated. The most suitable working temperature is reached when the metal is cherry-red. The blacksmith works his metal at this temperature and is able to do a lot more than just bend it.

1. Holding work in a vice

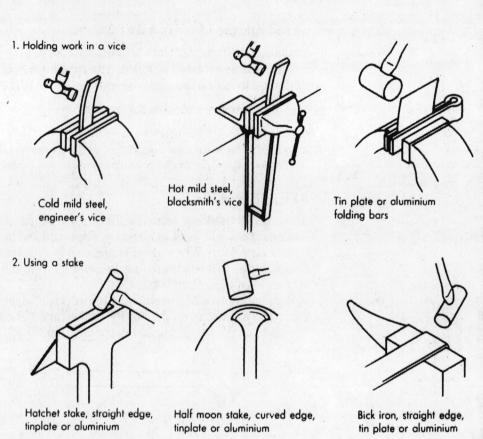

Cold mild steel,
engineer's vice

Hot mild steel,
blacksmith's vice

Tin plate or aluminium
folding bars

2. Using a stake

Hatchet stake, straight edge,
tinplate or aluminium

Half moon stake, curved edge,
tinplate or aluminium

Bick iron, straight edge,
tin plate or aluminium

3. Using a jig: bending thermoplastics (hot).   This can often be done by hand and
the jig is needed to hold the work in position while it cools.

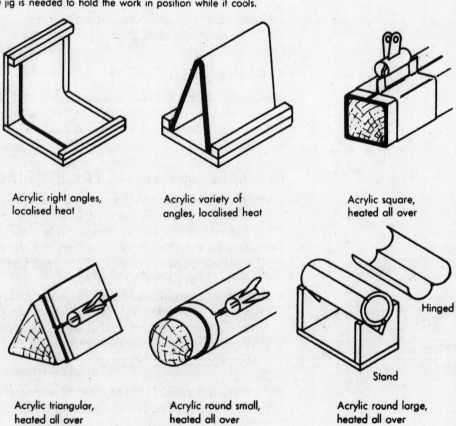

Acrylic right angles,
localised heat

Acrylic variety of
angles, localised heat

Acrylic square,
heated all over

Acrylic triangular,
heated all over

Acrylic round small,
heated all over

Acrylic round large,
heated all over

Hinged

Stand

Fig. 19.39

BEATING METAL TO SHAPE

Beating metal is a much more complex process than bending it. The forms that can result mean that the material has changed its shape in many directions and not just a single one as in bending (Fig 19.40).

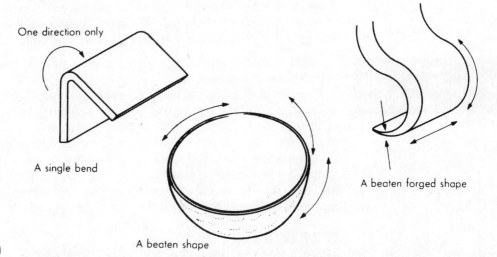

One direction only

A single bend

A beaten shape

A beaten forged shape

Fig. 19.40

Aluminium, copper and gilding metal are the most suitable materials for beaten work because they are malleable. This means that these metals will respond to being hit with a hammer or mallet. They will change their form without breaking.

As for bending, they will respond better if they are annealed. The process of hitting the metal has the effect of making it hard. The term "Work Hardening" is used to describe this effect. After a period of beating metal it should be annealed. In the process of making a shallow bowl it may be necessary to anneal the work three or four times.

When copper is annealed the surface is black due to the formation of an oxide during heating and cooling. Before the beating process can be continued the oxide has to be removed. This is done by immersing the work in a dilute acid. The process is known as "Pickling".

Pickling

This is only necessary for metals that form oxides when heated, e.g. gilding metal and copper. Aluminium does not form an oxide and therefore does not need to be "pickled" after annealing. The metal must be clean and free from oxide otherwise the beating process will hammer it into the surface and spoil the appearance of the finished work.

The *pickle* is kept in an earthenware dish or bath and covered with a wooden lid. The lid should have a clear label to show that the liquid is "ACID". After heating the copper or gilding metal it should be allowed to cool before putting it into the pickle bath. It should be picked up with tongs made from brass only. Steel tongs should not be used because the combination of the steel and the pickle will leave a stain on the work. After a few minutes the work can be carefully removed using the brass tongs and rinsed under flowing water from a tap. The loose remains of oxide should wash away leaving the clean copper exposed. Should there be any oxide still on the surface it may be necessary to return the work to the pickle for a while longer.

Aluminium does not require "pickling" but it will need rinsing in water to remove the burnt soap.

Mild steel, cast steel and wrought iron are best worked under a hammer when they are red hot. Though the shaping and forming is still carried out by beating, this type of work is referred to as "Forged Work". The metal is heated in a forge and it is from this that it gets its name.

FORGED WORK

The process involves working metal while it is red hot. As soon as the temperature of the metal falls, i.e. its colour is no longer red, it must be re-heated. Small-section material loses its heat readily and needs to be worked quickly. Larger-section material can retain its heat longer and allow more time for working. Hitting the metal when it is not red hot will cause small cracks to appear.

An oxide forms on the surface and should not be removed. It not only improves the appearance but it also provides a protective skin. This applies in particular to wrought iron work.

When forging cast steel, which is mainly concerned with the making of tools, e.g. chisels, punches, knives, scissors, shears, etc., the oxide will need to be removed from the surface when the steel has to be "tempered". This is done physically and not chemically. The surface is filed with an old file or ground on a grinding machine. Note that oxides are very hard and could easily take the "edge" off a new file very quickly.

10> HARDENING AND TEMPERING

Because these two processes are associated with cast steel it follows on naturally to include them in this section.

After all the shaping has been completed it is necessary to harden and temper the areas of the working part of the tool, i.e. the cutting edge of a chisel, the point of a centre punch, etc. Cast steel will harden if heated to red hot and suddenly quenched in tepid water or oil. It can be so hard that it becomes brittle and if, for example, the centre punch was left in this state it is possible for the working end of the punch to snap off when used to punch a mark in a piece of steel. To prevent this from happening and for the working end to still be sufficiently hard to make a mark, it is necessary to "Temper" the steel.

TEMPERING

The cast steel must be hardened *before* this process can be performed. The oxide left by the hardening process must be removed so that the silvery grey of the steel is exposed. Only the area near the working part needs to be prepared. The tool is then heated well behind the area to be tempered. The heat will conduct along the metal and this will be seen as an oxide on the cleaned surface.

At about 235 °C the oxide will be yellow. This will travel towards the working area. As the temperature rises so the colour of the oxide changes from yellow to dark-yellow, straw, pale-brown, dark-brown, purple and finally blue at 295 °C. The oxide colours will travel quite steadily and when the appropriate colour has reached the working end, the whole tool is quenched in cold water. If the colour bands are close together and the colours are travelling quickly, this means that too much heat was applied. The aim is to get wide bands of colour travelling slowly. You will then have more material tempered at the appropriate temper characteristic.

Tempering characteristics go from hard and tough (yellow oxide) to springy (blue oxide). For details of what tempering colour will result in obtaining the appropriate characteristics for different tools see Fig. 19.41.

Oxide colour	Temperature	Type of tool
Yellow	230°C	 Hammer face, Knife blade, Scriber
Dark yellow	245°C	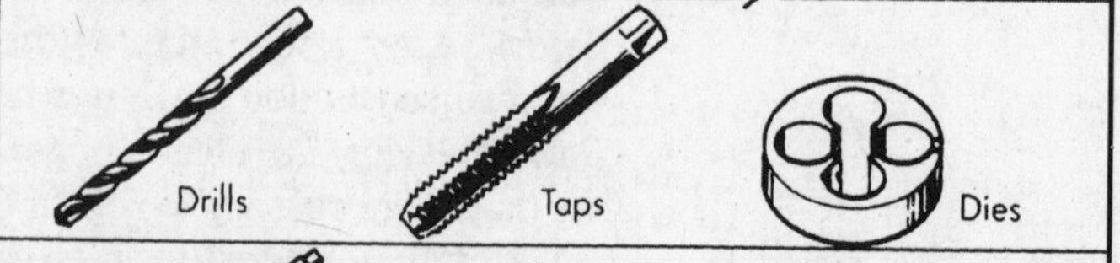 Drills, Taps, Dies
Pale brown	250°C	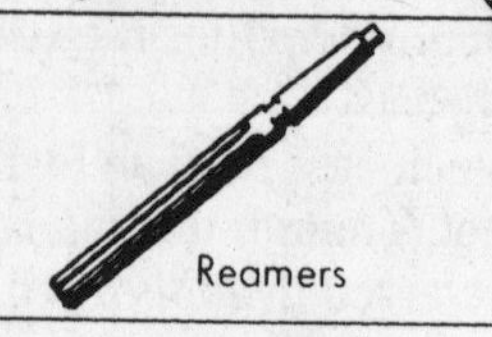 Reamers
Brown	260°C	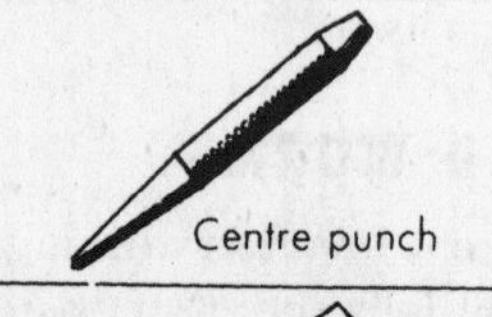 Centre punch
Dark brown	265°C	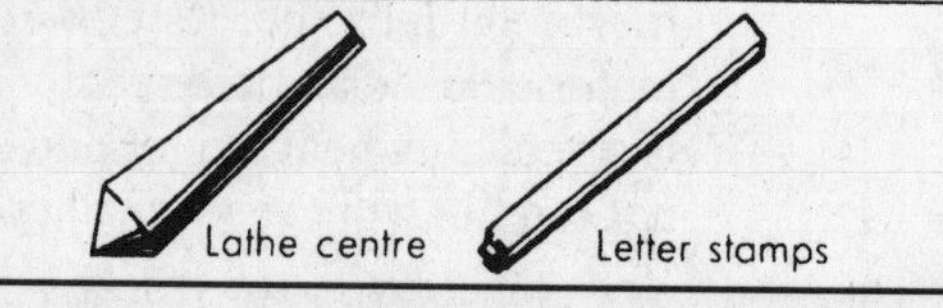 Lathe centre, Letter stamps

Fig. 19.41

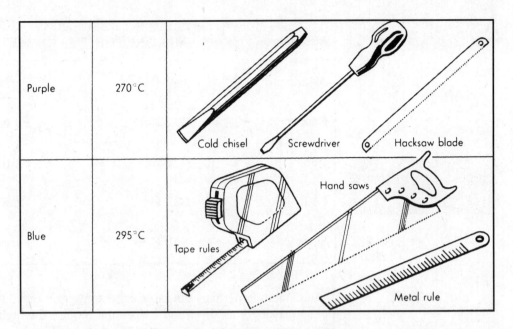

| Purple | 270°C | Cold chisel   Screwdriver   Hacksaw blade |
| Blue | 295°C | Tape rules   Hand saws   Metal rule |

Fig. 19.41 (continued)

A single tool may need different characteristics at different parts of the tool. For example, the cutting end of a cold chisel needs different characteristics than the end that has to withstand the impact of a hammer. If in tempering the cold chisel it was heated approximately 50 mm behind the cutting edge, this would mean that the heat source would be approximately 80 mm from the striking end. The heat would reach the cutting end first and the whole tool quenched in cold water would mean that the striking end would not be affected.

In such tools as rules, straight or tape, and hand saws it is important that the tool has a constant temper over all parts of the tool. Here the tool is heated in a muffle furnace set at 295 °C.

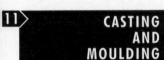

CASTING

When a material is in a liquid state it will flow until it meets a resistance. The water in a river flows and is kept on course by the banks of the river. If the liquid becomes solid it will keep the shape of that which prevents it from flowing. The water frozen in the river will keep the shape of the river while it is in a solid state. This principle can be applied to materials that have the capacity to:

a) flow in a liquid state;
b) become solid at atmospheric temperatures.

There are two ways in which this may be achieved:

1. Heating a material until it melts, and letting it cool to atmospheric temperature when it will become solid again;
2. Applying a chemical to a liquid that will cause it to set solid.

CASTING BY HEATING

Most metals are solid at atmospheric temperatures. The one metal that is not is mercury. Metals such as cast iron, aluminium, lead, silver, tin, copper and bronze, etc., can be melted by applying heat. They all have different melting points. It is necessary to know these so that the appropriate method of heating can be applied. See Table 19.4.

METAL	MELTING POINT	METHOD OF HEATING
Aluminium	660°C	Furnace and crucible
Copper	1,083°C	Furnace and crucible
Iron	1,533°C	Furnace and crucible
Lead	327°C	Brazing torch, electric ring
Silver	961°C	Furnace and crucible

Table 19.4

Aluminium is perhaps the most commonly used metal for casting in schools. It is not so expensive as silver and it does not require the high temperatures for melting that some metals need, e.g. copper and iron. Lead is still quite soft as a solid material and has limited use, but it is good where weight is an important aspect. So aluminium with its medium range melting point, its working qualities and its pleasing appearance is a favourite material for use in schools.

CASTING ALUMINIUM

Equipment

■ **Heating**: a crucible (the pot in which the aluminium is melted) and furnace are the major items. The furnace is heated by gas and forced air (Fig. 19.42).

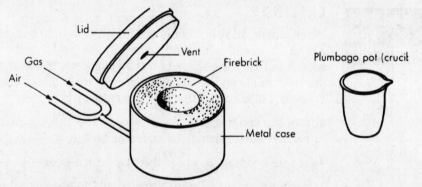

Fig. 19.42

■ **Clothing and holding equipment**: when working with very hot materials it is necessary to have tongs for handling the crucible and protective clothing. See page 158 for protective clothing.

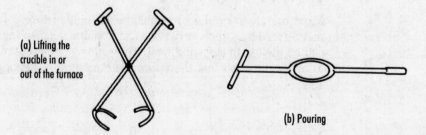

(a) Lifting the crucible in or out of the furnace

(b) Pouring

Fig. 19.43

■ **Flasks**: these keep the sand together and make it possible for a mould to be made. The most common sand casting process requires two flasks. A "Cope" and the "Drag" or top and bottom pair of flasks are needed. They can be made of wood or iron. On the inside edge is a groove which helps to keep the sand in the flask. The flasks must have handles at either end for lifting, and also locating pins for keeping the flasks together and round the correct way.

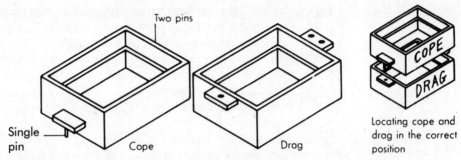

Fig. 19.44

Two pins

Single pin

Cope

Drag

Locating cope and drag in the correct position

Pattern

A form of the item to be made in aluminium is first made from wood. This is called a **pattern**. It is to be used to create the impression in the sand that will later be filled with molten aluminium. For some forms, a pattern can be made from a single form. For many forms it is necessary to make a split pattern to make it possible for it to be removed successfully from the sand.

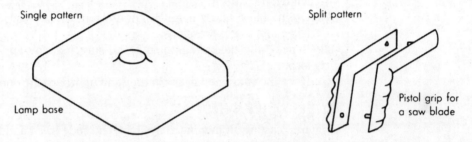

Single pattern

Split pattern

Lamp base

Pistol grip for a saw blade

Fig. 19.45

For a pattern to be removed from sand cleanly it must have the following:

a) a clean smooth surface;
b) radiused corners and edges;
c) a draft (a tapered slope to decrease the size at one end).

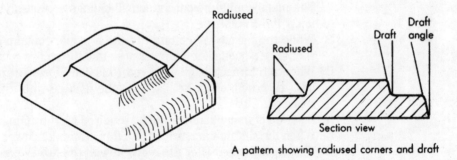

Radiused

Draft

Draft angle

Radiused

Section view

A pattern showing radiused corners and draft

Fig. 19.46

Preparing a sand mould

The sand is specially treated so that it will bond together under slight pressure. Squeezing it in the hand is a way of testing the sand to see if it is suitable. If it holds together it is satisfactory. If it crumbles, it is not fit for use in casting.

CASTING USING A "SPLIT PATTERN"

1. One half of the split pattern is placed in the centre of a ramming board.
2. A flask is then placed round the pattern. To assist the pattern to be withdrawn from the sand later in the process a sprinkling of a parting powder is evenly and thinly distributed.
3. Clean sand is then packed round the pattern until it is covered.
4. The flask is filled to just over the brim with sand.
5. The sand is lightly rammed.
6. The surplus sand is strickled off with a metal straight edge.
7. The flask and its contents can be lifted from the ramming board and turned over. The one half of the pattern is now visible.
8. Locate the other half of the flask on top of the flask now filled.

9. Locate the other half of the pattern.
10. Give the surface a light and even sprinkle of parting powder.
11. Place the riser sprue pin in position and secure with some sand.
12. Place the pouring sprue pin in position and secure with sand.
13. Cover the pattern with clean sand taking care not to move the sprue pins.
14. Completely fill the flask with sand and lightly ram.
15. Strickle off any surplus sand.
16. Cut a pouring basin near the pouring sprue hole. (This is the larger diameter pin of the two.)
17. Scoop out a channel leading to the pin.
18. Carefully remove the two pins.
19. Round off the edge of the pouring hole so that no sand can be washed into the hole during the pouring operation.
20. Lift and turn the top flask over and place on a flat clean surface.
21. Carefully remove the pattern from the sand.
22. Cut a channel in the drag flask from the position marks left by the sprue pins.
23. Remove the second half of the split pattern.
24. Round off any sharp edges left by the channel leading to and from the impression left by the pattern.
25. Lightly blow with a hand bellows to remove any particles of sand that may have fallen into the impressions.
26. Replace the flasks together. Make sure that the ends match by looking at the locating pins.
27. Place the combined flasks in the sand pit where the pouring will take place.

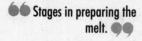
Stages in a split pattern.

Preparing the melt

The best casting aluminium alloys have the code LM 4 and LM 6:

- LM 4 is an alloy of 3% copper, 5% silicon and the remainder aluminium and trace elements.
- LM 6 is an alloy of 12% silicon and the remainder aluminium and trace elements.

Unidentified "off-cuts" of aluminium may be used but the quality of the casting cannot be guaranteed.

1. The metal should be cut into small chunks so that no pieces protrude above the top of the crucible.
2. While the furnace is getting hot the crucible containing the metal to be melted should be placed near the furnace so that the chill is removed.
3. When the furnace is glowing red (this can be seen through the vent hole in the lid), the crucible can be placed in the furnace with the lifting tongs, and the lid replaced.
4. A period of many minutes will be required for the aluminium to melt.
5. When the aluminium has melted a flux is sprinkled over the surface.
6. The dross formed after the reaction with the flux is scooped off with a refractory-coated ladle. A silvery liquid is then revealed.
7. Lift the crucible from the furnace.
8. When the melt has been made up with scrap material it should be degassed. A degassing tablet is placed on the surface of the melt and pushed below the surface with a bell shaped plunger. A vigorous bubbling takes place and gases are given off. When the reaction has stopped the plunger can be removed.
   Note that the degassing process gives off irritating fumes and should be done while the air extracting system is switched on or the doors and windows are open.
9. The crucible should now be transferred to the pouring tongs.
10. The person going to control the pouring (usually the teacher) should hold the "T"-shaped end.
11. The other end may be held by the pupil (both people should be wearing appropriate protective clothing).
12. The holder of the "T"-shaped end is responsible for all movements and gives the instructions.
13. The crucible is steadily held with the lip over the pouring basin.
14. The melt is poured into the basin allowing it to flow steadily into the pouring sprue hole.

Stages in preparing the melt.

15. When the melt is seen rising up the riser hole the pouring is gently eased off.
16. The crucible is then returned to a safe place in the sand pit alongside the flasks, or back to the furnace if more pouring is to be done later.
17. The flask and its contents are left to cool until the melt has solidified.
18. The contents of the flask are removed over the sand tray or bin.
19. If the work is completely cool it may be handled and the remaining sand brushed away.
20. Saw off the unwanted metal and clean off any flashing with a file.

The casting is now ready for the next stage in its production.

CASTING BY ADDING A CHEMICAL

Many of the resin plastics are in a liquid state at atmospheric temperature and will only become solid when:

a) exposed to air;
b) a chemical is added.

Many of the two-part adhesives like Araldite will become solid when the resin and the "hardener" are mixed together. If a resin mixed with a "hardener" is poured into a mould, it will retain the shape of the mould when cured (set hard). This technique is called **Cold Casting**.

Cold casting procedure

The moulds can be "rigid" or "flexible". A "rigid" mould is one that cannot be bent or twisted and is made from such materials as wood, metal, and glass, etc. A "flexible" mould is one that can be bent, twisted, and stretched without damage to its original form. These moulds can be made from latex liquid rubber; silicone rubber; gelflex, a two part polyurethane elastomer, etc. Plasticine can also be used but has to be re-shaped after each casting process.

Rigid moulds can be used for embedding or encapsulation of objects in resin. For the casting to be released it is necessary for the mould to have:

a) a draft of approximately 2°;   c) no undercuts;
b) slightly radiused corners;   d) the sides treated with a release agent, e.g. silicone wax.

Flexible moulds are made from latex, a rubber which can be stretched to release the casting. They are particularly suited for casting detailed work and forms that have "under-cuts". The mould is ready for use.

CASTING IN A RIGID MOULD

Embedding resin is a crystal-clear resin and is used for encapsulating objects of interest, such as leaves, insects, coins, watch parts, etc. The procedure varies slightly according to whether or not the object floats in a liquid.

Stage 1 Prepare a small quantity of embedding resin by adding a liquid catalyst. Approximately 2% catalyst will start the chemical process of curing (setting hard).

Stage 2 Pour the resin into the mould and cover with a piece of paper. The paper will prevent the dust in the air from settling on the surface of the resin.

Stage 3 When the resin has cured place the object centrally.

Stage 4 Prepare a small quantity of resin by adding 2% catalyst as before. If the object is light and floats, only pour in sufficient resin to run round its surface. This will then set and keep the object in position. Another quantity of resin can be prepared to completely cover the object. If the object does not float then it can be covered in one step only.

Curing time

Resins are normally available as "Preactivated". This means that an activator has been added to the resin to make it *cure* at room temperature when a catalyst has been added. As soon as a resin container has been opened for use, the process of curing begins. This means that the resin would eventually cure, just in the same way as a tin of paint begins to go hard when the lid has been removed.

Shelf life

Under normal room temperatures it would take more than a year for the resin to become solid. It is necessary for the manufacturer to indicate on the label a "shelf life" (a useful working life) for the product. This is to tell you that it will be unusable after a certain date. The shelf life of resins can vary between 6 and 12 months.

Preactivated resin

The curing time for a resin that has been preactivated and a catalyst added is approximately 1 hour for it to become set but the curing process continues for several months before it becomes really hard.

Non-preactivated resin

If an activator has not been added by the manufacturer, this can be done in the workshop at the same time as preparing the resin with the catalyst for a casting. Only 0.25%–0.50% activator is required, but the preactivator should be carefully added to the resin first and thoroughly mixed before adding the catalyst. Activator and catalyst should never come directly into contact because the chemical reaction is highly active and dangerous. One reason for buying preactivated resins is to avoid the risk of someone mixing the two chemicals.

Exothermic heat

The chemical reaction that takes place when a catalyst has been added to a preactivated resin gives off heat. The bulkier the casting and the larger the amount of resin used can be the cause for the casting getting hot. In extreme cases the reaction can cause a fire. It is important that very little heat is generated in embedding casting to preserve the clarity of the resin when it is cured. By not keeping strictly to the mixing ratios specified by the manufacturer and trying to produce oversized castings too quickly it is possible for the resin to craze.

CASTING IN A FLEXIBLE MOULD

Flexible moulds can be bought or they can be made. It is much more interesting and demanding to make your own mould.

Making a mould

As with the hot casting process with aluminium, it is necessary to have a pattern from which a mould can be made. The pattern can be a single pattern because the mould will be flexible and will be able to be stretched and removed from the pattern. It can be made from wood, clay, plasticine, or plaster of paris, metal, etc. The material should be:

a) easy to work;
b) easy to obtain a good finish;
c) readily responsive to carving or shaping.

Remember the quality of the casting is only as good as the quality of the mould. If absorbent materials are used they should be sealed with a coat of varnish.

Plaques, chess pieces, small sculptures, etc., can be made using this process.

The pattern is suspended or dipped in a container of the prepared flexible resin and allowed to "dry".

The main **advantages** of using this method of casting are:

1. The process can be repeated many times without the need to make a fresh mould.
2. Shapes with fine detail and undercuts can be produced.
3. No heat is required.

The **disadvantages** are:

1. The size of the castings is limited.
2. Only one casting can be made at a time which takes a minimum of one hour to produce.
3. It is easy to be wasteful; resin cannot be re-used if too much has been prepared.

Fillers

These are powders that can be added to the resin in the preparation stage. They can be metallic powders such as bronze or aluminium to give the final product a metallic finish.

Colouring

There are two types of pigment:

1. opaque (cannot be seen through);
2. translucent (light can pass through).

These are added to the resin in its preparation and thoroughly mixed in to produce an even colour. Lightly stirred pigments can produce an attractive result in the final product; similar to that seen in coloured marbles.

CHOOSING A METHOD OF CASTING

The method may be decided by what is available. If, however, there is a choice, then the following points will need to be considered:

1. The function of the component or product to be made. Is it an engineering component that has to withstand wear, leverage, or pressure and be of a high precision quality? Or is it an item of artistic visual quality?
2. Size.
3. Quantity to be produced.
4. The fineness of the surface detail.
5. Will there be any under-cuts?

MOULDING

If you think of *casting* as a process where only gravity is used for the liquid state material to enter a mould, then moulding is a process where a pressure or force is applied.

INJECTION MOULDING

A thermosoftening plastics material is heated in a heating chamber until it reaches a fluid state and then it is forced into a mould. An injection moulding machine like the one illustrated in Fig. 5.17 is required for this process. The very long handle provides the leverage and the pressure needed to inject the plastics material into the mould. The size of the mould must not exceed the capacity of the heating chamber. The fluid material is injected in a single downward movement of the handle. Before a second pull on the handle can be made the heating chamber has to be recharged with pellets and given time to melt. By this time the plastics injected into the mould will have cooled and returned to a solid state, blocking the entrance so that no more plastics may be injected.

MOULDS

Because of the high pressure needed for injection moulding, most moulds are made from metal. Mild steel or aluminium is commonly used. Split moulds are most suitable. Once the plastics material has filled the mould it can be removed from the vice of the injection moulding machine and the moulding taken out of the mould. Protective gloves will be needed because although the plastics will have cooled slightly it will still be too hot to hold by hand. The two halves of the split mould are located by the two pins in one half and by the two holes in the other half.

THE ESSENTIAL DESIGN FEATURES OF A SPLIT MOULD ARE:

a) The two halves of the mould should match perfectly.
b) It should be easy to part the two halves.
c) There should be no under-cuts.
d) The entrance for the plastics should be on the split.
e) The entrance hole should match the nozzle of the machine.
f) The cavity space of the mould should be less than the capacity of the injection moulding machine.
g) The heat of the plastics material should not affect the mould.
h) The surface of the mould should be highly polished.

66 The answers to many questions can be set out in this way. 99

PREPARING A MOULD READY FOR INJECTING

There are two factors that need to be attended to before injecting:

1. Make sure that the mould is warm so that the molten plastics do not chill and set too early.
2. Apply a thick smear of oil to the surface of the mould. This will ensure an easy release of the moulding.

Suitable moulding materials are listed in Table 19.5.

Table 19.5

MATERIAL	APPROX. MELTING POINT
Nylon	190°C – 220°C
Polyethylene	190°C – 220°C
Polystyrene	200°C
Polypropylene	250°C

Safety

When dealing with very hot materials it is essential that the following precautions are taken:

Safety precautions

1. Only use dry pellets of thermoplastics.
2. Only use clean materials.
3. Ensure that the correct heat setting is used.
4. Close the clear see-through guard round the mould.
5. Wear goggles.
6. Wear heat resistant gloves.
7. Wear a protective apron.

Hot plastics have a nasty habit of clinging. If there is any moisture in the plastics, steam is formed and spitting may occur. This is why it is necessary for precautions to be taken. Under normal circumstances this is a safe and reliable method of moulding and accidents are rare.

BLOW MOULDING

Blow moulding into a space

A sheet of thermoplastics material is heated in an oven. The material becomes soft and pliable. It is quickly transferred to a blow moulding jig and air is blown against the surface. The soft plastic rises in a hemisphere. The blowing is stopped and the air is trapped by the valve and the contact the plastic has with the jig. The material cools and sets. The hemisphere or dome is released from the jig as soon as it is cool enough to handle. The unwanted material is trimmed, the edges are scraped and polished and the dome is complete. The dome may be used as a food cover or, if large enough, could form part of an exhibition case. The most suitable material is acrylic. The workable temperature is between 150°C and 160 °C.

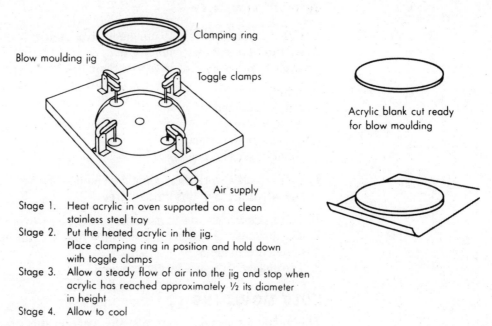

Clamping ring

Blow moulding jig

Toggle clamps

Air supply

Acrylic blank cut ready
for blow moulding

Stage 1. Heat acrylic in oven supported on a clean
          stainless steel tray
Stage 2. Put the heated acrylic in the jig.
          Place clamping ring in position and hold down
          with toggle clamps
Stage 3. Allow a steady flow of air into the jig and stop when
          acrylic has reached approximately ½ its diameter
          in height
Stage 4. Allow to cool

Fig. 19.47

Blowing into a mould

For this process a hollow or female mould is required. The shape of the mould can be
readily turned on the woodworker's lathe. Also an oven for heating the thermoplastics
material and air supply is needed.

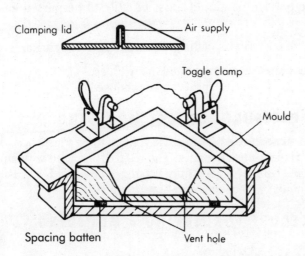

Clamping lid   Air supply

Toggle clamp

Mould

Fig. 19.48   Spacing batten   Vent hole

The mould is placed in a jig that makes it possible for the heated thermoplastics
material to be held in position while the air pressure is applied. The material takes up
the form of the mould and sets in this position quite quickly. See Fig. 19.48.

The **advantages** of this process are:

a) Identical shapes can be produced.
b) With several sheets of thermoplastic heated, the process can be repeated in a short
   space of time.
c) Different moulds can be used.

The most suitable material is 4 mm-6 mm thick acrylic sheet.

VACUUM FORMING

Instead of forcing a sheet of thermoplastics material by blowing, the reverse action is
applied, i. e. air is removed and the material is drawn onto a mould.

This process requires a vacuum pump, a heat source and a mould. A vacuum
forming machine has these three elements built into it and production of mouldings
from this equipment is efficient and speedy. There are different sizes of machine that
will take different sizes of sheet. A useful size machine will take a cut sheet size of 254
mm x 458 mm. The maximum thickness of sheet is 2.0 mm.

Suitable materials

1. **polystyrene:** 0.5 mm, 1.0 mm and 2.0 mm thick;
2. **extruded acrylic:** 2.0 mm thick.

The design of the moulds have to include the following features:

a) a draft;
b) radiused corners;
c) no under-cuts;
d) clean smooth surfaces;
e) venting holes in recesses.

For very shallow work there should be no need for venting.

The **advantages** of this process are:

1. The process is clean and the machines are easy to operate.
2. The process can be repeated very quickly, an excellent machine for batch production of items.
3. The quality of the product is excellent.

COLD MOULDING

The moulding principles are just the same in this process as in the hot moulding processes. They are:

1. The material to be formed must be in a fluid or malleable state at the time of moulding.
2. A pattern or mould is required to determine the form the moulding is to adopt.
3. The pattern or mould must be able to be parted easily when the process is complete.

The characteristics of the process are also very similar:

a) The process can be repeated many times.
b) Objects of identical form can be produced.

LOW PRESSURE CONTACT MOULDING

This is sometimes known as Glass Reinforced Plastics work. A resin is used to bond layers of glass fibre together. The resin is prepared with an activator and a catalyst so that it will cure. The glass fibre is tamped down with a brush to make it adopt the form of the mould. Hence the term "low pressure".

PROCEDURE FOR MAKING A MOULDING

Making the mould

There are two types of mould:

1. a *negative* mould for producing a smooth surface on the outer surface of the moulding;
2. a *positive* mould for producing a smooth surface on the inside of a moulding.

It must be remembered that one surface will be rough and one will be smooth. The surface that is in contact with the mould will be smooth and the top surface will be rough. The term rough is quite relative and the quality of the finished surface is dependent upon the skill of the person doing the work (Fig. 19.49).

Fig. 19.49

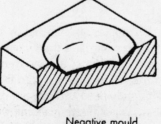

Negative mould
and moulding

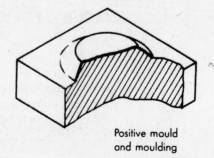

Positive mould
and moulding

Moulds are best made from wood; it is an easy material to shape, the surface can be made smooth and it will accept a finish to give a high quality surface. The moulds must have:

1. a draft;
2. no under-cuts;
3. rounded corners;
4. a clean and highly polished surface.

Fig 19.49 shows a mould that could be used for the production of small trays. The one on the left will produce a smooth finish to the under surface of the tray and the one on the right a smooth surface to the inner and upper surface.

"LAYING UP"

The method of **laying up** has to follow a number of stages. They are:

The stages in laying up.

1. Apply a silicone wax release agent to the contact surface of the mould.
2. Cut the sheet fibre glass mat to just a little larger than the mould.
3. Coat the mould with a gel coat resin that has been prepared with a catalyst.
4. Allow the gel coat to just cure. (*Note*: if a coloured moulding is required a pigment may be added to the gel resin and thoroughly mixed for an even colour.)
5. Prepare a quantity of general purpose resin, sufficient for a single coating of the mould.
6. Coat the mould and apply the glass fibre mat. The mat should be tamped down with a brush until the resin is forced through the mat. It is then allowed to cure.
7. If the finish surface needs to be made a little smoother the next layer of glass fibre mat can be a tissue mat which is made from very fine strands of glass.
8. The moulding can be removed from the mould after it has had ample time to cure (approximately 24 hours).
9. The edges are trimmed with a heavy-duty pair of scissors and smoothed with a file and abrasive paper.

There are times when a split mould needs to be made. The model yacht shown in Fig. 19.50 has an under-cut and in such cases a split mould has to be made. To make a split mould a "plug" (a wooden pattern) has to be made first. The plug is then used to make the mould. The "laying up" process is the same as that already given. The only modification is that the mould is to be made in two halves. This can be done by cutting the "plug" in half along its length. Each half is then glued to a board. A second board is glued at right-angles along what will be the deck surface. A positive mould is then made of each half (Fig. 19.51). The two halves are trimmed and holes are drilled in the lip so that the two halves can be held together by small nuts and screws.

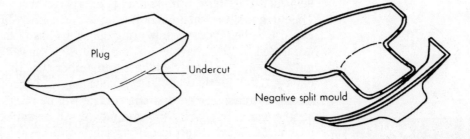

Fig. 19.50

Plug

Undercut

Negative split mould

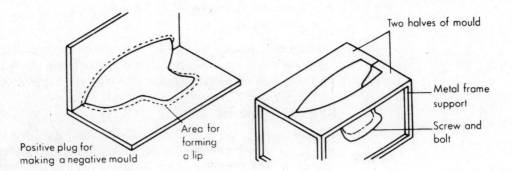

Two halves of mould

Metal frame support

Screw and bolt

Positive plug for making a negative mould

Area for forming a lip

Fig. 19.51

Procedure for making a moulding from a split mould

1. Follow stages 1–9 given for "laying up" in the two separate moulds.
2. Trim the edges of the moulding carefully with a craft knife, making sure not to damage the mould.
3. Mix some gel-resin, pigment and catalyst.
4. Apply a coating of the mix to the trimmed edges of the moulding.
5. Bring the two halves together and fix them with the nuts and screws.
6. Cut a length of glass ribbon a little longer than the edges to be joined and tamp it in position with a brush along the join. The gel-resin prepared in 3 can be added to ensure that a good join has been made.
7. The join is left for approximately 24 hours.
8. The screws and nuts are removed and the moulding is released from the mould.

The **advantages** of "Laying up" as a cold moulding process are:

Advantages and disadvantages

1. The finished product is light and strong.
2. A pigmented gel-coat should mean that there will be no need for a finish to be applied throughout the life of the product, i. e. low maintenance cost.
3. The product is water resistant.
4. Damage can be readily repaired.
5. Many identical products can be made.

The **disadvantages** of "Laying up" as a cold moulding process are:

1. A strong smell is given off with the preparation of the resin.
2. Protective clothing must be worn.
3. A mask must be worn.
4. A barrier cream must be used on the hands.
5. Despite the precautions taken some skin irritation can be expected.
6. It may take several hours or even several days for a moulding to be made.
7. The chemicals used must be stored in metal cabinets at cool temperatures.
8. The resins have a limited shelf life.

Whenever a choice of process is necessary all the advantages and disadvantages should be considered. Making lists such as those given throughout this chapter is helpful. Though some lists may contain more disadvantages than advantages this does not mean that the process should not be used. It is necessary to rate the items listed as "high priority" and "low priority".

Looking at the list of advantages above items 1. and 3. must be rated as being of high priority for the hull of a yacht. The list of disadvantages 1–8 does not contain a high-priority factor. The exception to this would be of course if the user of the resins, etc., had a breathing handicap or a highly sensitive skin, in which case the process could not even be considered. The advantages outlined on page 328, item 1 might suggest that vacuum forming is a better process to consider in this case.

Getting into the habit of comparing the advantages and disadvantages of processes can also be helpful when answering questions in an examination paper. Whenever you are asked to give reasons for a choice they must be based upon the advantages outweighing the disadvantages. Remember that there is no perfect solution to a choice, only one that has least disadvantages. A good choice is one with very few disadvantages.

12 SURFACE TREATMENT

There are three good reasons why a **surface** should be treated:

1. to provide protection;
2. to improve appearance;
3. to improve performance.

Many materials are affected by water, moisture, dryness, insect attack, fungi attack, ultraviolet light and chemical contact, etc. For most situations there is a surface treatment that will protect a material to prolong its active life.

PROTECTION OF WOOD

Solid timber is prone to the effects of water, moisture, dryness, insect attack, and fungi attack. To help it withstand some of these enemies, timber is *seasoned*. This means that the moisture content of the freshly felled tree is reduced to a level that makes it unattractive to insects and fungi. Most living organisms require moisture to survive and seek places that are able to supply this demand. A seasoned piece of timber will always try to balance its moisture content with its surroundings. A seasoned piece of timber with a moisture content of 11% will maintain that level in a centrally heated building where the air has a moisture content of 11%. Should the moisture content of the air rise to 15%–20%, then the timber will attempt to absorb moisture so that its own moisture level will be the same. The taking in of extra moisture makes the timber swell slightly. If the absorption is not even, then while one portion is swelling, another may be quite still, with the result that there will be a stress in the timber, causing a warp or split. The *reverse* can happen where a timber with a high moisture content is trying to match the much lower level moisture content of the air.

Sealing can be used to protect wood. If the pores of the timber are blocked, moisture cannot be taken in or given off. This can be done by applying a "finish".

WOOD FINISHES

> Wood finishes often protect and improve the appearance.

Finishes are available as wax polish, polyurethane lacquer, coloured polyurethane enamel, French Polish and teak oil, etc. All these offer some protection but have to be freshly applied every two or three years. Wax polishing needs to be done more frequently.

Most wood finishes are concerned with protection *and* improving appearance. The grain and colouring in timber make it a unique material. No two pieces of timber are the same and different timbers respond to different treatment.

Before a finish can be applied, the surface of the timber has to be smooth and clean. The surface left by a sharp and finely set smoothing plane is ideal. Glass papering and sanding processes can produce a good finish and may be chosen as a method where the skills of using a smoothing plane are not available. Only the orbital sander, illustrated in Fig. 9.6 is suitable for producing a fine finish on timber that is going to be treated with a clear varnish or lacquer. Other sanding tools or machines tend to leave scratches that will be made more obvious by the reflecting surfaces of the lacquer.

Oiling

Some timbers have natural oils. These are partly lost in the seasoning process and the colouring in the grain appears lost. A rub with raw linseed oil helps to restore the colour and pattern of many hardwood timbers. While Teak oil is more suited for Teak and such wood as Afromosia, the rubbing helps to improve the finish.

Waxing

This is often applied with a cloth but spray wax polishes are also available. Both polishes require some rubbing and the rubbing in a circular motion is most commonly used. The portable polishing mop can be of value and takes some of the hard work out of rubbing by hand. If the layer of wax gets too thick it should be "cut" back with a very fine grade of steel wool.

Most timbers respond well to a wax finish. Carnauba wax is very hard. Pressing a small piece on revolving work on a turner's lathe generates sufficient heat to make it soft for easy spreading. It can be burnished with a handful of shavings to produce an excellent finish.

Silicone wax is easy to apply and adds a protection to a surface likely to have tea or coffee spilt on it.

Varnishing

This is commonly used for a finish on wood that is used either indoors or outdoors. The varnishes with the higher proportion of oil are for outdoor use.

Lacquering

These have a cellulose or polyurethane base. The cellulose lacquer is quick and easy to apply by spraying. A build-up of several layers produces a high gloss finish. The results may be compared with French Polishing but they tend to craze and do not last as long as the highly skilful application of French Polish. It is not possible to repair damaged surfaces successfully. All the lacquer has to be removed and the wood thoroughly cleaned and made smooth to start the process again.

Polyurethane lacquers are very tough and able to withstand heat, water, spirits and much knocking about. They can be easily repaired. The lacquers are available as one-pack or two-pack varieties. The two-pack varieties have a resin and a catalyst that have to be mixed just before application. The catalyst starts the curing action and has to be used immediately. Careful estimates of how much is needed must be made to avoid waste. The final finish is extremely tough. Single packs have a resin and catalyst already prepared and only when the lacquer is exposed to air does the process of curing begin. The finish is tough but not as resistant to knocks as the two-pack variety.

French polishing

True *French Polishing* is a highly skilled craft. The quality of finish is very dependent on the skill of the craftsman. It has been replaced with materials that are easily and quickly applied. Though the cellulose lacquers give a similar quality of finish, they do not last as long.

Painting

Paint offers a protection for wood. It is opaque and coloured with a pigment so that once on the wood the grain, colour and features of the wood can no longer be seen. As a guide, *hardwoods* usually have an attractive appearance and are treated with a clear type of finish; *softwoods* have a less attractive appearance and are treated with an opaque coloured finish. Therefore paint is much more commonly used on softwoods. Many manufactured timber products such as hardboard, general purpose plywood, blockboards, etc., are painted. The type of surface finish can vary from high gloss to matt. The colour range is very wide and matching colours can be obtained in matt or gloss finish.

Most paints that are applied by a brush have an oil base. The thinner paints have a cellulose base and are applied by brush or spraying techniques.

Polyurethane paints are similar to the lacquers except they have a pigment added to provide an opaque coloured finish.

Emulsion paints can be used on wood but because they have a water base the wood should be sealed first.

Staining

Applying a *stain* to wood usually results in the wood becoming darker in colour and the grain being still visible. It changes the appearance but does not offer any protection. A light staining often emphasises the features of an interesting grain pattern. Too many coats of stain loses this feature. The common colour range of dyes are based on reds and browns but green and blue dyes are also available.

Black dyes are used to make such woods as Sycamore, Beech, and Birch simulate a wood called Ebony. Ebony is a naturally black timber that is not readily available but is very attractive. Darkening hardwoods is one way of imitating ebony and has been given the name "Ebonising".

Since dyes do not offer protection a coat of matt polyurethane may be applied. Extra coats may be added to give extra protection. For a good quality finish the surface should be rubbed down with very fine steel wool (00 or 000 grade).

To improve performance

This factor is often overlooked when thinking of finishes that are applied to products made from wood. Some surfaces must not be slippery, while others need to be slippery. The success or failure of a sliding panel in grooves, or a drawer on runners could depend upon the finish used on the wood. Beeswax is commonly used for polishing wood. It produces a high polish and a limited resistance to slipping. Paraffin wax improves the slipping quality and if rubbed on sliding parts of wood can improve the function of sliding panels and drawers. The wax finish that provides some grip is best used on wooden floors, trays etc.

Preserving

Wood that is exposed to all kinds of weather needs protection. Where the quality of finish is not important a wood preservative can be applied directly to a sawn finished surface. Creosote is commonly used. It has a strong smell and readily leaves a mark on anything that comes in contact with it. For effective use as a preservative, the wood is submerged in the creosote to allow it to become soaked. Industrial methods of pressure penetration are even better. Where it is just applied with a brush the process will need to be repeated regularly.

Some wood preservatives are coloured with a green or brown dye and are suitable for garden furniture. No mark or stain is left if touched and there is very little smell. They do not harm plants and can be used on fences or frames where plants climb.

PROTECTION OF METAL

METAL FINISHES

Many **metals** require protection from corrosion. Alloys of iron such as mild steel, tool steel, cast iron, etc., have a high tendency to rust. Metals such as copper and aluminium also corrode but usually at a much slower rate. Metals such as gold, silver, zinc, tin and lead do not corrode and therefore do not need protection.

Some non-corrosive metals can be used to protect the highly corrosive metals by an industrial process known as plating. A thin layer of a non-corrosive metal is used to cover the surface of a corrosive metal. For example:

a) Tin is used to protect mild steel – tinplate sheet.
b) Zinc is used to protect mild steel – zinc coated sheet.
c) Silver is used to protect copper – silver plating.
d) Chromium is used to protect a variety of metals – chromium plating.

a) and b) are examples of situations where protection is important and appearance not important.
c) and d) are examples of situations where protection and appearance are important.

Enamelling

This is a process where a glass powder is sprayed on a metal surface, heated to red heat and the glass powder melts and fuses to the surface of the metal. This has a practical application in enamelling kitchen sinks, pans and baths, etc., and an aesthetic application in the creative work of enamelling where the metal is more a means of supporting the enamel, as in many items of jewellery.

The creative use of enamels can be carried out in the school workshop. The coating of metal sinks etc. can only be done industrially.

Anodising

Though commonly thought of as an industrial process, small quantities can be done in schools.

Anodising is carried out on aluminium. It consists of depositing a film of aluminium hydroxide on the surface. The aluminium hydroxide is able to absorb dyes, so that a piece of work made from aluminium may be protected and its appearance improved. The film is deposited by means of electrolysis. That is, the work is suspended in a liquid known as an electrolyte. A cathode is also suspended in the same electrolyte and a small electric current from a 12-volt battery is passed through the electrolyte via the cathode and the work for approximately half an hour. The work can then be washed in hot water that contains a dye.

Oxidation is the name given to the process of combining with oxygen. This is happening with most metals exposed to the atmosphere and can be readily seen on many ferrous metals as rust or a black scale. Metals such as copper or alloys like bronze and brass form oxides on the surface and this is seen as a green colouring, verdigris. This natural process provides some protection. Therefore it can be used under controlled conditions to finish some metals with an oxide. One such process is explained under "Anodising".

The tempering colours, explained on page 314, are different thicknesses of oxide and the tempering process can be adopted as a means of providing a protective finish. With careful control of the heat the heat source patterns may be created and trapped in position by quenching at the appropriate time. This can take place on bright mild steel and copper without seriously changing the character of the metal. For thicker and more protective oxides the metal can be heated to red heat and quenched in oil. Care must be taken to ensure that there is a sufficient quantity of oil to prevent it from burning. This process is suitable for products made of mild steel.

Plastics coating

This is a method of coating metal with a plastics material such as nylon or polythene. Clean metal is heated in an oven to approximately 300°C. It is then suspended from a thin wire in a Fluidiser, illustrated in Fig. 9.7, where the powder is in suspension and clings to the hot surface of the metal and begins to melt. The surface becomes evenly coated and hardens on cooling. A variety of colours is available so that the product may be colourful and protected.

Examples of industrially produced products dip coated in Polythene include such items as:

- garden furniture, hanging baskets, dish draining stands, milk bottle holders, etc.;
- cellulose acetate butyrate: motor car steering wheels, and hand rails and the temporary covering of tools and jigs, etc.;
- polyvinyl chloride: electrical fittings and some tools;
- nylon: motorway barriers and medical appliances.

Planishing

Some metals respond well to being hit with a hammer. They are malleable and the blow of a hammer will do two things:

1. It will leave an impression.
2. It will work harden the metal.

A highly polished hammer pein will leave a highly polished hammer mark. When the marks overlap, a whole surface can be highly polished. The individual blows of the hammering will be left as polished facets and will add to the appearance of the surface finish. The work hardening effect will make the surface a little more resistant to scratching. The most suitable materials for this process are: copper, aluminium and gilding metal when used in a school workshop, but precious metals such as gold and silver also may be finished with the hammer.

Lacquering

Metals that can be polished by rubbing with a mild abrasive such as Brasso or Silvo lose their shine after a few days and have to be constantly rubbed to restore their shine. A thin coating of a clear lacquer will help the shine to remain longer. The most commonly used metals are: copper, brass, and gilding metal.

Wire brushing

Most wrought iron work surfaces end up black. This is the oxide that has formed on the surface during the heating and hammering. It should not be removed because it provides a protective skin. A vigorous rubbing with a wire brush will not remove the skin but will bring a delightful sheen to the skin. This rubbing helps to show up the hammer marks and improve the appearance considerably.

Other finishes

Metals may be painted in the same way that wood may be painted. A protective undercoat to prevent corrosion is all that is necessary before applying the top coat or coats. Small surfaces are best painted using a brush. Large surfaces can be sprayed for high quality finish.

Hammer finish paints provide a finish that looks similar to metal that has been hammered and made shiny with a wire brush. Hence the name "hammer paint".

Crackle paints give the impression that the paint is rippled and crackled through overheating. This is a popular finish on metal parts of cameras, optical instruments etc. and is often matt black. This finish also hides blemishes on a surface and may be a good reason for its use. High gloss paints tend to show up blemishes and perhaps this is a good reason for not using a gloss paint.

PLASTICS

Many of the **plastics** materials that are used in the school workshops do not require a surface finish. The surfaces of sheet material such as acrylic are purchased with a protective covering. The quality of finish on these surfaces cannot be improved and thus the main aim is to avoid any marks getting on them during working. Marking out can be done on the covering and the cutting out can be done with the covering still in place. In many cases, the only areas that will need finishing are the edges. The covering will have to be removed for heat bending or forming and great care will have to be taken.

EDGE POLISHING ACRYLIC

All marks left from the saw, file or knife, have to be removed by the following stages:

1. draw filing with a clean fine toothed file;
2. scraping with a scraping tool;
3. rubbing down with a fine grade "wet and dry" abrasive;
4. rubbing with an acrylic polish;
5. light buffing with a clean lambs wool mop.

Each stage must be thoroughly done before going on to the next.

As a final stage the acrylic can be rubbed with an anti-static cleaner to reduce the attraction of dust particles.

CHOOSING A FINISH

This will depend on:

a) the material;
b) the purpose, i.e. protective against moisture, hot liquids, abrasions, etc., or appearance;
c) method of application;
d) the skill and experience of the person who is going to apply the finish;
e) available facilities.

A finish must satisfy three important conditions. It must:

1. be appropriate for the material;
2. produce the desired effect;
3. be safe to apply and be safe to the user.

Not all materials need an applied finish, e.g. plastic laminated surfaces, polythene, polyvinyl chloride, acrylic, silver, brass, copper, etc. They only need to be kept clean by wiping with a damp cloth. This information should be evident in a Design Folder or when answering questions in an examination to show that you are aware of this detail. Do not be tempted into thinking that every material must be painted, polished, lacquered, etc. An answer saying that: "This material does not need a protective coating because the surface is able to withstand knocking and its appearance would not be improved" is a quite valid answer.

13 SUMMARY CHART – FINISHES

	MATERIAL	Bees wax	Carnauba wax	Paraffin wax	Silicon wax	Teak oil	Raw linseed oil	Mineral oil	Varnish	Stain	Lacquer 'single pack'	Lacquer 'two pack'	Lacquer cellulose	French polish	Creosote	Wood preservative	Enamelling	Anodising	Plastics coating	Planishing	Wire brush	Tempering oxides	Red heat oxides	Hammer finish paint	Crackle finish paint	Emulsion paint	Polyurethane coloured	Cellulose coloured	Colouring pigment	Anti-static cleaner
WOOD	English beech	✓	✓	✓	✓					✓	✓	✓	✓																	
	Ramin	✓			✓		✓		✓		✓	✓	✓	✓																
	Teak					✓																								
	Obeche	✓			✓		✓		✓	✓	✓	✓	✓	✓																
	European redwood	✓		✓	✓				✓	✓	✓	✓	✓	✓	✓	✓											✓			
	Western red cedar									✓																				
	Hardboard																										✓	✓		
	Veneer boards (with attractive grain)	✓			✓				✓		✓	✓	✓	✓																
	Boards (general use medium quality)																										✓	✓		
METAL	Mild steel							✓									✓		✓		✓	✓	✓	✓	✓		✓			
	Carbon steel																				✓									
	Stainless steel																													
	Cast iron																										✓			
	Wrought iron																				✓		✓	✓						
	Aluminium																	✓		✓				✓			✓	✓		
	Copper								✓								✓			✓		✓								
	Brass								✓															✓						
	Gilding metal																			✓										
PLASTICS	Plastic Laminate																													
	Polyester Resin																												✓	
	Acrylic																													✓
	Nylon																													
	Polystyrene (opaque)																											✓		
	Polystyrene (expanded)																										✓			
	Polythene																													
	Polyvinyl chloride PVC																													
	Protection	✓			✓	✓		✓	✓		✓	✓		✓	✓	✓	✓	✓	✓					✓	✓		✓			
	Improve appearance	✓	✓		✓	✓	✓		✓	✓	✓	✓	✓	✓			✓	✓	✓	✓	✓	✓	✓	✓	✓	✓	✓	✓	✓	
	Improve performance			✓	✓							✓						✓	✓											✓

Fig. 19.52

REVIEW SHEET

■ In order to shape materials it is necessary to have the correct tool to do the job. Most tools are designed to cut particular materials, some are designed to be able to be used with a variety of materials. The most common cutting hand tool for resistant materials is the saw. Make three lists of saws that are designed to cut wood, metal and plastics.

	Wood Saws	Metal saws	Plastic saws
1.			
2.			
3.			
4.			
5.			

■ Explain why it is necessary to select a file according to:

a) the size of its teeth; _____

_____

_____

b) the length of the blade; _____

_____

_____

c) its cross-sectional shape. _____

_____

_____

■ There are designs of wood planes used to remove unwanted wood in specific situations. Name the plane that is used in the following situations and describe the design features of the plane that make it suitable:

a) to produce an excellent quality finish; _____

_____

_____

b) to remove fine and small amounts of wood; _____

_____

_____

c) to cut a groove 4 mm x 4 mm. _____

_____

_____

■ Material can also be removed to make holes using a drill bit and either a hand drill or a drilling machine. The drill bit does all the cutting action and the hand drill or drilling machine enable the drill bit to rotate under control. The choice of drill is governed by three factors. Can you state what these are?

Factor 1 _____

Factor 2 _____

Factor 3 _____

■ The speed at which the drill bit rotates is also governed by three factors. Can you state what these are?

Factor 1 _____

Factor 2 _____

Factor 3 _____

■ Name a suitable twist drill bit for cutting:

a) Wood; _____

b) Mild steel; _____

c) Stone; _____

■ The chisel is also a hand tool that is commonly used to remove unwanted material. Like the plane and the saw there are a variety of different designs of chisel to suit specific situations. In the following situations state which chisel you would select and give your reason why you think its special design makes it suitable.

General woodwork. _____

_____

_____

Cleaning in the corner of a dovetail joint. _____

_____

_____

Cutting a mortice. _____

_____

_____

Cutting metal sheet. _____

_____

_____

■ Bending material is another way of changing its form. Describe a method of bending wood that once bent it maintains its bent form.

_____

_____

_____

_____

■ Metal can also take on a new form when it is molten and is poured into a mould. Describe and illustrate the process of casting.
List and describe the important design features of a pattern to be used in sand casting.

_____

_____

_____

_____

■ When thermoplastics are heated they become soft and are able to be bent in a variety of forms. Name the equipment used to produce localised heating and describe how a flat piece of acrylic can be bent to form a right angle bend.

_____

_____

_____

AESTHETICS

GETTING STARTED

Aesthetics is to do with appearance. You are asked during the course to make judgements about the appearance of products. It is very easy to say "I like that. It looks good." It is not so easy to say *why* you think it looks good. You need to make a number of judgements and *give reasons*. This is particularly important in your **evaluation** of a product.

At first you look at the product *as a whole*. You gain an *overall* first impression. This first impression is important. It tells you that you like it, you do not like it, or it leaves you cold. The thing now is to try to find out *why* you respond the way you do. In order to do this it is necessary to *identify* those features that contribute to the *appearance* of any product, and then to take one feature at a time and make an evaluation judgement. You should then arrive at a number of answers which will help you to know *why* you responded the way you did when you gained your first impression.

Features that contribute to appearance include:

a) shape and form;
b) colour;
c) material;
d) texture;
e) proportion;
f) balance.

Though these features may be looked at individually, they should be compared with the rest of the product.

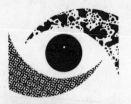

ESSENTIAL PRINCIPLES

1 ▷ SHAPE AND FORM

If you were making judgements that applied to a human being you would be making such observations as: "rather fat" or "thin" or "just right". You could of course make a number of observations about different parts and say, "the face is rounded, the hands and fingers are elegant and long", etc.

While the descriptions "fat" and "thin", do not always apply to a product, terms like "heavy", "light", etc., can be used to describe a chair or table. "The legs of the table were too light for the heavy top."

2 ▷ COLOUR

Not everyone can agree about colour. What appears to be attractive to one person is quite the opposite to someone else. Therefore whatever observations are made must be accepted. The important part is the **reason**: "The matt black finish to the metal legs of the table made a pleasing contrast with the reddish-brown of the wooden top." A "pleasing contrast" is a perfectly good reason. Colours can "blend" or "harmonise". "The pale-blue upholstery of the chair blended well with the brown warmth of the wood."

3 ▷ MATERIAL

The beauty of wood is commonly admired. If a product is so designed and suitably finished to take advantage of this quality the chances are that its appearance will be described as being "aesthetically pleasing'. Wood can be described as being a "warm" material, possibly because at one time it was a living material. The wide variation of types of timber can mean that some are more popular than others. The majority of interesting and pleasing timbers come from the hardwoods, e.g. Oak, Walnut, Elm, Cherry, Mahogany, etc.

The beauty and attraction of metal is often found in its shiny quality. Therefore such materials as gold, silver, platinum, copper, gilding metal and aluminium are often chosen for this quality alone. Steel is not thought of as a material that has a pleasing appearance. It is very functional and does little to inspire comment. This is one reason why an opaque finish is commonly used on most products made from steel. The quality of appearance rests with the finish and not with the features of the material.

Very strong colours can be used in the production of many plastics materials. Those that can combine colour with shine are very striking and can be used effectively, e.g. acrylic. Colourless acrylic is also attractive, particularly when it can be shaped from thick sizes and is highly polished. The refraction of light produces interesting colour bands and it can be used with good effect in curved forms. Clear resins can also be effectively used in this way but the effort needed to get a high quality finish is considerable.

4 ▷ TEXTURE

A surface can have a variety of grades of texture from being very rough to being very smooth. It has been mentioned that shiny surfaces have considerable appeal. Many of the applied finishes such as paint, varnish, etc., set out to provide a shiny surface. Matt or semi-matt finishes are also available and produce an appealing appearance irrespective of colour, or lack of colour. Too much high gloss can be unsettling, so if some surfaces or parts of surfaces have a rough texture, the combined effect can be pleasing.

5 ▷ PROPORTION

There are some shapes and forms that are more pleasing than others. The relationship between length and width, height and width can by very pleasing and feel right. "If it looks right the proportions are right" is something you may have heard your teacher say. This is very much a feeling and not very helpful when you want to know exactly what is a pleasing proportion. We have inherited knowledge from the ancient Greeks, a proportion known as the "*Golden Mean*". It is a proportion they used in their building. The height and width, or height and length of the temples were all based upon the proportions of the "Golden Mean".

THE GOLDEN MEAN

The proportions can be *calculated mathematically* or *constructed geometrically*.

The "Golden Mean" is reputed to have been *mathematically* calculated in the 13th century by a man called Leonardo Fibonacci. He produced a series of numbers in which the addition of the previous two numbers gives the next number, e.g:

❝ Be familiar with the 'Golden Mean'. ❞

$1 + 1 = 2, 1 + 2 = 3, 2 + 3 = 5, 3 + 5 = 8, 5 + 8 = 13, 8 + 13 = 21$ etc.

If this is written as a series it will appear like this:

1, 1, 2, 3, 5, 8, 13, 21, 34, 55, 89, 144, 233, 377, etc.

Use any two numbers that are next to one another in this list and you have a proportion that is approximately equal to the "Golden Mean". The higher the numbers, the greater the accuracy.

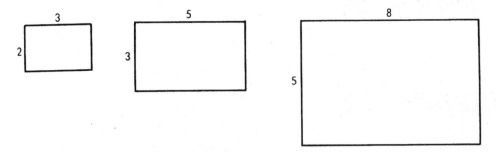

Fig. 20.1

The "Golden Mean" may be constructed *geometrically*:

1. Start by drawing a right-angle triangle. The length of *AB* is twice the length of *AC*.
2. Set a compass equal to *AC*. From *C* draw an arc to cut *CB* and call it *D*. Set the compass to *BD* and from *B* draw an arc. Draw a line at right-angles to *AB* from *B*. Where the line and the arc meet label it *E*.
3. The length of lines *AB* and *BE* are equal in proportion to the "Golden Mean".
4. The rest of the rectangle can be completed (Fig. 20.2).

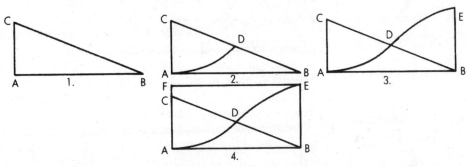

Fig. 20.2

The use of this method is restricted by the size of the compass. This can be overcome for intermediate-size work by using a trammel or a piece of batten with a nail at one end and a pencil in a hole at the required distance.

The outline proportion of an object can be made to the "Golden Mean" proportions and areas within the outline can be subdivided to the same proportions. The total effect is usually one of harmony.

Proportion is also related to the *use of material*. The proportion of width and thickness will depend on the *strength* of the material being used. A leg for a chair made from wood needs to be made from a larger-section piece of material than one made from metal tube. If the sizes were the same for both materials the legs in one chair would either be too heavy or too thin in the other. Much thinner proportions may be used with metal than with wood because metal has greater strength than wood.

The drawing on page 165 shows a folding picnic chair. The frame is made from tubular steel. Imagine making the same size chair from wood. The cross-section sizes would have to be larger to provide the strength required to take the weight of a person. This would not only produce a heavier chair, it would look heavy even if the weight of the chairs were the same. The term "heavy" can apply to appearance as well as being an actual description of weight. Similarly, the term "light" can be used to describe appearance. The two descriptions can apply to a single product. "The top rail of the stool looks far too heavy and the bottom rail looks far too light", could be an observation and a comment in an evaluation of a design for a stool. In other words the proportion does not look right. This feeling for what looks right and what looks wrong is something that comes with experience and understanding of materials.

Proportion plays an important part in construction. If you are joining two pieces of wood together by nailing, you select a nail that is in proportion to the size of the wood being joined. Similarly the proportions of a mortice and tenon joint must be suitable for the sizes of wood being joined (Fig. 20.3).

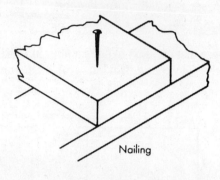

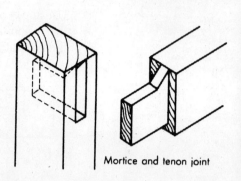

Fig. 20.3

Construction is often shown as a design feature so it is important for the proportions to be correct for strength and for their appearance.

6 ▷ BALANCE

Balance is concerned with the distribution of weight. When you walk or run your legs and arms move. When your left leg moves forward your right arm moves backward. When your right leg moves forward your left arm moves backward. This rhythm of movement helps you to maintain your balance.

An expert ice skater relies considerably upon good balance and it is a pleasing experience to watch an ice skater who can skate well. The movements are smooth and flowing. Watching someone who *cannot* skate well is not such a pleasing experience, and can make you feel a little uneasy. Photographs of skaters in action also give a tremendous feeling of balance. So the feeling of balance is not confined to something that is moving. The sculptor could capture the movement of the skater leaning over at an angle and *still* capture the feeling of balance.

Objects give a feeling of balance. Most buildings are built to stand upright and we take little notice until we see one that is leaning to one side and then we feel slightly uneasy. The leaning tower of Pisa is famous for its *lack* of balance and the feeling of uneasiness that is experienced by looking at it.

Balance is more than being able to remain upright. It is a visual experience. What is it that tells us that the skater is well balanced and the building is not?

When we look at things we may identify balance in three different ways:

1. symmetry;
2. asymmetry;
3. radial balance.

SYMMETRY

This is seen in natural and geometric forms. The one half is a mirror image of the other half.

When we see something that is symmetrical we feel at ease. The balance is visually acceptable.

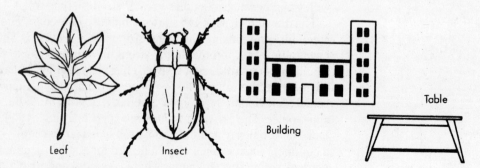

Fig. 20.4   Leaf   Insect   Building   Table

ASYMMETRY

This is also seen in natural and geometric forms. The two halves are not the same yet an acceptable visual balance is achieved.

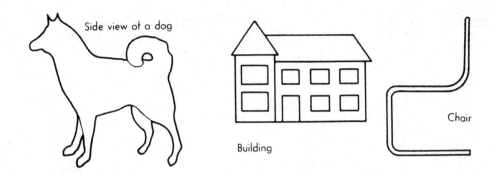

Fig. 20.5

RADIAL BALANCE

Lines that radiate from a centre are very acceptable visually. This also occurs in natural and geometric forms and gives a feeling of balance.

Fig. 20.6

CREATING A FEELING OF MOVEMENT

Even in static drawings, structures and sculpture a feeling of movement can be created by the use of line and form. Figures 20.7 and 20.8 overleaf are examples where a student is designing a trophy for a sailing club. Much of the line work is sweeping and flowing much in the same way as waves and wind move. Look at the sails for the trophy. Though they are to be made from a rigid material eventually, they all have the feeling that there is a force acting upon them to adopt this bellowing form.

7 > SUMMARY

When making aesthetic judgements we do two things:

1. judge the object as a whole and form a first impression;
2. make a judgement about six different aspects: shape and form, colour, material, texture, proportion, and balance.

Carrying out these two stages will help you to form an opinion and to be able to say *why* you like or do not like an object. The *reasoning* is more important than the conclusion. Accept the points of view that:

a) What is pleasing to you is not necessarily pleasing to someone else.
b) You are expressing an opinion about those things you like and do not like.

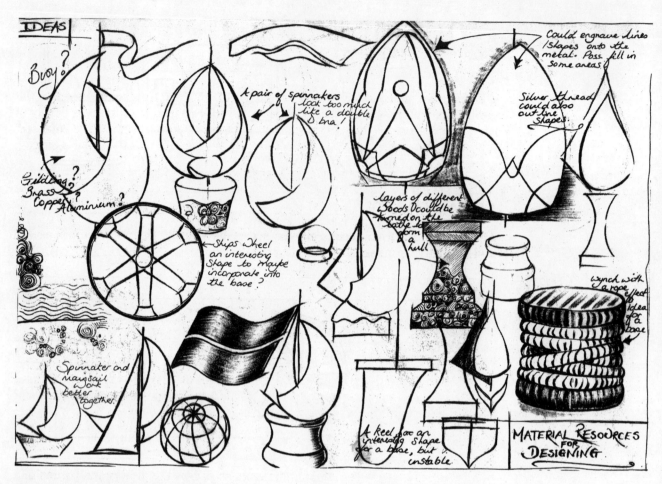

Fig. 20.7 Original drawing by Debbie Colenso

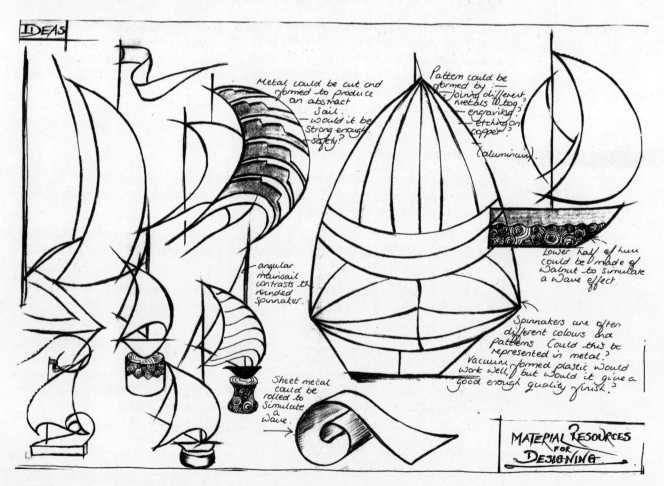

Fig. 20.8 Original drawing by Debbie Colenso

REVIEW SHEET

■ Objects are often judged by their appearance. Something that looks pleasant to the eye is often said to be aesthetically pleasing. If you were going to assess the quality of appearance of a variety of objects, what set of criteria would you use? List five important criteria that you could use.

1. _____

_____

2. _____

_____

3. _____

_____

4. _____

_____

5. _____

_____

■ Certain proportions are said to be pleasing i.e. they do not offend the eye, and these have been calculated mathematically. What is the name given to these calculations and who is credited with being their originator?

_____

_____

■ By producing carefully measured drawings show how the pleasing proportion of a rectangle is a) calculated and b) geometrically constructed.
Calculation.

Geometric Construction.

■ Materials have their own aesthetic quality. The colour and grain of many hardwoods have their own natural beauty but for a material like plastic or metal they do not have a natural beauty and require a treatment to enhance their visual appeal.

Describe a treatment that would enhance the appearance of a piece of oak.

_____

_____

_____

_____

■ Describe a treatment or finish that would enhance the appearance of a bowl made from copper.

_____

_____

_____

_____

■ Describe a treatment or finish that would enhance the appearance of an acrylic jewellery case.

_____

_____

_____

_____

■ Balance and symmetry is evident in natural and man made products. Draw two objects, one that illustrates natural symmetry and the other that illustrates geometric symmetry.

Natural Symmetry   Geometric Symmetry

■

■ Asymmetry can also produce pleasing forms naturally and in man-made products. Draw an example of each.

Natural Asymmetry   Man-made Asymmetry

■ In order to appreciate what we believe to be visually acceptable we also need to know what is visually unacceptable. If something is top heavy we have the uneasy feeling that it may fall over. In which case we would say that the object is not pleasing to look at. There are many other factors that would contribute to an object being considered not attractive. Some might even considered to be ugly. Identify an object that you consider to be ugly and list the features that contribute to its ugliness.

_____

_____

_____

_____

_____

_____

_____

_____

_____

_____

ASSESSMENT

GETTING STARTED

At the beginning of the course the two people most concerned with assessing your work are you and your teacher. You both look through the work that has been completed and assess the progress that has been made.

Coursework is mainly concerned with designing and making. Therefore the points that have to be assessed fall under two main headings: your ability to *design* and your ability to *make*. Of course there is a third heading: your ability to *communicate* what you have thought and done to those around you.

What must you and your teacher look for when assessing your ability to design and make? We consider this, before turning to the externally set examinations, and the points looked for in these by the examiners.

COURSEWORK

Often before you start to think of a project for GCSE you will ask the question:

"What is a suitable project for the examination?"

This is very difficult to answer and will depend upon a range of factors:

- Your ability and experience   – how well are you doing on the course?
  - did you do a DT Foundation course?
  - are you taking other GCSE subjects which help your Technology?
- Do you have to work with one teacher only?
- Which optional modules have you studied?

66 Points to bear in mind when finding a project. 99

- Will you be able to have any outside (e.g. industrial) assistance/advice with your project?
- What facilities and materials do you have available?
- How much time can you give?
- Will there be a cost limit on your project?
- Does your idea meet the aims and assessment objectives of the syllabus you are taking?
- Do you feel you are able to do the project you have chosen?

All of these factors must be considered **before** you start any project. The answers will obviously be dependent upon your own ideas and interests, what your school offers and the choices your teachers make. So it is almost impossible to give suggestions of suitable projects. Of course, providing your project meets the aims and assessment objectives of the syllabus you are taking, then it **is** suitable. If you have any doubts, your teacher will advise you. Some examining groups produce a sample project list to give you some ideas, though these lists are not seen as exclusive. Have a look through the list below.

LIST OF SELECTED MAJOR PRACTICAL PROJECTS

This list is not intended to be prescriptive or exhaustive; it is offered simply as an indication of the wide range of possibilities for practical projects.

PNEUMATIC

66 Some practical suggestions for projects. 99

1. **Metalwork or jewellery vice**	pneumatically operated by one or two double acting cylinders.
2. **Car park barrier**	pneumatic operation – coin operating mechanism – automatically closing after car has passed.
3. **Plastic forming press**	pneumatic press to form plastic trays, dishes or containers.
4. **Food slicer**	pneumatically controlled machine to slice food – cheese, fruit, bread.
5. **Hacksaw**	pneumatic hacksaw machine – possible pneumatic vice.
6. **Drinks dispenser**	machine to dispense fruit drinks automatically.
7. **Combination door lock**	a number of air bleeds which, when covered in the correct combination, open a door.
8. **Automatic door opener**	door mat triggers pressure sensitive valve.
9. **Automatic can opener**	machine to open beer or soft drink cans automatically.
10. **Automatic control of lathe**	cross slide feed – power from pneumatic cylinders – detection circuits.
11. **Lathe turret control**	pneumatic control of a lathe turret head to rotate lathe tools.
12. **Fabric tester**	fatigue test for fabrics – wire brush on pneumatic cylinder.
13. **Automatic control of drill press**	power tool drill with sequential controlled feed and vice.

14. **Pneumatic shaper**   shaping machine operated by pneumatic cylinder.

15. **Rocking horse**   GRP body of horse with pneumatic driven mechanism – suitable for children's playground.

16. **Printing press**   pneumatic printing press – sequential control to feed paper and operate press.

17. **Joint testing machine**   pneumatic machine for testing woodwork joints.

18. **Fluidic control**   fluidic control of any device such as a coin-in-the-slot dispenser of drinks or sweets.

19. **Flower watering device**   pneumatic device to water pot plants automatically.

20. **Guinness pouring machine**   pneumatic machine to take cap off bottle and pour from bottle.

ELECTRONIC

1. **Automatic counting device**   device to count people entering a room – possible use of photocells or photo transistors.

2. **Burglar alarm**   could be photocell device, or infra-red detector, micro switches, multivibrator alarm.

3. **Garage door opener**   automatically opens garage doors when motor car approaches.

4. **Smoke detector**   fire alarm to detect smoke.

5. **Rain alarm**   to detect when it is raining and wind in washing line.

6. **Amplifier**   for record player or cassette player or guitar – or as an intercom.

7. **Binary counter**   electronic machine to count in binary, with possible denary decoding.

8. **Electronic organ**   investigation of wave shapes and frequency from electronic organ using discrete components or integrated circuits.

9. **Frequency selective amplifier**   amplifier to control fluctuations of light in time with the frequency of musical input.

ELECTRICAL

1. **Bicycle ergonometer**   to determine power and efficiency of human body, using a bicycle.

2. **Plant propagator**   control of soil heating unit in greenhouse.

3. **Model railway controller**   transformer, rectifier, speed control.

4. **Battery charger**   power supply to charge car batteries with thermal overload facility.

INSTRUMENTATION

1. **Automatic weather station**
   a) anemometer to measure wind speed – possible analogue or digital display.
   b) wind direction indicator, possibly using LED's for display.
   c) measuring rainfall – possible use of strain gauges.
   d) measuring temperature – electronic thermometer using termistor or diode or transistor to sense temperature.

2. **Solar heater**   instrumentation of temperature fluctuation and recording.

3. **Tachometer**   to measure speed of rotation of lathe, or electric motor of kart engine – possible analogue or digital display.

4. **Measuring liquid level**   measuring to level of liquid in a tank – inflammable liquids, possible analogue or digital display.

5. **Seismograph**   device to record earthquakes or vibrations of traffic near motorway.

6. **Temperature measurement of casting metal**   to measure the temperature of molten metal used for casting in a school foundry.

MECHANICAL

1. **Coil winding machine**   a mechanical device to wind solenoid coils – possibly count number of turns and lay the wire evenly on the coil.
2. **Self steering device**   programmed mechanical vehicle that steers a predetermined course.
3. **Brake design for a kart**   design for a mechanical braking system on a kart.
4. **Toggle or cam press**   press to operate punch tools with toggle or cam or linkage action.
5. **Index machine**   device to index Hybridex strip through the drilling machine with $1/2$" indexing between holes.
6. **Weighing machine**   use of linkages to provide weighing machine mechanism – calibration.
7. **Vehicle**   model of vehicle steering suspension.
8. **Mechanical counting machine**   device to count tablets mechanically.

TEXTILES

1. **Clothes for female clergy**   Women are now being ordained. Designing a range of clothes for their use.
2. **Play system for children**   A system of clothes which can be adapted for any play situation by adding pads, inflation and decoration to a basic cape or overall.
3. **Home storage**   A storage system based on hanging bags and boxes made from canvas.
4. **Containers**   For specific sporting, leisure activities.

Further examples of suitable problems

1. A manufacturer needs to check if certain components on a production line are overweight. She wants to eject components that are too heavy but allow correct or underweight components to continue.
2. A roll of cartridge paper requires cutting accurately into equal lengths. The system can be started manually for each length of paper. The operator's safety is important.
3. A marksman shoots at a rifle target that is 25 metres away. He gets tired of walking up to the target to see if he has hit the bullseye. He is looking for a system that will indicate when he has scored on the bullseye only.
4. DIY enthusiasts often use electric drills on the floors or walls of their homes and are quite likely to puncture electric cables or central heating pipes. A system is needed to avoid this.
5. A disabled person, paralysed from the waist down, is often extremely strong in the arms. Canoeing would be a very popular sport for such a person if she could eject safely from the canoe cockpit.
6. Rockclimbers often spend their holidays on big mountains. Very seldom do they have the access to accurate localised weather forecasting that is necessary for safety.
7. School office staff are forever duplicating paper and counting it into batches for distribution to class groups. A lot of time and tedium would be saved if this process could be speeded up.
8. A manufacturer needs to automate a steam bending process with timber. He needs an "S" shaped length but finds that if he uses a simple clamping system it is difficult to prevent the timber moving lengthwise in the mould. He has to allow for this movement by using longer lengths than necessary and trim them up later. He would like to avoid this wastage each time.
9. A BMX racing enthusiast has to transport her bike to race meetings by car. She is looking for a reliable lightweight structure that could be clamped to an ordinary commercial roofrack.
10. A pupil who is keen on graphics wants a cheap airbrush system into which he can locate ordinary jumbo felt tip pens rather than the highly priced commercial alternatives.
11. People not long out of hospital, or the elderly, often have to take regular medication in the form of tablets. Being ill, they can easily forget what they have done and take an overdose. They need a dispenser that "remembers" when they took a tablet last.

Questions for consideration by candidates

These questions have been devised to assist candidates in preparing their project reports.

1. What is the title of your project?
2. What is your project brief?
3. Why did you choose this particular project?
4. Where did the idea for your project come from? (Teacher's suggestion; magazine search; something that you had read; TV; or something original.)
5. Have you considered other ways of solving your problem?
6. Have you considered the cost, in terms of time, equipment availability, of your project? How has this affected your final solution?
7. Have you set down a detailed specification for your project saying what it will do (and possibly what it will not do), over what range and what its requirements are?
8. Have you considered how you are going to test your project?
9. Have you the equipment to do this testing?
10. Will your project be safe for someone else to use? **Note: No accessible part of your project may be at mains voltage.**
11. How have you ensured your project is safe?
12. Have you made a timetable for the completion of your project?
13. Are there any special properties of the materials you have chosen which make them particularly suitable for your project?
14. How do you intend to present your final project? Will labelling/instructions be needed so that others can operate your project as you intend?
15. Is it going to be necessary for you to build prototypes?
16. Are you going to need to use any facilities from another department (e.g. a lathe if you work mainly in a science laboratory, or electrical meters etc. if you work mainly in a CD department)? Can this be arranged?
17. Will all parts of your project be readily accessible for testing and modification should it be necessary?
18. Have you considered how colour coding may help explain what you are doing?
19. Have you made sketches of parts of your construction to explain particularly important features?
20. Have you illustrated the tests you have carried out to check whether your project met its specification?
21. Have you made lists or tables of readings from the tests? Were they what you expected?
22. In the event of a problem, have you written details of checks on individual sections?
23. If you wish to make modifications to your project at this stage, what evidence can you provide of what you have achieved so far? Photographs, Sketches?
24. Have you listed the sources of ideas and information you have used such as magazines, books, teacher, etc? (Include name, author, publisher and page number.)
    This is essential.
25. Would it be clear from your project record that you have written the report in stages, as you have gone along, rather than after completion and evaluation of the project?
26. Have you tested the reliability of your project?
27. With hindsight, what aspects, if any, would you undertake differently if you were tackling the same project again?

2 ▷ DESIGN SKILLS

The method you use to solve a problem has been broken down into ten stages. Just to remind you (see Chapters 2, 3 and 6) they are:

1. identifying a need;
2. writing a design brief;
3. analysing a problem;
4. writing a specification;
5. finding out information;
6. thinking and recording a number of ideas;
7. developing ideas;
8. translating the ideas into a material form;
9. making a working drawing;
10. presenting an evaluation of the solution after it has been made.

The evidence of what you have done is contained in a "**Design Folio**". This is the folio that you and your teacher can look at to try and assess just how well you have performed in *each* of the ten stages.

It helps of course if you have a *well-organised* folio that shows the ten stages clearly. You can then assess each stage on four levels of performance. A "Progress and Assessment" table has been drawn up for you on page 350.

MEASURING PROGRESS

Only you and your teacher can tell how well you were able to identify a need. The teacher will know how much or how little assistance you were given to start the project. So the assessment here rests mainly with a *description* that best fits your situation. Then you can put a tick or colour in the appropriate box. You continue this process with your teacher until *every stage* has been assessed and a box has been ticked or coloured.

If this is your first project, you may find that in the first four stages you needed a lot of assistance and therefore that most of the boxes that are filled in are in columns 1 or 2. This is quite understandable when you are learning something new or when you find difficulty with a *particular stage*. When you are able to work more on your own and when you find the work less difficult for various stages you will discover that the boxes on the right are more likely to be filled in.

The aim is to get as many boxes filled in on the right-hand side as possible.

The first progress and assessment form that you and your teacher completed should be kept somewhere safe. It is a record of your achievement and can be compared with the assessments that are made on *future* progress and assessment forms. You will probably fill in three of these during the course. They will be a complete record of your coursework and can show where progress has been made if you manage to move from the columns on the left towards those on the right. It will also show that you have maintained your standard if you stay in a column and finally it will show any deterioration in the quality of your work if you move to the left of any column you have previously occupied.

The second area to be assessed is your ability to "make".

3 **MAKING SKILLS**
The ability to make a product from hard materials such as wood, metal and plastics, requires a number of different skills. Some are acquired by *practice*, e.g. measuring, sawing, chiselling, fitting and finishing, etc. Other skills are acquired by *thinking*, e.g. planning, organising and selecting processes that are safe.

The quality of the product is often a good indication of the ability of the person or persons who produced it. Before it can be used for assessment it must be authenticated, i.e. there must be *proof* that the work is your own. This should not be difficult in the case of work done in school, but if work is done elsewhere your parents must guarantee that the work was carried out by you.

MEASURING PROGRESS

What then must you and your teacher look for when assessing your making skills? Irrespective of the quality of the design, this aspect is assessed independently.

A Progress and Assessment form has been set out on page 351 in the same way as the one on page 350 (Fig. 21.1).

The making skills are not just limited to the marking out, cutting and shaping skills, etc. They also include the ability to *plan* a sequence of operations so that you use your time to the best advantage and a continuous flow of activity is achieved. For example, all the possible cutting, fitting and finishing must be completed before glueing parts together. While the glue is setting on some components, you should see if it is possible to work on another part. Careful planning should help you to always be busy.

Selecting the appropriate tools or machine is an important skill. Using the correct tool for the job is an important step in producing a good result. Once you have selected the appropriate tool, it is necessary to be able to *use* the tool correctly.

Accuracy is seen in two ways; how well the parts *fit together*, and how well the finished sizes *agree with the working drawing*. When the parts are assembled they all have a function to perform, e.g. the legs of a small table must offer *stability and support* for the weight expected to be carried; the legs of a folding chair must be able to *fold away* when required.

Most items require a *finish*, whether a surface treatment or an applied protective coating. The quality of the finish is what is going to show and it could make or mar the appearance of a product. The finish must be appropriate to the material and to the function of the product.

4 COMMUNICATION SKILLS

Communication is an important skill and it too must be assessed. The Design Folio has already been looked at for the *design* skills, but it can also be looked at to assess your *communicating* skills. The most important factors in any communication are clarity, accuracy and economy. The ability to sketch so that you convey information clearly and accurately to others, with an economic use of line and tone, is an important skill in any designing activity. Therefore the points in which you will be assessed are presented on the Progress and Assessment record on page 352. Where possible, the language of communication is *drawing*. The *visual* image can often convey information more quickly and easily than words when trying to describe something that can be seen. For instance, it is much easier and quicker to *draw* a marking gauge than it is to *describe* it accurately.

Choosing the most appropriate *method* of drawing technique is important in making an *economic* use of time and materials. The sketch of an idea need only be an *outline* in pencil. Toning, colouring, and other techniques can be saved for later when the ideas have been developed. Annotated sketches are most valuable in the early stages. A note leading off the drawing, stating a process, a method of joining or the name of a material, etc., is also appropriate at this point. When the ideas *have* been developed in detail, other and more appropriate methods of communicating must be adopted. These may now include the techniques of toning and colouring to give a more finished visual impression of the product.

The *working drawing* must be precise in dimension and complete in detail. Traditionally this is presented in *orthographic projection*, using recommended *conventions* – a draughtsman's shorthand for drawing threads, dimensions, etc. While it is still one of the best ways of presenting a working drawing it is not the only way information of a precise nature need be conveyed. Exploded Isometric Projections, drawn to scale, can be most effective.

The answer to the question given at the beginning of the chapter is that you and your teacher are involved with assessing the coursework. This means that between 30% and 50% of the marks are influenced by you and your teacher's assessment.

5 CONVERTING DESCRIPTIONS INTO MARKS

The Progress and Assessment Record Sheets give a description in *four columns*. The descriptions can be given a 0–5 value in column 1, 6–10 value in column 2, 11–15 value in column 3, and 16–20 value in column 4. Adding the marks given against each stage will give a total for *each completed Progress and Assessment Record Sheet*. For *each completed project* an assessment will be made. The total marks awarded for each project are then added together to give a *grand total*. This mark is then used by your teacher to put all the pupils in your class, and those in other classes, into an order of merit. This is when those with the high marks go to the top of the list and those with low marks go to the bottom end of the list.

6 MODERATING THE MARKS

This is done by a visiting *moderator*. The job that the moderator has to do is to see whether the marks awarded by the school compare in standard with those awarded by the Examining Board. If the marks awarded by the school agree with those awarded by

DESIGN: ''PROGRESS AND ASSESSMENT RECORD''

STAGE	1	2	3	4
1 Need identified	Required considerable help to get started	Required some help to get started	Required just a little help to get started	Identified a 'need' without help
2 Design brief	Had to be given a Design Brief	Some help was necessary	With a little help was able to write a Design Brief	Able to write a clear sound Design Brief
3 Analysis	Very little understanding or no analysis given	Identified a few details with some help	Only a little help was given to get started	Able to analyse a problem and to write a clear analysis
4 Specification	Little or no specific detail given	Details had to be given before a specification could be written	Could identify some detail and write down requirements	Able to identify and write down clearly specific requirements
5 Research	Very little effort was made	Uses cuttings from a catalogue	Uses catalogue cuttings with notes. Visits libraries, makes some notes and sketches of things seen observed on visits	Thoroughly investigates and records information. Makes good use of annotated sketches of things
6 Ideas	Has a single idea and no desire to look further	Has one or two very similar ideas	Has some ideas and is prepared to look at alternatives but not to go into detail	Thinks broadly and develops several alternative possibilities
7 Devel. of ideas	Drawings lack detail and often in 2-D only	Some attempt to show detail in 3-D	Shows a reasonable amount of detail in drawings for ideas to be understood	Shows sufficient detail in a drawing to demonstrate a principle or function
8 Construction	Has very little idea of how materials are joined	Shows some construction but not always appropriate for the material	Constructional detail detail quite sound and mostly appropriate for the situation	Details of construction clear and appropriate for the material
9 Working drawings	Very little detail	Some information given relating to main sizes and material used	With a little more detail given, the solution could be made	All the details are given from which the idea can be made e.g. sizes, material, cutting list
10 Evalutation	Little or no comment made	Identifies some good and bad points	Identifies most good and bad points. Has little or no recommendations to make for improvements	A thorough and detailed evaluation of the solution and appropriate recommendations given for improvements

Name ....

Project Title ....

Date ....

Fig. 21.1

MAKING: ''PROGRESS AND ASSESSMENT RECORD''

STAGE	1	2	3	4
Planning	Shows little concern for the need to plan ahead	Has some idea of future needs	Able to plan most stages in a logical order	Carefully plans each stage of making on a logical sequence
Selecting tools/machines	Can select a few machines/tools that are appropriate for the function they are intended	Able to select some	Able to select most	Able to select the appropriate tools and machinery
Ability to use tools/machines	Can use tools and machines when they have been set by someone else	Can set up the commonly used machines and able to adjust marking out and measuring tools	Has the ability to 'set up' most machines and tools that are available	Has the ability to 'set up' a machine ready for use
Accuracy	Only vaguely resembles details given in the 'Working Drawing'	A fair resemblance to the details given in the 'Working Drawing'	Able to produce a product that agrees with many dimensions given in a 'Working Drawing'	Able to produce a product that reasonably agrees with all dimensions given in a 'Working Drawing'
Assembly	Some parts are put totether and very few really function well	Some parts are put together and function fairly well	Most parts are held together well but function only fairly well	All components are together and function well
Finish	Only the minimum attention has been given to any form of finish	Some attention has been given to finish of parts that are normally seen	Most parts have been given attention including parts not normally seen	Gives a general feeling of quality. Surface treatment sensitive and appropriate

Name ....

Project Title ....

Date ....

Fig. 21.1 (continued)

COMMUNICATION: "PROGRESS AND ASSESSMENT"

STAGE	1	2	3	4
Transform ideas into drawings and notes	Drawings elementary. Limited information and minimum notes	Some aspects are reasonably effective	Can draw reasonably effectively	Can draw effectively and economically
Select appropriate means of communication	Limited in variety. Tends to use a single method throughout	Has two or three well-tried approaches that are used with little discrimination	Makes some discrimination and selects wisely	Selects and discriminates between a wide range of techniques
Convey information	Able to convey little information	Able to convey some information clearly	Able to convey most information cleary	Able to convey information clearly and precisely
Convey ideas	Able to convey a few ideas	Able to convey some ideas using technical terms	Able to convey most information using appropriate technical terms	Able to use appropriate technical terms and symbols
Presentation	Takes little care	Takes some care	Takes care	Takes meticulous care
Organisation	Few stages identifiable and little semblance of order	Some stages recognisable and in some semblance of order	Most stages identifiable and arranged in a logical sequence	All stages labelled and arranged in a logical sequence

Name ....   Project Title ....   Date ....

Fig. 21.2

the Board, then no change will be made. If the marks awarded by the school are *too low* then the moderator will *raise* the school's mark until they agree with the Board's. Similarly if the marks are *too high* an adjustment will be made to bring the marks *down* and into line. This procedure happens in every school to make sure that you obtain the correct award.

EXAMINATIONS

7 MARKING THE EXAMINATION SCRIPTS

These are marked by a team of examiners who all have to work to a mark scheme. The mark scheme tells the examiner how many marks are available for each question and part of a question. It also indicates the type of answers that will get high marks, medium marks, low marks or nothing.

8 STANDARDISING THE MARKS

Once the examiners have marked 30–50 scripts they have to meet with the Chief Examiner and read through each question. If the examiners find that some pupils are giving different answers from those on the mark scheme, the answers are discussed and a decision is made as to whether or not they should be acceptable. Once a decision is made all the examiners will give marks according to what has been agreed. This process is known as "*Standardisation*" and it is done to make sure that all examiners are marking to the same standard.

The examiners return the marked scripts to the Board Office. The scripts are then checked again to see that the adding is correct. Any obvious corrections are made at the office. Those that cannot be resolved are sent to the *Chief Examiner* for marking and checking.

The Chief Examiner is then sent a *sample* of each examiner's scripts to check that the examiners have been marking consistently to the same standard. If the Chief Examiner detects that some examiners mark a little hard or a little leniently the marks can be adjusted so that all scripts are marked to the one standard.

This marking procedure applies to all papers that are marked by examiners. In this subject the Design Paper and the Technology Paper are marked this way.

9 AWARDING THE GRADES

The marks you gained for the coursework, the set project and the examination papers are added together to give a final total mark. It is the responsibility of a Chief Moderator, a Chief Examiner and a Subject Officer of the Board, to compare the figures with sample coursework and scripts. The team are all very experienced people in the subject and have an idea of what should be expected from a pupil to obtain a particular grade. A *grade description* list is used, similar to those you saw in the "Progress and Assessment Records" on pages 350, 351, and 352. This helps the team to select the work and scripts so that a grade can be awarded. Once the *bottom* standard of work for a grade has been decided, the mark awarded for that sample work is noted and it becomes known as a "cut-off" point. Cut-off points are established for *each grade boundary*. The marks that fall *between* the cut-off points are the marks that will determine the final grade.

LOOKING AT SAMPLE SCRIPTS

Looking at sample scripts that have been submitted for marking and assessment, with comments made by an examiner, is perhaps the best way for you to find out how to prepare yourself.

10 DESIGN PAPER

The Examination Boards each have slightly different ways of testing your ability to *design*. You must keep this in mind when you look at the samples.

The University of London Examinations and Assessment Council gives information in January of the year in which the examination is held. It informs the candidates about a *design theme* and the *three design problems* set on the theme. Only one problem is to be attempted and the work has to be completed by 20 March. The *solution* to the problem has to be *made* and forms the *Realisation* part of the examination.

A *Research Folio* is necessary for this examination. It will contain the source of information that will be used to help solve the chosen problem. The Folio will not be marked as part of the Design Paper, but it will be assessed as part of the *Realisation*.

The work that forms the *Designing* is done on A3 size paper supplied by the Examining Board.

The Theme for this sample paper was:
"SIMPLE ENERGY CONVERSIONS Problem 1: MOTOR POWER TOY"

Fig. 21.3 gives details of the basic system available to give a safe power source for a toy having moving parts. The toy is to be self-contained in that battery, switch and motor are on, or within, the toy itself. The toy can be designed for any particular age group, but the age group must be specified in your design brief.

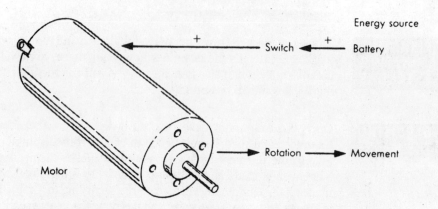

Fig. 21.3

STUDENT'S ANSWER – EXAMINER'S COMMENTS

The six diagrams in Fig. 21.4 are of pages taken from a Research Folio. They were prepared to supply the source information for the design and realisation part of the examination.

SHEET NO 1

The problem is clearly stated. A good start. The areas for investigation are also clearly stated and appropriate for the task. Writing in ink and taking care with the quality of printing makes for easy reading and understanding. The use of language is economic and adequate.

This is an example of a good start and the examiner was obviously impressed. There is nothing so effective as getting off to a good start.

SHEET NO 2

The information about mechanisms is clearly presented. The quality of the drawings is appropriate and the notes supply that extra information to help gain a fuller understanding. The range of mechanisms drawn is adequate for this problem.

The drawings are, if anything, too well done for this part of the preparation. Only in the sense that the time taken to complete drawings to this standard could perhaps be spent on other more important aspects. If you can draw quickly then a little time spent in tidying up may be an advantage.

SHEET NO 3

The shape and form of the electronic components to be used is helpful but since most of these are standard components it would have been an advantage to know at least overall sizes. The lead from the battery should not be attached to the spindle. I would have liked to have seen more written detail indicating where the switches might be incorporated in a toy design, e.g. internally or externally.

The examiner has picked up the need for sizes. If this is to be used as a source of information that comment is most valid. Weight could be another factor for consideration. Again such detail can be justifiably part of the investigation.

SHEETS 4, 5, AND 6

It is nice to see that the thoughts centre round the needs of the child. The ages are clearly stated and the levels of child development have been carefully identified. It is not clear whether the toys illustrated are examples of toys used by children 1–2 years, 2–3 years, or 3–5 years or ideas of toys for children in these age ranges. The good and skilful use of pencil and colour pencil show a good range of toys. The use of pictures cut from a catalogue were helpful and it was pleasing to see that this technique of recording information was not over done. This Research Folio contains almost enough information for a start to be made on the designing of a toy. It is very well organised and a pleasure to read.

The examiner has said it all. It is an excellent example of an economic selection of information that will be useful in the designing of a child's toy.

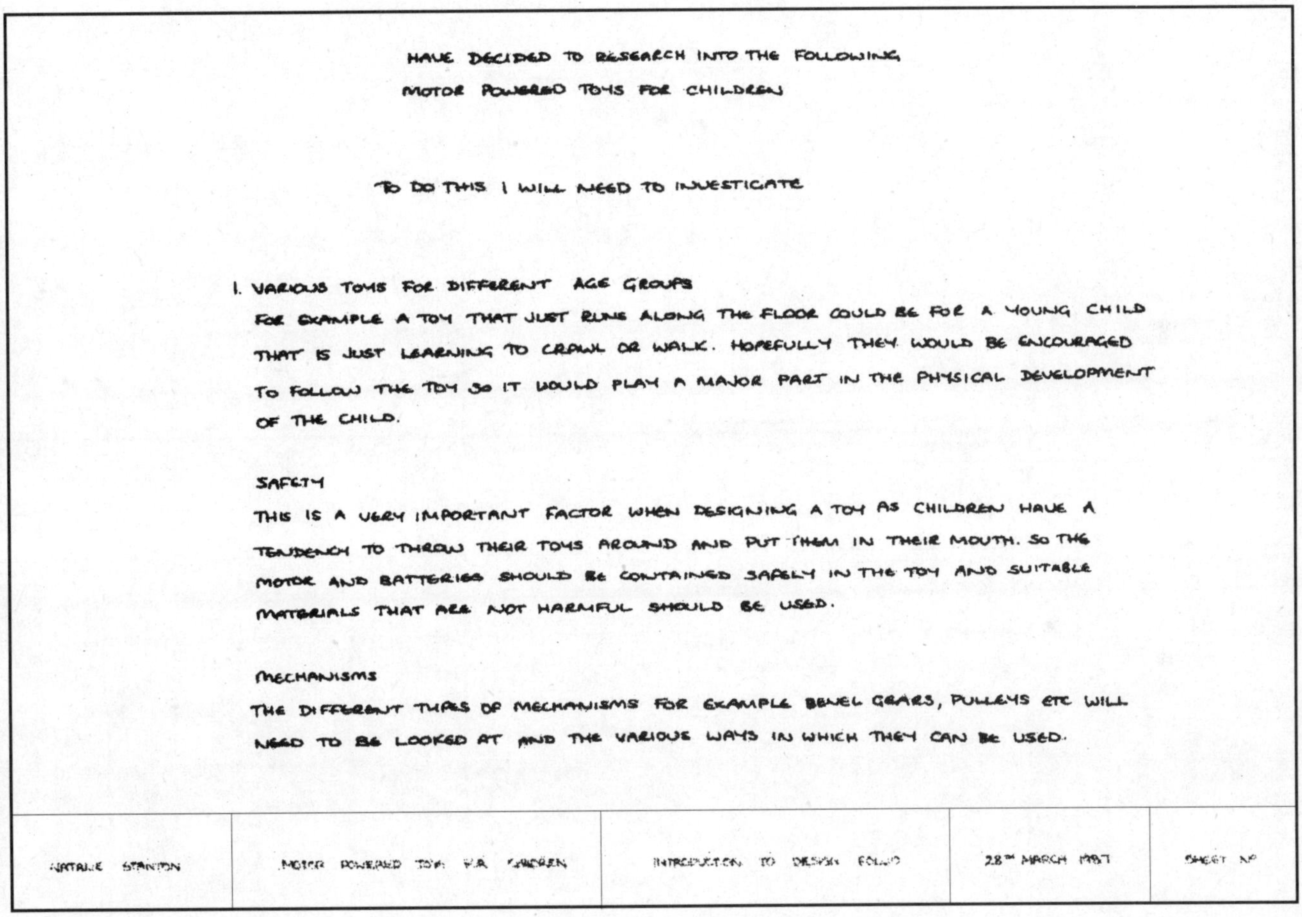

HAVE DECIDED TO RESEARCH INTO THE FOLLOWING
MOTOR POWERED TOYS FOR CHILDREN

TO DO THIS I WILL NEED TO INVESTIGATE

1. VARIOUS TOYS FOR DIFFERENT AGE GROUPS
FOR EXAMPLE A TOY THAT JUST RUNS ALONG THE FLOOR COULD BE FOR A YOUNG CHILD
THAT IS JUST LEARNING TO CRAWL OR WALK. HOPEFULLY THEY WOULD BE ENCOURAGED
TO FOLLOW THE TOY SO IT WOULD PLAY A MAJOR PART IN THE PHYSICAL DEVELOPMENT
OF THE CHILD.

SAFETY
THIS IS A VERY IMPORTANT FACTOR WHEN DESIGNING A TOY AS CHILDREN HAVE A
TENDENCY TO THROW THEIR TOYS AROUND AND PUT THEM IN THEIR MOUTH. SO THE
MOTOR AND BATTERIES SHOULD BE CONTAINED SAFELY IN THE TOY AND SUITABLE
MATERIALS THAT ARE NOT HARMFUL SHOULD BE USED.

MECHANISMS
THE DIFFERENT TYPES OF MECHANISMS FOR EXAMPLE BEVEL GEARS, PULLEYS ETC WILL
NEED TO BE LOOKED AT AND THE VARIOUS WAYS IN WHICH THEY CAN BE USED.

| NATALIE STANTON | MOTOR POWERED TOY FOR CHILDREN | INTRODUCTION TO DESIGN FOLIO | 28TH MARCH 1987 | SHEET Nº |

Fig. 21.4

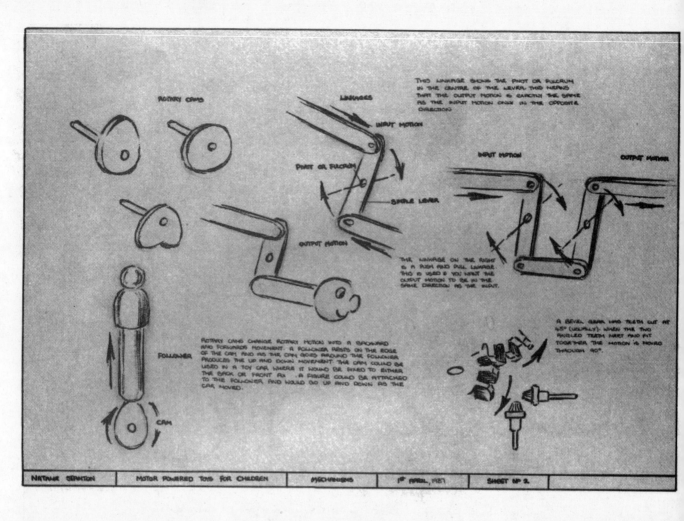

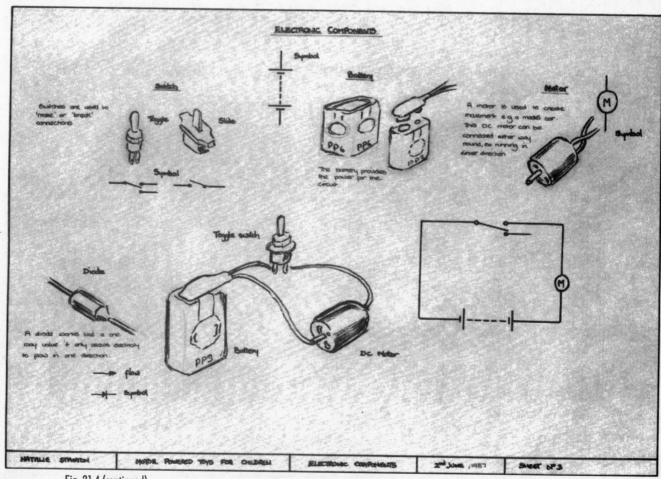

Fig. 21.4 (continued)

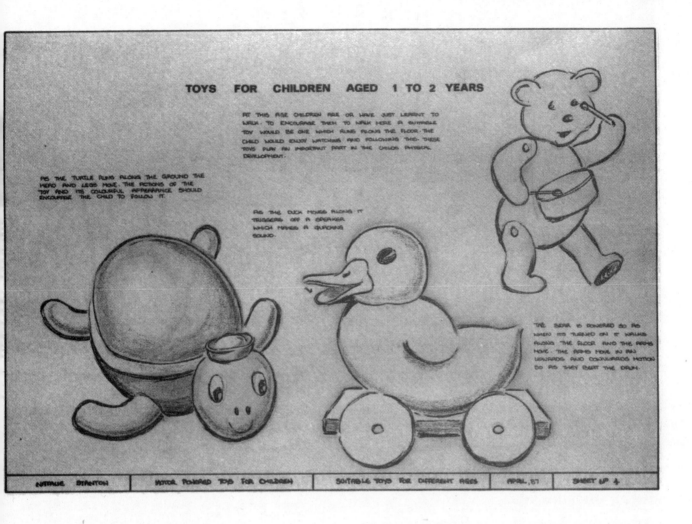

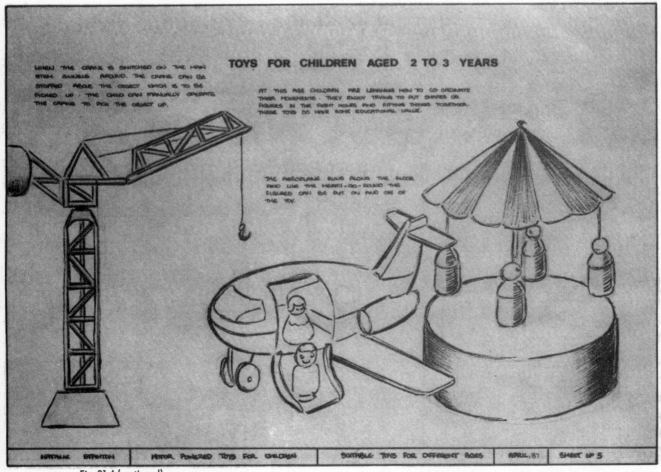

Fig. 21.4 (continued)

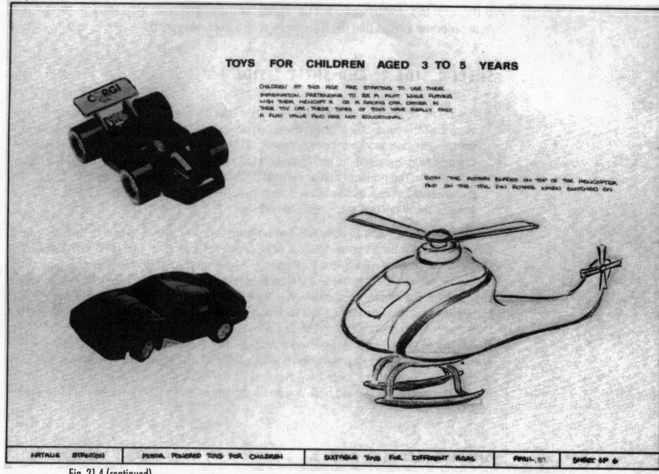

Fig. 21.4 (continued)

You have seen the results of producing a *Research Folio*. Now the same candidate tackles the problem of **designing** a suitable toy using the information contained in the Research Folio. The work has to be presented on the four sheets of A3 drawing paper that are supplied by the Examining Board.

The layout of the paper is similar to a formal examination in that there are spaces for writing in your Centre No., Candidate No., Name, etc., and every page is numbered. The four sheets are supplied individually so that they may be used on a drawing board.

On the left-hand side at the top of the sheet is the first instruction.

SHEET 1, SIDE 1

The front sheet is correctly filled in.

1. a) The problem is stated clearly, briefly and precisely.
   b) The summary of the investigation has been written neatly, and precisely. An economic use of words, with all the relevant areas adequately covered.
   c) The important points have been identified and neatly tabulated 1–5.

   The whole page shows that care and thought has been taken to present the information as succinctly as possible without being too brief.

The examiner was rightly impressed with this sheet. The candidate had done precisely what had been asked and did it very well. The layout was excellent and the information was relevant to the problem. The one important area that appears to have been overlooked is the need to know the speed of the spindle of the electric motor and how to use gears of an appropriate size so that the toy moved at an acceptable speed.

SHEET 1 SIDE 2, AND SHEET 2 SIDE 1

A wide range of excellent alternative ideas are neatly displayed on both sheets. They show that the candidate is imaginative and prepared to try out a number of possibilities before selecting an idea for development. The notes gave information about movement. It would have been helpful had some notes referred to how appropriate each idea was as a solution to the problem. Then it would be clear how a choice was made for development. Ticks were not used, as instructed at the top of the sheet 2 side 1, to indicate the ideas that were going to be used.

The examiner was right to point out that not sufficient attention was paid to thoughts about the suitability of each design idea. A brief comment indicating the good or weak design features would have shown the examiner just how much thought had been given to each idea. The balance of the crane is a technical problem, but the hook is something that should have received a comment in connection with safety. The speed at which the mobile with the letters and numbers rotate is a technical problem that would need to be resolved. Is a motor necessary in such a toy? This is a question that might have been asked in the notes. Is a child aged between 9 months and 2 years really interested in letters and numbers? Had questions like these been posed, and briefly answered, the *reason* for selection would have been clear. These two sheets have reached an excellent standard of graphics and design ideas. The points mentioned here are just suggestions as to where further improvements could be made.

SHEET 3, SIDES 1 AND 2

The quality of the drawing skills is very high. This candidate did not need the help of an isometric grid and rightly chose not to use it. The depth of detail is superb and sufficient for a model to be made. The notes to support the reason for selection should have been made on sheet 2. However, it would appear that the toy is already made since the notes refer to the toys "not being robust enough due to the restriction of the materials and processes available to me".

The notes do suggest that the toy might have been made. Also it would explain how the drawings are so detailed. To make a drawing of a toy that can be seen is much easier than drawing from your imagination. The intention should be that the drawings are worked out first and the product made from the drawing.

SHEET 4

A very competent use of Orthographic Projection has been made and the difficulties of getting the drawing onto the paper have been mainly overcome. A third view might have been an advantage had there been space. A good use of conventions to indicate centre lines and hidden detail. Dimensional detail a little sparse. A good use was made of identifying the parts using a letter press technique which corresponded with a well prepared cutting list.

All the sections of the paper were attempted and the total script represented an excellent response. There is no single way of answering this type of paper. The important things to ask yourself are:

1. Have all the stages been attempted?
2. Have I done what is required for each stage?
3. Have I presented my work so that someone else can follow what I have done?

The stages for designing are given on page 350. By reading the comments in column 4 you will have an idea of what is expected to get a top grade. The example you have seen on pages 355 to 358 fits comfortably in a top grade description.

Paper Ref. No.

1151/1.0

Centre No.	Candidate No.

Surname and Initials (Block letters)

Signature

Date

London
EXAMINATIONS
UNIVERSITY OF LONDON EXAMINATIONS & ASSESSMENT COUNCIL

GCSE

Summer 1994

CDT:
Design & Realisation

Paper 1.0: Design

DESIGN ANSWER SHEETS
To be completed and despatched to the examiner by
31 March 1994

INSTRUCTIONS TO CANDIDATES

In the boxes above, write your centre number, candidate number, surname and initials, signature and the date.

Use these sheets to develop your answer to the problem chosen from Paper 1.0.

You may use colour and any other graphic techniques. Annotate your sketches. The working drawing(s) should be in proportion and must include a cutting list.

All dimensions to be in millimetres.

When the design work has been completed all four sheets must be fastened together and handed to the teacher for despatch to the examiner.

54249 FV 140 1 1151
© 1994 University of London Examinations & Assessment Council

For Examiner's use only	
1	
2	
3	
4	
5	
6	
SPG	
Total	

1. (a) State the problem chosen

   Motor driven toy suitable for a 9 month to 2 year old child

   (b) Summary of your investigation (Folio)

   In this project I have researched into the
   following areas

   1. *The importance of play*
   2. *Suitability of toys for different stages in the childs development*
   3. *Popular themes relating to childrens tv programmes / literature*
   4. *Investigations relating to;*
      i. *Gear and pulley systems*
      ii. *Mechanisms, levers and linkages*
      iii. *Simple energy conversion systems.*
      and how these can be related to the areas stated above.

   (c) Analysis of the Problem
   List the important points that you will consider in preparing your design

   Important factors
   1. *Safety*
      The toy should be made as safe as possible whether its for a 2 year old or a 10 year old. As its a motor driven toy it would be much safer if the mechanics were contained in the toy (lockable compartment) so that the child could not harm themself by touching or getting there finger caught.
   2. *Colour*
      The colour of the toy is important because if the toy doesn't look appealing then the child won't play with it. Eg. the toy would be better if it was painted in primary colours rather than a pale grey.
   3. *Mechanics*
      The mechanisms should look good and make the toy look interesting. They should be safe and if the toy is for a young child then they should be able to withstand a fair amount of bashing about and not break instantly
   4. *Materials*
      The toy should be made out of strong materials that will not break easily. Also children often put toys in their mouth so the finishing of the toy is most important eg if the toy is being painted non-toxic paints should be used. It is also important that there is no sharp edges when the toy is finished.
   5. *The toy should be suitable for the age group I have stated.*

   PTO

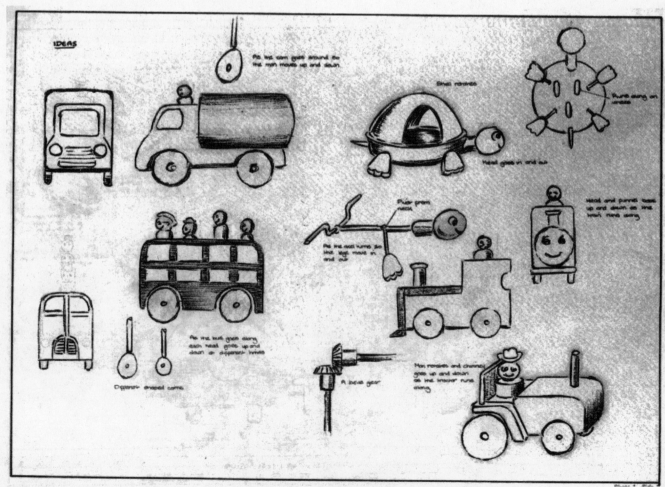

Fig. 21.5

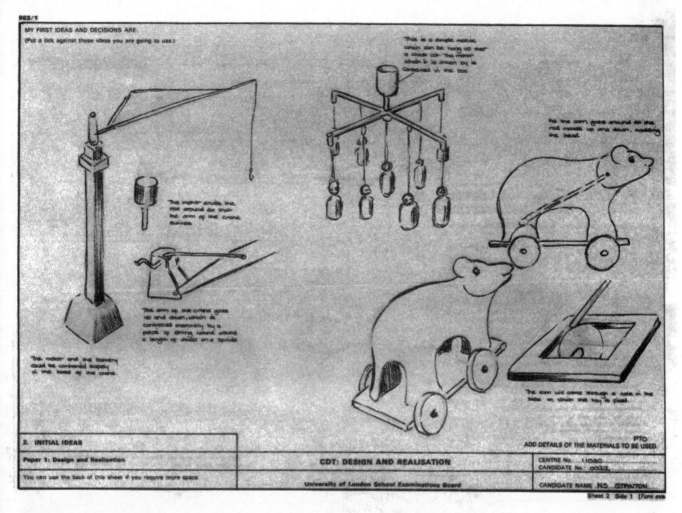

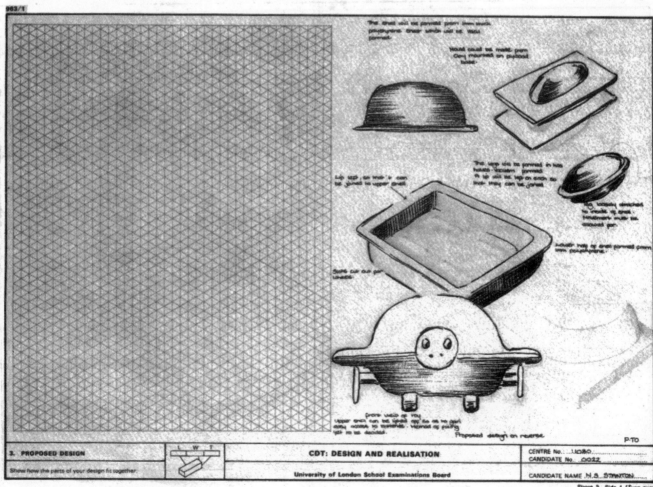

Fig. 21.5 (continued)

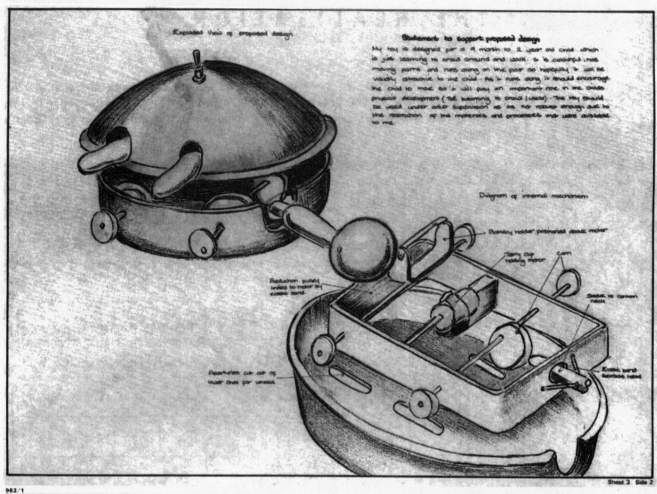

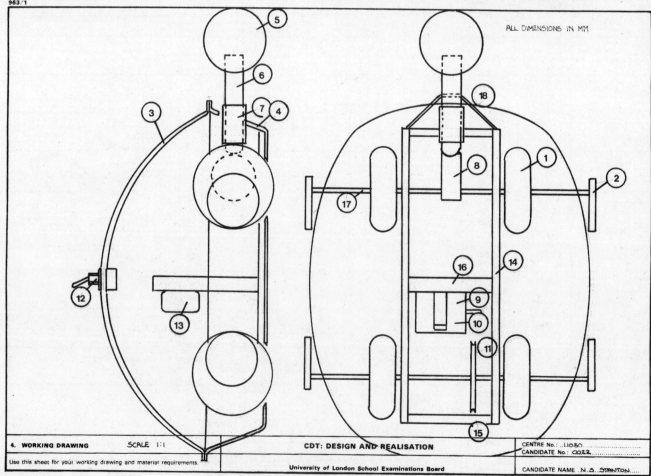

Fig. 21.5 (continued)

As soon as the work has been completed for Paper 1, so work can start on the **realisation**. The working drawing and the cutting list must be available for you to use, so if you have sent the Paper I to the examining board you will have to work from a photocopy.

Part	L	W	T	Nº Off	Material	Description
1	Ø50			4	Plastic	Balloon wheels
2	Ø30		3	4	Plywood	Cam
3	Refer to drawing			1	Polystyrene	Vacuum formed upper shell
4	Refer to drawing			1	Polystyrene	Vacuum formed lower shell
5	Ø40			1	Plastic	Head
6	58	Ø12		1	Dowel	Neck
7	20	Ø15		1	Aluminium	Sleeve
8	Ø26		12	1	Plywood	Cam
9				1		3 volt electric Motor
10				1		Terry Clip
11				1	Plastic	Reduction pulley
12				1		Switch
13	Ø40		3	1	Plastic	Battery holder
14	172	39	5	2	Softwood	
15	50	39	5	2	Softwood	
16	64	49		1		
17	175	Ø2		2	Welding rod	front and back axles
18				1	Rubber	Elastic band

CUTTING LIST

Fig. 21.6

The realisation is marked by your teacher and he or she will have a mark scheme similar to the one used to assess the realisation of your coursework. See page 201 for details of such a scheme.

Throughout the time you take to make your solution, your teacher will be assessing the stages listed in the first column. You will not be involved in discussing your assessment but you should let your teacher see *planning notes* showing the stages you wish to follow and the equipment you are going to need. This will be helpful to the teacher who may have to make arrangements for certain materials and equipment to be available for your use.

12 > EXTERNAL MODERATION OF THE REALISATION

When the visiting moderator assesses your coursework, your realisation will also be moderated. The marks arrived at by your teacher will be given to the moderator. Aspects of planning, selecting tools and your ability to set up equipment ready for use can only be judged by the person who saw you *do* these things (i.e. your teacher), so the visiting moderator will only be able to assess what can be *seen*. Accuracy, assembly and finish of the realisation are the things that can be seen. If your teacher has been too mean or too generous with *these* aspects, then the moderator will make whatever adjustment if any is necessary.

The photograph shown alongside is the Realisation of the solution to the child's motor driven toy. From just looking at the photograph, which is not an ideal way of assessing a piece of work, it is fair to say that:

a) The product resembles the details given in the working drawing, and appears to be accurately made.
b) All parts are assembled together.
c) The finish is colourful and appropriate and appears to be very well executed.

On this basis the realisation would fit in column 4 of the assessment sheet on page 351. If the teacher's assessment of the planning, selection and use of tools and equipment also fell in column 4, then the mark would be unchanged.

Fig. 21.7

EVALUATION

The evaluation cannot obviously be made until *after* the Realisation has been completed. It should be available for the visiting moderator to see. An appropriate place to keep it is in the Research Folio.

13 > ASSESSMENT OF THE EVALUATION

For guidance refer to page 116 and read the section on "Evaluation of a one-off product". Below are the Visiting Assessor's comments on the Student's evaluation.

VISITING ASSESSOR'S COMMENTS

The layout and quality of presentation is excellent. A summary of the Design Brief and a photograph of the realisation (see above) is an excellent feature of the presentation. The comments in the evaluation are pertinent to some of the design weaknesses but there were very few recommendations to show how improvements could be made. There was no reference to how well the realisation suited the needs of the child. This was an important point made in the analysis which was worthy of comment in the Evaluation. The evaluation was not clearly identified and it was necessary to ring the different parts. (See page 117). A disappointing level of evaluation after such an excellent first impression.

Had the candidate listed the five statements made in the analysis of the problem, page 360, and presented them as questions to be answered, this could have produced an excellent evaluation. While the quality of presentation is high, this evaluation avoided tackling the more thoughtful considerations in detail and therefore would be graded as an average response.

SAMPLE QUESTION PAPERS AND RESPONSES

4 ▷ TECHNOLOGY

All **Technology** papers are marked by an examiner. It will not be the same examiner who marked your design paper, but the procedures for marking and checking, etc., will be very similar. Much of the detail about the structure of the paper is dealt with in Chapter 4.

MULTIPLE CHOICE QUESTIONS

Q1   Aesthetics means:

    A   measuring human beings
    B   pleasing appearance
    C   decoration
    D   applying a finish   (1)

Q2   An example of a fossil fuel is:

    A   coal
    B   coke
    C   wood
    D   methane   (1)

Q3   An example of an alloy is:

    A   silver
    B   mercury
    C   lead
    D   brass   (1)

This type of question is only to be found in the IGCSE Technology Papers at present and may be used in GCSE Technology in the future. If this does happen then the centres taking these papers would be informed. In answering this type of question make sure you follow the instructions. You may be required to tick the correct answer or under-line the correct answer. A correct answer will be awarded the mark given in the brackets.

MULTIPLE CHOICE ANSWERS

The answers to the above questions are: 1 B, 2 A, 3 D.

SHORT ANSWER QUESTIONS

Short answer questions can be easily identified. When they are set they usually:

a) form the first part of the examination paper;
b) have a low number of marks for each question;
c) have to be attempted;
d) have to be answered in a booklet;
e) require briefly worded answers, sometimes with a sketch or completion of an existing question;
f) have lines on which to write answers. (Note the length of the line or lines is an indication of the length of the answer.)

Below is a typical type of short answer question.

QUESTION 1

a) The diagram shows a small wire nail in a piece of wood. Name the tool you would use to remove the nail.
   Claw hammer   (1)
b) On the diagram, sketch the tool you have named. Show clearly how it is used to remove the nail.   (2)
c) Show on the diagram any precautions you would take to protect the surface of the wood while the nail is being removed.   (1)

                                                                              (WJEC)

ANSWER 1

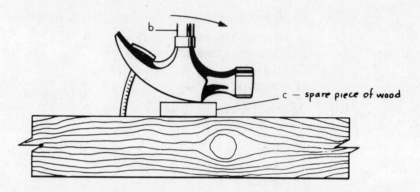

Fig. 21.8

a) There are two possible answers and you would only give one answer even if you know both. You will only be given credit for one answer. So do not waste your time by putting down more information than you need. Just write "Claw Hammer" or "Pincers". Note "Pincers" *not* "Pinchers" as they are often mistakenly called. It is unlikely that you would lose marks for an error of this kind particularly when there is only (1) mark. However, you are assessed upon your ability to spell, punctuate and use a sentence structure that is grammatically correct, so within this context you would be penalised.
b) Just add the detail of the tool named in a) but first read the rest of the question because the position you draw the tool will determine the space that is needed for *c*).
c) The drawing of a spare piece of wood in the position shown is sufficient to get the one mark. The written label and the letter "c" is added just to make sure that the examiner knows which part of the question is being answered.

The following two questions are concerned with your knowledge and understanding of drilling. The first question asks for a drawing to be completed, the other for a chart to be completed.

QUESTION 2

The diagram below shows a pillar drilling machine with guards removed. Draw the belt in position on the pulleys for drilling a 2mm diameter hole.

                                                                             (ULEAC)

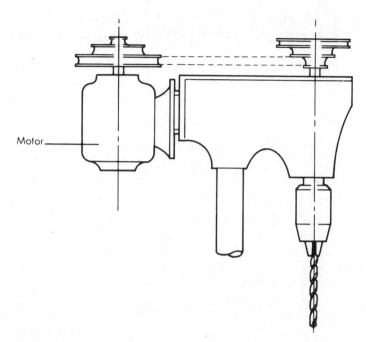

Fig. 21.9

ANSWER 2

In answering Question 2, you have to decide two things. The first is the speed of the drill and the second is how to make the drill achieve the speed you have decided. As a guide you can say:

■ "Small drill – fast speed." "Large drill – slow speed."

To obtain the speed you want, think of the pulley on the drilling machine because it is that one that rotates either slowly or quickly. The pulley on the motor always rotates at one speed; the speed of the motor.

■ "Small drill – small pulley." "Large drill – large pulley."
      (fast)   (slow)

The answer is for the belt to be on the small pulley wheel as shown in the dotted line.

QUESTION 3

Complete the table below by naming the correct cutting tool for **each** process for **each** of the three materials.

(ULEAC)

Process	Materials		
	Hardwood	Mild steel	Acrylic sheet
a) Cutting 3mm thick sheet material			
b) Making a 10mm diameter hole through 12mm thick material			
c) Preparing an edge from which to work			

Fig. 21.10

ANSWER 3

The question is concerned with materials and how the characteristics of the material influences the choice of tool to be used. Some general guide lines in selecting a drill twist bit will help. Try to remember that:

- Soft materials can be drilled with soft steel drills, i.e. carbon steel, CS.
- Hard materials can be drilled with hard steel drills, i.e. high speed steel, HSS.

Plastics materials may be drilled using CS or HSS twist drills, but the thermosetting plastics prefer a slow helix twist and the thermoplastics prefer a fast helix twist. With one exception to the rule, acrylic, a thermoplastics material prefers a slow helix.

a) Here the following should be given:

- hardwood   carbon steel twist drill;
- mild steel   high speed steel twist drill;
- acrylic   slow helix twist drill, CS or HSS.

b) Here it would appear that the same answers could be provided as for a) and be quite acceptable. But, with the increase in size of hole, there are other types of hole cutting devices that would be preferred. For hardwood, a range of centre bits are available, e.g. Screw Centre Bit, Jennings Bit, and Forstner Bit. Any of these would be more suitable than a twist drill. Twist drills used on metals can go to much larger sizes than 10 mm and there is no alternative drilling bit, therefore a 10 mm twist drill HSS must be the answer. The smallest hole cutter is 12.5 mm diameter, therefore this leaves the only cutting tool as the 10 mm twist drill with the slow helix.

c) Preparing an edge from which to work when using hardwood must be the Jack plane. It is the tool designed for planing surfaces smooth, flat and true. Preparing mild steel is a second-cut hand or flat file. The thickness or sizes of the materials have not been given. The answers can therefore apply to the most common situations. If you find that you are giving the same answer to two different parts of a question, do look carefully to see if a different answer is being looked for. Most questions are designed to cover a wide area, rather than a narrow one that will produce the same answer several times.

INCREASE OF DIFFICULTY

Though the short answer questions are not awarded the higher range of marks as are the longer questions they do get more and more demanding. Question 1 on page 372 carried 4 marks; now we look at one question that carries 7 marks. This steady increase is used by ULEAC, MEG and WJEC. It may also occur in papers produced by the other Examining Boards.

Your understanding of mechanisms is tested in a number of ways and completing diagrams is a commonly used method. In part b) of question 4 an example is given. Draw in the piece or pieces that are missing. Make sure you indicate the pivoting point and put an arrow to indicate the direction of movement. In this question you are not asked to put the arrows in, but it should help you to check that your answer is correct.

QUESTION 4 AND SAMPLE ANSWER

a) Name **one** common object where the drive system consists of a "chain and sprockets".

Bicycle

(1)

b) The Figure below shows diagrams of simple mechanisms that could be used in children's toys. Complete the diagrams – by adding one or more components such as levers, pulleys, cams, drive belts, gears and so on.
Moving part A in the direction shown by the arrows, must move part B in the direction shown by the arrows. (8)

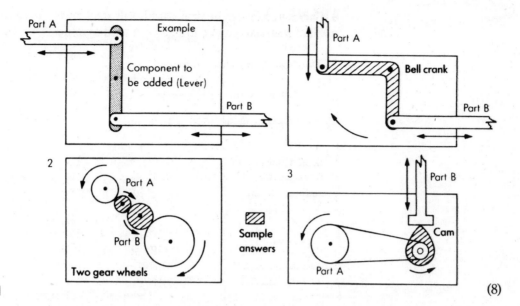

Fig. 21.11   (8)

Question 5 is the last question of a short answer section and the mark given. It is also reasonable to expect to have to take a little longer in answering this question.

QUESTION 5

The main terms (stages) in a design process are given below. Put the terms in their correct order, and explain each.

TERMS – CUTTING LIST; DESIGN BRIEF; EVALUATION; GENERATION OF
IDEAS; MAKING; RESEARCH; WORKING DRAWING; PRODUCT
DESIGN SPECIFICATION; PLANNING AND ORGANISATION;
DEVELOPMENT OF AN IDEA.

(ULEAC)

ANSWER 5

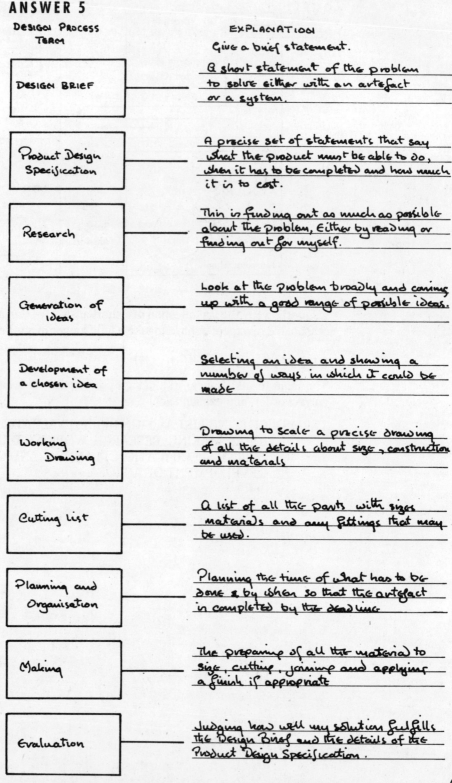

Fig. 21.12

(20)

You should, throughout the course, become very familiar with these terms as a result of your experience in solving problems. So all you have to do is to think of the *stages* you went through to design a product or project.

When going through the list to work out the correct order you will realise that not all stages are included. You could put a tick by each of the terms, when it is transferred to the boxes down the lefthand side, so that it is clear which terms are left. The order in the example is the most common sequence.

Question 6 gives you a similar type of question from another Examining Group.

QUESTION 6

1. a) Name the soft, lightweight timber that is used for making models.

     (1)

   b) Name the lightweight, silvery white metal that is often cast into shape.

     (1)

2. a) Name **one** common object in or around the home that is normally made from polythene

     (1)

   b) A piece of acrylic sheet, 3 mm thick, is to be bent to a 90 degree angle. What piece of equipment would be used to heat the acrylic sheet?

     (1)

3. a) Why is wood "seasoned" before it can be used to make things?

     (1)

   b) A table decoration is to be made from several pieces of copper. Name **one** heat process that could be used to join the pieces.

     (1)

4. Name the tool you would use for marking a line parallel to the straight edge of
   i) a piece of mild steel,

     (1)

   ii) a piece of pine.

     (1)

5. a) When wood turning, face protection must be worn. Describe **one** other safety precaution you would observe.

     (1)

   b) Why is it dangerous to pour molten metal into a sand mould that is very damp?
     (1)

6. What would be a suitable finish for the following objects:
   i) a decorative indoor plant stand made from mild steel;

     (1)

   ii) a mahogany coffee table?

     (1)

7. a) What do you understand by the term *veneer*?

     (1)

   b) What do you understand by the term *extrusion*?

     (1)
     (WJEC)

EXPECTED ANSWERS

1a) Balsa, b) Aluminium. 2a) bag, b) strip heater. 3a) To reduce the moisture content and prevent it from being attacked by woodworm. b) silver soldering. 4 i) Odd-leg caliper. ii) Marking gauge. 5a) Make sure there is no loose clothing. b) steam may be formed. 6 i) Polyurethane paint, ii) Cellulose lacquer. 7a) A thin sheet of wood, b) a material such as aluminium that has to be forced through a die.

ANSWERING THE LONG QUESTIONS

These long questions usually appear in a separate section of the paper and you do have a choice. Because they are longer you do not have to answer so many questions as in the first section. Two or three questions often have to be attempted in this section. Once you have decided to attempt a question, *all* parts of it must be answered.

   The questions are so arranged that you start off with short answers. The further you go into the question, the more difficult it gets and the answers have to be a little more detailed and longer. Question 1 below about the push-along toy shows this clearly by the distribution of the marks for each part of the question.

QUESTION 1: A PUSH-ALONG TOY

Young children enjoy playing with very simple toys.
Figure 21.3 shows the outline of a simple car and a model person.

Materials

a) Name **one** specific wood that could be used to make the car body.   (2)
b) Name **one** other material that could be used to make the car body.   (2)
c) Name **two** specific materials that could be used to make the wheels.   (4)

Processes

d) Choose one material from those you have named. Use diagrams and notes to explain, step by step, how you would make the car body.   (8)
e) Using notes and diagrams, explain how you would fit the wheels – firmly and safely.   (4)

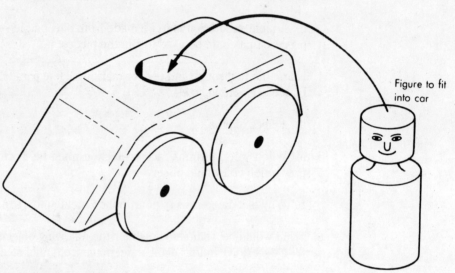

Figure to fit into car

Fig. 21.13

SAMPLE ANSWER 1

a) beech;
b) polystyrene;
c) acrylic, aluminium;
d) car body to be made from sheet polystyrene.

Step 1 Make a pattern of the car body from wood

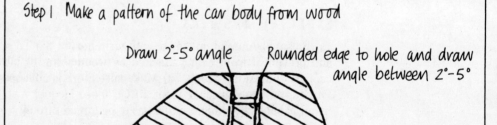

Draw 2°-5° angle   Rounded edge to hole and draw angle between 2°-5°

Air Evacuation hole

Step 2 Cut sheet of polystyrene to fit the clamping frame. Mount in frame and heat until soft.

Step 3 Bring the soft polystyrene sheet down over the pattern and switch the vacuum pump on.

Step 4 Reverse action to blow to release the moulded sheet from the pattern.

Step 5 Thin edges.

Fig. 21.14

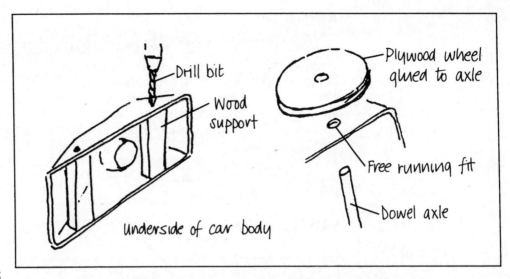

Fig. 21.15

QUESTION 2: A BOOK RACK FOR A PRIMARY SCHOOL

A primary school teacher needs to store several sets of books in the classroom. Each book is 180 mm x 120 mm x 8 mm. There are 30 books in each set.

Figure 21.16 shows the outline of a simple book rack. Ten of these are to be made in your DT workshop.

Materials

a) Name **two** different materials that could be used to make the end supports – part A, (for example: a **specific** metal; wood; plastic or some other material). State the thickness of materials you would use. (4)

b) Name **two** different materials that could be used to make the two horizontal pieces – part B, (for example: a **specific** metal; wood; plastic or some other material). State the diameters of both materials. (4)

Processes

c) Choose **one** of the materials you have named for the end supports. Use notes and diagrams to show, step by step, how you would make a pair of end supports. Include in your answer details of
   i)   marking-out,
   ii) removing the waste,
   iii) finishing the edges. (6)

d) Choose **one** of the materials you have named for the horizontal pieces. Use diagrams and notes to explain, step by step, how you would join these to the end supports. (6)

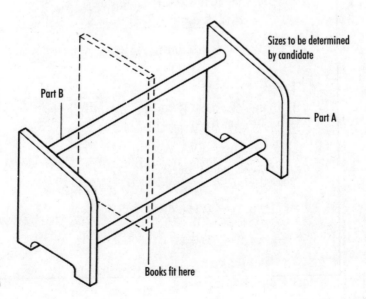

Fig. 21.16

Notes

Part a). Notice that two words are in heavy print. This is to draw your attention to two important points. Only name two different materials and be specific, i.e. give the *full* name of a material. When you are required to state a measurement, always give the *units* of measurement. Figures on their own are not sufficient.

Part b). There is no need to consider the materials given in a). So the choice is wide open, but do watch for the question in part d) that asks you to go into more detail on your choice here. This is why it is important to read *all* the question.

Part c). Here you have to relate your answer to one of the materials you have named in a). Choose a material with which you are most familiar and show how you would use it to make part A. Use diagrams where possible.

Part d). Same procedure as c)

SAMPLE ANSWER 2

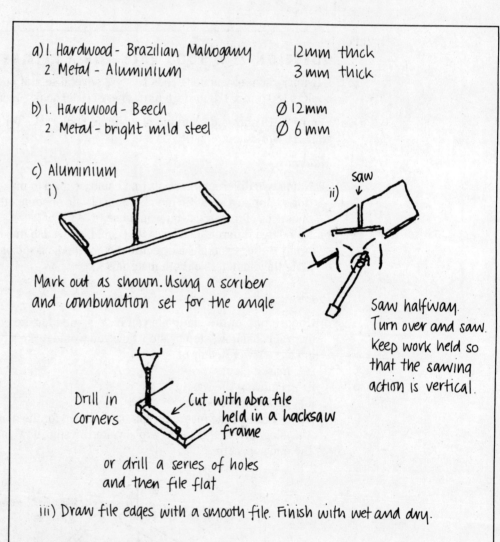

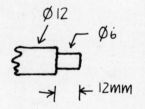

Fig. 21.17

QUESTION 3 AND SAMPLE ANSWERS

CONTROL SYSTEMS   Valves

*If you choose this question,
attempt all parts of it.*

(a) Several control devices are shown in the picture. Make **two** lists of those illustrated sorting them into those that are controlled directly, and those that are controlled remotely.

(10 marks)

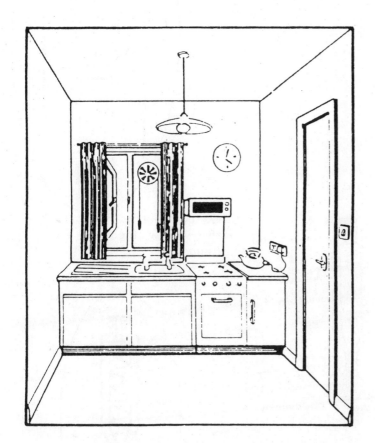

CONTROLLED DIRECTLY
Hot & cold water tap
Window latch
Door handle
Cupboard handle
Ventilation Cord

CONTROLLED REMOTELY
Electric light
Electric Kettle
Oven temperature
Clock
Self ignition gas ring

(b) The diagram below shows a control system for supplying cold water in a house system.

(i) Which of the valves (**A, B, C, D** and **E**) will need to be turned off to repair the washing machine?

      E

(ii) What could be repaired if valve **D** is turned off?

      Sink and Washing Machine

(iii) What problem might arise if the pipe bursts between the washbasin and the bath?

Valve B would be turned off & the Wash basin and bath would be out of use.

Fig. 21.18

BICYCLE PUMP

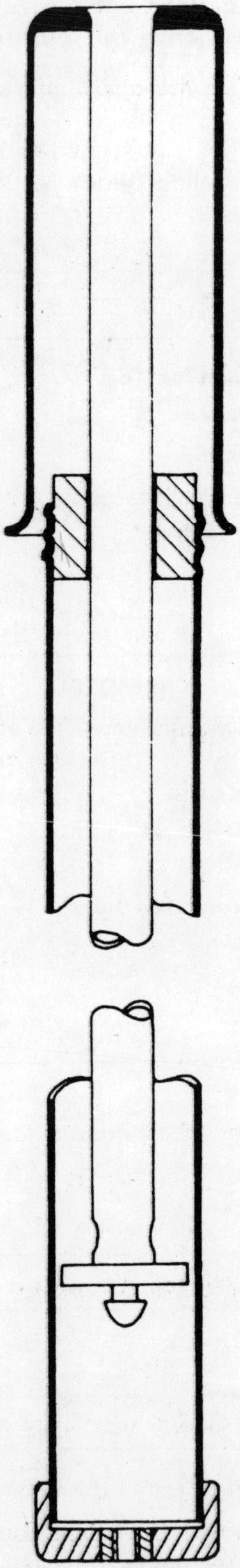

(i) Draw in the leather washer/valve on the pump.

(ii) Draw in the spring on the pump.

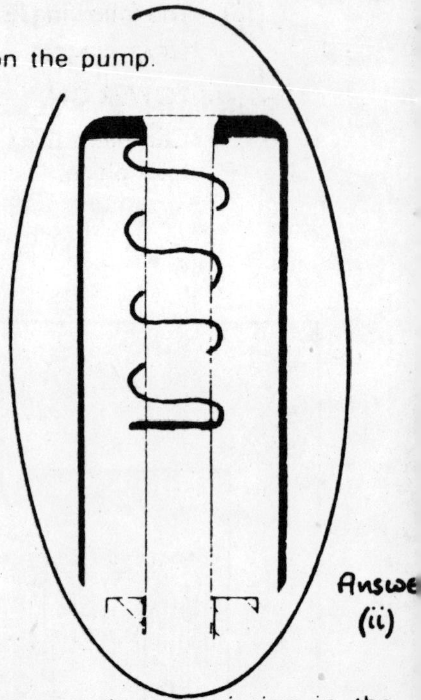

Answer (ii)

FOOTBALL VALVE

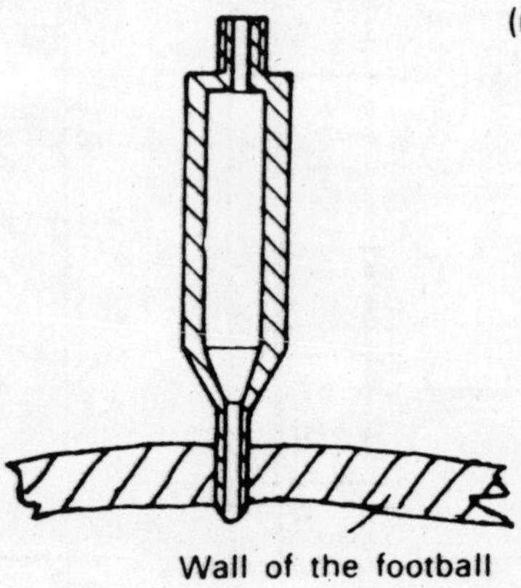

(iii) Two components are missing in the valve. Draw them in their correct position.

(11 marks)

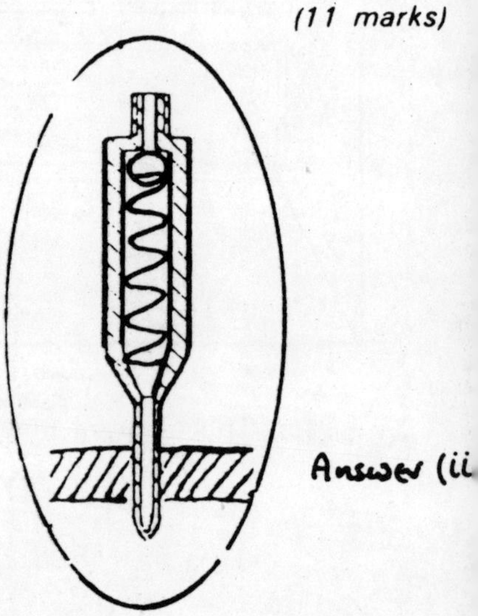

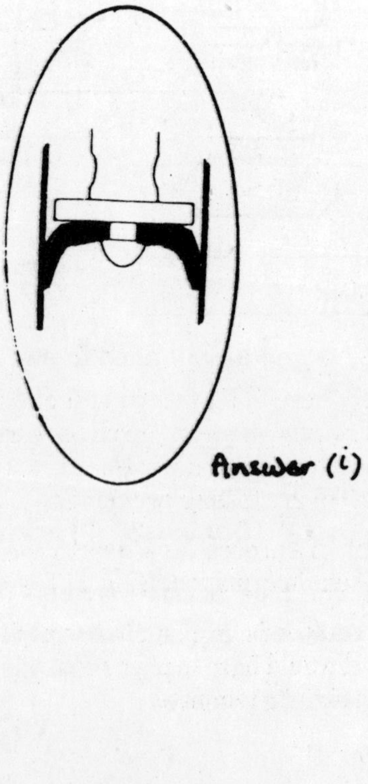

Wall of the football

Answer (ii)

Answer (i)

(Question continued overleaf)

Fig. 21.19

(d) The following list describes the operations carried out, when water has to be boiled using a kettle
HEAT SENSO   WATER IN   TAP OFF   QUANTITY SENSOR   POWER OFF   TAP ON
POWER ON.

Complete the flow diagram below to show the correct order in which the operations should take place.   *4 marks)*

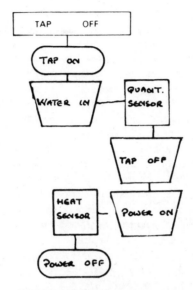

(e) Prepare a FLOW CHART for making and pouring a cup of tea. Assume all kitchenware is empty.
(16 marks)

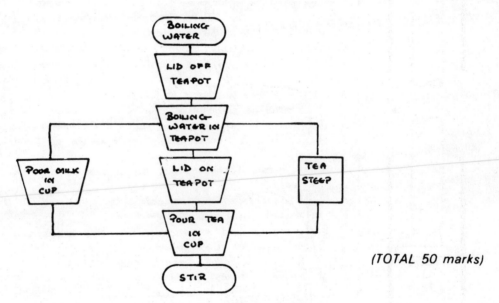

(TOTAL 50 marks)

Fig. 21.20

Notes

All the written answers have to be written in the spaces provided. Drawing is done on the drawings. The drawing answers given in part (c) of the sample question are presented in the ellipse: to show you what was given in the question and what has been added. Part d) and part c) are testing two things:

1. Your ability to think of a process as a sequence of logical steps.
2. Your ability to present information using a Flow Chart diagram.

Because such questions do exist in examination papers it would be sensible to use a flow chart template, but you would have to check that this is acceptable. The answer given in the sample is with the aid of a template.

15> DESIGN

QUESTION 1

More detailed comments are made by the Examiner at the end of the student's answer.

1. *(a)* State the problem chosen. Design a working model of an electricity generating system powered by wind, water or human means which utilises its output to demonstrate an everyday use for electricity.

(b) Summary of your Investigation (Folio). The folio investigated the possibility of using wind, water or human power to generate electricity on a small scale. The suitability, simplicity of construction and efficiency were noted. Practical investigation provided performance graphs for two possible dynamos and the study of industrial, experimental and small scale methods of generation showed that;

Human Power is very versatile and is used to perform many tasks of energy conversion. However, when harnesed to generate electricity it can only be sustained for a very limited period of time.

Wind Power was shown, by the construction of a model, to only be effective in generating electricity when the driving propeller is very large.

Water Power provides the most scope as more than ten basically different methods of generation are available with hundreds more variations. Water generators are more compact than wind generators and high efficiencies can be gained.

The folio provided a good insight and some firm ideas for the design project.

(c) Analysis of the Problem.

List the important points that you will consider in preparing your design.

A generator is required to power a small d.c. motor. Sufficient power must be generated to light a small bulb or produce an audible sound or provide heat. The generator must be able to run off domestic water pressure or a compressed air supply; human power is another possibility. In order for the generator to fulfill these requirements it must achieve the following;

① It must be sufficiently powerful to drive a dynamo.
② It must be efficient and reliable in use.
③ Simplicity of construction is essential as time for realisation is limited.
④ The materials chosen must be appropriate to their use and cost effective.
⑤ The generator must be compatible with and in proportion to the standard d.c. motor/dynamo.
⑥ Aesthetics and ergonomics are not necessary requirements.
⑦ The size of the generator is not restricted, however it should be kept within sensible limits.
⑧ Surface finishes should be such that the generator is protected from rust and dirt and should be easy to maintain.
⑨ The generator should be safe in operation; toxic paints or materials should be avoided and sharp edges should be rounded.

66 Could be much more brief. **99**

66 Too much writing. Use an a), b), c), d), style. **99**

66 Better. **99**

Fig. 21.21

Analysis Continued.

One aspect of the generator which must be carefully examined and analised is the question of speed, torque and gears.

The folio examined ways in which the output from the dynamo could be increased; two of which involved re-building the dynamo which was ruled out, but the other one was quite simply to increase the speed of rotation of the motor/dynamo. This is where the complicated balance between speed, torque and gearing comes in. Industrial turbine generators are able to produce both high speeds and high levels of torque which means that they are able to gear their 'dynamos' or 'alternators' UP so that the greatest amount of power is generated. Small scale generators, however, present the problem that although they are able to produce high speeds, they are not able to produce high levels of torque.

TORQUE IS THE MOMENT OF A FORCE WHICH PRODUCES ROTATION OR TORSION.

This means that if the level of torque being produced by the generator is low, the resistance of the dynamo may be enough to stall the generator.

Such items as a clutch which can be used to engage the dynamo when the generator has run up to speed, and a flywheel which will maintain rotational momentum would help 'smooth out' and maintain the action of the generator. However, these devices (especially the clutch) would be difficult to make, but the flywheel could be turned quite accuratly on the lathe. These items might, however, cause drag which must be avoided for the generator to work well.

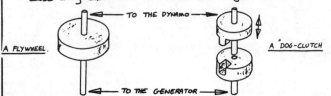

A FLYWHEEL   TO THE DYNAMO   A "DOG-CLUTCH"

TO THE GENERATOR

Fig. 21.22

Depending upon the speed and the torque of the generator it may or may not be necessary to use gears. The following diagrams are simplifications of what would happen if the generator was geared.

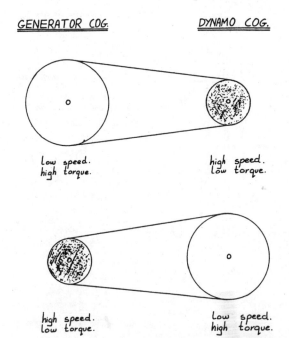

GENERATOR COG.   DYNAMO COG.

low speed.   high speed.
high torque.   low torque.

high speed.   low speed.
low torque.   high torque.

Many of the generators shown in the initial ideas stage may have a large cog on the generator and a small cog on the dynamo. It has been assumed, therefore, that the necessary levels of torque are available.

Sheet 1 Side 2

1181/1

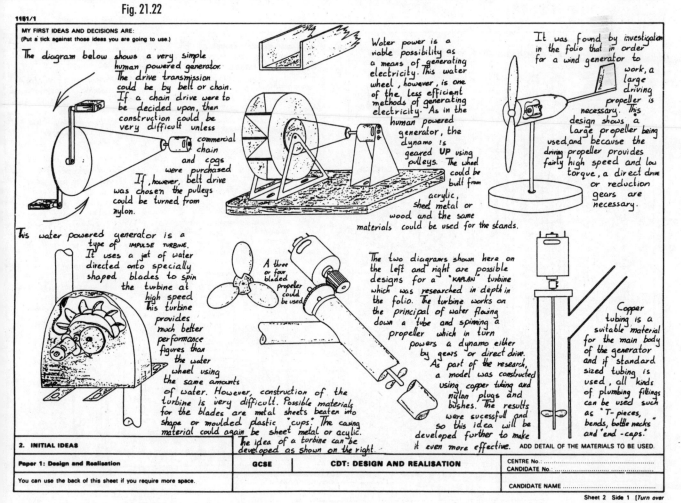

MY FIRST IDEAS AND DECISIONS ARE:
(Put a tick against those ideas you are going to use.)

The diagram below shows a very simple human powered generator. The drive transmission could be by belt or chain. If a chain drive were to be decided upon, then construction could be very difficult unless commercial chain and cogs were purchased. If, however, belt drive was chosen the pulleys could be turned from nylon.

Water power is a viable possibility as a means of generating electricity. This water wheel, however, is one of the less efficient methods of generating electricity. As in the human powered generator, the dynamo is geared UP using pulleys. The wheel could be built from acrylic, shed metal or wood and the same materials could be used for the stands.

It was found by investigation in the folio that in order for a wind generator to work, a large driving propeller is necessary. This design shows a large propeller being used, and because the driving propeller provides fairly high speed and low torque, a direct drive or reduction gears are necessary.

This water powered generator is a type of IMPULSE TURBINE. It uses a jet of water directed onto specially shaped blades to spin the turbine at high speed. This turbine provides much better performance figures than the water wheel using the same amounts of water. However, construction of the turbine is very difficult. Possible materials for the blades are metal sheets beaten into shape or moulded plastic 'cups'. The casing material could again be sheet metal or acylic. The idea of a turbine can be developed as shown on the right.

A three or four bladed propeller could be used.

The two diagrams shown here on the left and right are possible designs for a "KAPLAN" turbine which was researched in depth in the folio. The turbine works on the principal of water flowing down a tube and spining a propeller which in turn powers a dynamo either by gears or direct drive. As part of the research, a model was constructed using copper tubing and nylon plugs and bushes. The results were sucessfull and so this idea will be developed further to make it even more effective.

Copper tubing is a suitable material for the main body of the generator and if standard sized tubing is used, all kinds of plumbing fittings can be used such as "T-pieces," bends, bottle necks and "end-caps."

ADD DETAIL OF THE MATERIALS TO BE USED.

2. INITIAL IDEAS

Paper 1: Design and Realisation	GCSE	CDT: DESIGN AND REALISATION	CENTRE No. .... CANDIDATE No. ....
You can use the back of this sheet if you require more space.			CANDIDATE NAME ....

Sheet 2 Side 1 [Turn over

Fig. 21.23

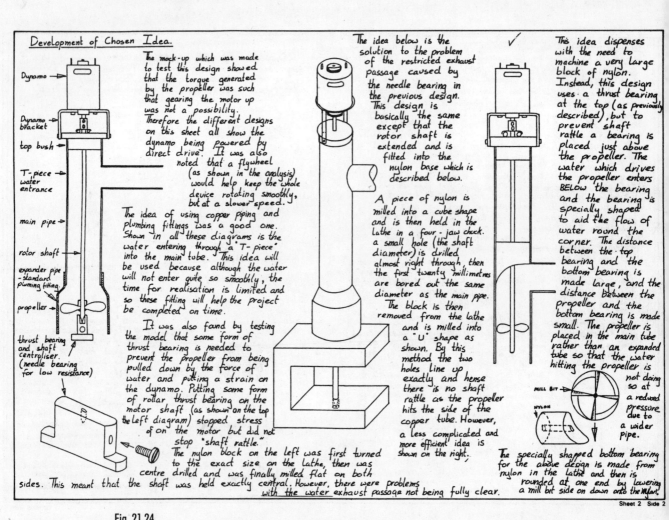

Development of Chosen Idea.

The mock-up which was made to test this design showed that the torque generated by the propeller was such that gearing the motor up was not a possibility. Therefore the different designs on this sheet all show the dynamo being powered by direct drive. It was also noted that a flywheel (as shown in the analysis) would help keep the whole device rotating smoothly, but at a slower speed.

The idea of using copper piping and plumbing fittings was a good one. Shown in all these diagrams is the water entering through a "T-piece" into the main tube. This idea will be used because although the water will not enter quite so smoothly, the time for realisation is limited and so these fitting will help the project be completed on time.

It was also found by testing the model that some form of thrust bearing is needed to prevent the propeller from being pulled down by the force of water and putting a strain on the dynamo. Putting some form of rollar thrust bearing on the motor shaft (as shown on the top the left diagram) stopped stress of on the motor but did not stop "shaft rattle." The nylon block on the left was first turned to the exact size on the lathe, then was centre drilled and was finally milled flat on both sides. This meant that the shaft was held exactly central. However, there were problems with the water exhaust passage not being fully clear.

Labels (left diagram): Dynamo, Dynamo bracket, top bush, T-piece water entrance, main pipe, rotor shaft, expander pipe - standard plumbing fitting, propeller, thrust bearing and shaft centraliser. (needle bearing for low resistance)

The idea below is the solution to the problem of the restricted exhaust passage caused by the needle bearing in the previous design. This design is basically the same except that the rotor shaft is extended and is fitted into the nylon base which is described below.

A piece of nylon is milled into a cube shape and is then held in the lathe in a four-jaw chuck. A small hole (the shaft diameter) is drilled almost right through, then the first twenty millimetres are bored out the same diameter as the main pipe. The block is then removed from the lathe and is milled into a "U" shape as shown. By this method the two holes line up exactly and hence there is no shaft rattle as the propeller hits the side of the copper tube. However, a less complicated and more efficient idea is shown on the right.

This idea dispenses with the need to machine a very large block of nylon. Instead, this design uses a thrust bearing at the top (as previously described), but to prevent shaft rattle a bearing is placed just above the propeller. The water which drives the propeller enters BELOW the bearing and the bearing is specially shaped to aid the flow of water round the corner. The distance between the top bearing and the bottom bearing is made large, and the distance between the propeller and the bottom bearing is made small. The propeller is placed in the main tube rather than an expanded tube so that the water hitting the propeller is not doing so at a reduced pressure due to a wider pipe.

MILL BIT   NYLON

The specially shaped bottom bearing for the above design is made from nylon in the lathe and then is rounded at one end by lowering a mill bit side on down onto the Milan.

Sheet 2   Side 2

Fig. 21.24

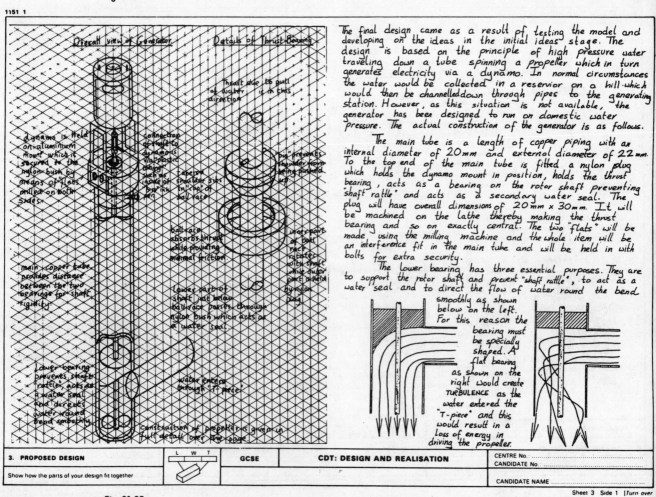

1151 1

Overall view of Generator   Details of Thrust Bearing

The final design came as a result of testing the model and developing on the ideas in the initial ideas stage. The design is based on the principle of high pressure water traveling down a tube spinning a propeller which in turn generates electricity via a dynamo. In normal circumstances the water would be collected in a reservoir on a hill which would then be channelled down through pipes to the generating station. However, as this situation is not available, the generator has been designed to run on domestic water pressure. The actual construction of the generator is as follows.

The main tube is a length of copper piping with an internal diameter of 20mm and external diameter of 22mm. To the top end of the main tube is fitted a nylon plug which holds the dynamo mount in position, holds the thrust bearing, acts as a bearing on the rotor shaft preventing "shaft rattle" and acts as a secondary water seal. The plug will have overall dimensions of 20mm x 30mm. It will be machined on the lathe thereby making the thrust bearing and so on exactly central. The two "flats" will be made using the milling machine and the whole item will be an interference fit in the main tube and will be held in with bolts for extra security.

The lower bearing has three essential purposes. They are to support the rotor shaft and prevent "shaft rattle", to act as a water seal and to direct the flow of water round the bend smoothly as shown below on the left. For this reason the bearing must be specially shaped. A flat bearing as shown on the right would create TURBULENCE as the water entered the "T-piece" and this would result in a loss of energy in driving the propeller.

3. PROPOSED DESIGN		GCSE	CDT: DESIGN AND REALISATION	CENTRE No. ....
Show how the parts of your design fit together	L W T			CANDIDATE No. ....
				CANDIDATE NAME ....

Sheet 3   Side 1   [Turn over

Fig. 21.25

The construction of the lower bearing is very simple; it will be turned on the lathe to the overall dimensions of 20mm x 20mm (20mm being the diameter). Then, using the milling machine it will be made into the curved shape shown below. Nylon is an ideal material since it is easy to machine, is very hard, tough and rigid, is a very good bearing surface since it is self lubricating, is resistant to oil, fuels and chemicals and finally it has good fatigue resistance with very low levels of wear and friction.

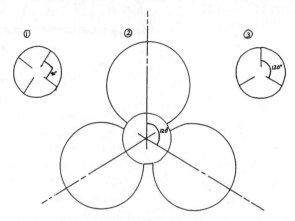

Since the nylon can not be left in the copper tube when the "T-piece" is being soldered on, the following method of installing the bearing could be used.

blunt instrument → eg. steel bar

nylon bearing → is pushed down main tube.

special plastic clip to hold standard plumbing tubing.

main tube and "T-piece" have been soldered together.

self tapping screw or bolt used to secure nylon bearing.

The bearing must be pushed down the main tube and into the "T-piece" once the soldering has been completed and the whole unit has cooled down. The bearing has to enter from the top of the main tube and not from the bottom of the "T-piece" because it will be necessary to use a "blunt instrument" as the nylon is an interference fit and pushing the curved end of the bearing may result in damage. Once the bearing is in the correct position, a hole can be drilled through the copper tubing and into the nylon. The hole can either be "tapped" and the correct bolt inserted or a self tapping screw can be used in the bare hole. This will prevent the bearing from ever becoming dislodged from its correct position. Also shown is a readily available plastic clip which could be used with some others to hold the generator on a stand.

The propeller is the component of the generator that is rotated by the flow of water. A great amount of efficiency can be lost or gained through the propeller. So, much care and attention must be paid to its design. The test model used a three bladed "clover-leaf" design propeller. It was constructed (and soldered) so that the rotor shaft went through a hole in the centre of the flat cut-out propeller (similar to that in picture ②) and into a small "boss" which had been turned on the lathe. This was then soldered and once cool, the blades were carefully bent to a fairly steep angle. Experiments were also conducted with other designs, such as the four bladed propeller (as in picture ①) and the three bladed "unshaped" propeller (as in picture ②).

The results of the experiment showed that the three bladed propellers performed better than the four bladed, but not much difference was noted between the different styles of three bladed propeller.

For these reasons, a three bladed propeller will be used in the final design and it will have the same constructional details.

Sheet 3 Side 2

1151/1

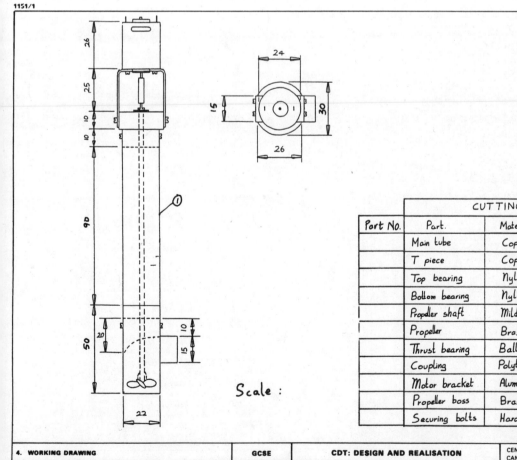

Scale :

Part No.	Part.	Material.	Nº off.	L.	W.	T.
	Main tube	Copper	1	118	⌀ 22	
	T piece	Copper	1	50	⌀22 ⌀15	
	Top bearing	Nylon	1	20	⌀30 ⌀20	
	Bottom bearing	Nylon	1	20	⌀20	
	Propeller shaft	Mild steel	1	170	⌀3	
	Propeller	Brass	1	18	18	1
	Thrust bearing	Ball race	1	4	⌀9·5	
	Coupling	Polythene tube	1	15	⌀3	
	Motor bracket	Aluminium	1	100	15	2
	Propeller boss	Brass	1	8	⌀5	
	Securing bolts	Hardened steel	12	5	VARIOUS.	

CUTTING LIST.

4. WORKING DRAWING	GCSE	CDT: DESIGN AND REALISATION	CENTRE No. ....
			CANDIDATE No. ....
Use this sheet for your working drawing and material requirements.			CANDIDATE NAME ....

Sheet 4

Fig. 21.26

EXAMINER'S COMMENTS

1. a)   Your statement could be much more brief, e.g. "Generating System".

   b) Investigation. This again is far too long and far too many words have been used. List the details a), b), c), d), etc.:
   a) Wind – natural, compressor.
   b) Water – stream, tap.
   c) Human – handle, crank.
   d) Gears – ratios, speed.
   e) Torque – pulley systems, forces.

   c) **Analysis** Points 1-9 Very important and appropriate. The continuation should really form part of your investigations and remain in your "Research Folio".
   First ideas A good range of ideas – your notes could be much more succinct (brief). Try labelling your drawings and do not describe in writing that which is very clearly illustrated in a drawing. Your drawings are clear, full of detail and convey all the information that is necessary.
   Chosen Idea Your notes form the investigation and need not be written here. Drawings are very clear and well detailed.
   Proposed Design Your drawings are excellent and do not need to be described in writing. You are duplicating work unnecessarily.
   Working Drawing Very clear and neatly drawn. Dimension figures should be; on the left of a vertical dimension line and at 90° to the line, above a horizontal line. Scale of drawing should be given. Cutting list – neatly presented. A part number would make it easier to identify each part.

INDEX